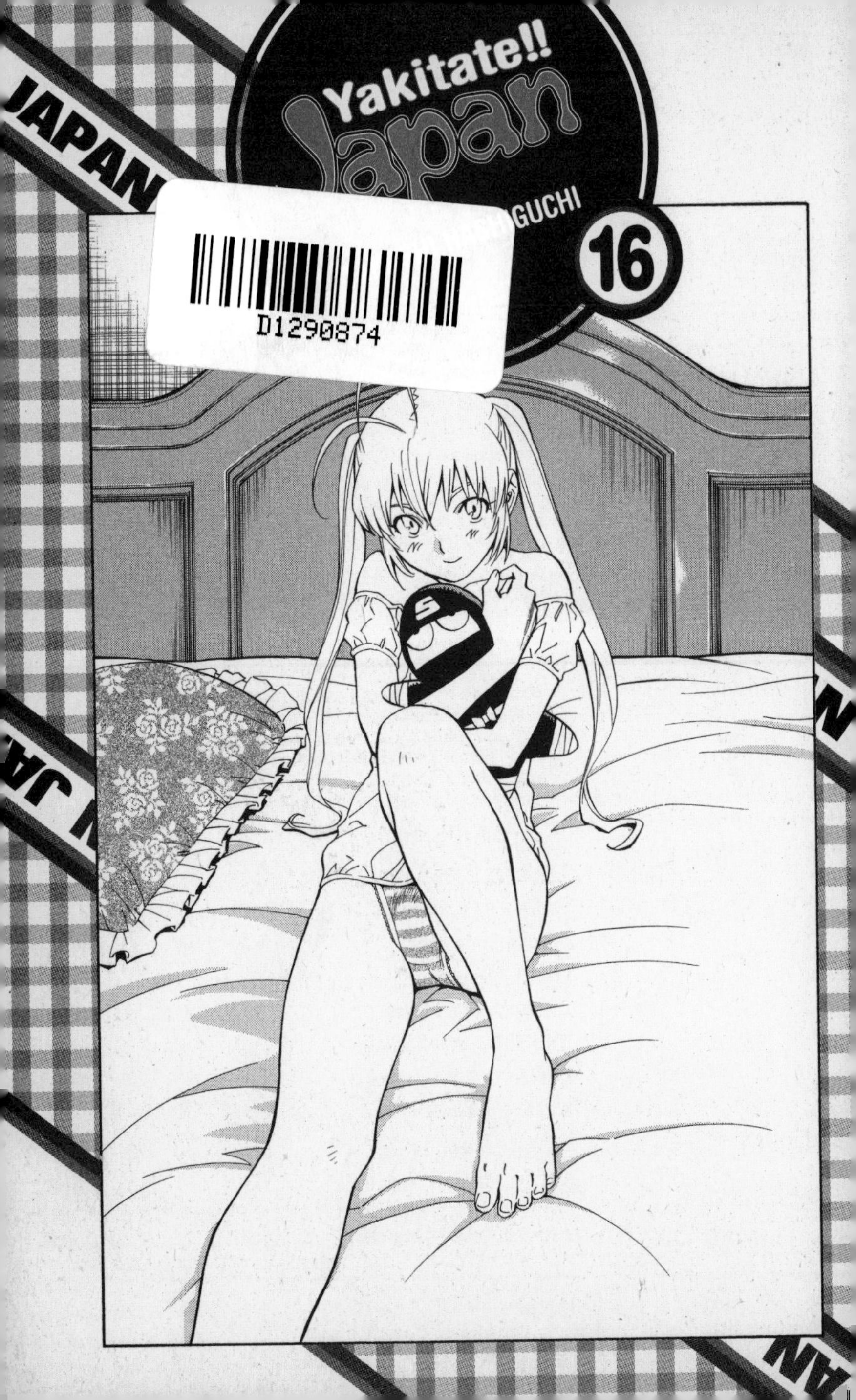
Yakitate!!
Japan
GUCHI
16
JAPAN
JAPAN

YAKITATE!! JAPAN
16
VIZ Media Edition
★The Story Thus Far★

It is a dark time for the bakery. Even though Pantasia's bread craftsmen took the Monaco Cup, St. Pierre's sinister Kirisaki trumped their victory by buying a controlling interest in Pantasia!

While our heroes have enough winnings from Monaco to create a new bakery, Tsukino is unwilling to abandon her grandfather's legacy and surrender Pantasia. After a unanimous vote, the team decides to accept Kirisaki's challenge and fight to win Pantasia back the only way they know how—in bread baking battles!

Kirisaki's challenge is a cooking competition on live TV called "Yakitate!! 25" that will pit Pantasia's bakers against St. Pierre's in a series of battles across Japan. The catch—the contestants' breads must epitomize local flavors in order to create regional breads for host cities. And the show's host is none other than Kuroyanagi, who retired from baking altogether to pursue professional tasting.

In the first match, Team Pantasia faces off against pin-up boy Tsubozuka of the celebrity cooking group CMAP. While Tsubozuka and his patron Yukino focus on the host city's celebrated Super-Tuna, our heroes innovate with a bread that combines Azuma's outside-the-box thinking, Kanmuri's encyclopedic knowledge of ingredients and Kawachi's "disgusting" technique. The result: a fabulous "Chawanmushi" bread made with purple sea urchin and the ultimate cage-free eggs.

CONTENTS

Story 134	The Three Arrows	3
Story 135	Forbidden Fruit Reaction	27
Story 136	Spooky Serendipity	45
Story 137	Loosening Juice	63
Story 138	A Strange Beast Enters	81
Story 139	Mere Acting Won't Suffice!	99
Story 140	Rapport with the Haniwas	119
Story 141	Noodle Nonsense	137
Story 142	Enter the Ninja!	155
Story 143	A Thing That's Curved	173

Research Assistance: "Pan No Mimi," Koichi Uchimura/ Miyazaki Sun Salt Inc. /Writer, Shigeyuki Kimura

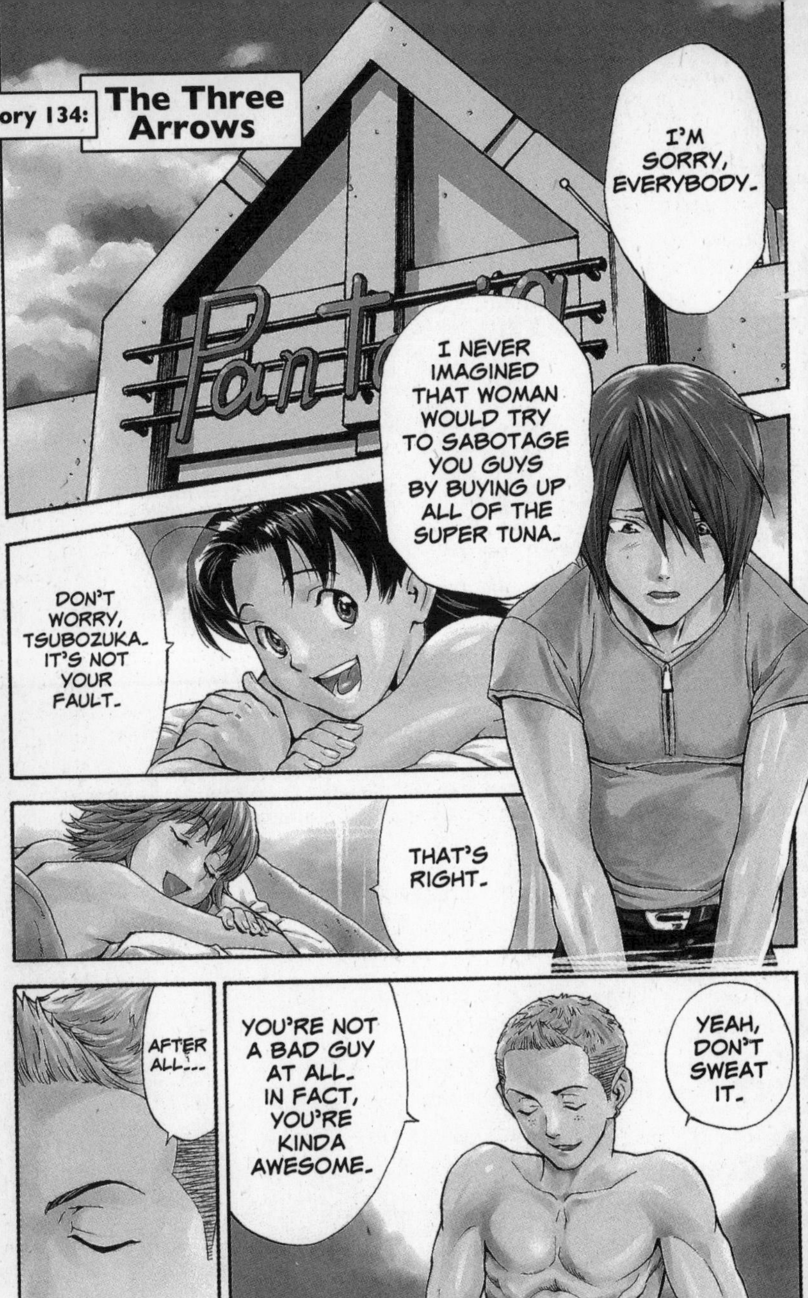
Story 134: The Three Arrows
I'M SORRY, EVERYBODY.
I NEVER IMAGINED THAT WOMAN WOULD TRY TO SABOTAGE YOU GUYS BY BUYING UP ALL OF THE SUPER TUNA.
DON'T WORRY, TSUBOZUKA. IT'S NOT YOUR FAULT.
THAT'S RIGHT.
YEAH, DON'T SWEAT IT.
YOU'RE NOT A BAD GUY AT ALL. IN FACT, YOU'RE KINDA AWESOME.
AFTER ALL...

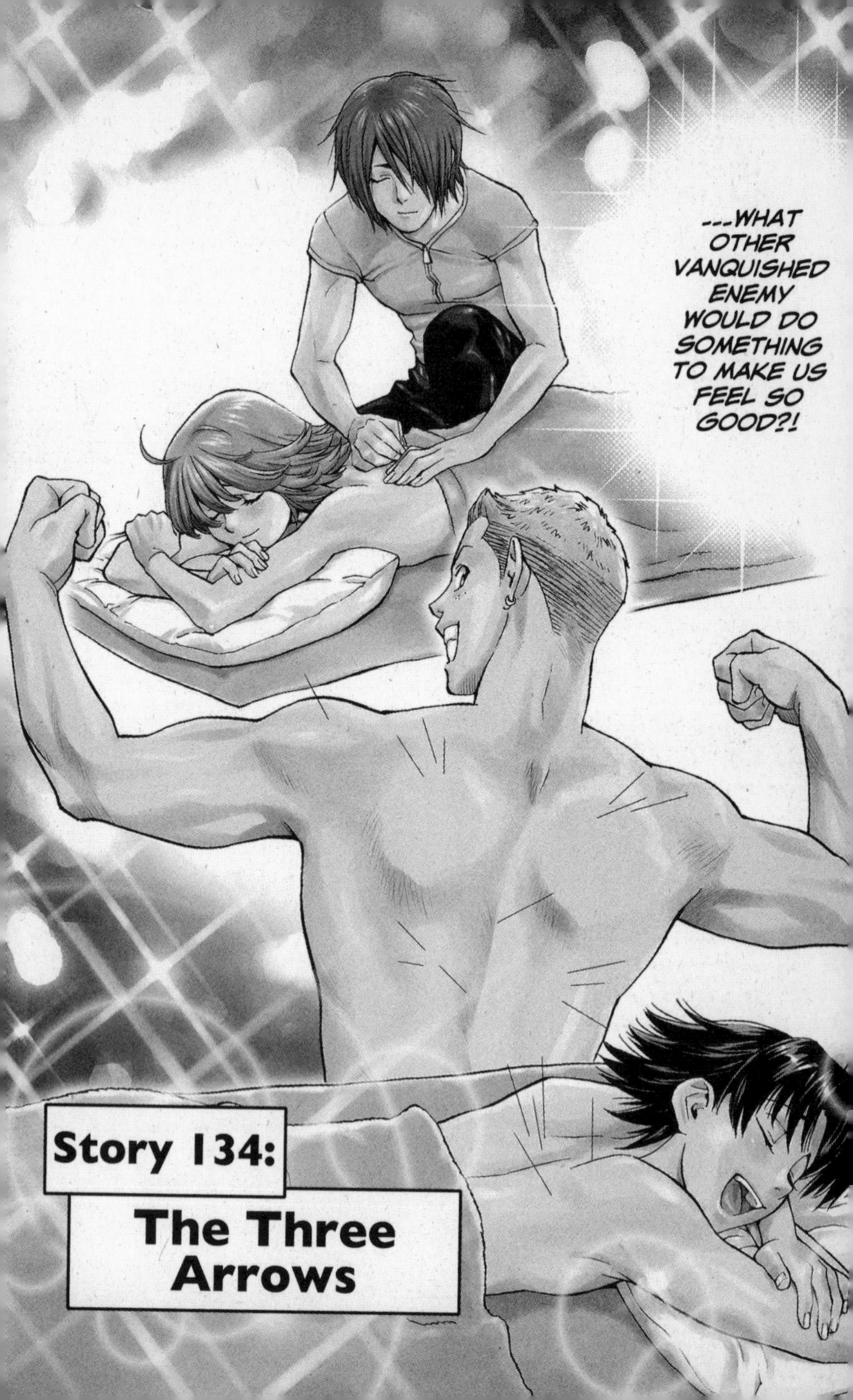
---WHAT OTHER VANQUISHED ENEMY WOULD DO SOMETHING TO MAKE US FEEL SO GOOD?!
Story 134:
The Three Arrows

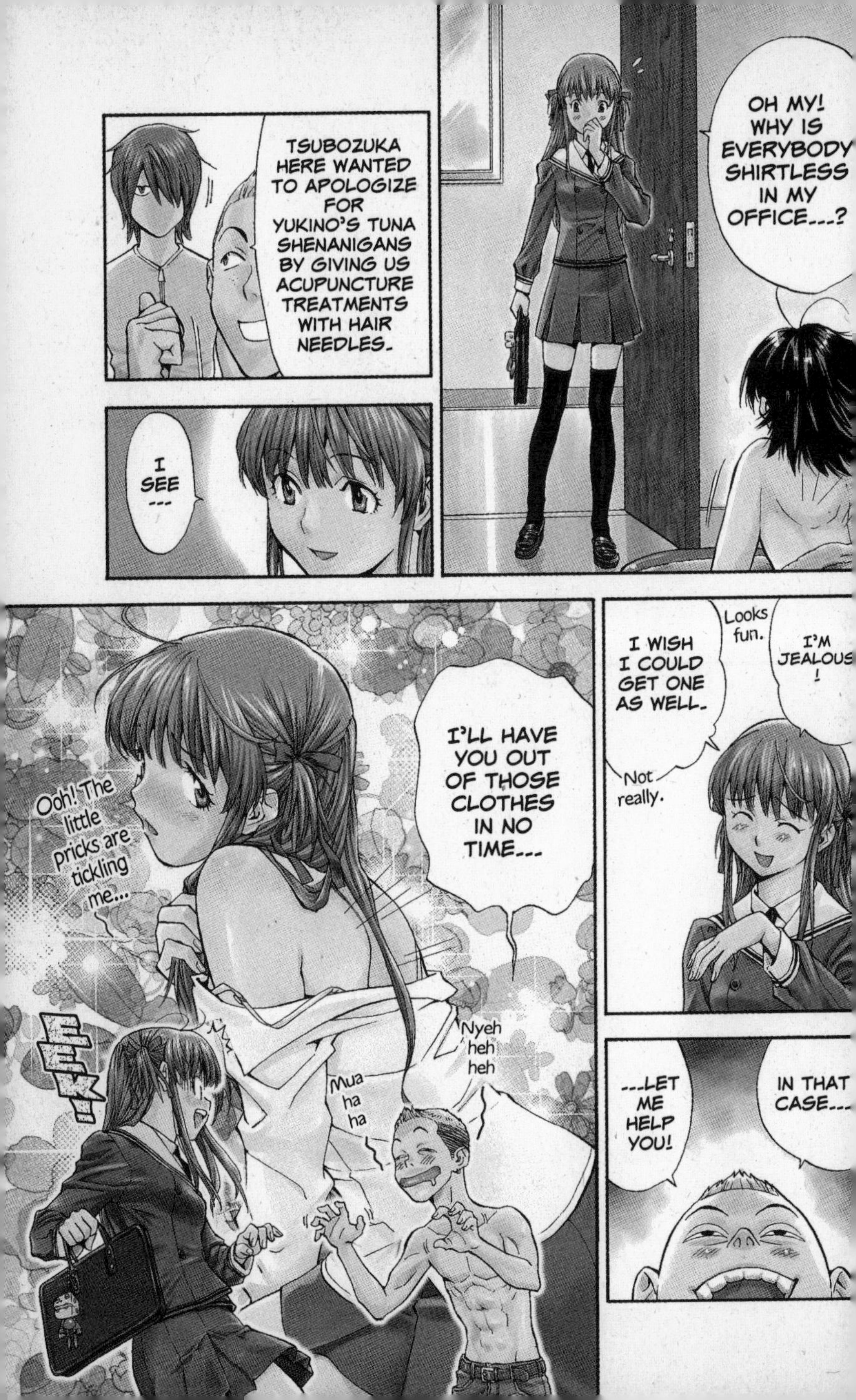
OH MY! WHY IS EVERYBODY SHIRTLESS IN MY OFFICE...?
TSUBOZUKA HERE WANTED TO APOLOGIZE FOR YUKINO'S TUNA SHENANIGANS BY GIVING US ACUPUNCTURE TREATMENTS WITH HAIR NEEDLES.
I SEE...
I'M JEALOUS!
Looks fun.
I WISH I COULD GET ONE AS WELL.
Not really.
IN THAT CASE...
...LET ME HELP YOU!
I'LL HAVE YOU OUT OF THOSE CLOTHES IN NO TIME...
Nyeh heh heh
Mua ha ha
Ooh! The little pricks are tickling me...
EEK!

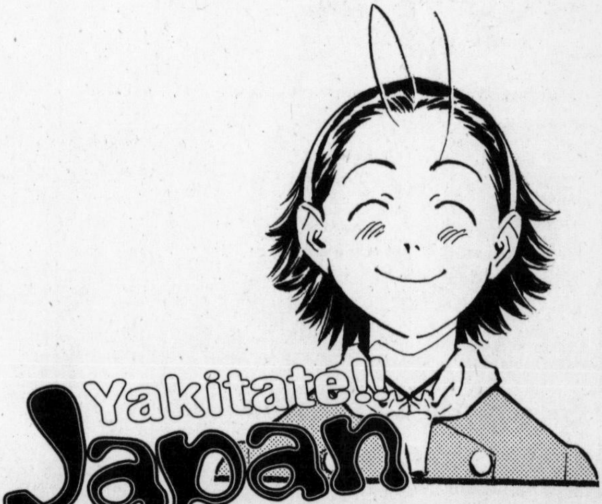
Yakitate!!
Japan

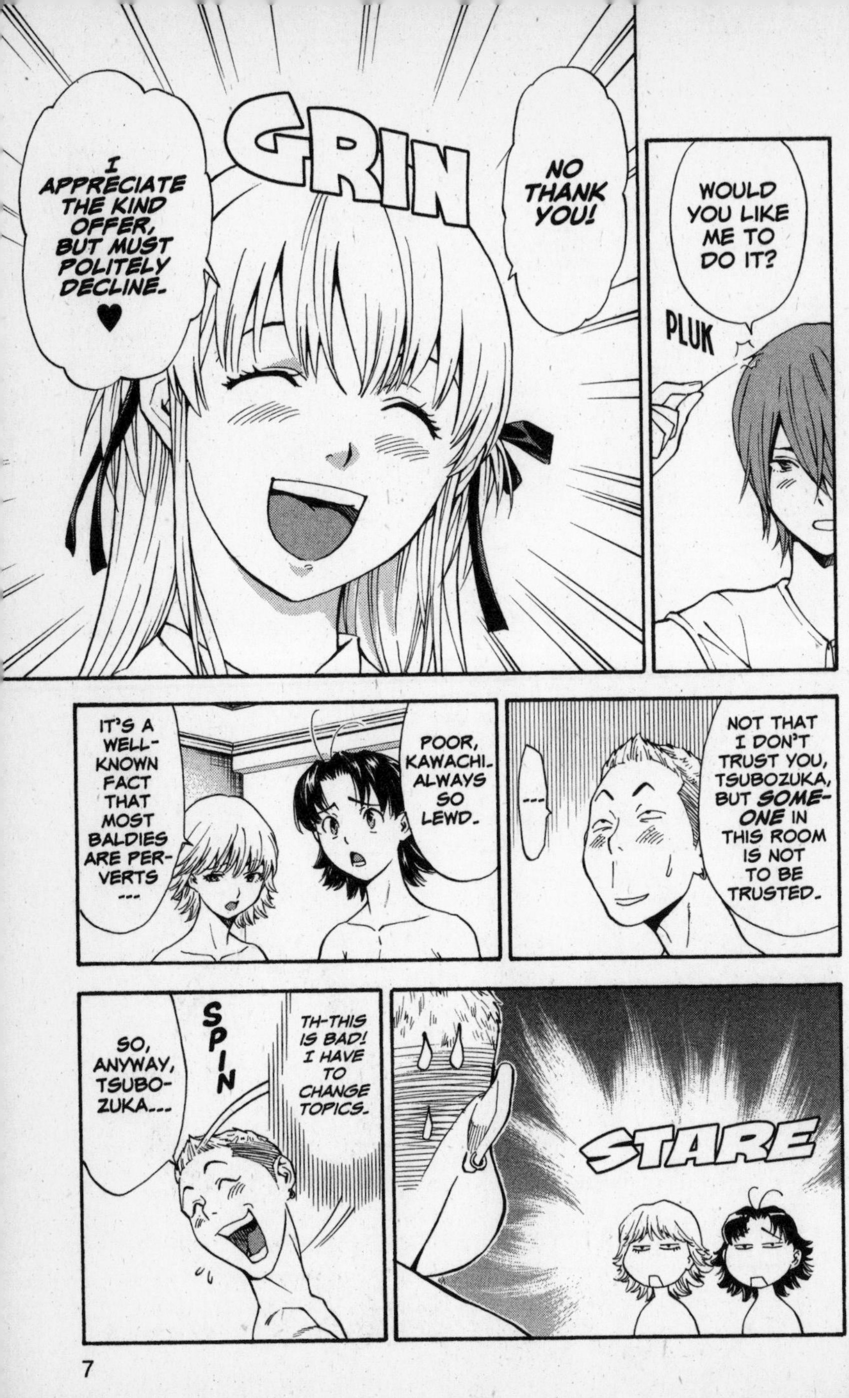
WOULD YOU LIKE ME TO DO IT?
PLUK
NO THANK YOU!
GRIN
I APPRECIATE THE KIND OFFER, BUT MUST POLITELY DECLINE. ♥
NOT THAT I DON'T TRUST YOU, TSUBOZUKA, BUT *SOME-ONE* IN THIS ROOM IS NOT TO BE TRUSTED.
...
POOR, KAWACHI. ALWAYS SO LEWD.
IT'S A WELL-KNOWN FACT THAT MOST BALDIES ARE PER-VERTS...
STARE
TH-THIS IS BAD! I HAVE TO CHANGE TOPICS.
SPIN
SO, ANYWAY, TSUBO-ZUKA...

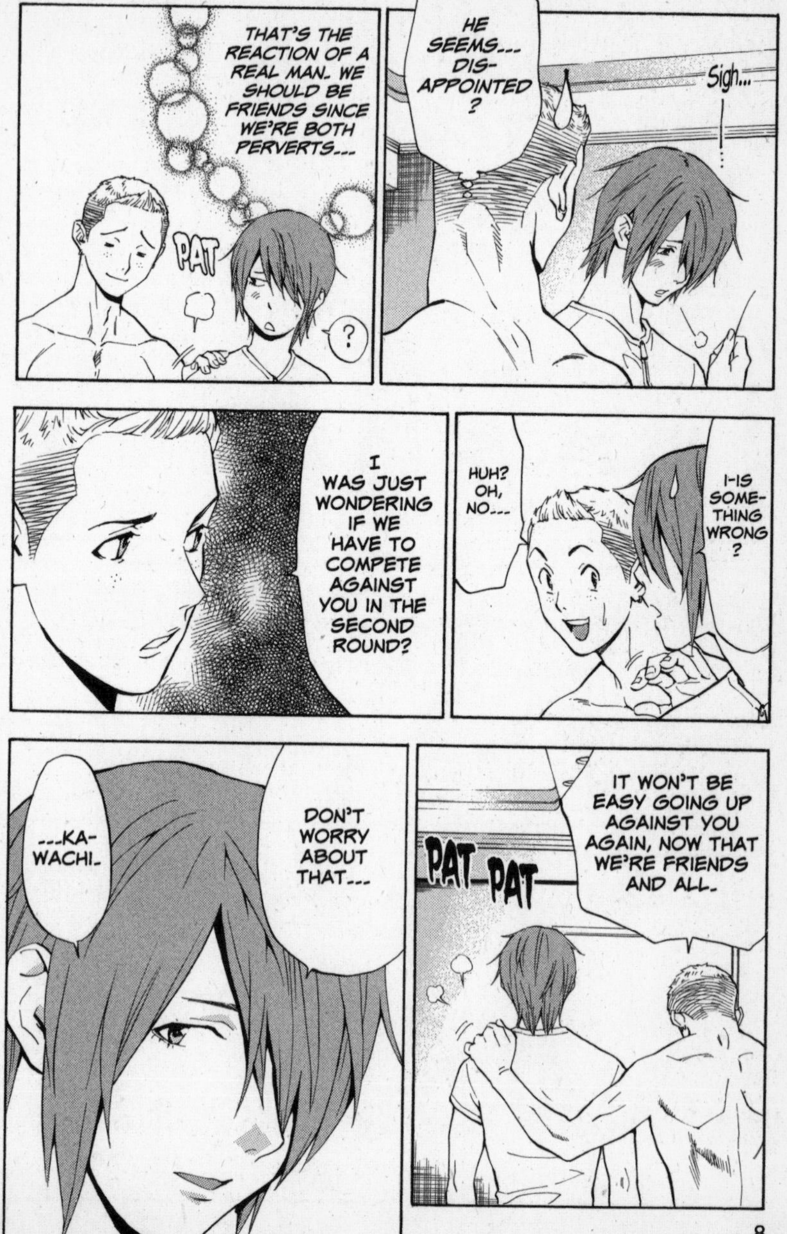
HE SEEMS... DIS-APPOINTED?
Sigh...
THAT'S THE REACTION OF A REAL MAN. WE SHOULD BE FRIENDS SINCE WE'RE BOTH PERVERTS...
PAT
?
I-IS SOME-THING WRONG?
HUH? OH, NO...
I WAS JUST WONDERING IF WE HAVE TO COMPETE AGAINST YOU IN THE SECOND ROUND?
IT WON'T BE EASY GOING UP AGAINST YOU AGAIN, NOW THAT WE'RE FRIENDS AND ALL.
PAT PAT
DON'T WORRY ABOUT THAT...
...KA-WACHI.

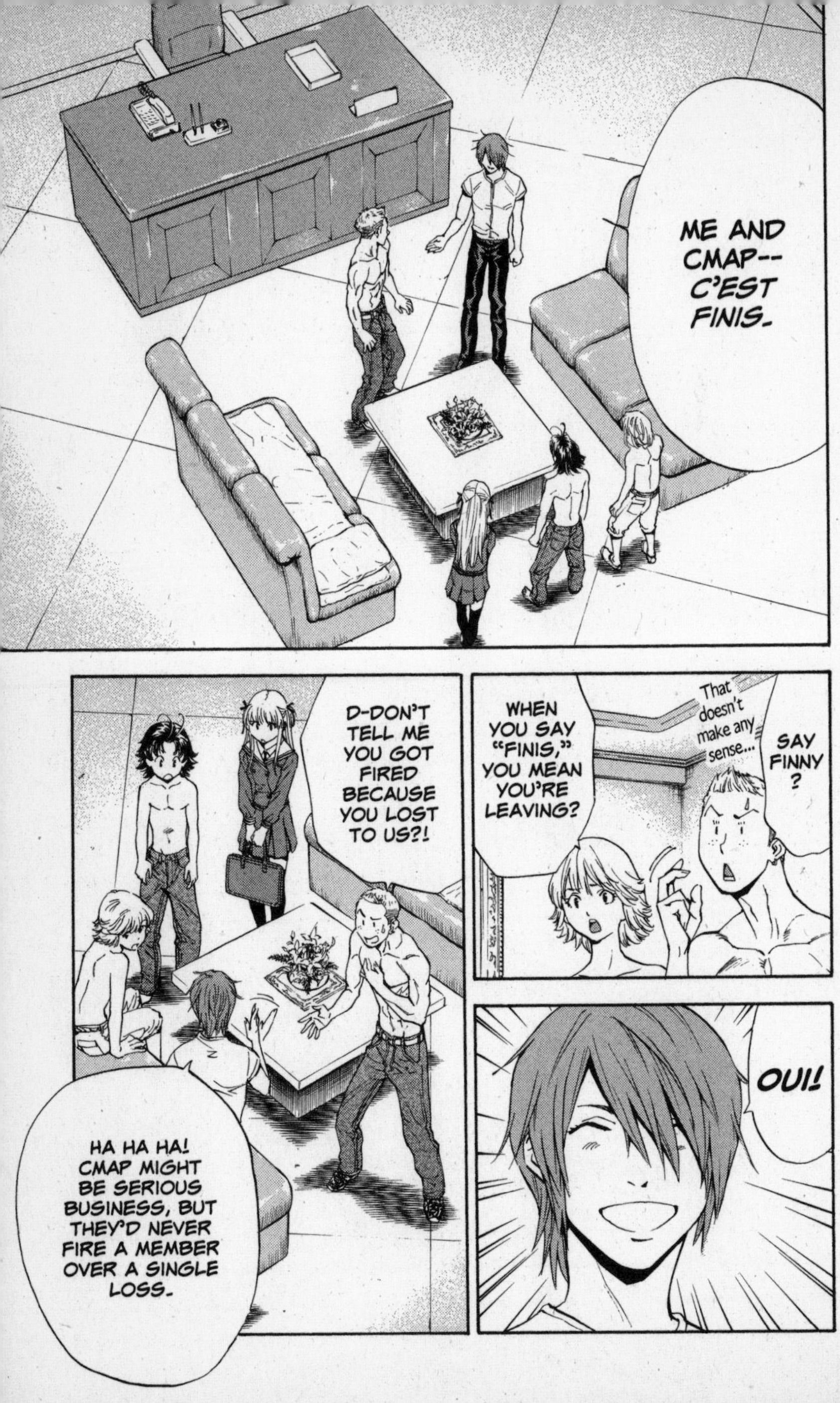
ME AND CMAP-- C'EST FINIS.
SAY FINNY?
That doesn't make any sense...
WHEN YOU SAY "FINIS," YOU MEAN YOU'RE LEAVING?
OUI!
D-DON'T TELL ME YOU GOT FIRED BECAUSE YOU LOST TO US?!
HA HA HA! CMAP MIGHT BE SERIOUS BUSINESS, BUT THEY'D NEVER FIRE A MEMBER OVER A SINGLE LOSS.

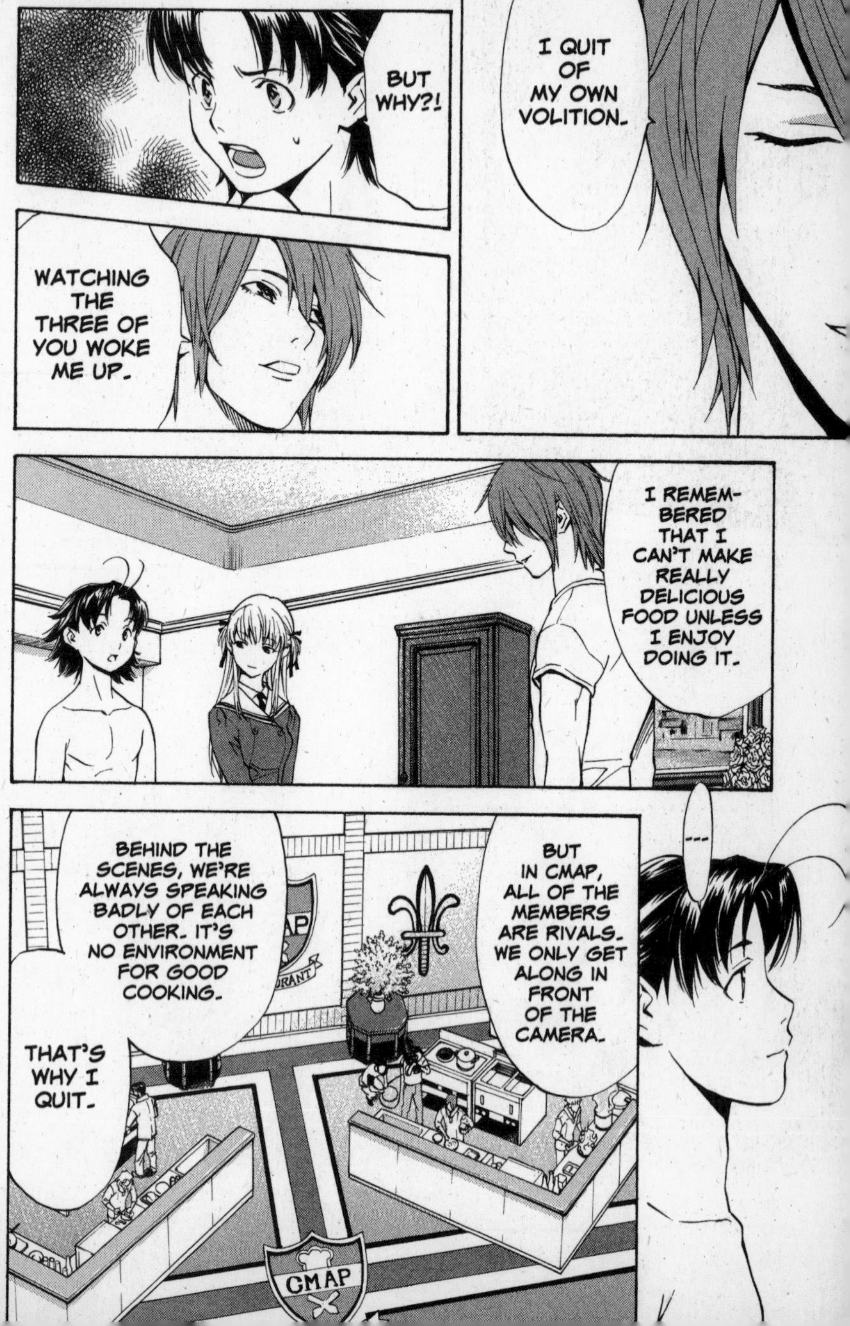
I QUIT OF MY OWN VOLITION.
BUT WHY?!
WATCHING THE THREE OF YOU WOKE ME UP.
I REMEMBERED THAT I CAN'T MAKE REALLY DELICIOUS FOOD UNLESS I ENJOY DOING IT.
...
BUT IN CMAP, ALL OF THE MEMBERS ARE RIVALS. WE ONLY GET ALONG IN FRONT OF THE CAMERA.
BEHIND THE SCENES, WE'RE ALWAYS SPEAKING BADLY OF EACH OTHER. IT'S NO ENVIRONMENT FOR GOOD COOKING.
THAT'S WHY I QUIT.
CMAP

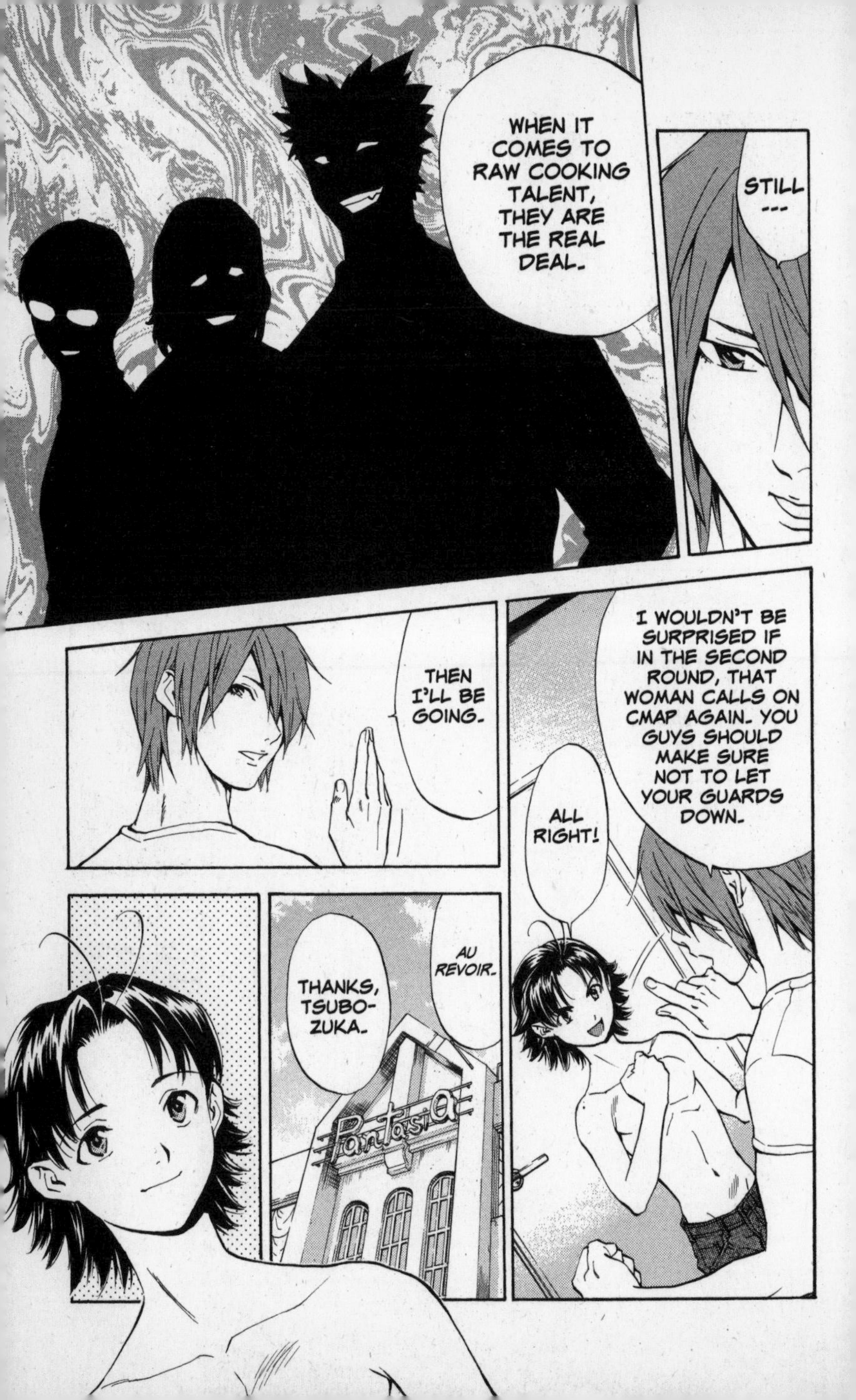
STILL ---
WHEN IT COMES TO RAW COOKING TALENT, THEY ARE THE REAL DEAL.
I WOULDN'T BE SURPRISED IF IN THE SECOND ROUND, THAT WOMAN CALLS ON CMAP AGAIN. YOU GUYS SHOULD MAKE SURE NOT TO LET YOUR GUARDS DOWN.
ALL RIGHT!
THEN I'LL BE GOING.
AU REVOIR.
THANKS, TSUBO-ZUKA.
PantasiA

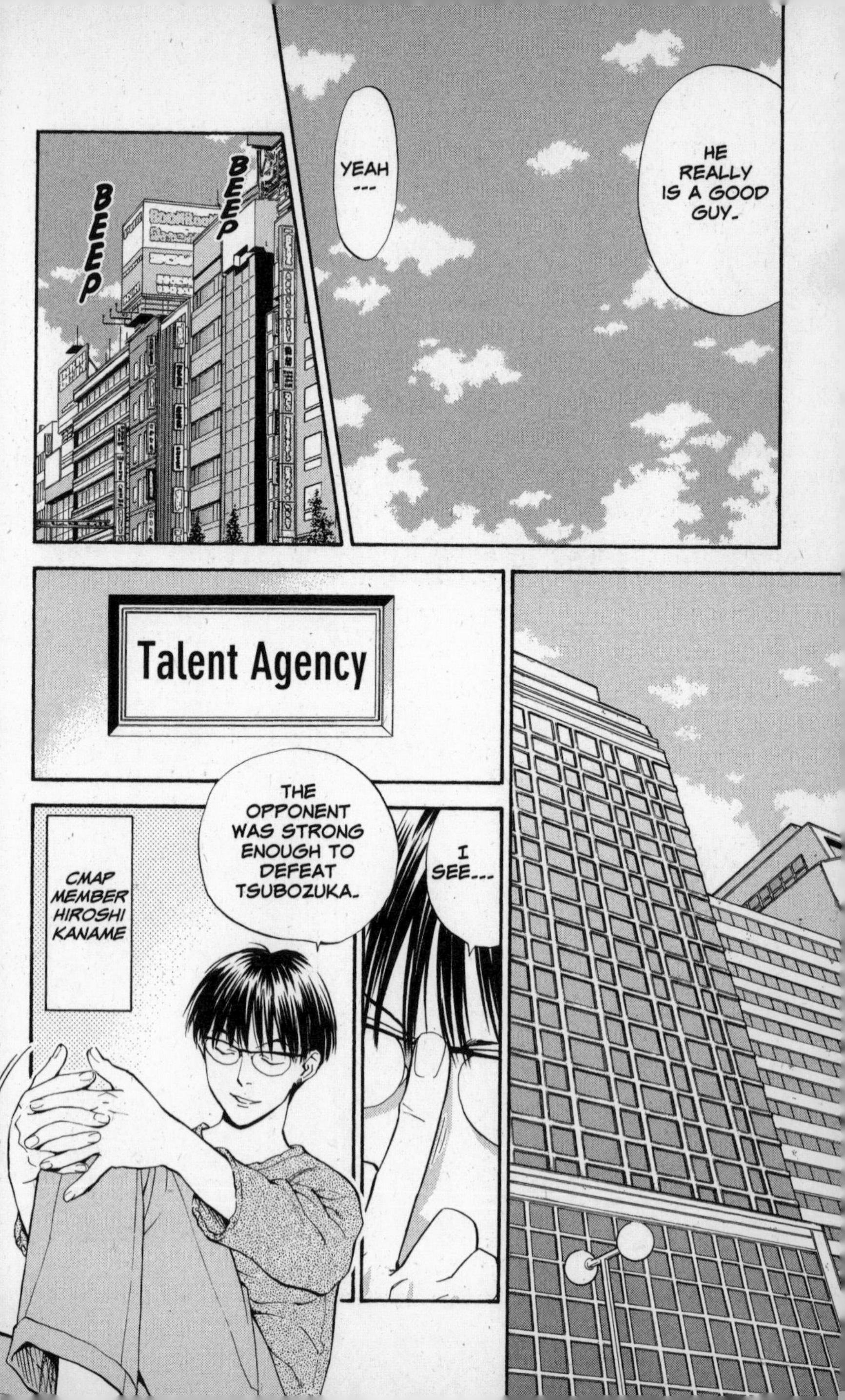
HE REALLY IS A GOOD GUY.
YEAH ---
BEEP
BEEP
Talent Agency
I SEE...
THE OPPONENT WAS STRONG ENOUGH TO DEFEAT TSUBOZUKA.
CMAP MEMBER HIROSHI KANAME

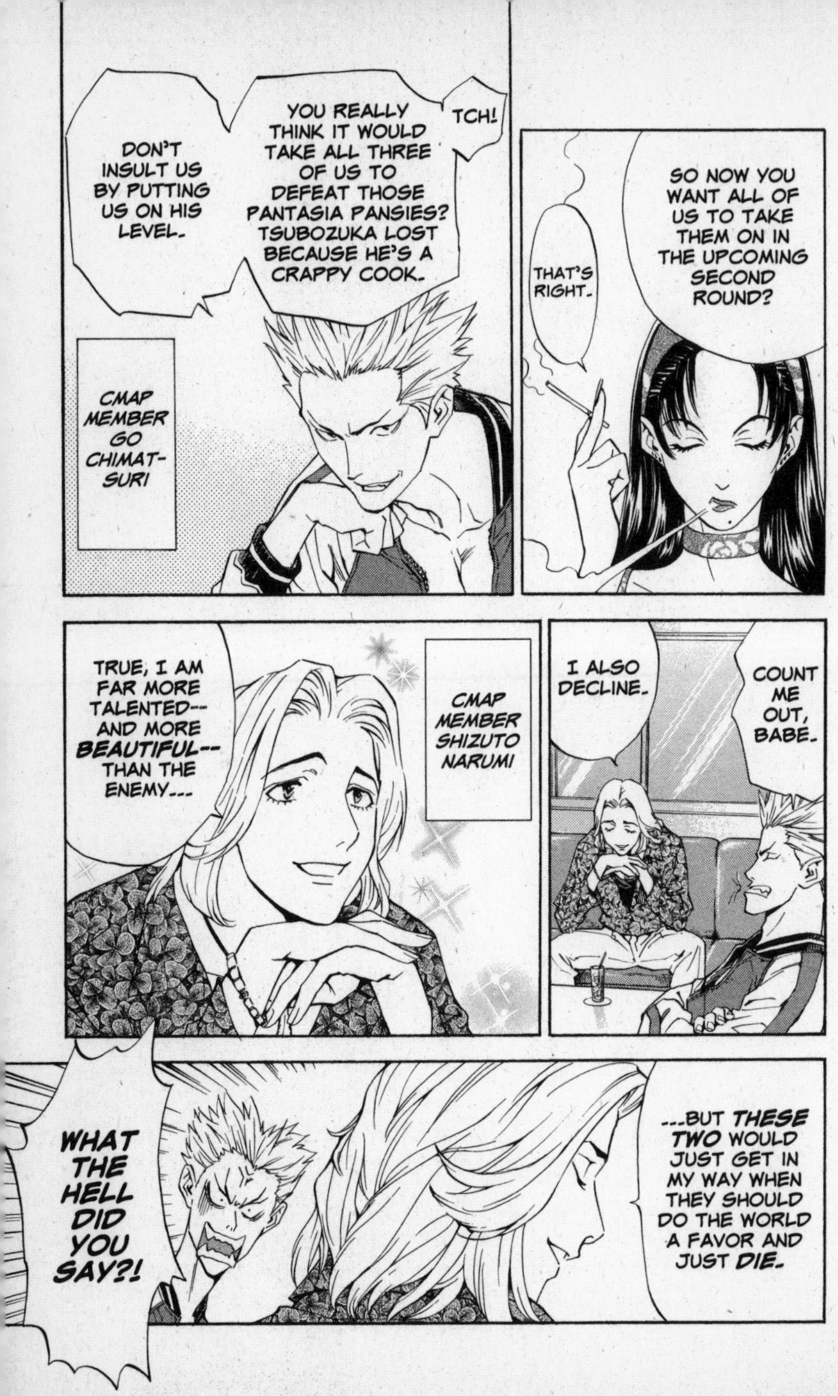
SO NOW YOU WANT ALL OF US TO TAKE THEM ON IN THE UPCOMING SECOND ROUND?
THAT'S RIGHT.
TCH!
YOU REALLY THINK IT WOULD TAKE ALL THREE OF US TO DEFEAT THOSE PANTASIA PANSIES? TSUBOZUKA LOST BECAUSE HE'S A CRAPPY COOK.
DON'T INSULT US BY PUTTING US ON HIS LEVEL.
CMAP MEMBER GO CHIMATSURI
COUNT ME OUT, BABE.
I ALSO DECLINE.
CMAP MEMBER SHIZUTO NARUMI
TRUE, I AM FAR MORE TALENTED-- AND MORE BEAUTIFUL-- THAN THE ENEMY...
...BUT THESE TWO WOULD JUST GET IN MY WAY WHEN THEY SHOULD DO THE WORLD A FAVOR AND JUST DIE.
WHAT THE HELL DID YOU SAY?!

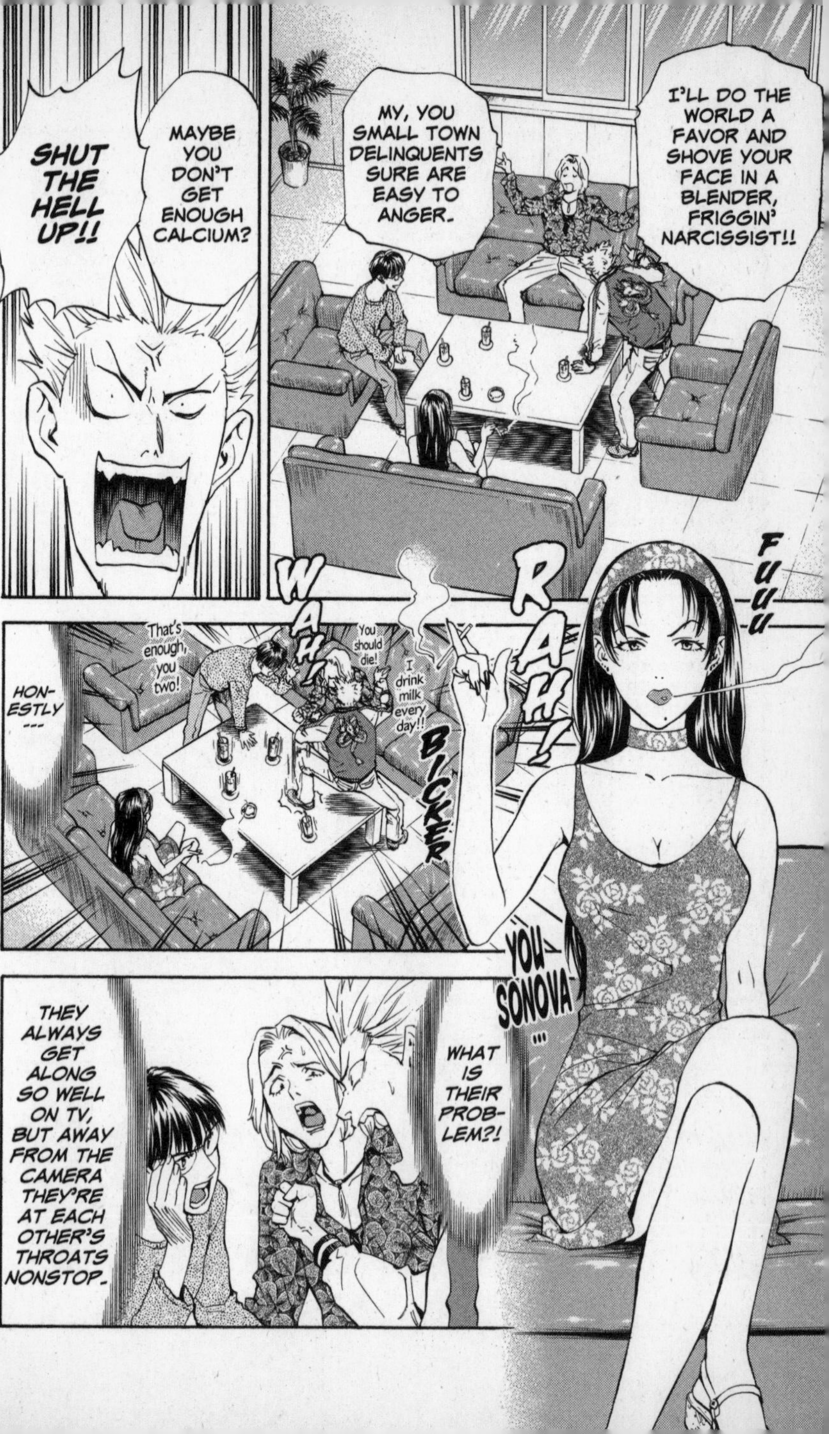
I'LL DO THE WORLD A FAVOR AND SHOVE YOUR FACE IN A BLENDER, FRIGGIN' NARCISSIST!!
MY, YOU SMALL TOWN DELINQUENTS SURE ARE EASY TO ANGER.
MAYBE YOU DON'T GET ENOUGH CALCIUM?
SHUT THE HELL UP!!
FUUUU
RAH!
WAH!
You should die!
I drink milk every day!!
That's enough, you two!
BICKER
YOU SONOVA...
HON-ESTLY---
WHAT IS THEIR PROB-LEM?!
THEY ALWAYS GET ALONG SO WELL ON TV, BUT AWAY FROM THE CAMERA THEY'RE AT EACH OTHER'S THROATS NONSTOP.

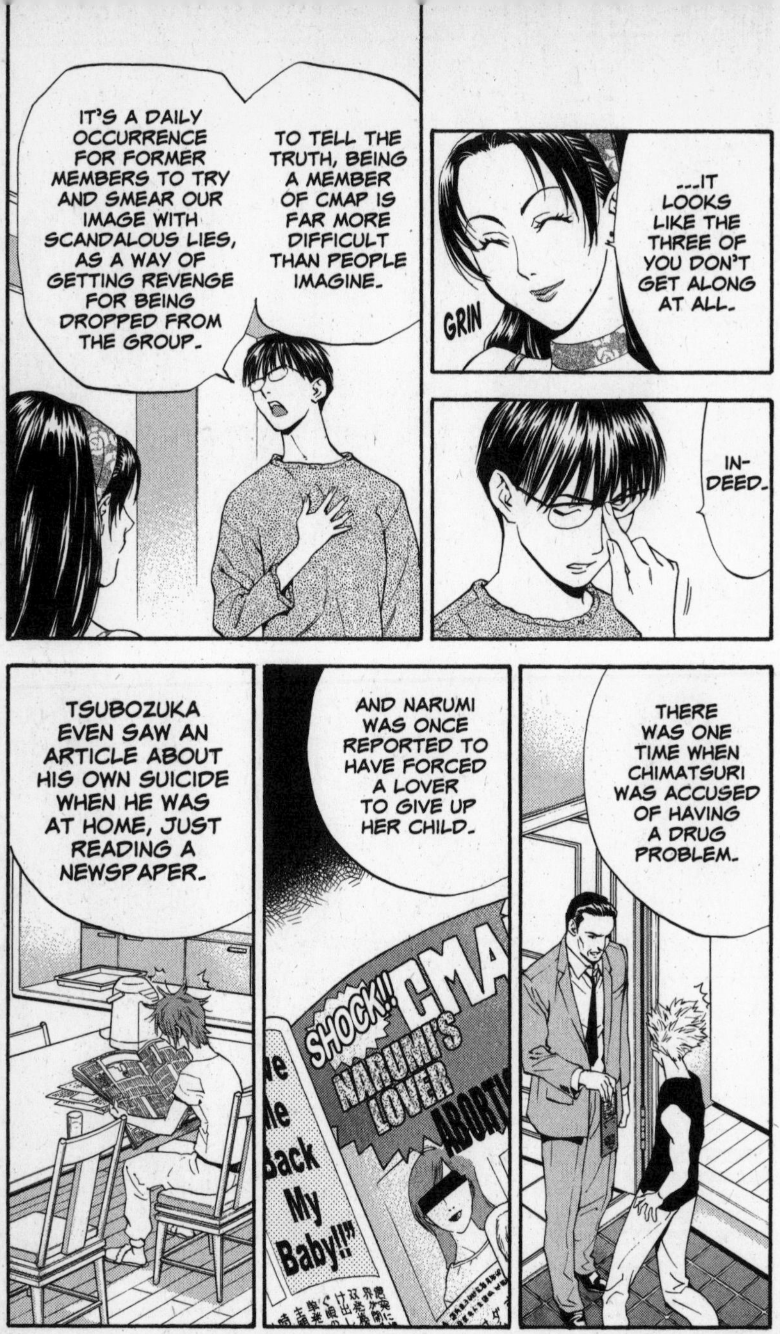

...IT LOOKS LIKE THE THREE OF YOU DON'T GET ALONG AT ALL.
GRIN
IN-DEED.
TO TELL THE TRUTH, BEING A MEMBER OF CMAP IS FAR MORE DIFFICULT THAN PEOPLE IMAGINE.
IT'S A DAILY OCCURRENCE FOR FORMER MEMBERS TO TRY AND SMEAR OUR IMAGE WITH SCANDALOUS LIES, AS A WAY OF GETTING REVENGE FOR BEING DROPPED FROM THE GROUP.
THERE WAS ONE TIME WHEN CHIMATSURI WAS ACCUSED OF HAVING A DRUG PROBLEM.
AND NARUMI WAS ONCE REPORTED TO HAVE FORCED A LOVER TO GIVE UP HER CHILD.
SHOCK!!
NARUMI'S LOVER
Back My Baby!!"
TSUBOZUKA EVEN SAW AN ARTICLE ABOUT HIS OWN SUICIDE WHEN HE WAS AT HOME, JUST READING A NEWSPAPER.

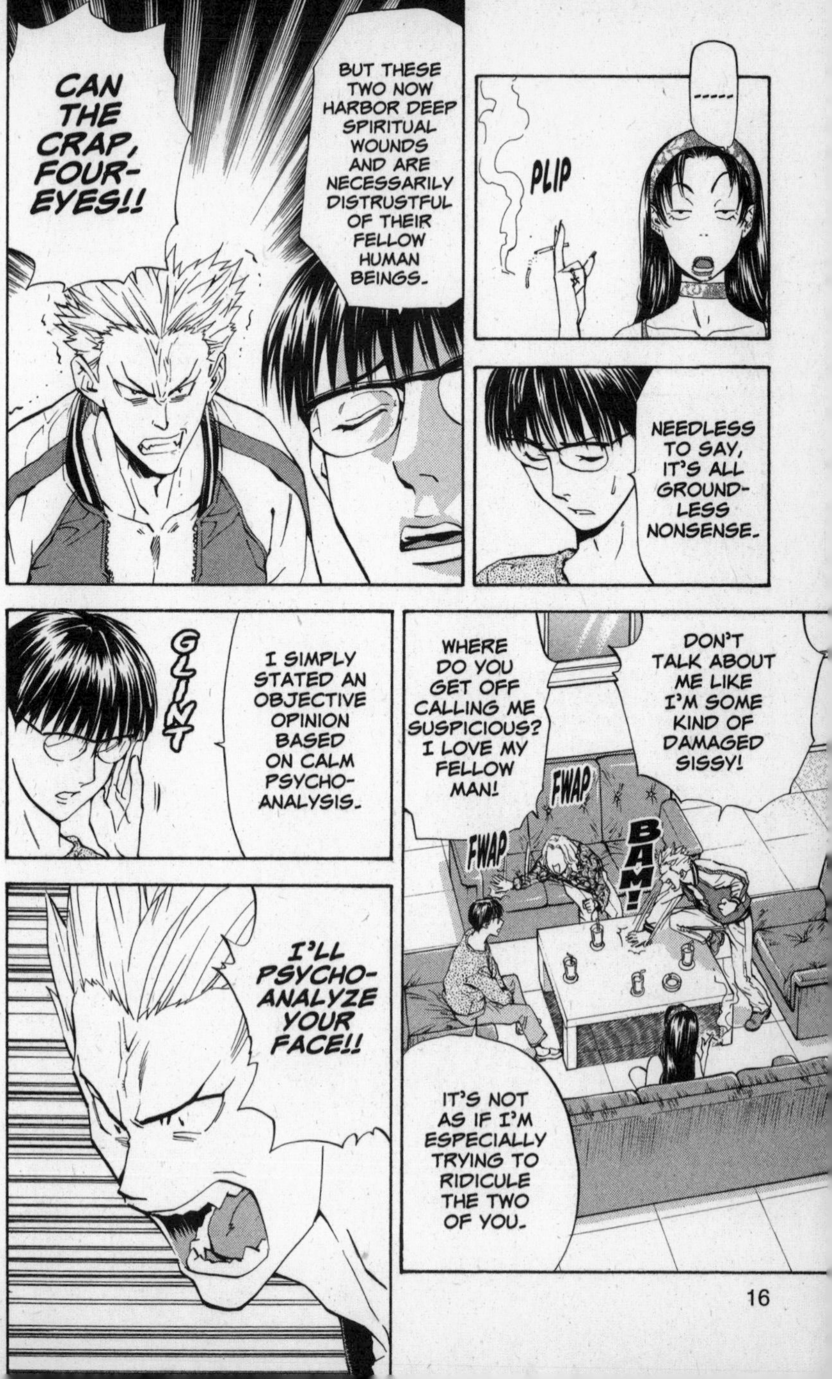

PLIP
NEEDLESS TO SAY, IT'S ALL GROUNDLESS NONSENSE.
BUT THESE TWO NOW HARBOR DEEP SPIRITUAL WOUNDS AND ARE NECESSARILY DISTRUSTFUL OF THEIR FELLOW HUMAN BEINGS.
CAN THE CRAP, FOUR-EYES!!
DON'T TALK ABOUT ME LIKE I'M SOME KIND OF DAMAGED SISSY!
WHERE DO YOU GET OFF CALLING ME SUSPICIOUS? I LOVE MY FELLOW MAN!
FWAP
BAM!
FWAP
IT'S NOT AS IF I'M ESPECIALLY TRYING TO RIDICULE THE TWO OF YOU.
I SIMPLY STATED AN OBJECTIVE OPINION BASED ON CALM PSYCHO-ANALYSIS.
GLINT
I'LL PSYCHO-ANALYZE YOUR FACE!!

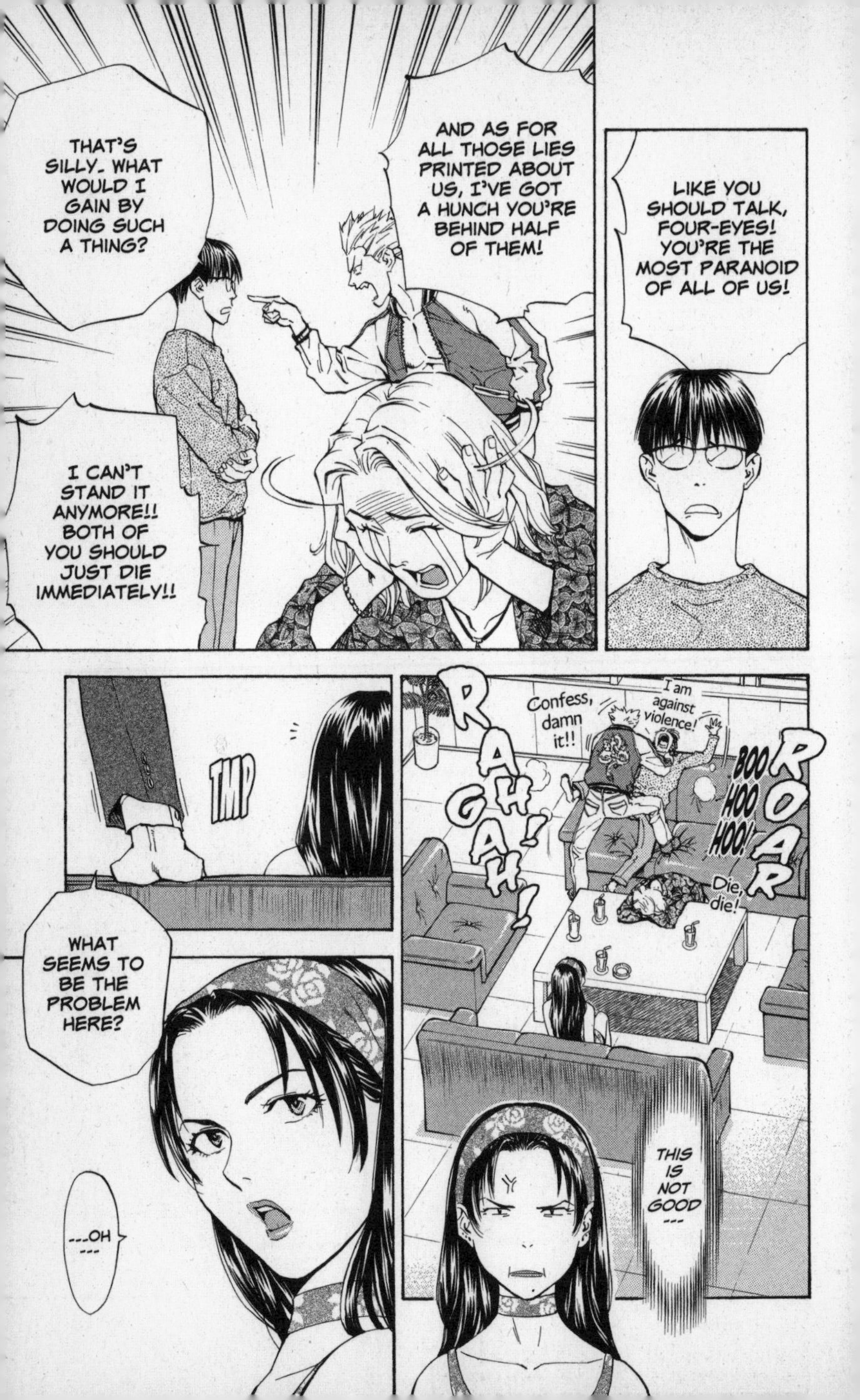
LIKE YOU SHOULD TALK, FOUR-EYES! YOU'RE THE MOST PARANOID OF ALL OF US!
AND AS FOR ALL THOSE LIES PRINTED ABOUT US, I'VE GOT A HUNCH YOU'RE BEHIND HALF OF THEM!
THAT'S SILLY. WHAT WOULD I GAIN BY DOING SUCH A THING?
I CAN'T STAND IT ANYMORE!! BOTH OF YOU SHOULD JUST DIE IMMEDIATELY!!
ROAR
BOO HOO HOO!
I am against violence!
Confess, damn it!!
RAGH GAH! AH!
Die, die!
THIS IS NOT GOOD ---
TMP
WHAT SEEMS TO BE THE PROBLEM HERE?
---OH ---

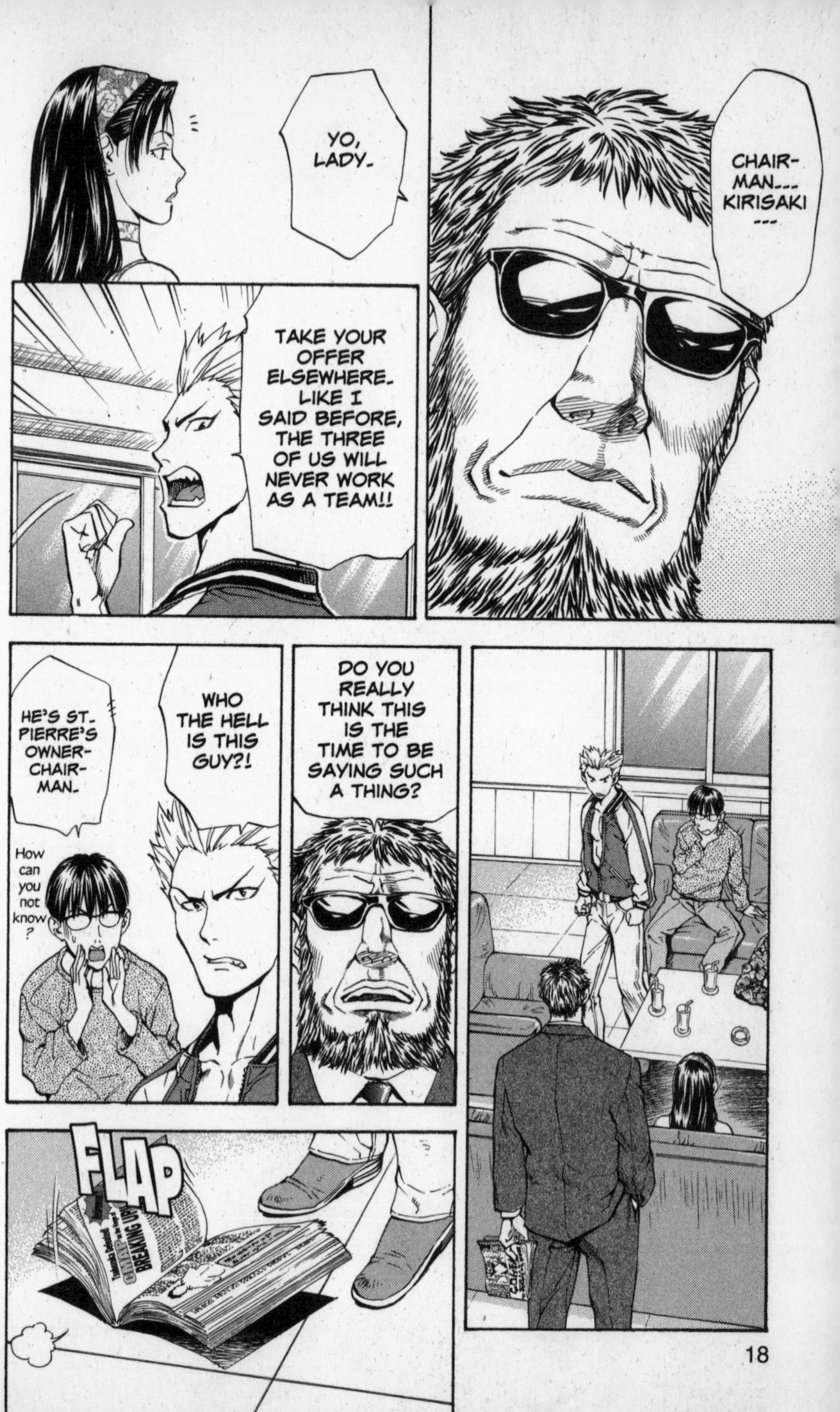
CHAIR-MAN... KIRISAKI ...
YO, LADY.
TAKE YOUR OFFER ELSEWHERE. LIKE I SAID BEFORE, THE THREE OF US WILL NEVER WORK AS A TEAM!!
DO YOU REALLY THINK THIS IS THE TIME TO BE SAYING SUCH A THING?
WHO THE HELL IS THIS GUY?!
HE'S ST. PIERRE'S OWNER-CHAIRMAN.
How can you not know?
FLAP
BREAKING UP!

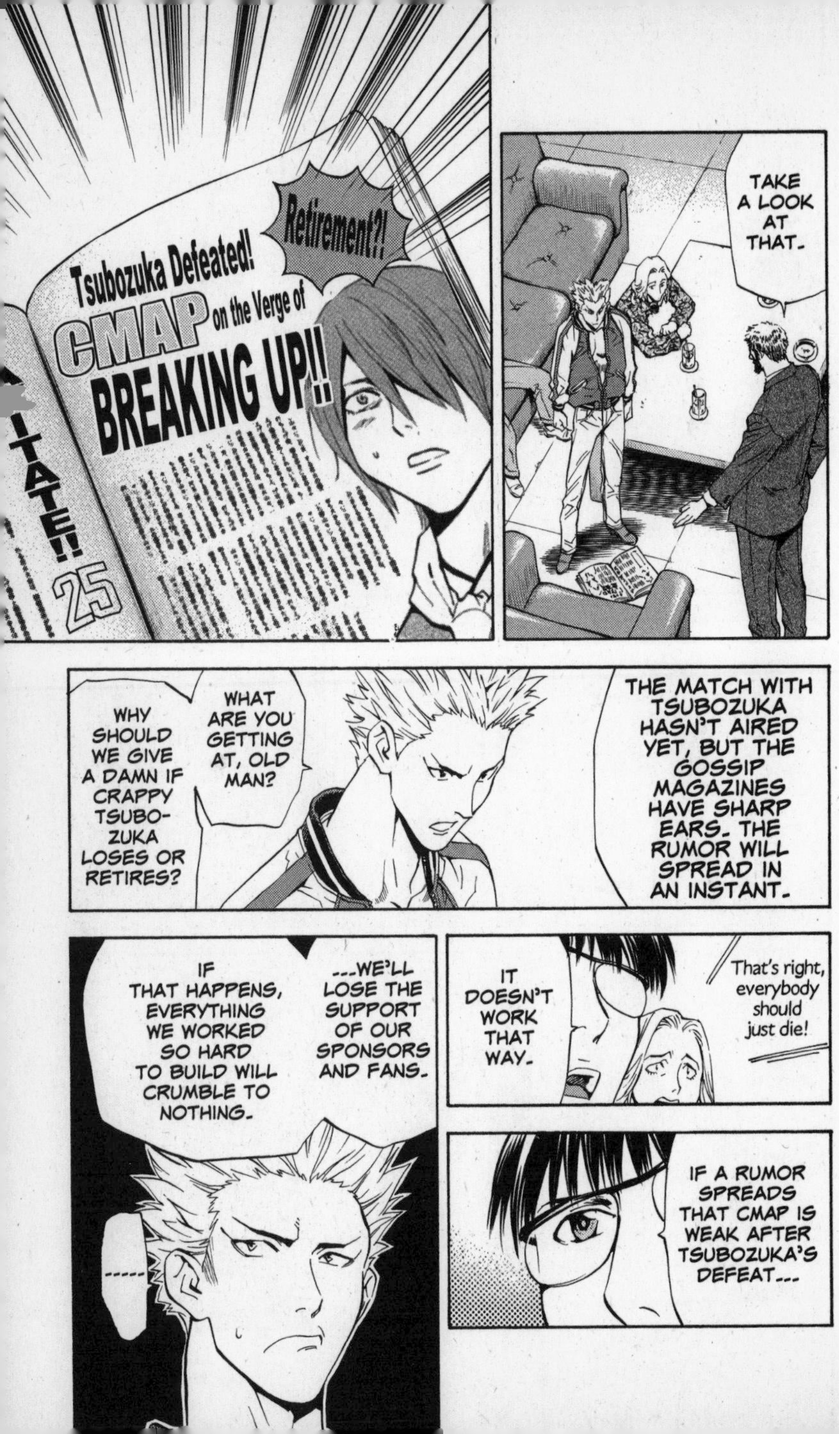
TAKE A LOOK AT THAT.
Retirement?!
Tsubozuka Defeated!
CMAP on the Verge of BREAKING UP!!
TATE!!
25
THE MATCH WITH TSUBOZUKA HASN'T AIRED YET, BUT THE GOSSIP MAGAZINES HAVE SHARP EARS. THE RUMOR WILL SPREAD IN AN INSTANT.
WHAT ARE YOU GETTING AT, OLD MAN?
WHY SHOULD WE GIVE A DAMN IF CRAPPY TSUBOZUKA LOSES OR RETIRES?
That's right, everybody should just die!
IT DOESN'T WORK THAT WAY.
IF A RUMOR SPREADS THAT CMAP IS WEAK AFTER TSUBOZUKA'S DEFEAT...
...WE'LL LOSE THE SUPPORT OF OUR SPONSORS AND FANS.
IF THAT HAPPENS, EVERYTHING WE WORKED SO HARD TO BUILD WILL CRUMBLE TO NOTHING.
.....

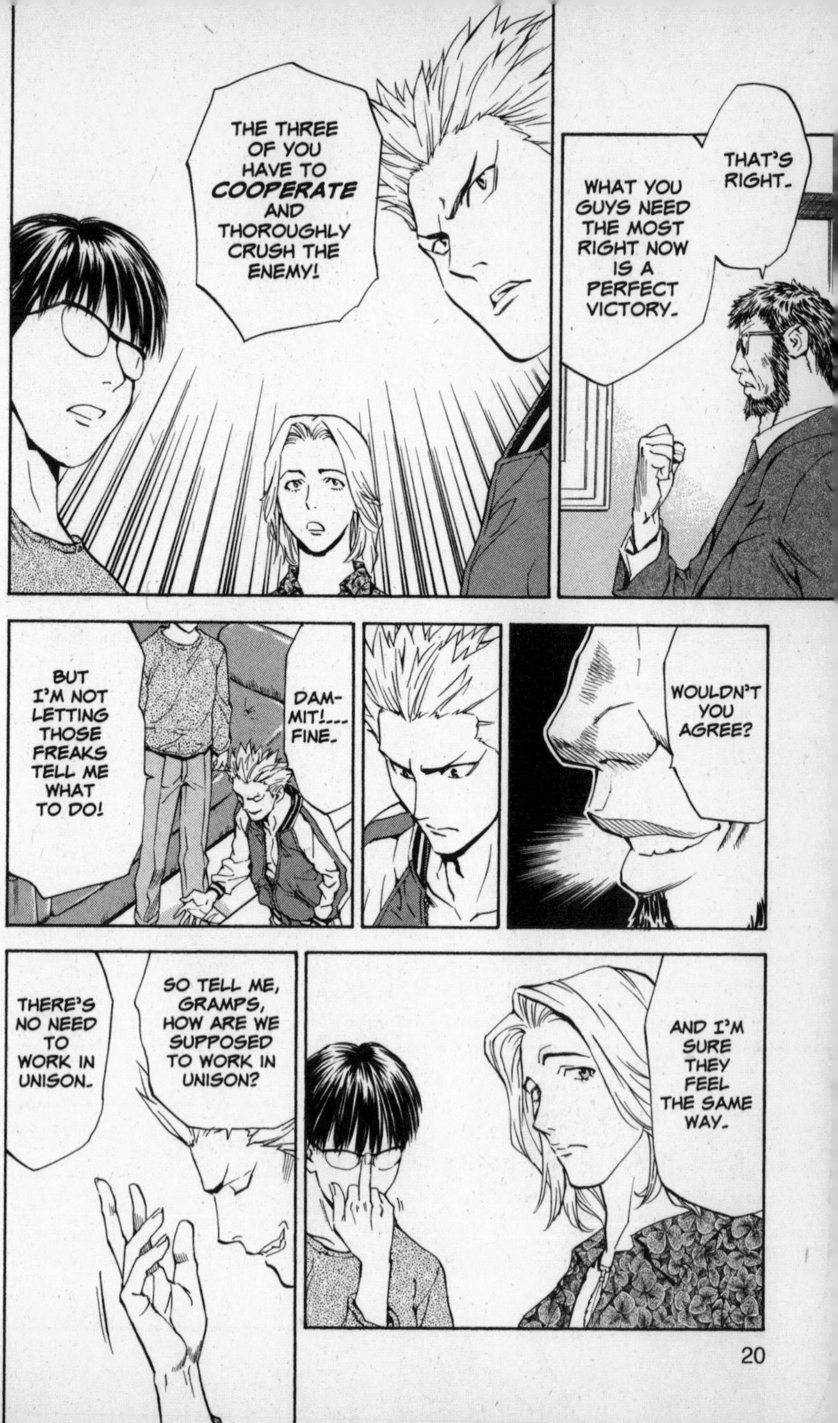
THAT'S RIGHT.
WHAT YOU GUYS NEED THE MOST RIGHT NOW IS A PERFECT VICTORY.
THE THREE OF YOU HAVE TO *COOPERATE* AND THOROUGHLY CRUSH THE ENEMY!
WOULDN'T YOU AGREE?
DAM-MIT!... FINE.
BUT I'M NOT LETTING THOSE FREAKS TELL ME WHAT TO DO!
AND I'M SURE THEY FEEL THE SAME WAY.
SO TELL ME, GRAMPS, HOW ARE WE SUPPOSED TO WORK IN UNISON?
THERE'S NO NEED TO WORK IN UNISON.

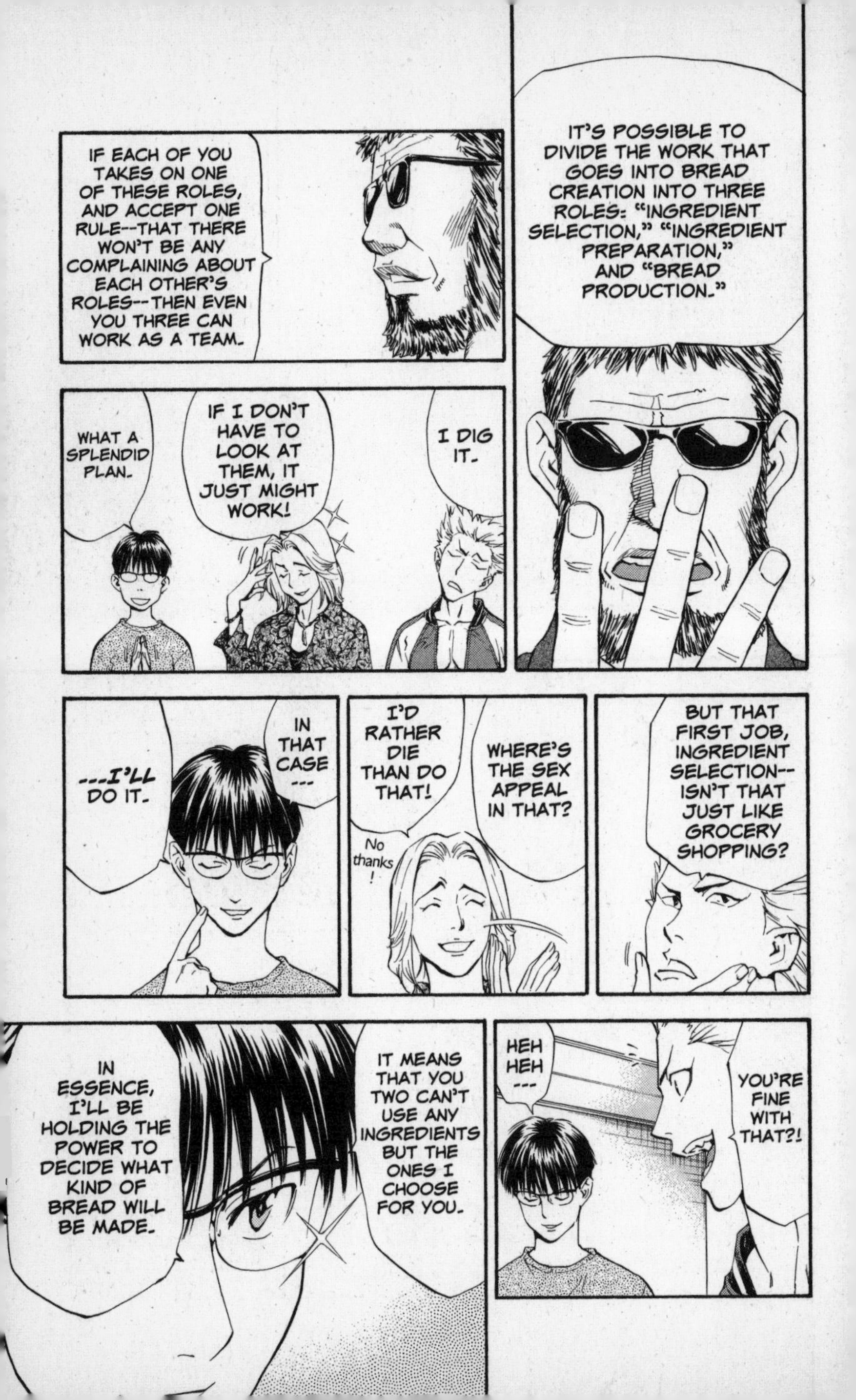
IT'S POSSIBLE TO DIVIDE THE WORK THAT GOES INTO BREAD CREATION INTO THREE ROLES: "INGREDIENT SELECTION," "INGREDIENT PREPARATION," AND "BREAD PRODUCTION."
IF EACH OF YOU TAKES ON ONE OF THESE ROLES, AND ACCEPT ONE RULE--THAT THERE WON'T BE ANY COMPLAINING ABOUT EACH OTHER'S ROLES--THEN EVEN YOU THREE CAN WORK AS A TEAM.
I DIG IT.
IF I DON'T HAVE TO LOOK AT THEM, IT JUST MIGHT WORK!
WHAT A SPLENDID PLAN.
BUT THAT FIRST JOB, INGREDIENT SELECTION-- ISN'T THAT JUST LIKE GROCERY SHOPPING?
WHERE'S THE SEX APPEAL IN THAT?
I'D RATHER DIE THAN DO THAT!
No thanks!
IN THAT CASE---
---I'LL DO IT.
YOU'RE FINE WITH THAT?!
HEH HEH---
IT MEANS THAT YOU TWO CAN'T USE ANY INGREDIENTS BUT THE ONES I CHOOSE FOR YOU.
IN ESSENCE, I'LL BE HOLDING THE POWER TO DECIDE WHAT KIND OF BREAD WILL BE MADE.

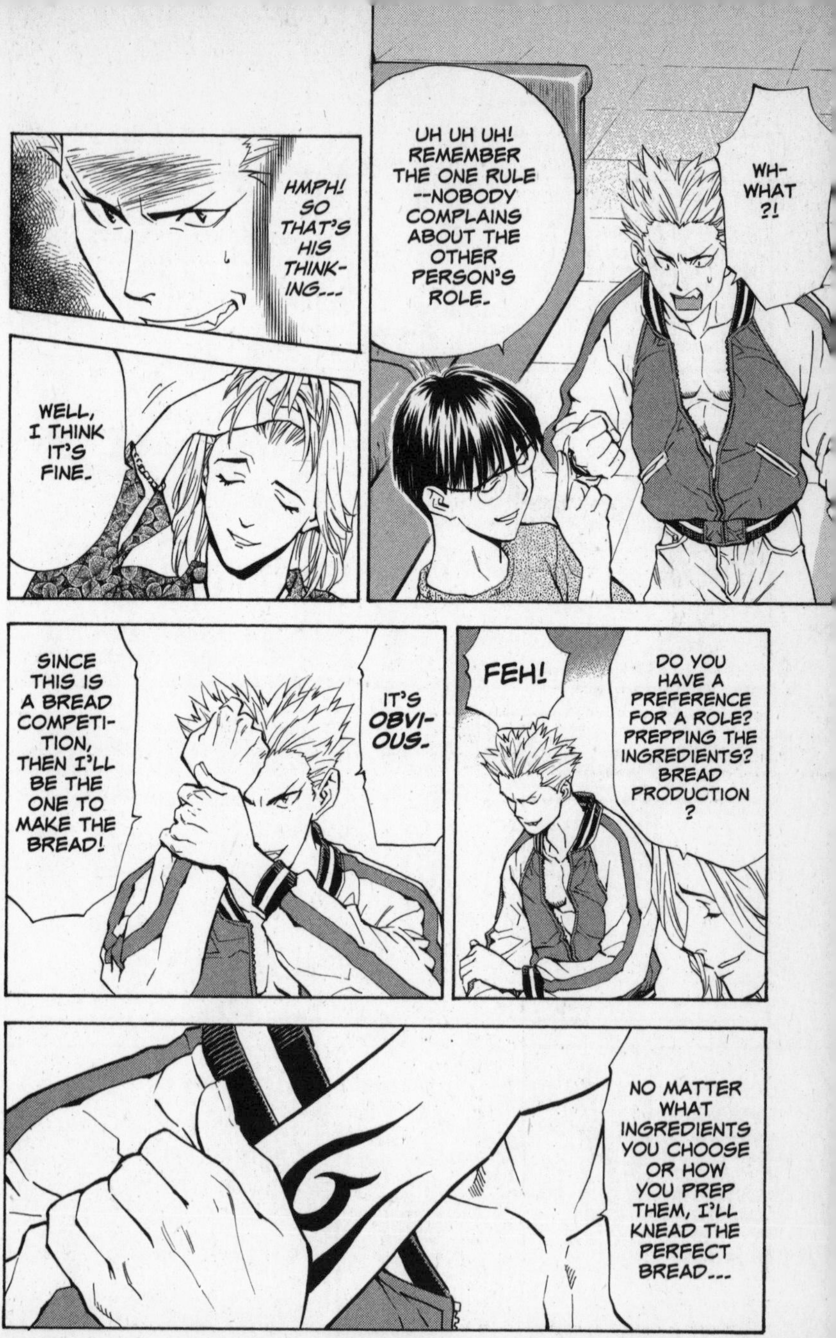
WH-WHAT?!
UH UH UH! REMEMBER THE ONE RULE --NOBODY COMPLAINS ABOUT THE OTHER PERSON'S ROLE.
HMPH! SO THAT'S HIS THINKING...
WELL, I THINK IT'S FINE.
DO YOU HAVE A PREFERENCE FOR A ROLE? PREPPING THE INGREDIENTS? BREAD PRODUCTION?
FEH!
IT'S OBVIOUS.
SINCE THIS IS A BREAD COMPETITION, THEN I'LL BE THE ONE TO MAKE THE BREAD!
NO MATTER WHAT INGREDIENTS YOU CHOOSE OR HOW YOU PREP THEM, I'LL KNEAD THE PERFECT BREAD...

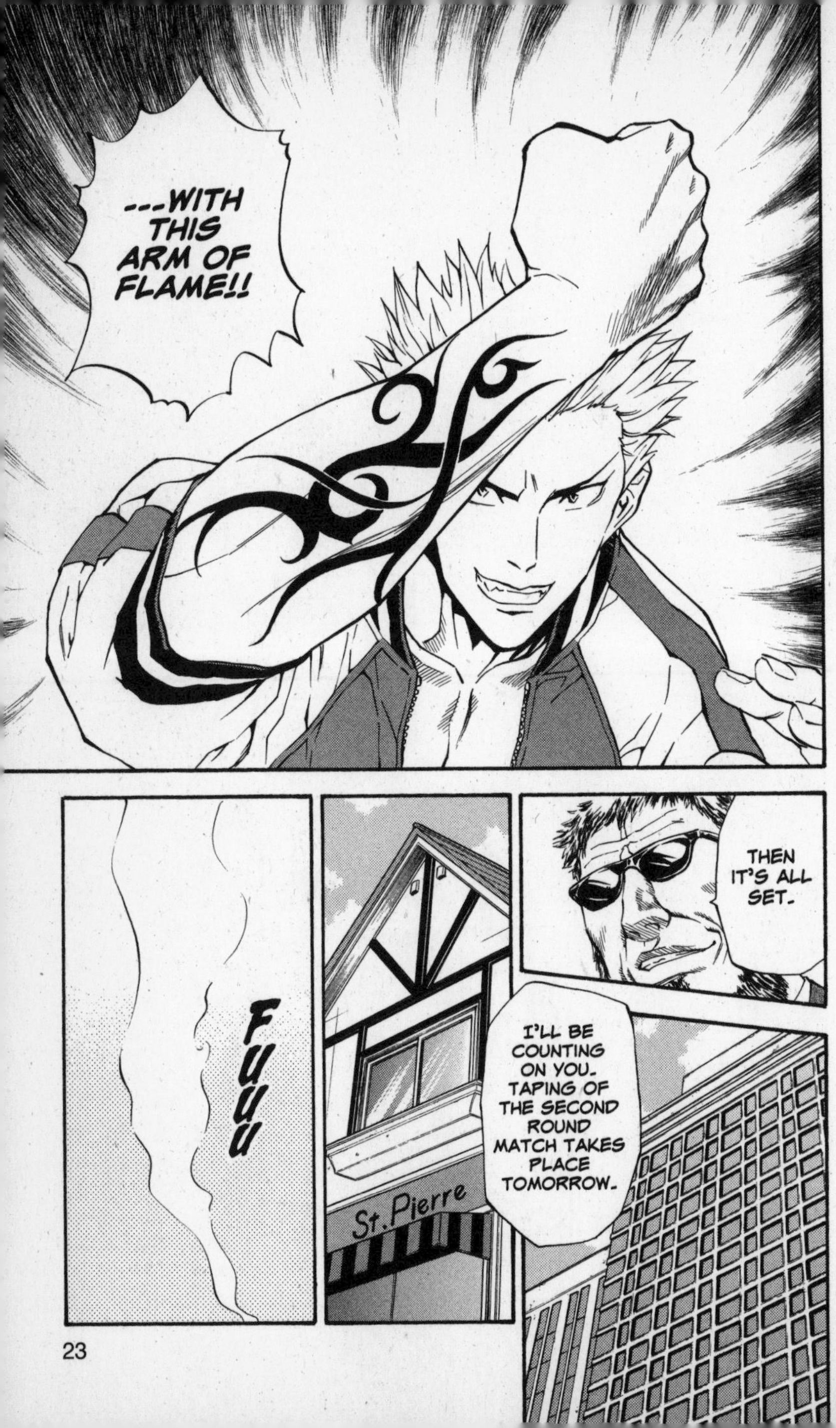
---WITH THIS ARM OF FLAME!!
THEN IT'S ALL SET.
I'LL BE COUNTING ON YOU. TAPING OF THE SECOND ROUND MATCH TAKES PLACE TOMORROW.
St. Pierre
FUUU

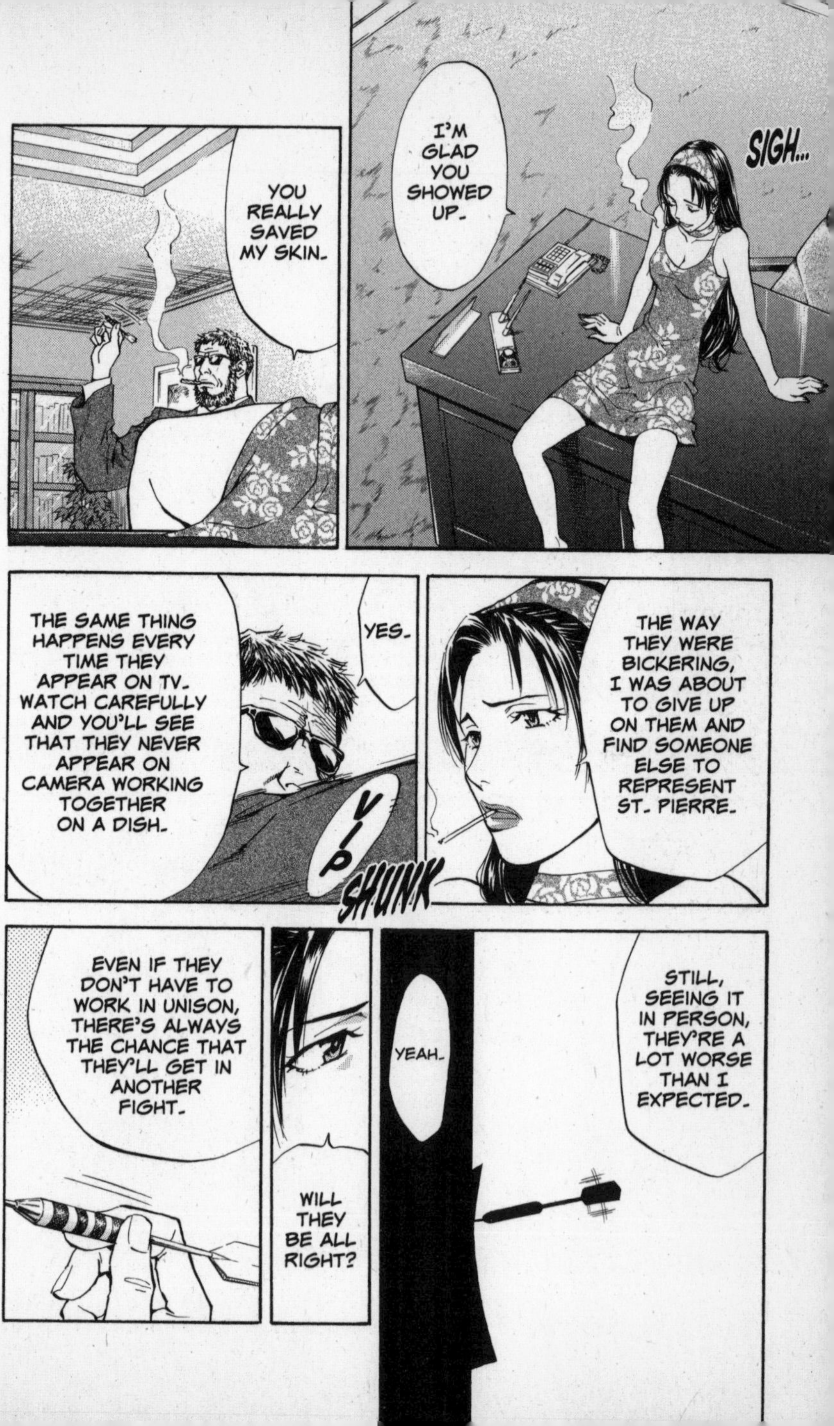
SIGH...
I'M GLAD YOU SHOWED UP.
YOU REALLY SAVED MY SKIN.
THE WAY THEY WERE BICKERING, I WAS ABOUT TO GIVE UP ON THEM AND FIND SOMEONE ELSE TO REPRESENT ST. PIERRE.
YES.
THE SAME THING HAPPENS EVERY TIME THEY APPEAR ON TV. WATCH CAREFULLY AND YOU'LL SEE THAT THEY NEVER APPEAR ON CAMERA WORKING TOGETHER ON A DISH.
VIP
SHUNK
STILL, SEEING IT IN PERSON, THEY'RE A LOT WORSE THAN I EXPECTED.
YEAH.
WILL THEY BE ALL RIGHT?
EVEN IF THEY DON'T HAVE TO WORK IN UNISON, THERE'S ALWAYS THE CHANCE THAT THEY'LL GET IN ANOTHER FIGHT.

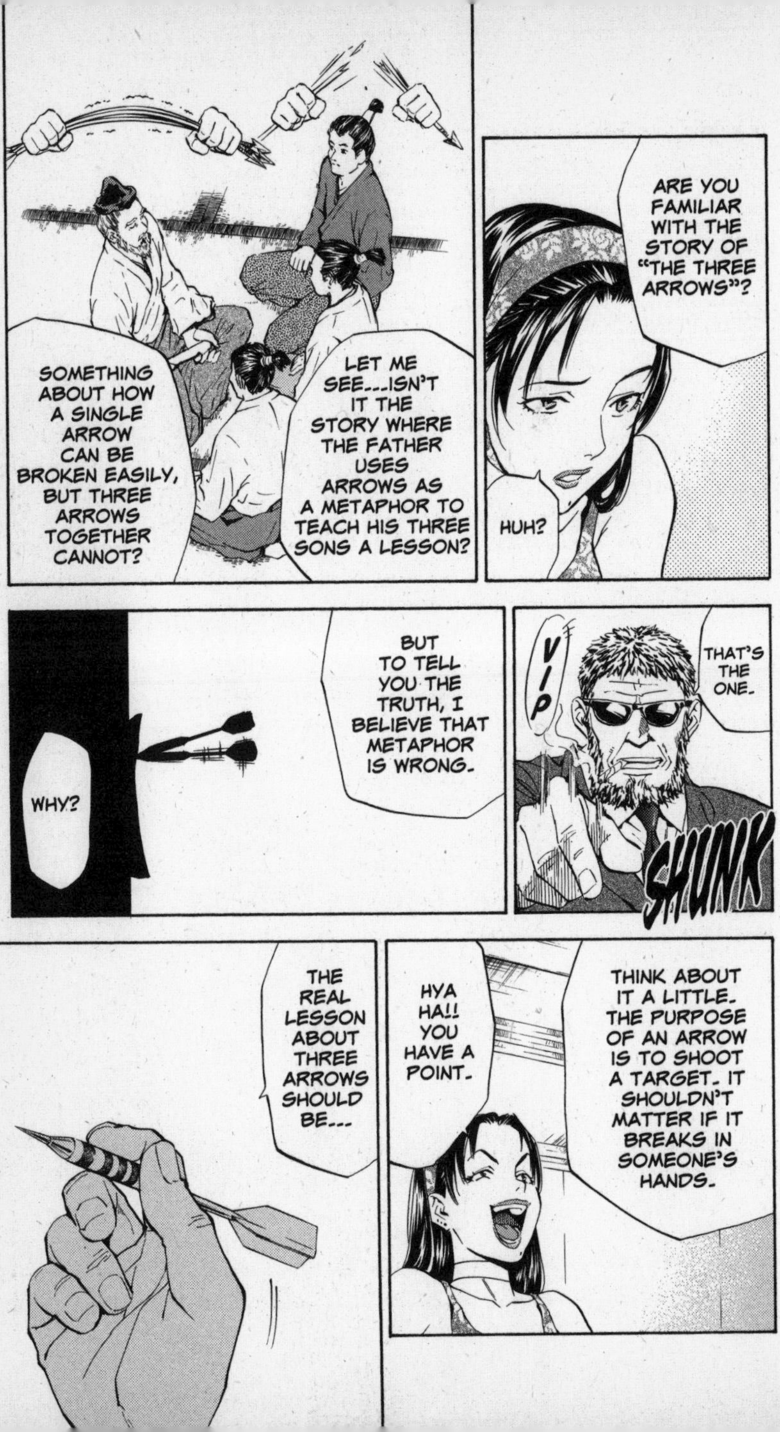
ARE YOU FAMILIAR WITH THE STORY OF "THE THREE ARROWS"?
HUH?
LET ME SEE...ISN'T IT THE STORY WHERE THE FATHER USES ARROWS AS A METAPHOR TO TEACH HIS THREE SONS A LESSON?
SOMETHING ABOUT HOW A SINGLE ARROW CAN BE BROKEN EASILY, BUT THREE ARROWS TOGETHER CANNOT?
VIP
THAT'S THE ONE.
SHUNK
BUT TO TELL YOU THE TRUTH, I BELIEVE THAT METAPHOR IS WRONG.
WHY?
THINK ABOUT IT A LITTLE. THE PURPOSE OF AN ARROW IS TO SHOOT A TARGET. IT SHOULDN'T MATTER IF IT BREAKS IN SOMEONE'S HANDS.
HYA HA!! YOU HAVE A POINT.
THE REAL LESSON ABOUT THREE ARROWS SHOULD BE...

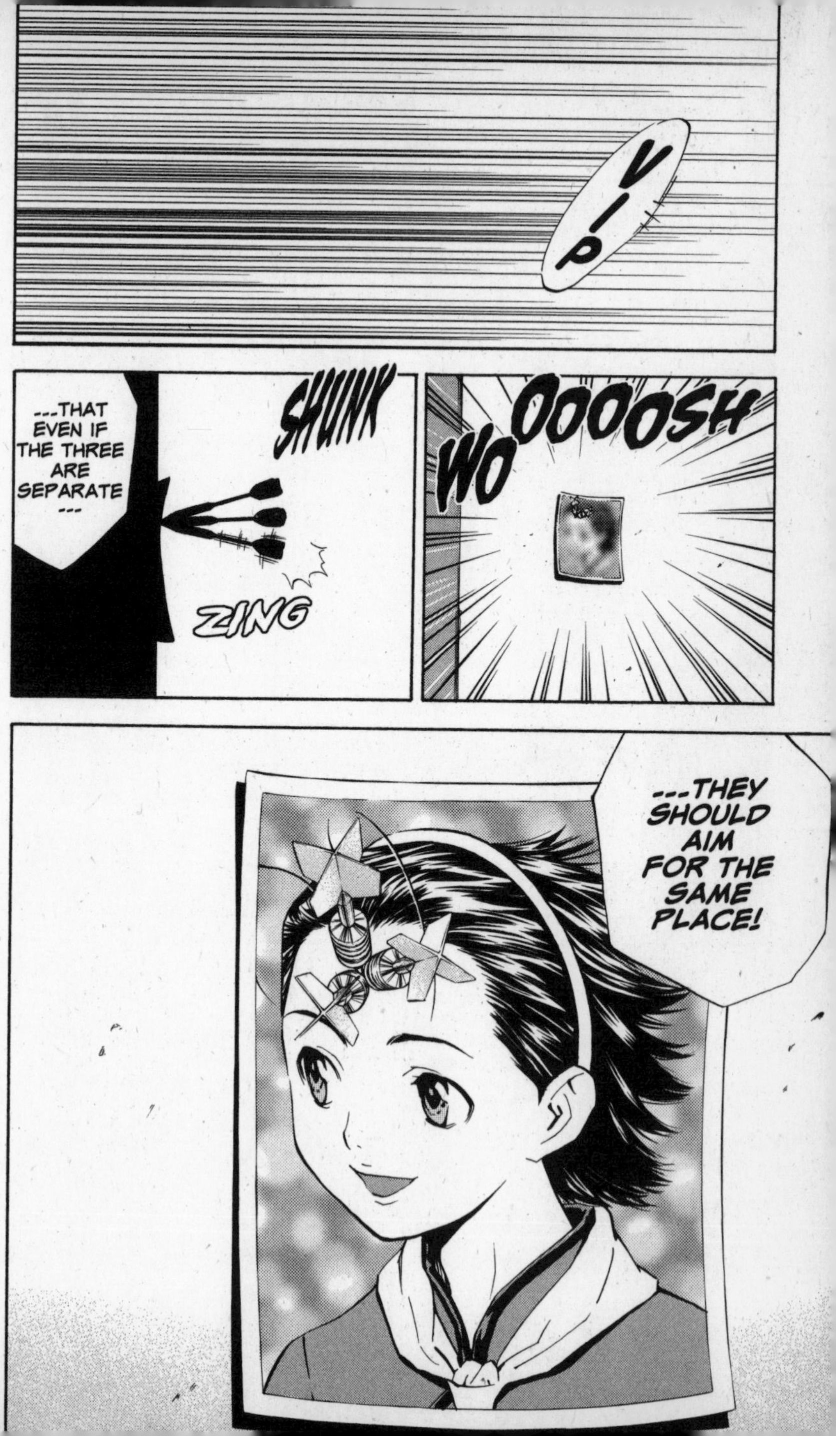
VIP
WOOOOOSH
---THAT EVEN IF THE THREE ARE SEPARATE ---
SHUNK
ZING
---THEY SHOULD AIM FOR THE SAME PLACE!

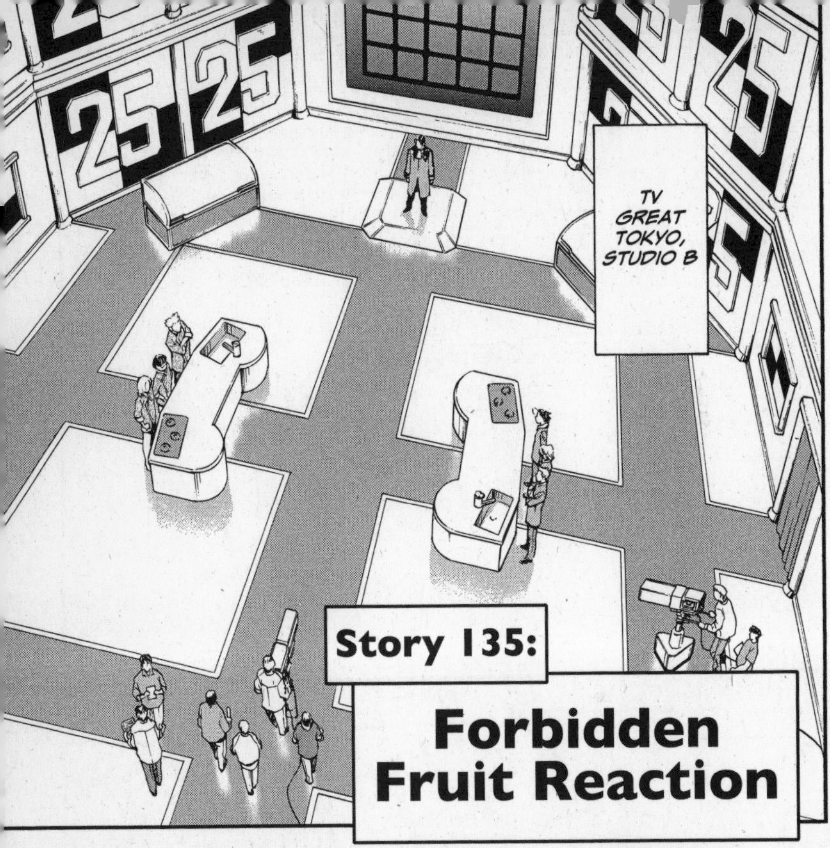
TV GREAT TOKYO, STUDIO B
Story 135:
Forbidden Fruit Reaction
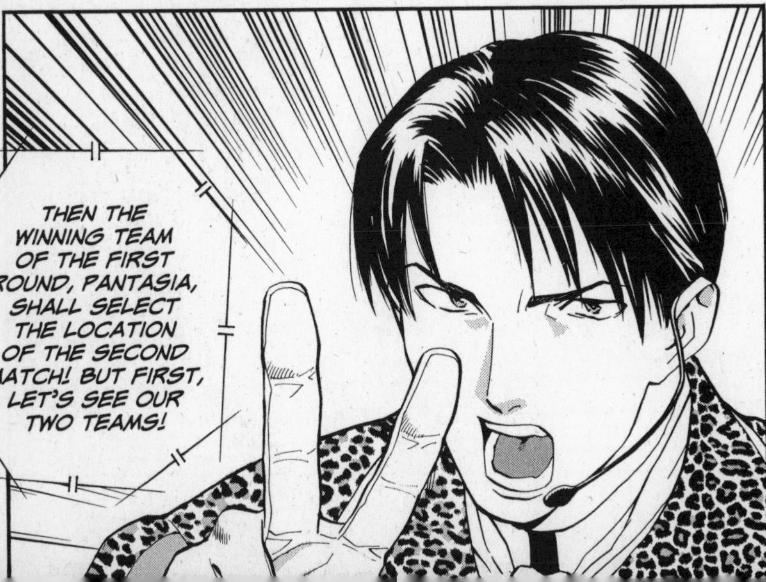
THEN THE WINNING TEAM OF THE FIRST ROUND, PANTASIA, SHALL SELECT THE LOCATION OF THE SECOND MATCH! BUT FIRST, LET'S SEE OUR TWO TEAMS!

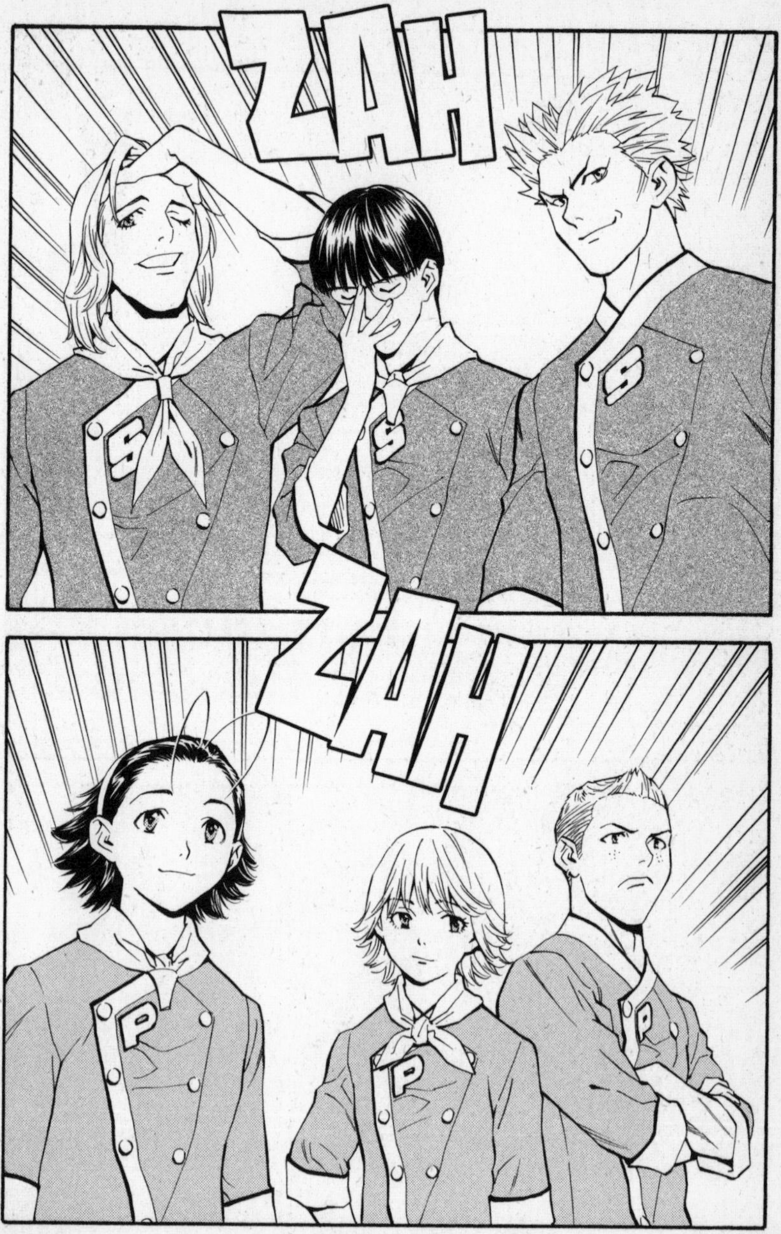
ZAH
ZAH

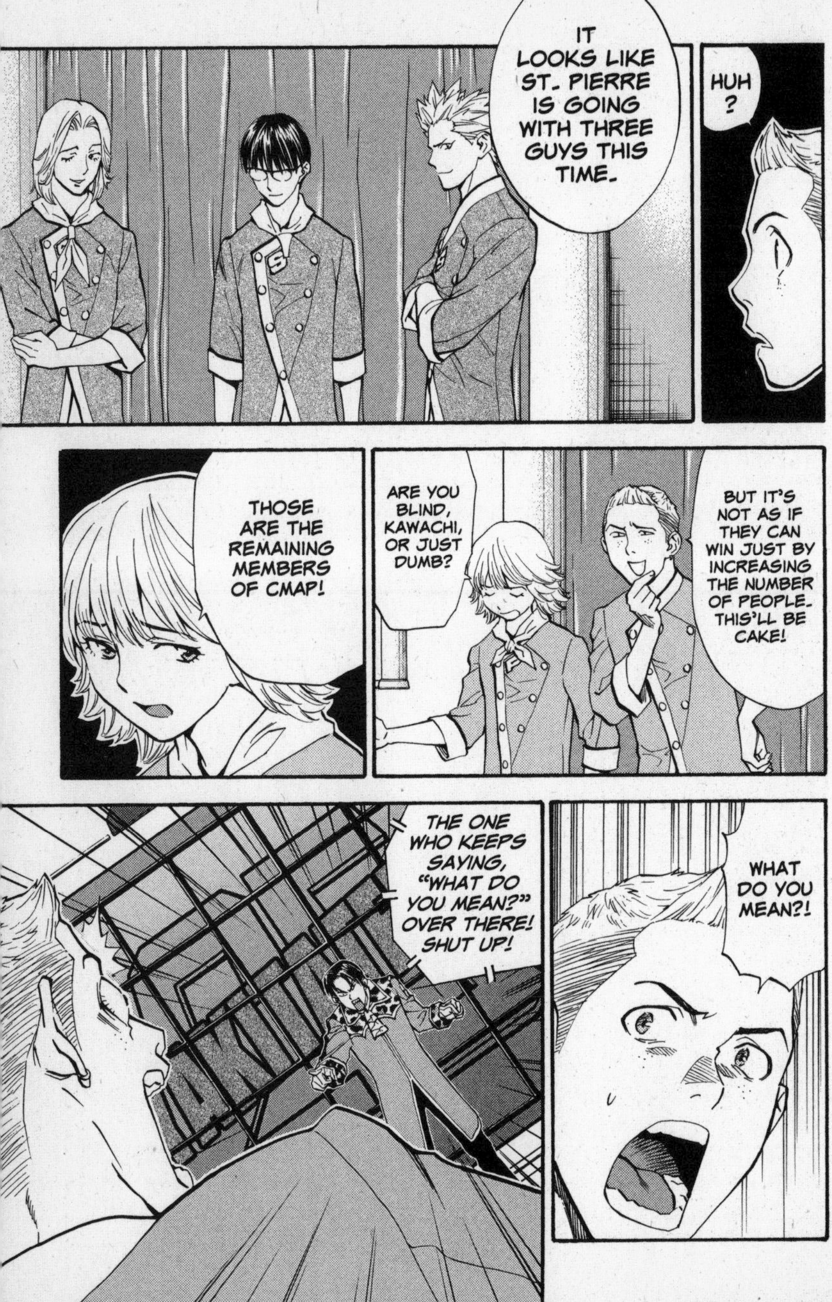
HUH?
IT LOOKS LIKE ST. PIERRE IS GOING WITH THREE GUYS THIS TIME.
BUT IT'S NOT AS IF THEY CAN WIN JUST BY INCREASING THE NUMBER OF PEOPLE. THIS'LL BE CAKE!
ARE YOU BLIND, KAWACHI, OR JUST DUMB?
THOSE ARE THE REMAINING MEMBERS OF CMAP!
WHAT DO YOU MEAN?!
THE ONE WHO KEEPS SAYING, "WHAT DO YOU MEAN?" OVER THERE! SHUT UP!

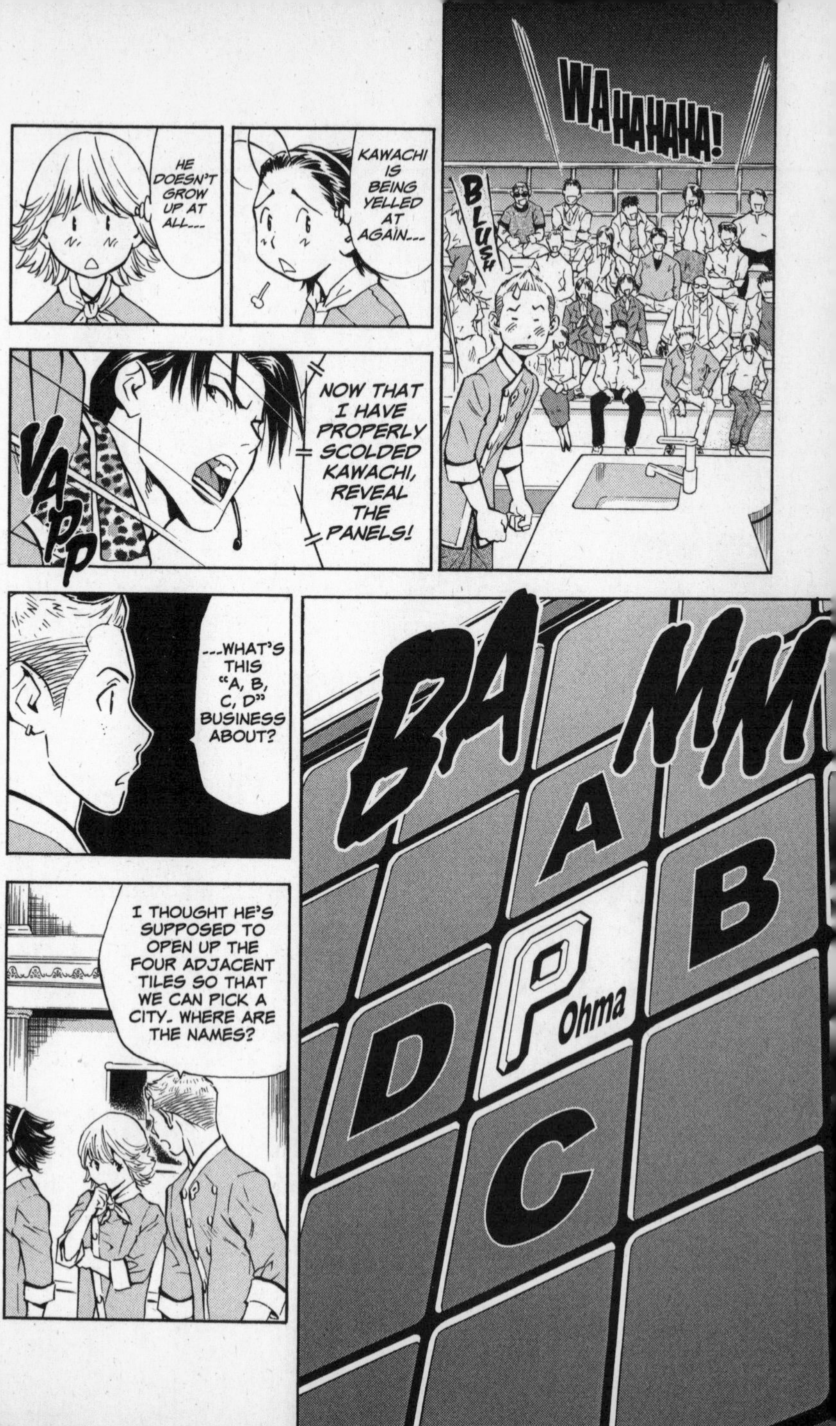
WAHAHAHA!
BLUSH
KAWACHI IS BEING YELLED AT AGAIN...
HE DOESN'T GROW UP AT ALL...
NOW THAT I HAVE PROPERLY SCOLDED KAWACHI, REVEAL THE PANELS!
VAPP
BAMM
A
B
P
Ohma
D
C
...WHAT'S THIS "A, B, C, D" BUSINESS ABOUT?
I THOUGHT HE'S SUPPOSED TO OPEN UP THE FOUR ADJACENT TILES SO THAT WE CAN PICK A CITY. WHERE ARE THE NAMES?

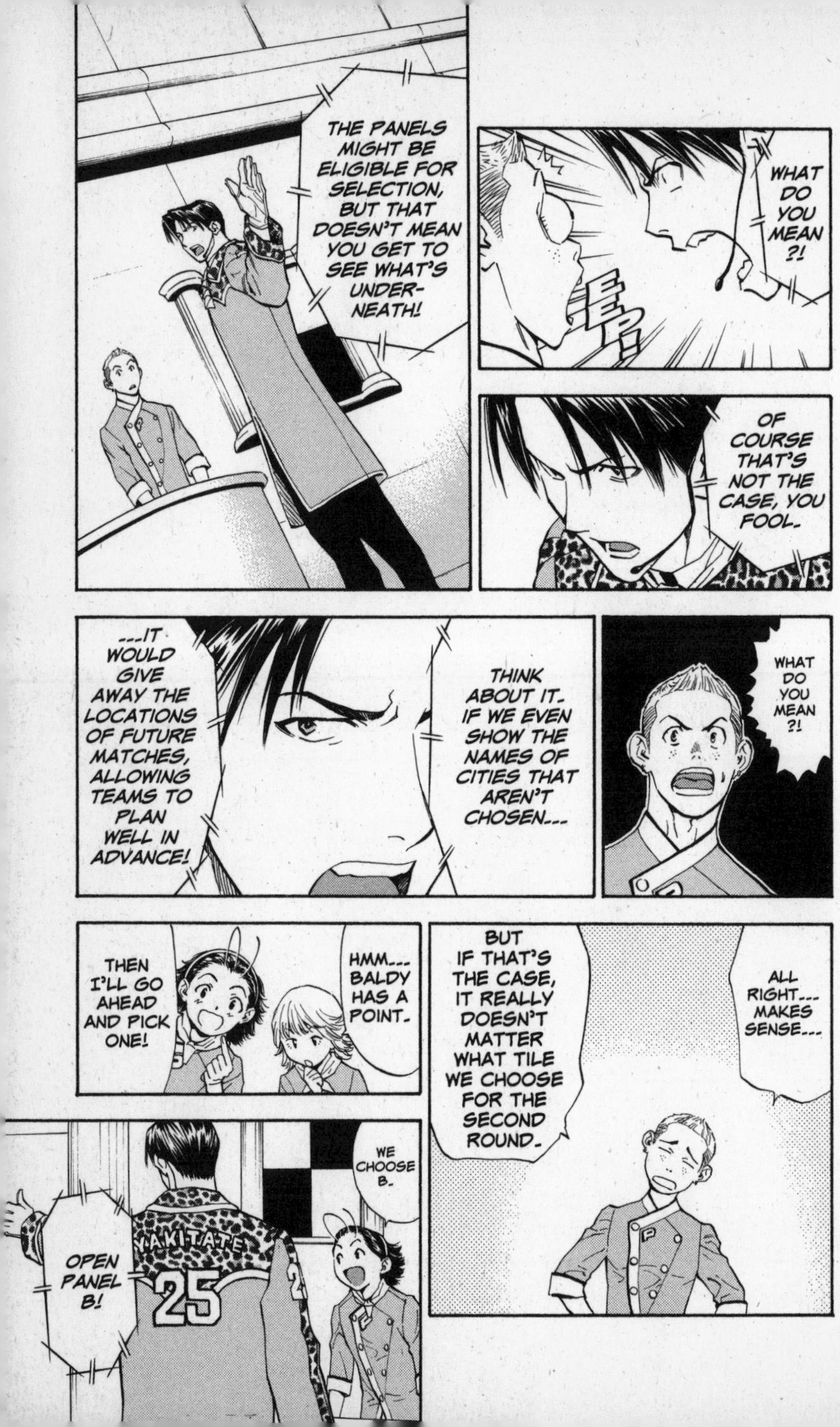
WHAT DO YOU MEAN?!
EEP!
OF COURSE THAT'S NOT THE CASE, YOU FOOL.
THE PANELS MIGHT BE ELIGIBLE FOR SELECTION, BUT THAT DOESN'T MEAN YOU GET TO SEE WHAT'S UNDER-NEATH!
WHAT DO YOU MEAN?!
THINK ABOUT IT. IF WE EVEN SHOW THE NAMES OF CITIES THAT AREN'T CHOSEN...
...IT WOULD GIVE AWAY THE LOCATIONS OF FUTURE MATCHES, ALLOWING TEAMS TO PLAN WELL IN ADVANCE!
ALL RIGHT... MAKES SENSE...
BUT IF THAT'S THE CASE, IT REALLY DOESN'T MATTER WHAT TILE WE CHOOSE FOR THE SECOND ROUND.
HMM... BALDY HAS A POINT.
THEN I'LL GO AHEAD AND PICK ONE!
WE CHOOSE B.
YAKITATE
25
OPEN PANEL B!

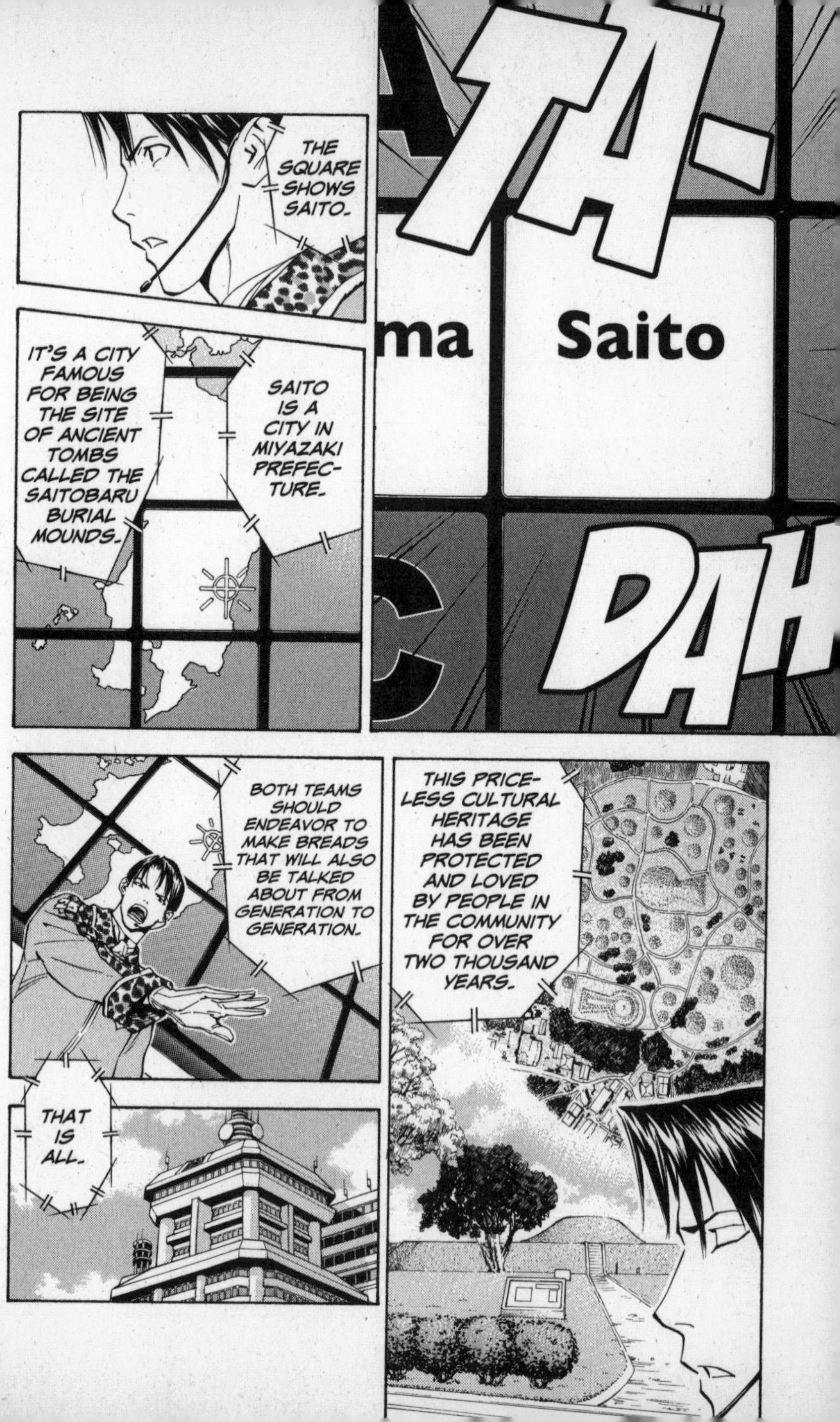
TA-
ma
Saito
DAH
THE SQUARE SHOWS SAITO.
SAITO IS A CITY IN MIYAZAKI PREFECTURE.
IT'S A CITY FAMOUS FOR BEING THE SITE OF ANCIENT TOMBS CALLED THE SAITOBARU BURIAL MOUNDS.
THIS PRICELESS CULTURAL HERITAGE HAS BEEN PROTECTED AND LOVED BY PEOPLE IN THE COMMUNITY FOR OVER TWO THOUSAND YEARS.
BOTH TEAMS SHOULD ENDEAVOR TO MAKE BREADS THAT WILL ALSO BE TALKED ABOUT FROM GENERATION TO GENERATION.
THAT IS ALL.

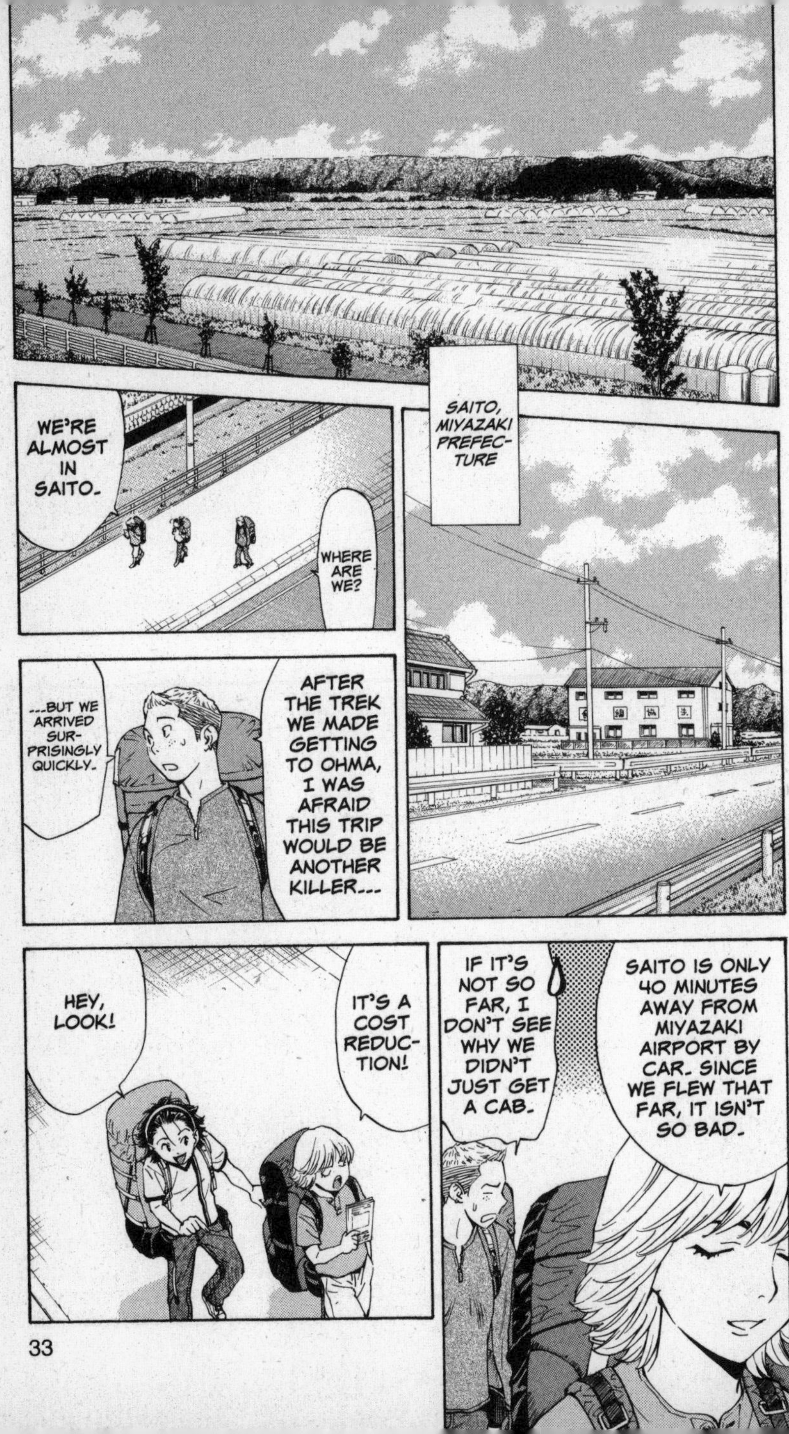

SAITO, MIYAZAKI PREFECTURE
WHERE ARE WE?
WE'RE ALMOST IN SAITO.
AFTER THE TREK WE MADE GETTING TO OHMA, I WAS AFRAID THIS TRIP WOULD BE ANOTHER KILLER...
...BUT WE ARRIVED SURPRISINGLY QUICKLY.
SAITO IS ONLY 40 MINUTES AWAY FROM MIYAZAKI AIRPORT BY CAR. SINCE WE FLEW THAT FAR, IT ISN'T SO BAD.
IF IT'S NOT SO FAR, I DON'T SEE WHY WE DIDN'T JUST GET A CAB.
IT'S A COST REDUCTION!
HEY, LOOK!

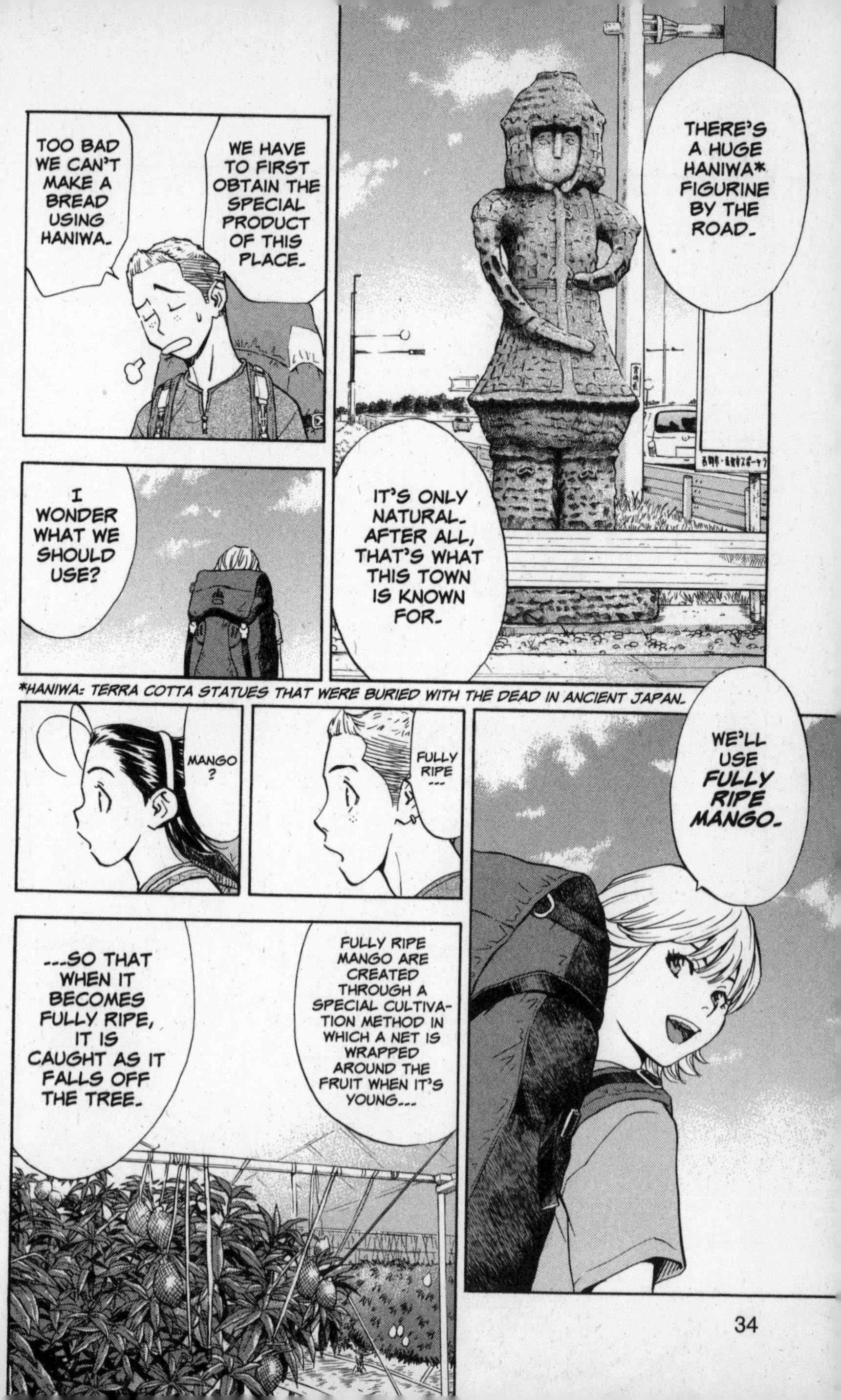
THERE'S A HUGE HANIWA* FIGURINE BY THE ROAD.
IT'S ONLY NATURAL. AFTER ALL, THAT'S WHAT THIS TOWN IS KNOWN FOR.
WE HAVE TO FIRST OBTAIN THE SPECIAL PRODUCT OF THIS PLACE.
TOO BAD WE CAN'T MAKE A BREAD USING HANIWA.
I WONDER WHAT WE SHOULD USE?
*HANIWA: TERRA COTTA STATUES THAT WERE BURIED WITH THE DEAD IN ANCIENT JAPAN.
WE'LL USE *FULLY RIPE MANGO.*
FULLY RIPE...
MANGO?
FULLY RIPE MANGO ARE CREATED THROUGH A SPECIAL CULTIVATION METHOD IN WHICH A NET IS WRAPPED AROUND THE FRUIT WHEN IT'S YOUNG...
...SO THAT WHEN IT BECOMES FULLY RIPE, IT IS CAUGHT AS IT FALLS OFF THE TREE.

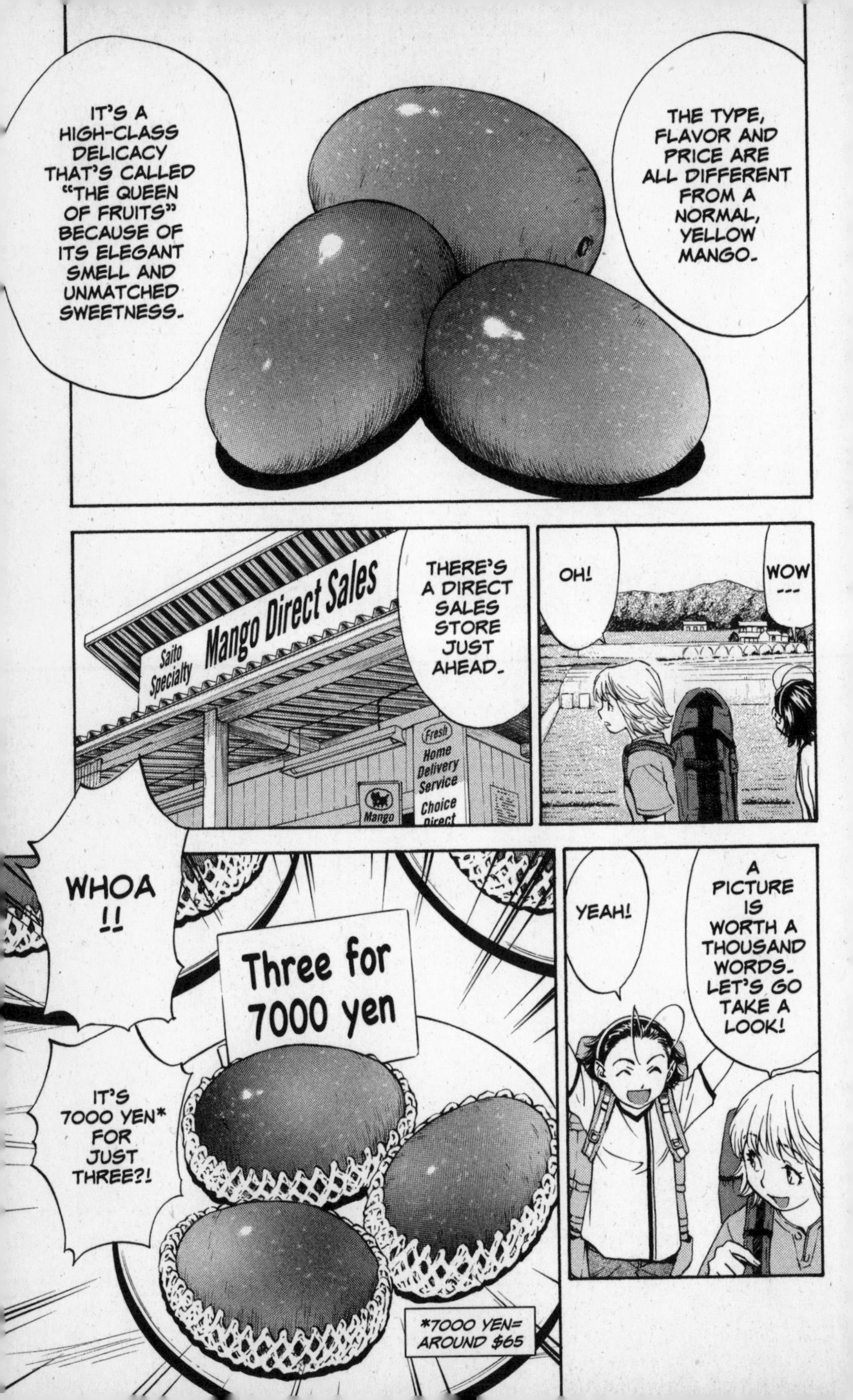
THE TYPE, FLAVOR AND PRICE ARE ALL DIFFERENT FROM A NORMAL, YELLOW MANGO.
IT'S A HIGH-CLASS DELICACY THAT'S CALLED "THE QUEEN OF FRUITS" BECAUSE OF ITS ELEGANT SMELL AND UNMATCHED SWEETNESS.
WOW---
OH!
THERE'S A DIRECT SALES STORE JUST AHEAD.
Mango Direct Sales
Saito Specialty
Fresh
Home Delivery Service
Choice
Mango
A PICTURE IS WORTH A THOUSAND WORDS. LET'S GO TAKE A LOOK!
YEAH!
WHOA!!
Three for 7000 yen
IT'S 7000 YEN* FOR JUST THREE?!
*7000 YEN= AROUND $65

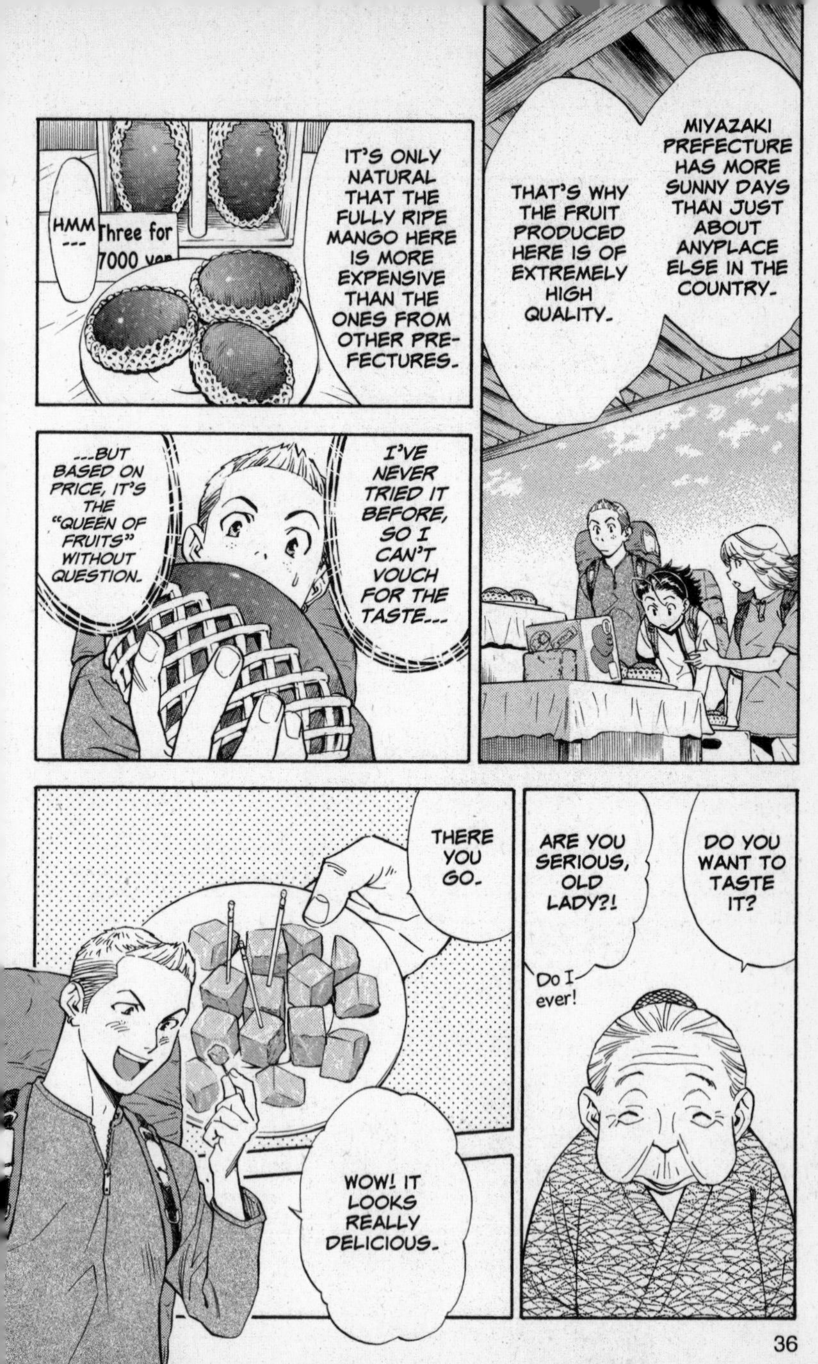
MIYAZAKI PREFECTURE HAS MORE SUNNY DAYS THAN JUST ABOUT ANYPLACE ELSE IN THE COUNTRY.
THAT'S WHY THE FRUIT PRODUCED HERE IS OF EXTREMELY HIGH QUALITY.
IT'S ONLY NATURAL THAT THE FULLY RIPE MANGO HERE IS MORE EXPENSIVE THAN THE ONES FROM OTHER PRE-FECTURES.
HMM---
Three for 7000 yen
I'VE NEVER TRIED IT BEFORE, SO I CAN'T VOUCH FOR THE TASTE---
---BUT BASED ON PRICE, IT'S THE "QUEEN OF FRUITS" WITHOUT QUESTION.
DO YOU WANT TO TASTE IT?
ARE YOU SERIOUS, OLD LADY?!
Do I ever!
THERE YOU GO.
WOW! IT LOOKS REALLY DELICIOUS.

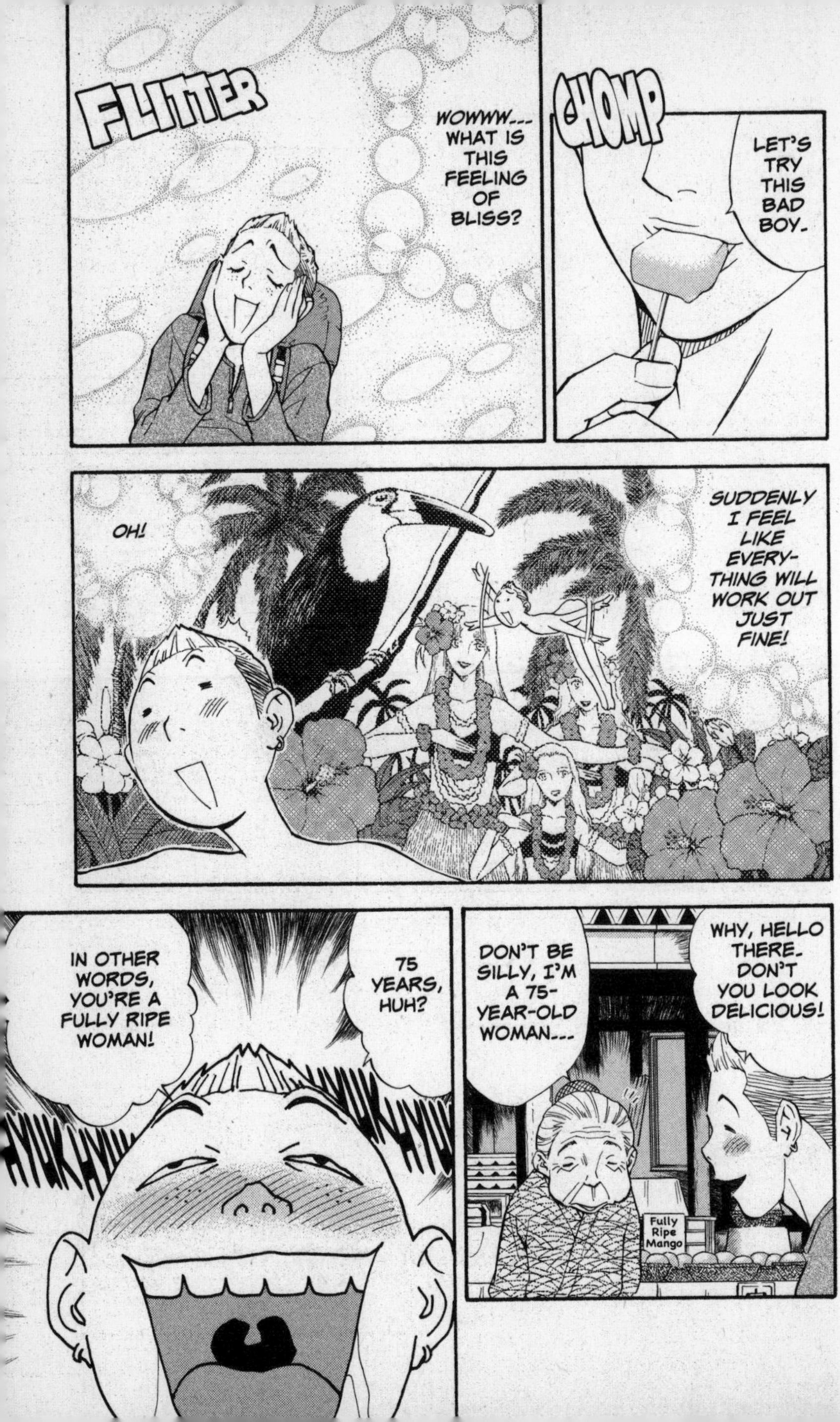
CHOMP
LET'S TRY THIS BAD BOY.
FLITTER
WOWWW... WHAT IS THIS FEELING OF BLISS?
SUDDENLY I FEEL LIKE EVERYTHING WILL WORK OUT JUST FINE!
OH!
WHY, HELLO THERE. DON'T YOU LOOK DELICIOUS!
DON'T BE SILLY, I'M A 75-YEAR-OLD WOMAN...
Fully Ripe Mango
75 YEARS, HUH?
IN OTHER WORDS, YOU'RE A FULLY RIPE WOMAN!
HYUK HYUK
HYUK HYUK

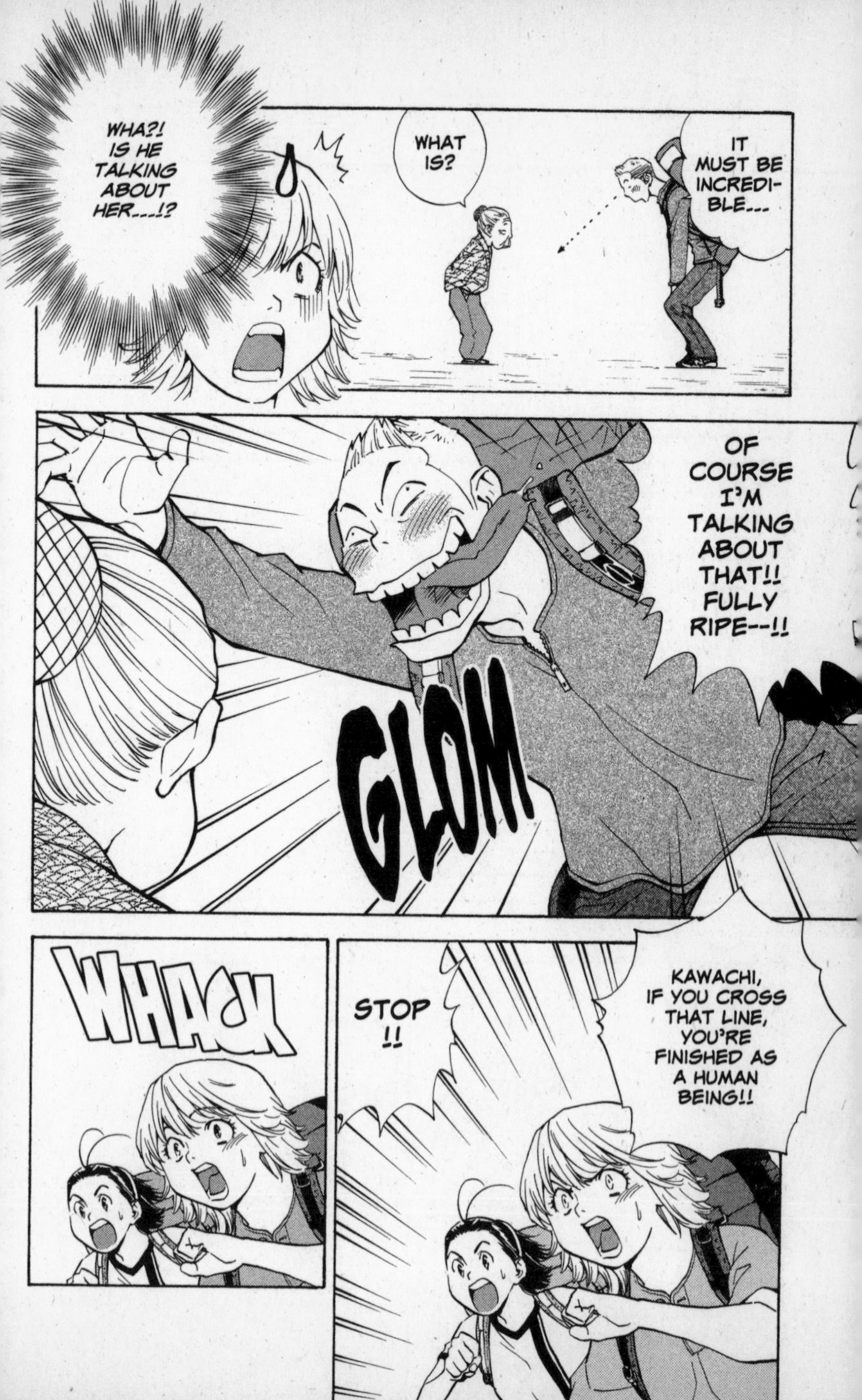
IT MUST BE INCREDIBLE...
WHAT IS?
WHA?! IS HE TALKING ABOUT HER...!?
OF COURSE I'M TALKING ABOUT THAT!! FULLY RIPE--!!
GLOM
KAWACHI, IF YOU CROSS THAT LINE, YOU'RE FINISHED AS A HUMAN BEING!!
STOP!!
WHACK

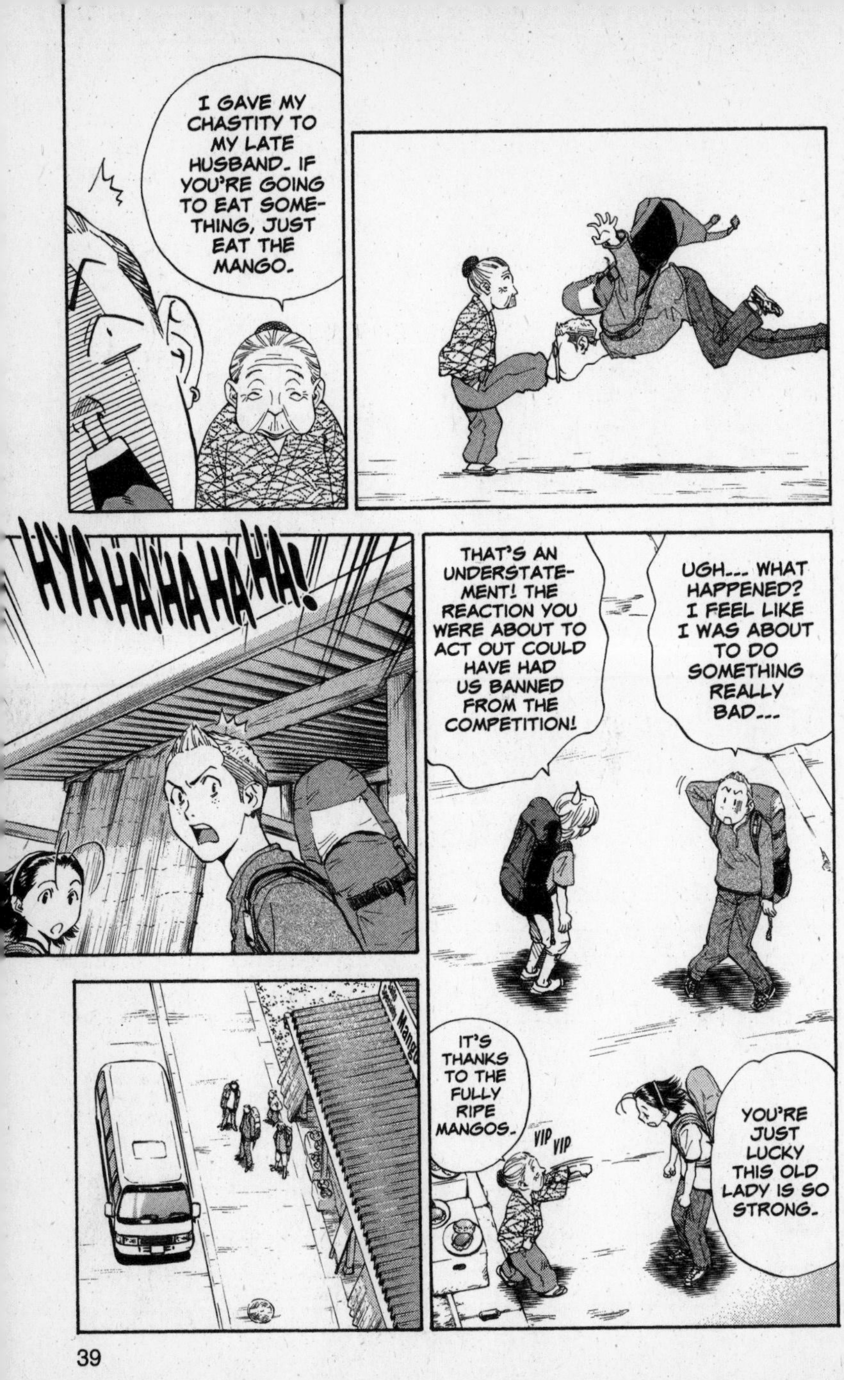
I GAVE MY CHASTITY TO MY LATE HUSBAND. IF YOU'RE GOING TO EAT SOMETHING, JUST EAT THE MANGO.
UGH... WHAT HAPPENED? I FEEL LIKE I WAS ABOUT TO DO SOMETHING REALLY BAD...
THAT'S AN UNDERSTATEMENT! THE REACTION YOU WERE ABOUT TO ACT OUT COULD HAVE HAD US BANNED FROM THE COMPETITION!
YOU'RE JUST LUCKY THIS OLD LADY IS SO STRONG.
VIP VIP
IT'S THANKS TO THE FULLY RIPE MANGOS.
HYAHAHAHAHAHA!

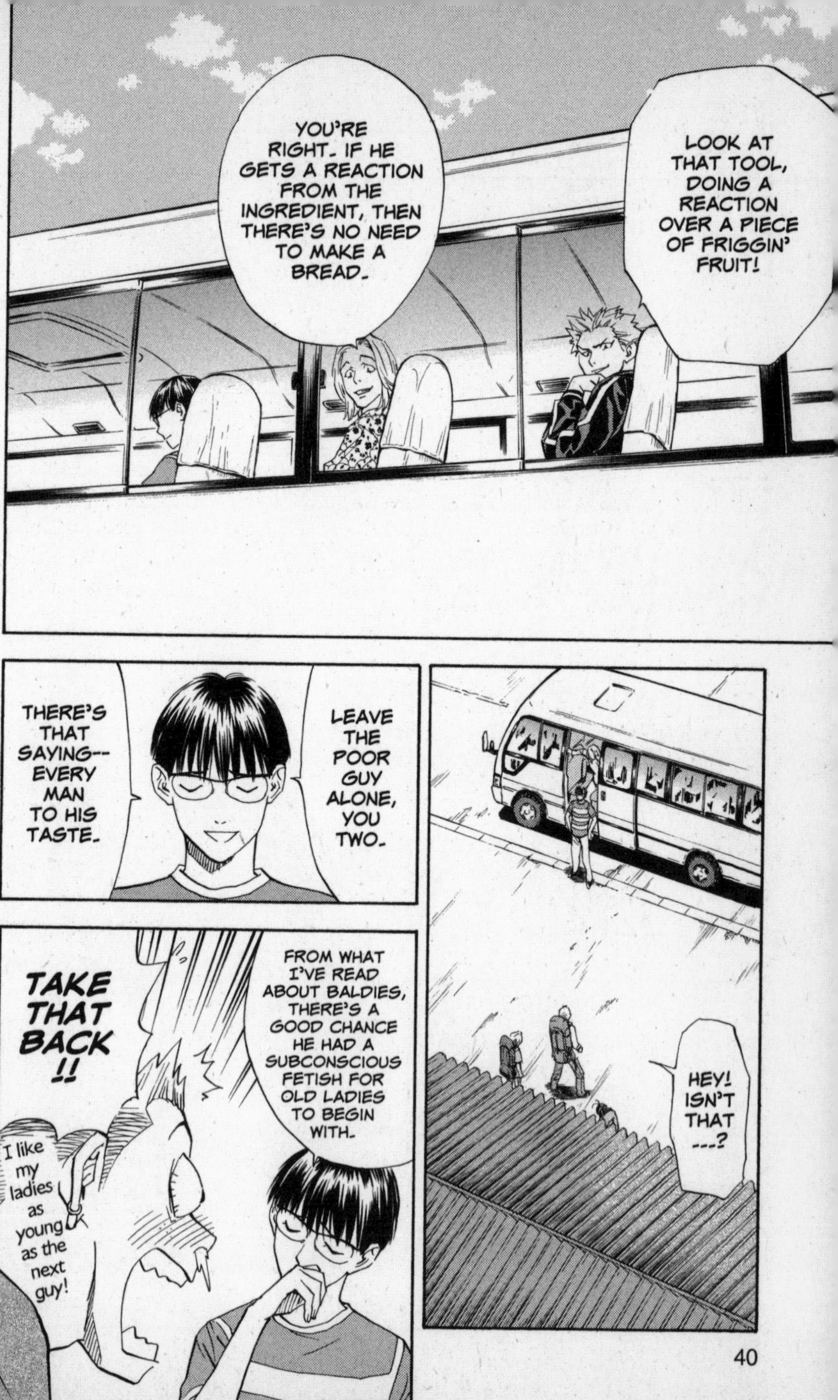
LOOK AT THAT TOOL, DOING A REACTION OVER A PIECE OF FRIGGIN' FRUIT!
YOU'RE RIGHT. IF HE GETS A REACTION FROM THE INGREDIENT, THEN THERE'S NO NEED TO MAKE A BREAD.
HEY! ISN'T THAT ...?
LEAVE THE POOR GUY ALONE, YOU TWO.
THERE'S THAT SAYING-- EVERY MAN TO HIS TASTE.
FROM WHAT I'VE READ ABOUT BALDIES, THERE'S A GOOD CHANCE HE HAD A SUBCONSCIOUS FETISH FOR OLD LADIES TO BEGIN WITH.
TAKE THAT BACK!!
I like my ladies as young as the next guy!

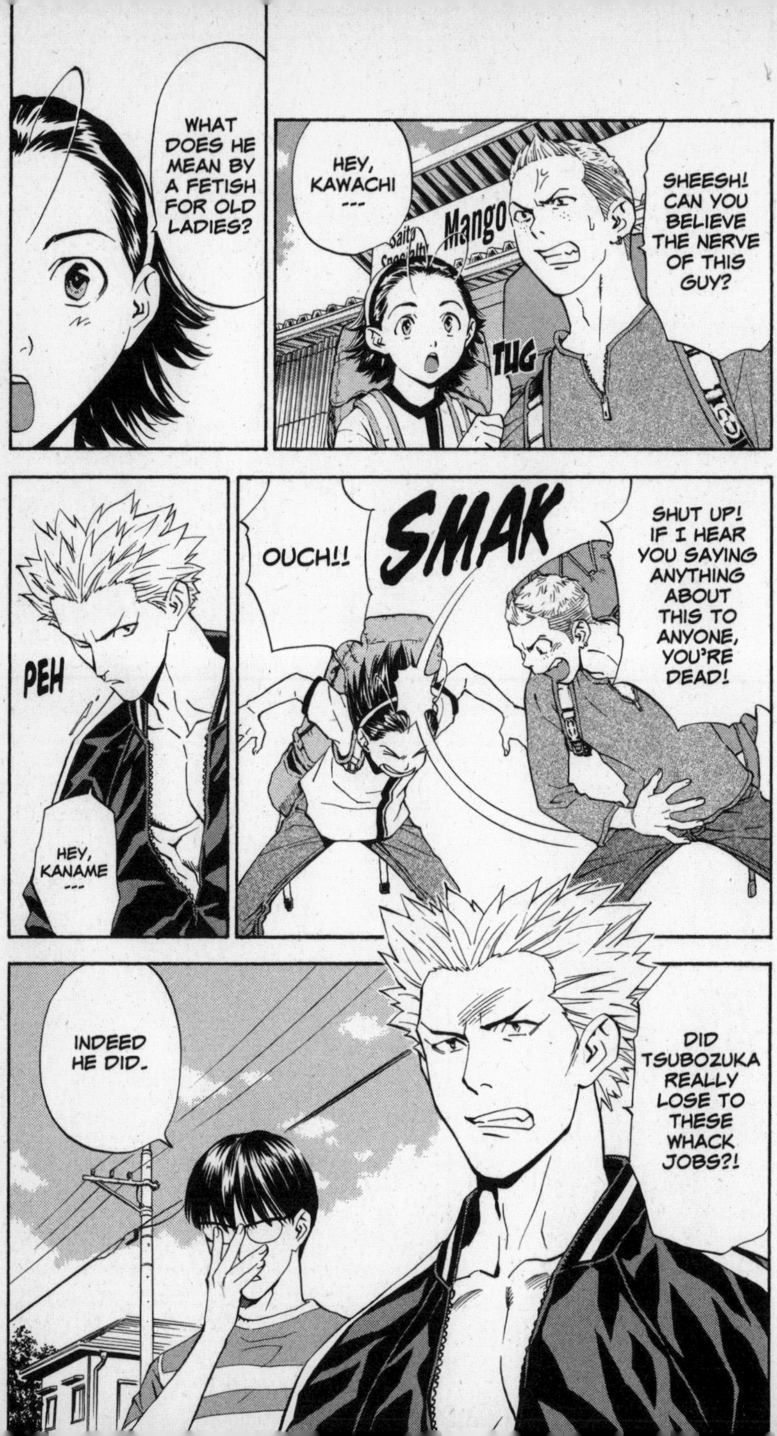
SHEESH! CAN YOU BELIEVE THE NERVE OF THIS GUY?
HEY, KAWACHI ---
Mango
TUG
WHAT DOES HE MEAN BY A FETISH FOR OLD LADIES?
SHUT UP! IF I HEAR YOU SAYING ANYTHING ABOUT THIS TO ANYONE, YOU'RE DEAD!
SMAK
OUCH!!
PEH
HEY, KANAME ---
DID TSUBOZUKA REALLY LOSE TO THESE WHACK JOBS?!
INDEED HE DID.

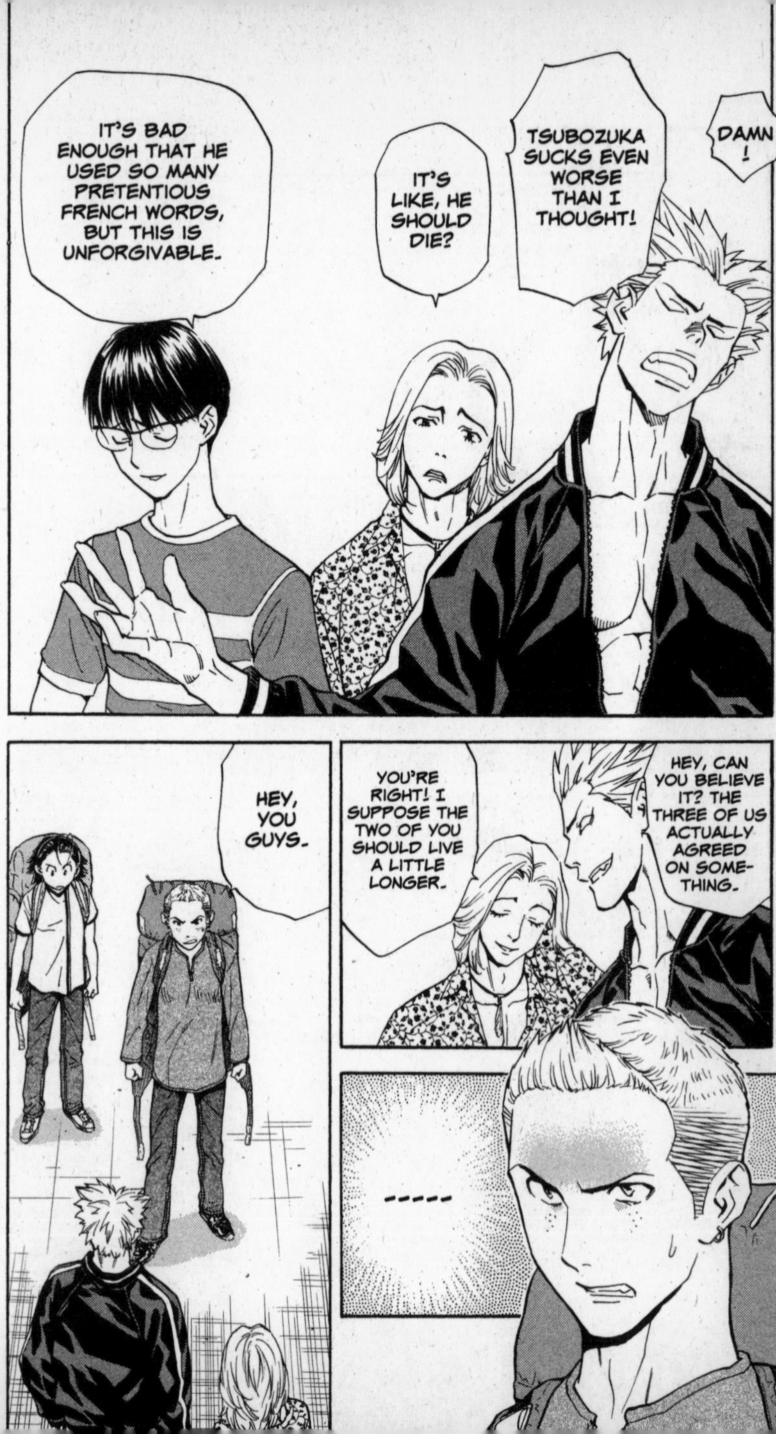
DAMN!
TSUBOZUKA SUCKS EVEN WORSE THAN I THOUGHT!
IT'S LIKE, HE SHOULD DIE?
IT'S BAD ENOUGH THAT HE USED SO MANY PRETENTIOUS FRENCH WORDS, BUT THIS IS UNFORGIVABLE.
HEY, CAN YOU BELIEVE IT? THE THREE OF US ACTUALLY AGREED ON SOME-THING.
YOU'RE RIGHT! I SUPPOSE THE TWO OF YOU SHOULD LIVE A LITTLE LONGER.

HEY, YOU GUYS.

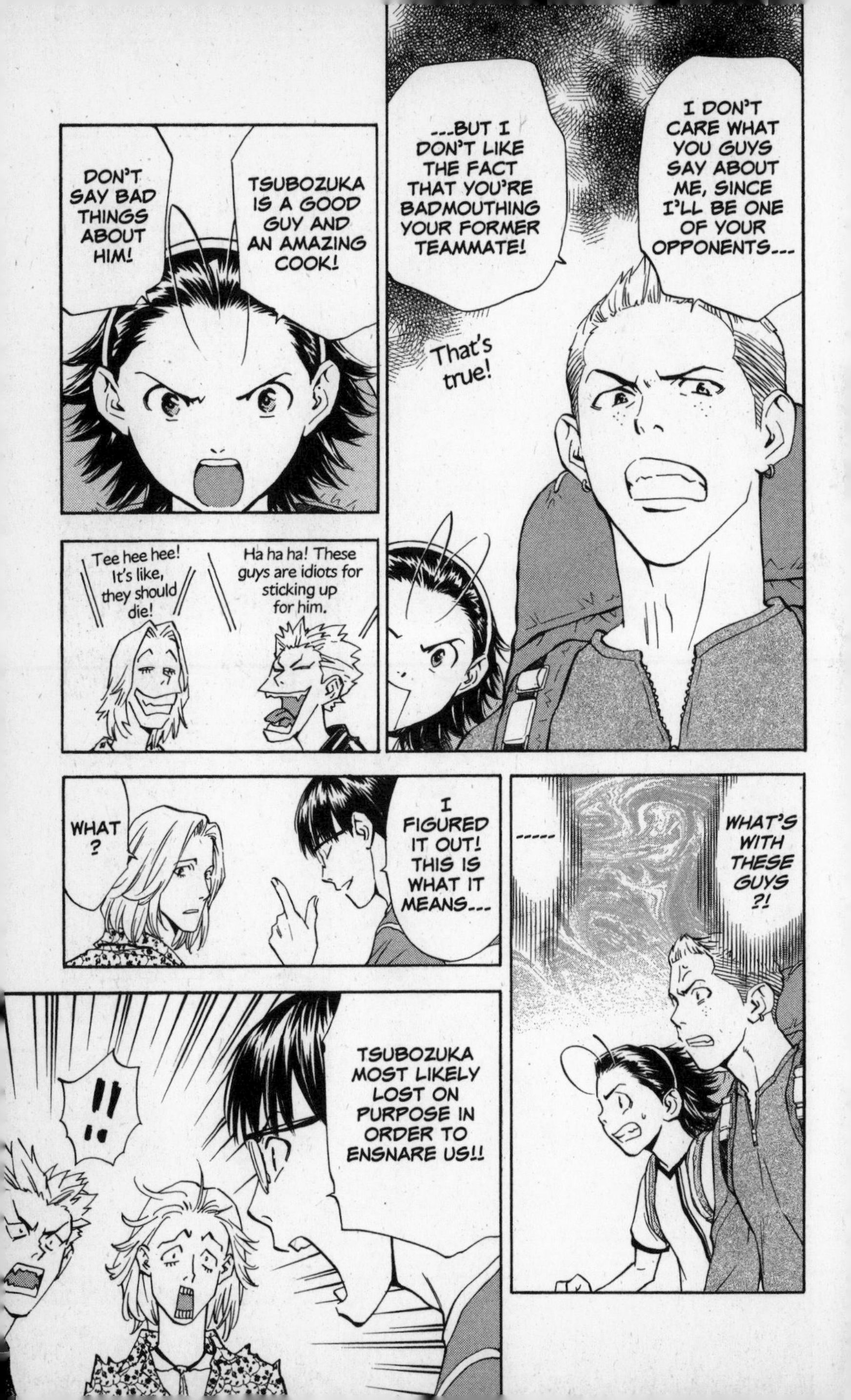

I DON'T CARE WHAT YOU GUYS SAY ABOUT ME, SINCE I'LL BE ONE OF YOUR OPPONENTS...
...BUT I DON'T LIKE THE FACT THAT YOU'RE BADMOUTHING YOUR FORMER TEAMMATE!
That's true!
TSUBOZUKA IS A GOOD GUY AND AN AMAZING COOK!
DON'T SAY BAD THINGS ABOUT HIM!
Ha ha ha! These guys are idiots for sticking up for him.
Tee hee hee! It's like, they should die!
WHAT'S WITH THESE GUYS ?!

I FIGURED IT OUT! THIS IS WHAT IT MEANS...
WHAT ?
TSUBOZUKA MOST LIKELY LOST ON PURPOSE IN ORDER TO ENSNARE US!!
!!

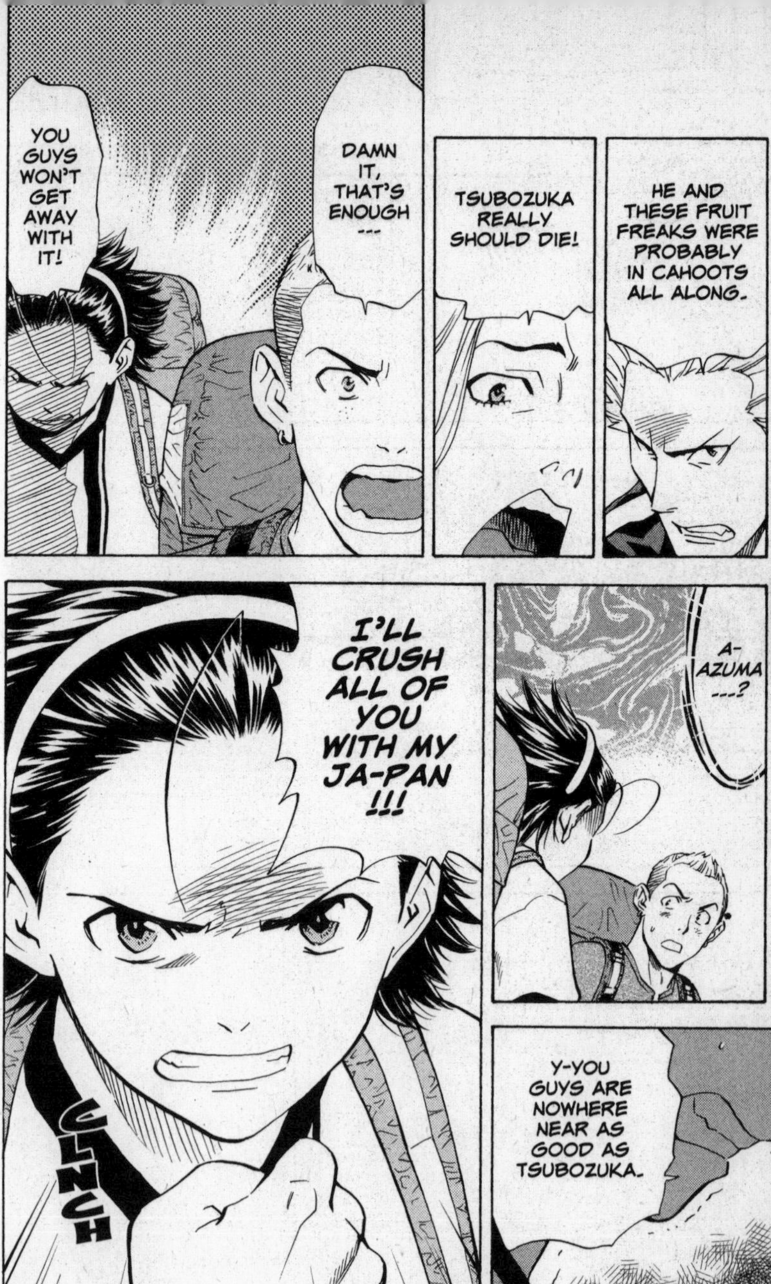
HE AND THESE FRUIT FREAKS WERE PROBABLY IN CAHOOTS ALL ALONG.
TSUBOZUKA REALLY SHOULD DIE!
DAMN IT, THAT'S ENOUGH---
YOU GUYS WON'T GET AWAY WITH IT!
A-AZUMA---?
Y-YOU GUYS ARE NOWHERE NEAR AS GOOD AS TSUBOZUKA.
I'LL CRUSH ALL OF YOU WITH MY JA-PAN!!!
CLNCH

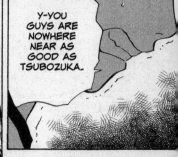

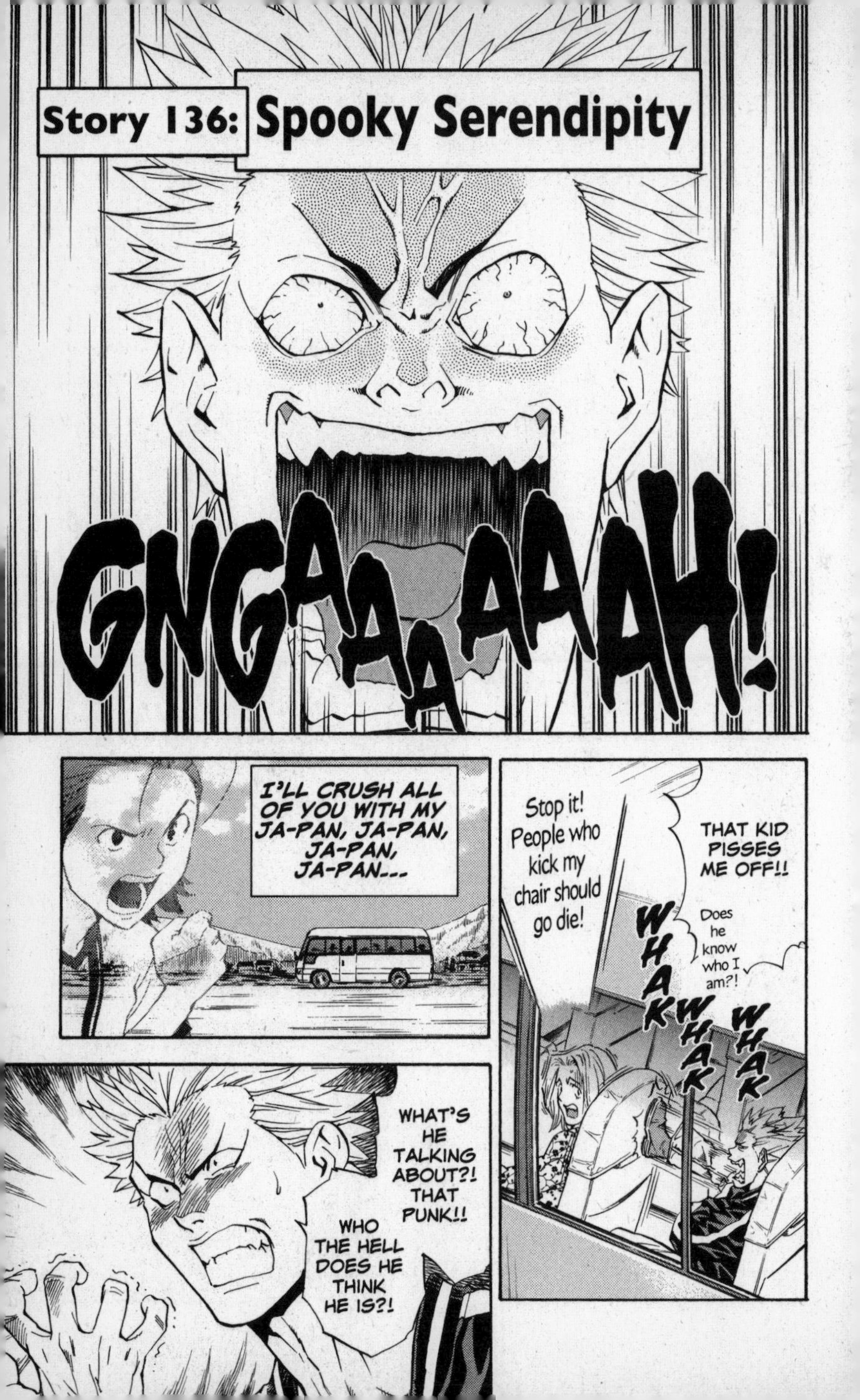
Story 136: Spooky Serendipity
GNGAAAAAH!
THAT KID PISSES ME OFF!!
Does he know who I am?!
Stop it! People who kick my chair should go die!
WHAK WHAK WHAK
I'LL CRUSH ALL OF YOU WITH MY JA-PAN, JA-PAN, JA-PAN, JA-PAN...
WHAT'S HE TALKING ABOUT?! THAT PUNK!!
WHO THE HELL DOES HE THINK HE IS?!

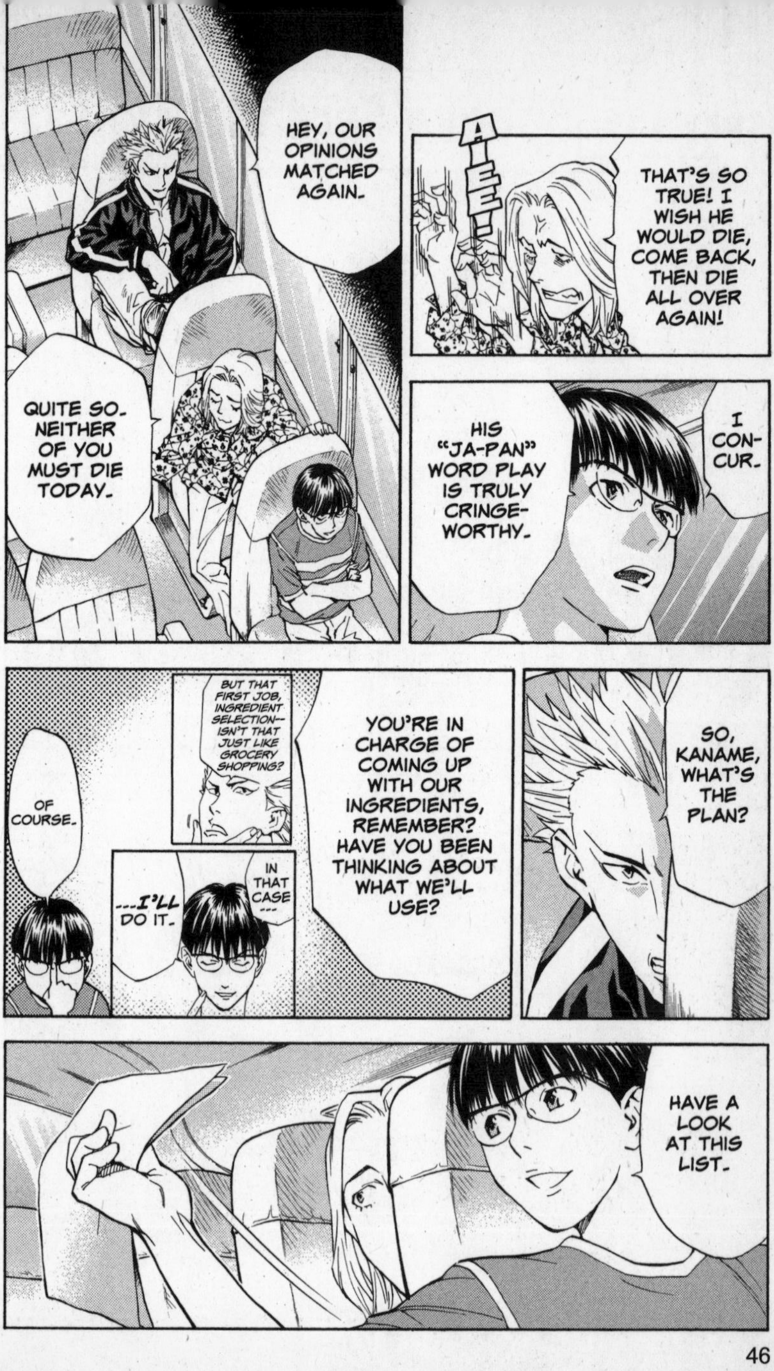
AIEE
THAT'S SO TRUE! I WISH HE WOULD DIE, COME BACK, THEN DIE ALL OVER AGAIN!
I CON-CUR.
HIS "JA-PAN" WORD PLAY IS TRULY CRINGE-WORTHY.
HEY, OUR OPINIONS MATCHED AGAIN.
QUITE SO. NEITHER OF YOU MUST DIE TODAY.
SO, KANAME, WHAT'S THE PLAN?
YOU'RE IN CHARGE OF COMING UP WITH OUR INGREDIENTS, REMEMBER? HAVE YOU BEEN THINKING ABOUT WHAT WE'LL USE?
BUT THAT FIRST JOB, INGREDIENT SELECTION--ISN'T THAT JUST LIKE GROCERY SHOPPING?
OF COURSE.
IN THAT CASE...
...I'LL DO IT.
HAVE A LOOK AT THIS LIST.

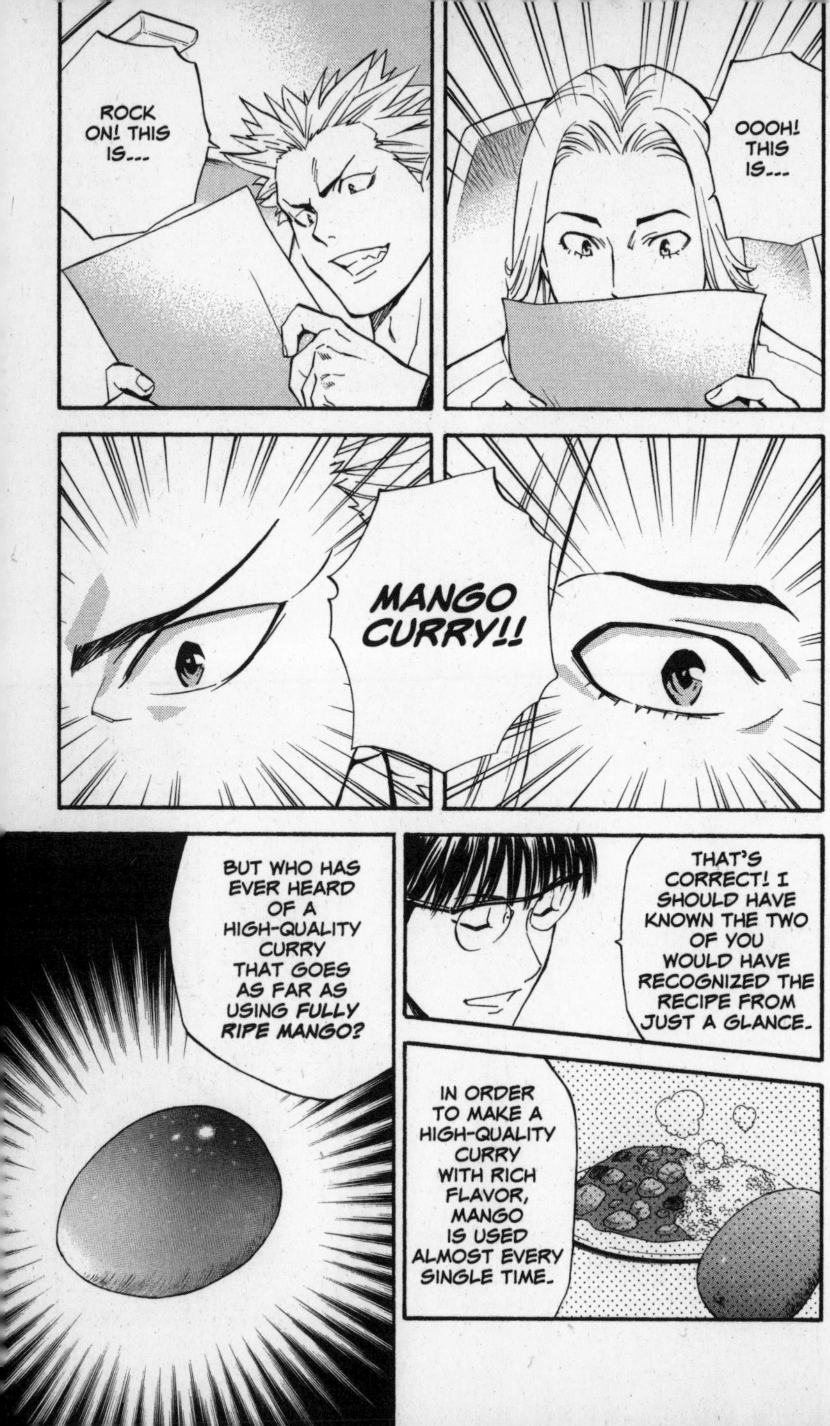
OOOH! THIS IS...
ROCK ON! THIS IS...
MANGO CURRY!!
THAT'S CORRECT! I SHOULD HAVE KNOWN THE TWO OF YOU WOULD HAVE RECOGNIZED THE RECIPE FROM JUST A GLANCE.
IN ORDER TO MAKE A HIGH-QUALITY CURRY WITH RICH FLAVOR, MANGO IS USED ALMOST EVERY SINGLE TIME.
BUT WHO HAS EVER HEARD OF A HIGH-QUALITY CURRY THAT GOES AS FAR AS USING *FULLY RIPE MANGO?*

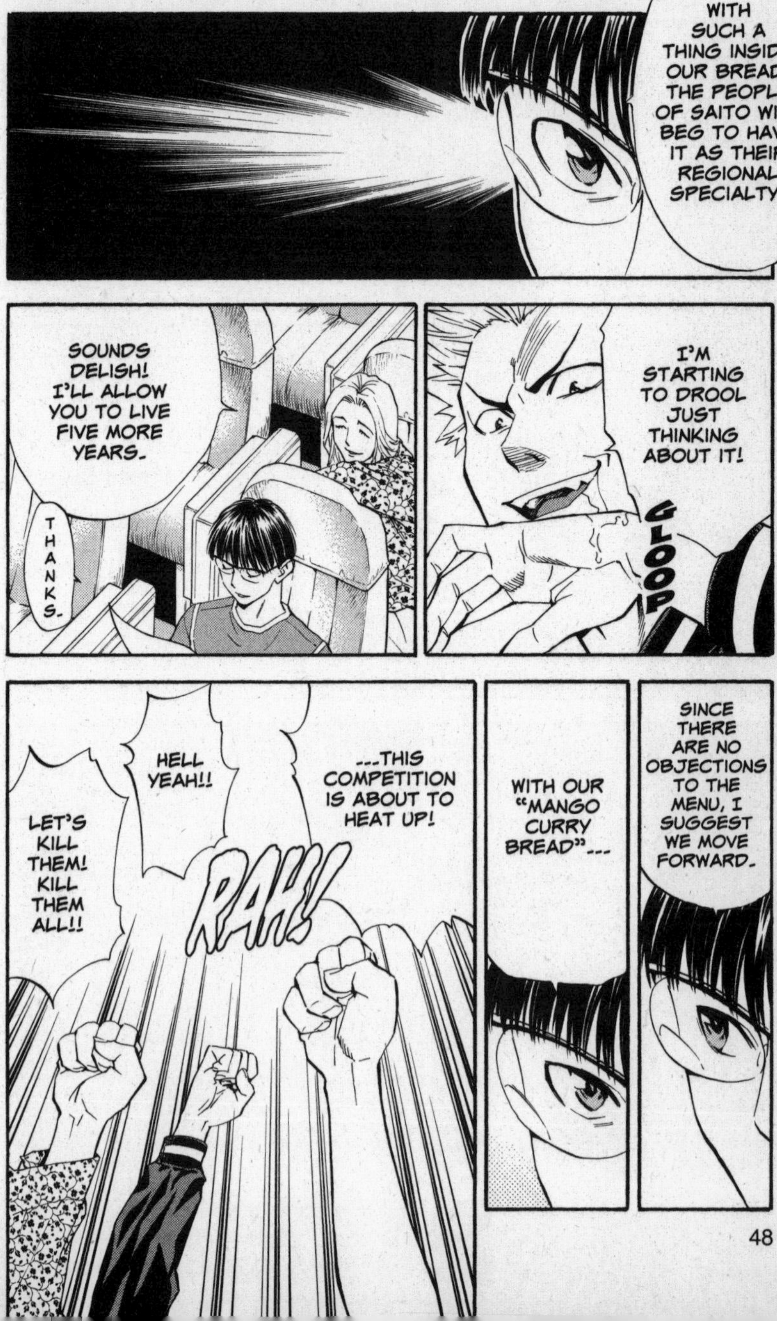
WITH SUCH A THING INSIDE OUR BREAD, THE PEOPLE OF SAITO WILL BEG TO HAVE IT AS THEIR REGIONAL SPECIALTY!
I'M STARTING TO DROOL JUST THINKING ABOUT IT!
GLOOP
SOUNDS DELISH! I'LL ALLOW YOU TO LIVE FIVE MORE YEARS.
THANKS.
SINCE THERE ARE NO OBJECTIONS TO THE MENU, I SUGGEST WE MOVE FORWARD.
WITH OUR "MANGO CURRY BREAD"...
...THIS COMPETITION IS ABOUT TO HEAT UP!
HELL YEAH!!
LET'S KILL THEM! KILL THEM ALL!!
RAH!

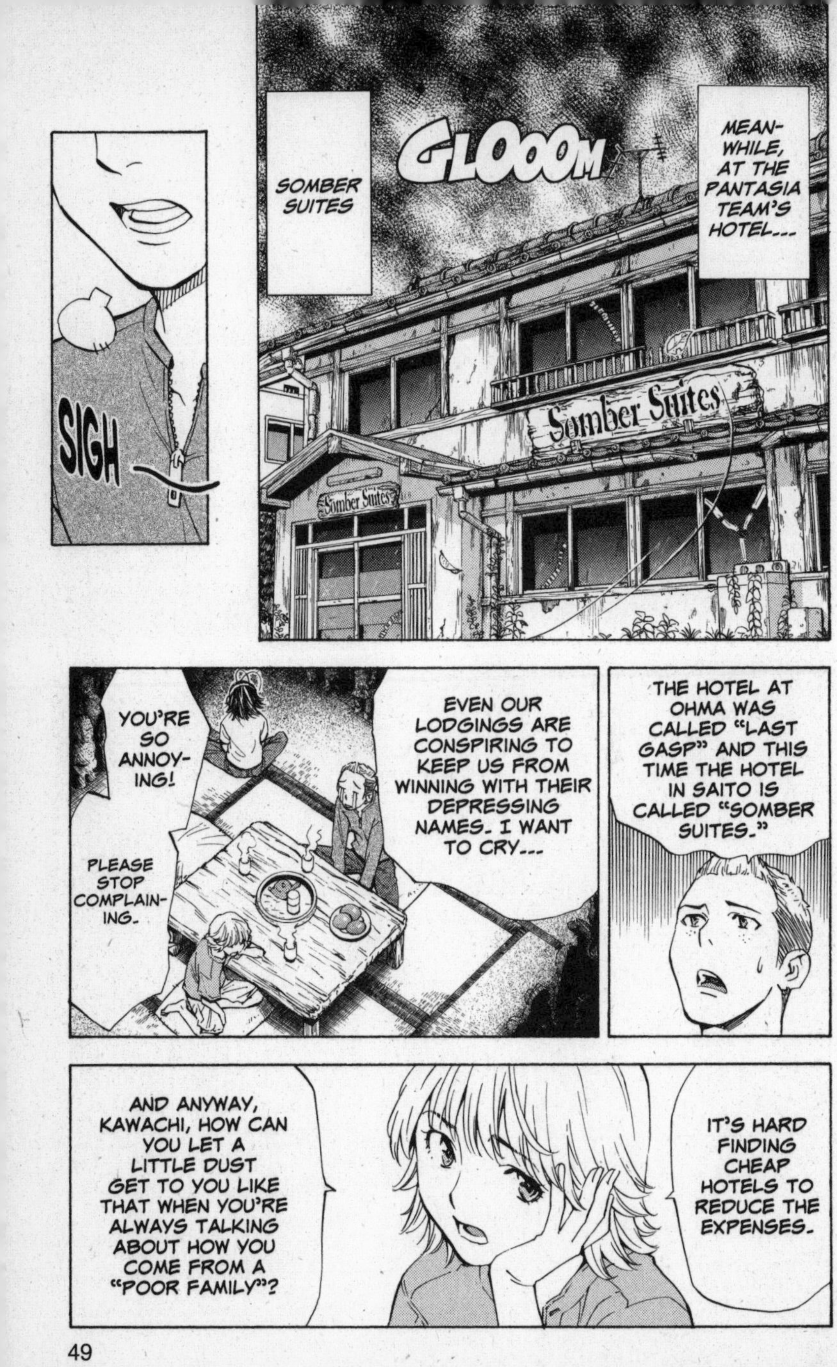
MEAN-WHILE, AT THE PANTASIA TEAM'S HOTEL...
GLOOOM
SOMBER SUITES
Somber Suites
Somber Suites
SIGH
THE HOTEL AT OHMA WAS CALLED "LAST GASP" AND THIS TIME THE HOTEL IN SAITO IS CALLED "SOMBER SUITES."
EVEN OUR LODGINGS ARE CONSPIRING TO KEEP US FROM WINNING WITH THEIR DEPRESSING NAMES. I WANT TO CRY...
YOU'RE SO ANNOY-ING!
PLEASE STOP COMPLAIN-ING.
IT'S HARD FINDING CHEAP HOTELS TO REDUCE THE EXPENSES.
AND ANYWAY, KAWACHI, HOW CAN YOU LET A LITTLE DUST GET TO YOU LIKE THAT WHEN YOU'RE ALWAYS TALKING ABOUT HOW YOU COME FROM A "POOR FAMILY"?

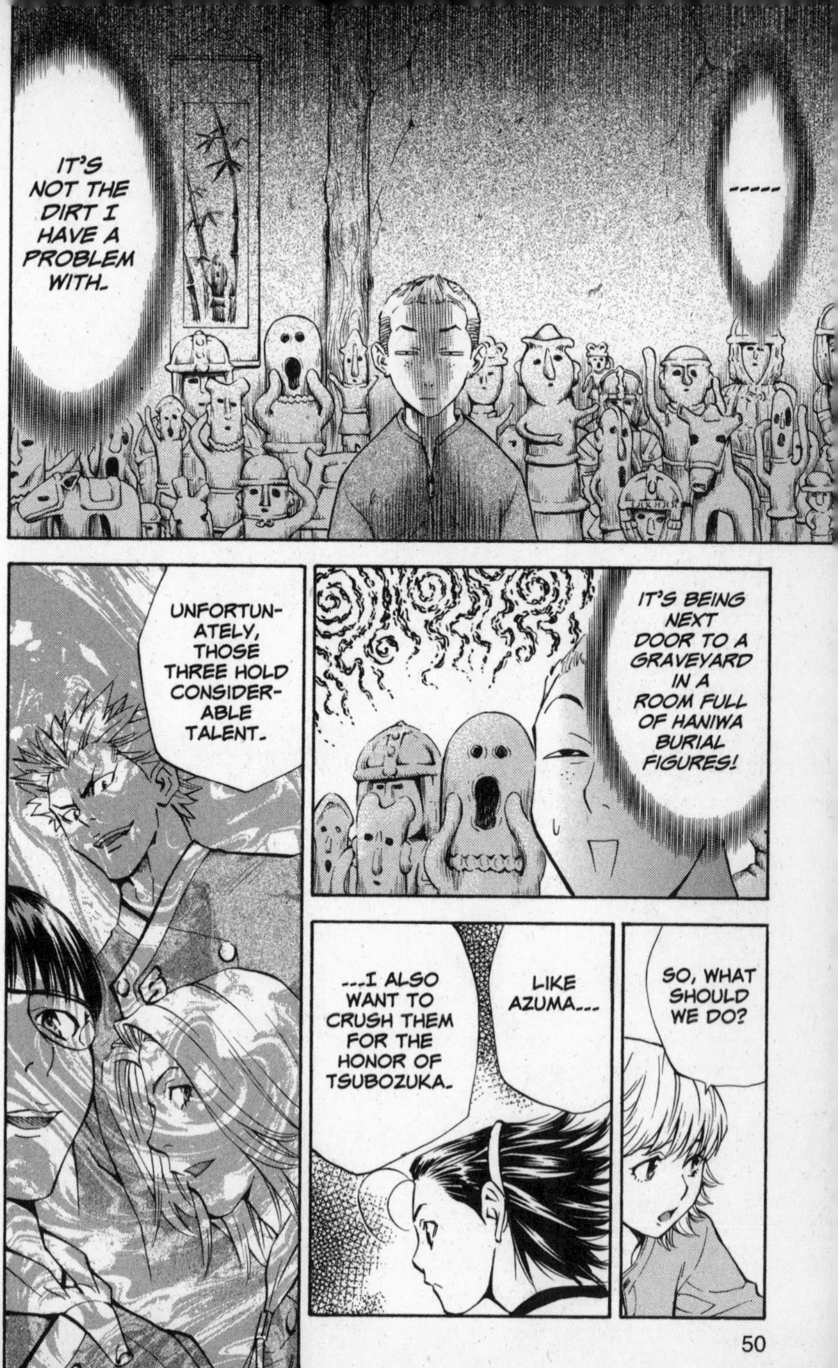

IT'S NOT THE DIRT I HAVE A PROBLEM WITH...
IT'S BEING NEXT DOOR TO A GRAVEYARD IN A ROOM FULL OF HANIWA BURIAL FIGURES!
SO, WHAT SHOULD WE DO?
LIKE AZUMA...
...I ALSO WANT TO CRUSH THEM FOR THE HONOR OF TSUBOZUKA...
UNFORTUN-ATELY, THOSE THREE HOLD CONSIDER-ABLE TALENT...

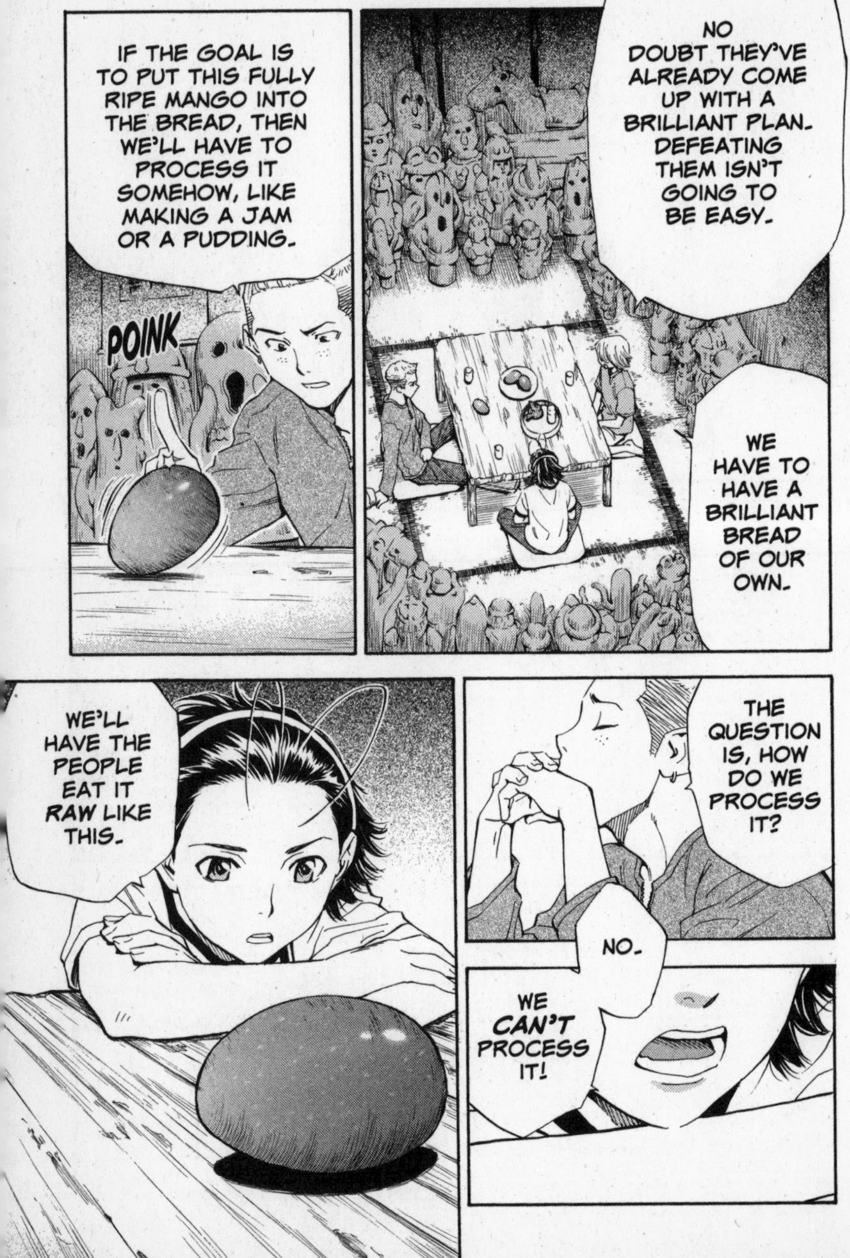
NO DOUBT THEY'VE ALREADY COME UP WITH A BRILLIANT PLAN. DEFEATING THEM ISN'T GOING TO BE EASY.
WE HAVE TO HAVE A BRILLIANT BREAD OF OUR OWN.
IF THE GOAL IS TO PUT THIS FULLY RIPE MANGO INTO THE BREAD, THEN WE'LL HAVE TO PROCESS IT SOMEHOW, LIKE MAKING A JAM OR A PUDDING.
POINK
THE QUESTION IS, HOW DO WE PROCESS IT?
NO.
WE CAN'T PROCESS IT!
WE'LL HAVE THE PEOPLE EAT IT RAW LIKE THIS.

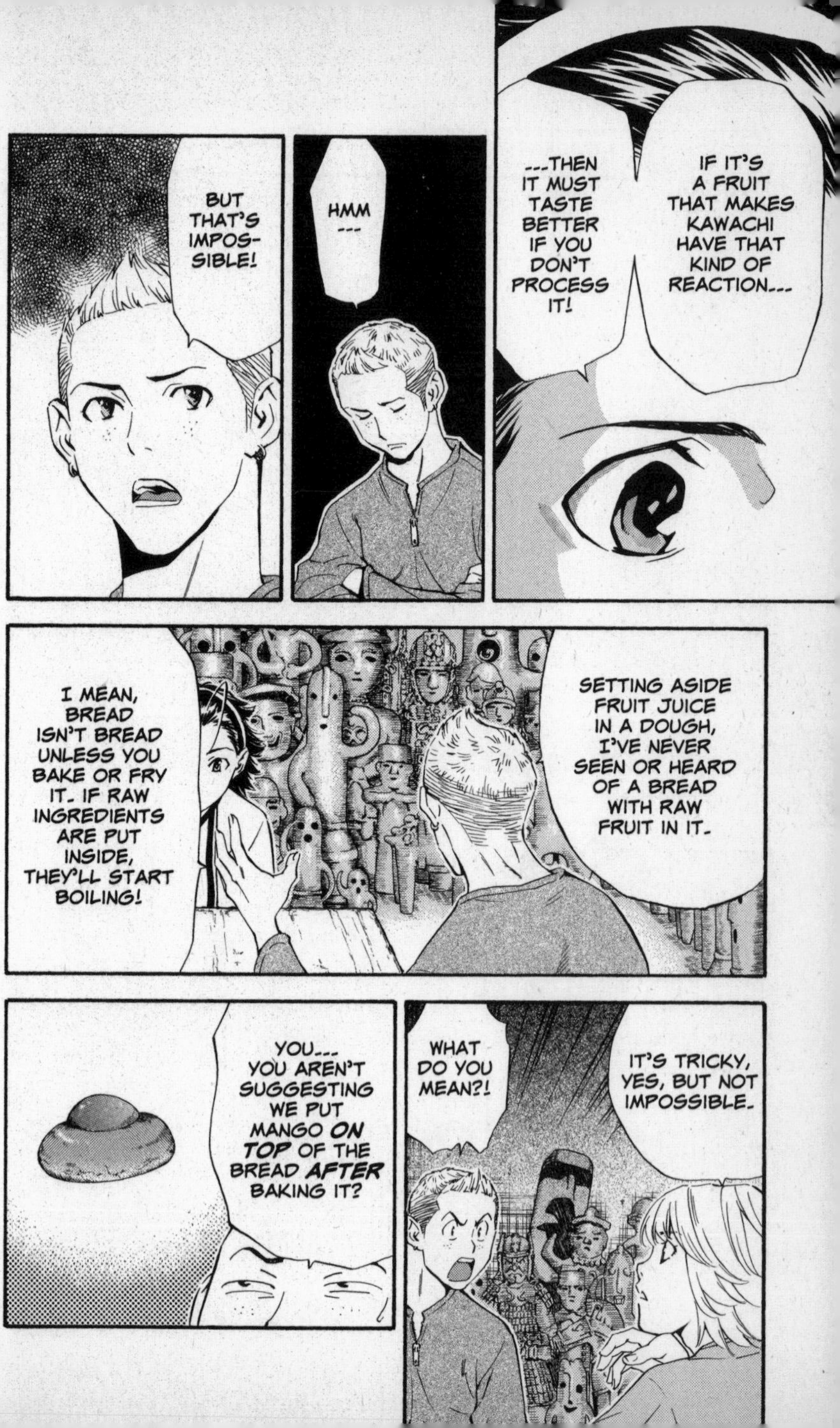
IF IT'S A FRUIT THAT MAKES KAWACHI HAVE THAT KIND OF REACTION...
...THEN IT MUST TASTE BETTER IF YOU DON'T PROCESS IT!
HMM...
BUT THAT'S IMPOS-SIBLE!
SETTING ASIDE FRUIT JUICE IN A DOUGH, I'VE NEVER SEEN OR HEARD OF A BREAD WITH RAW FRUIT IN IT.
I MEAN, BREAD ISN'T BREAD UNLESS YOU BAKE OR FRY IT. IF RAW INGREDIENTS ARE PUT INSIDE, THEY'LL START BOILING!
IT'S TRICKY, YES, BUT NOT IMPOSSIBLE.
WHAT DO YOU MEAN?!
YOU... YOU AREN'T SUGGESTING WE PUT MANGO *ON TOP* OF THE BREAD *AFTER* BAKING IT?

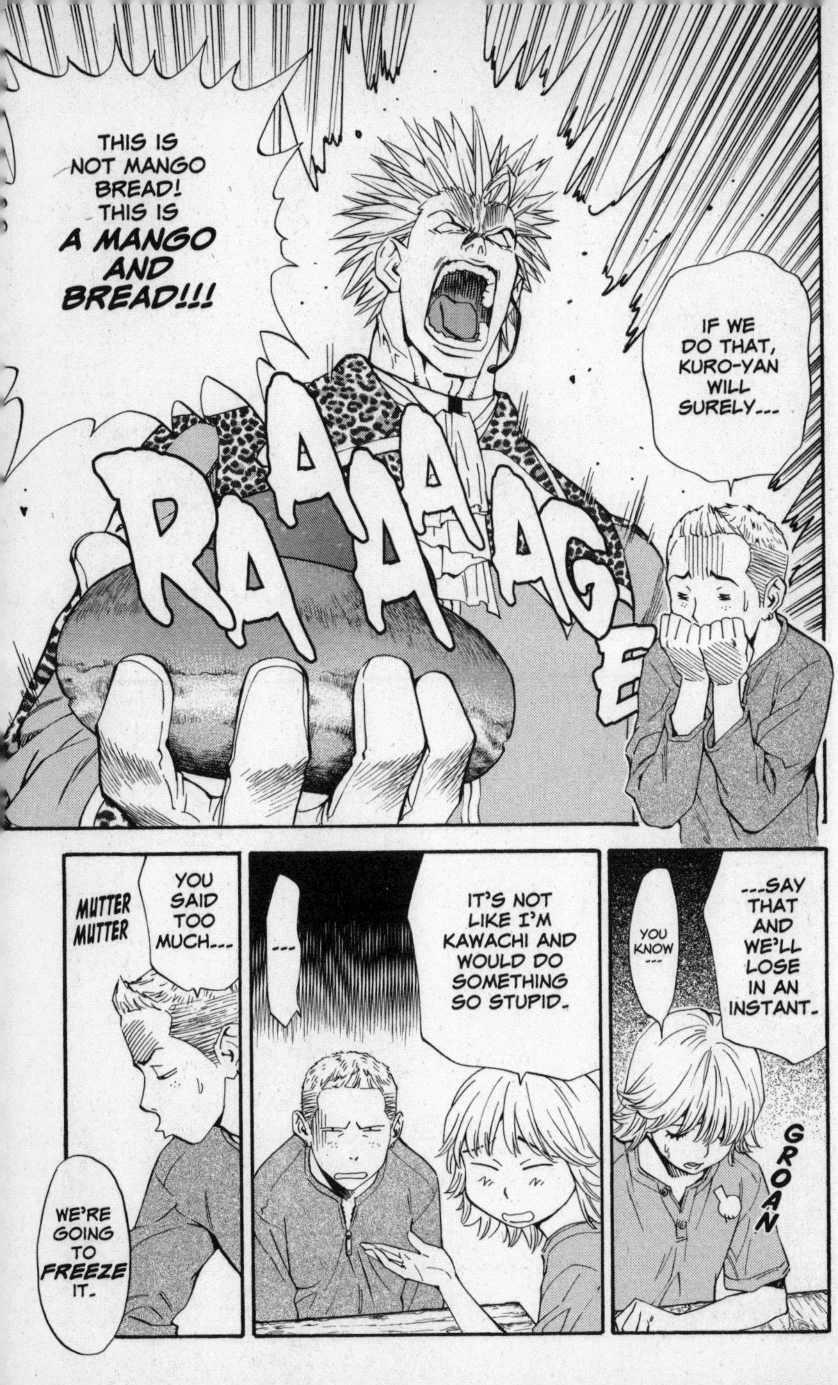
IF WE DO THAT, KURO-YAN WILL SURELY...
THIS IS NOT MANGO BREAD! THIS IS A MANGO AND BREAD!!!
RAAAAAGE
...SAY THAT AND WE'LL LOSE IN AN INSTANT.
YOU KNOW...
GROAN
IT'S NOT LIKE I'M KAWACHI AND WOULD DO SOMETHING SO STUPID.
...
YOU SAID TOO MUCH...
MUTTER MUTTER
WE'RE GOING TO FREEZE IT.

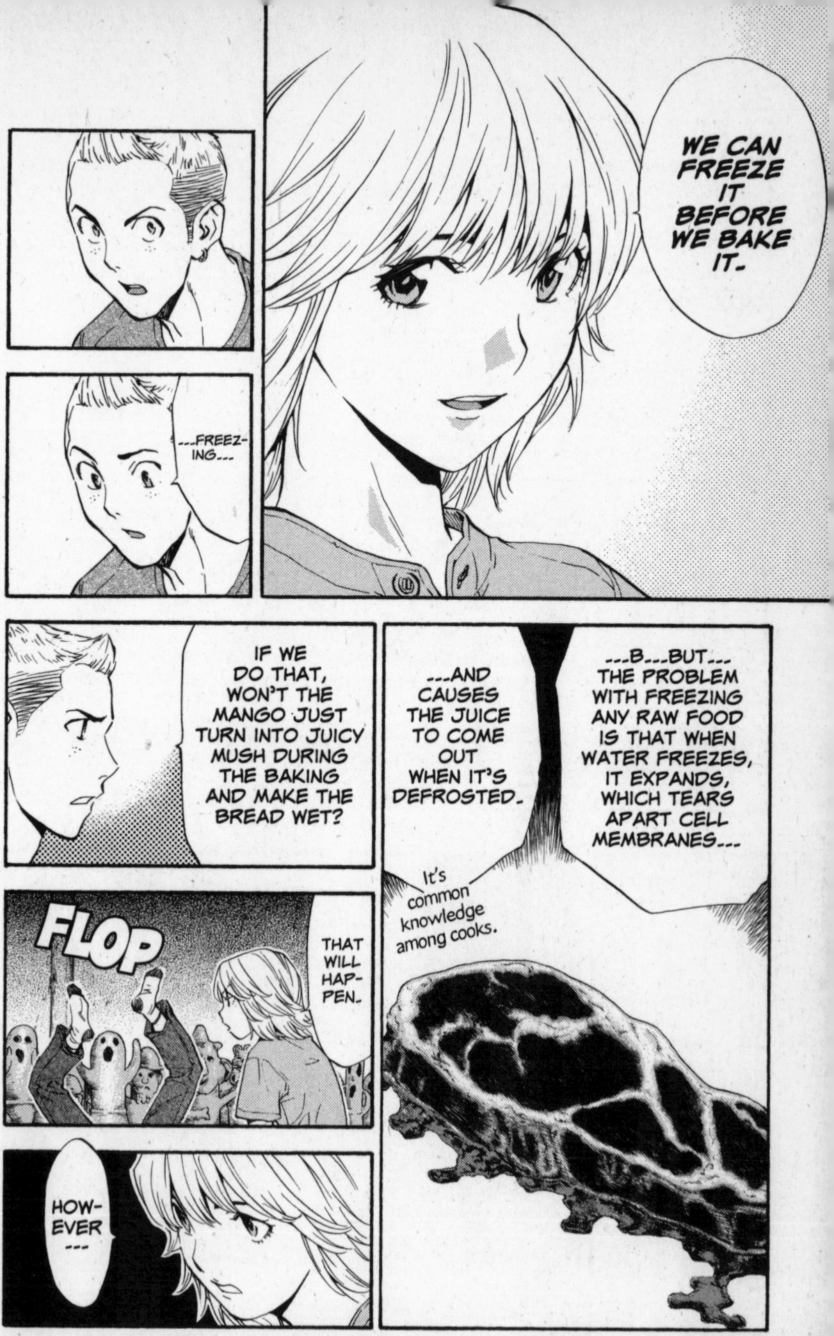
WE CAN FREEZE IT BEFORE WE BAKE IT.
...FREEZING...
...B...BUT... THE PROBLEM WITH FREEZING ANY RAW FOOD IS THAT WHEN WATER FREEZES, IT EXPANDS, WHICH TEARS APART CELL MEMBRANES...
...AND CAUSES THE JUICE TO COME OUT WHEN IT'S DEFROSTED.
It's common knowledge among cooks.
IF WE DO THAT, WON'T THE MANGO JUST TURN INTO JUICY MUSH DURING THE BAKING AND MAKE THE BREAD WET?
FLOP
THAT WILL HAPPEN.
HOWEVER---

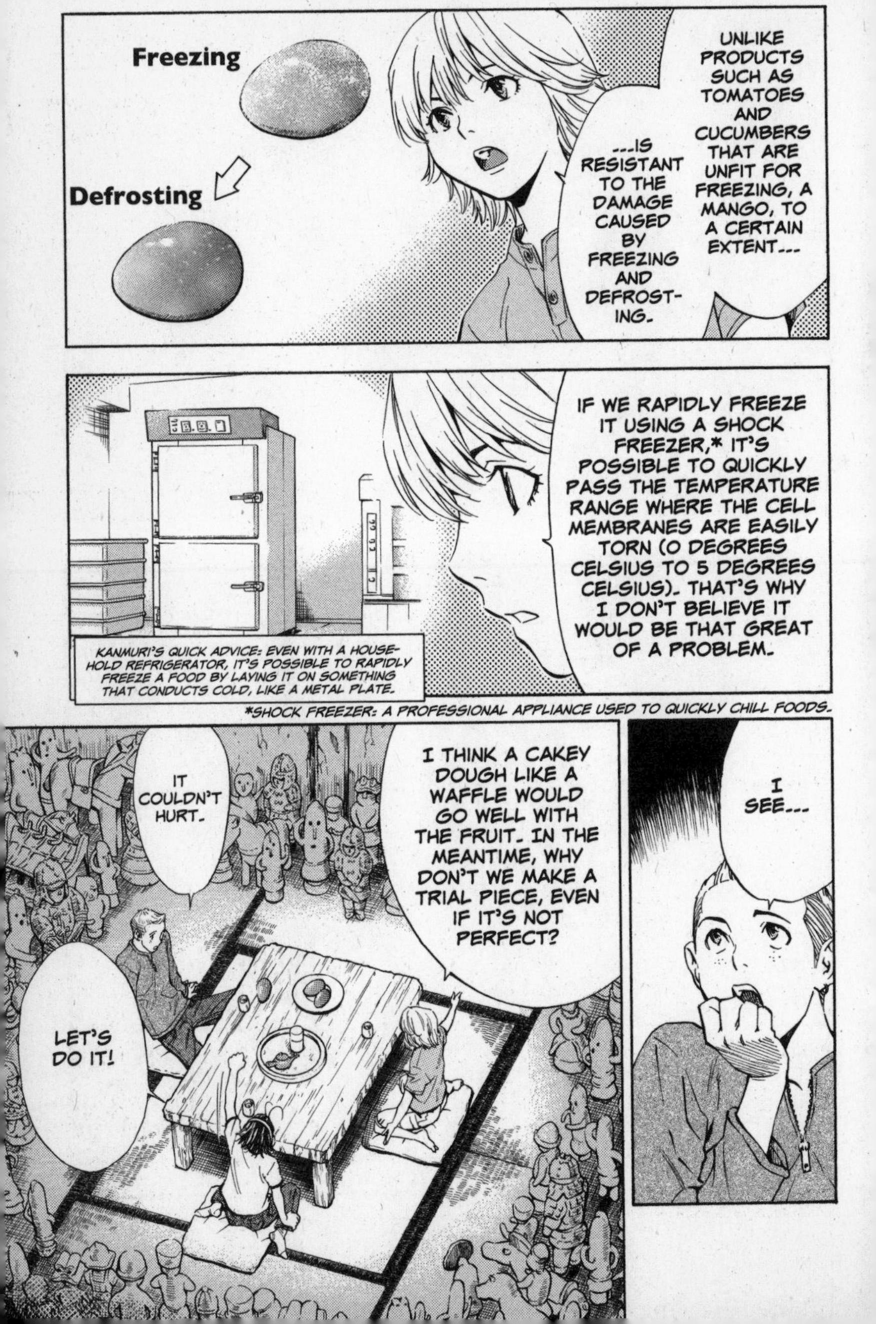
UNLIKE PRODUCTS SUCH AS TOMATOES AND CUCUMBERS THAT ARE UNFIT FOR FREEZING, A MANGO, TO A CERTAIN EXTENT...
...IS RESISTANT TO THE DAMAGE CAUSED BY FREEZING AND DEFROSTING.
Freezing
Defrosting
IF WE RAPIDLY FREEZE IT USING A SHOCK FREEZER,* IT'S POSSIBLE TO QUICKLY PASS THE TEMPERATURE RANGE WHERE THE CELL MEMBRANES ARE EASILY TORN (0 DEGREES CELSIUS TO 5 DEGREES CELSIUS). THAT'S WHY I DON'T BELIEVE IT WOULD BE THAT GREAT OF A PROBLEM.
KANMURI'S QUICK ADVICE: EVEN WITH A HOUSEHOLD REFRIGERATOR, IT'S POSSIBLE TO RAPIDLY FREEZE A FOOD BY LAYING IT ON SOMETHING THAT CONDUCTS COLD, LIKE A METAL PLATE.
*SHOCK FREEZER: A PROFESSIONAL APPLIANCE USED TO QUICKLY CHILL FOODS.
I SEE...
I THINK A CAKEY DOUGH LIKE A WAFFLE WOULD GO WELL WITH THE FRUIT. IN THE MEANTIME, WHY DON'T WE MAKE A TRIAL PIECE, EVEN IF IT'S NOT PERFECT?
IT COULDN'T HURT.
LET'S DO IT!

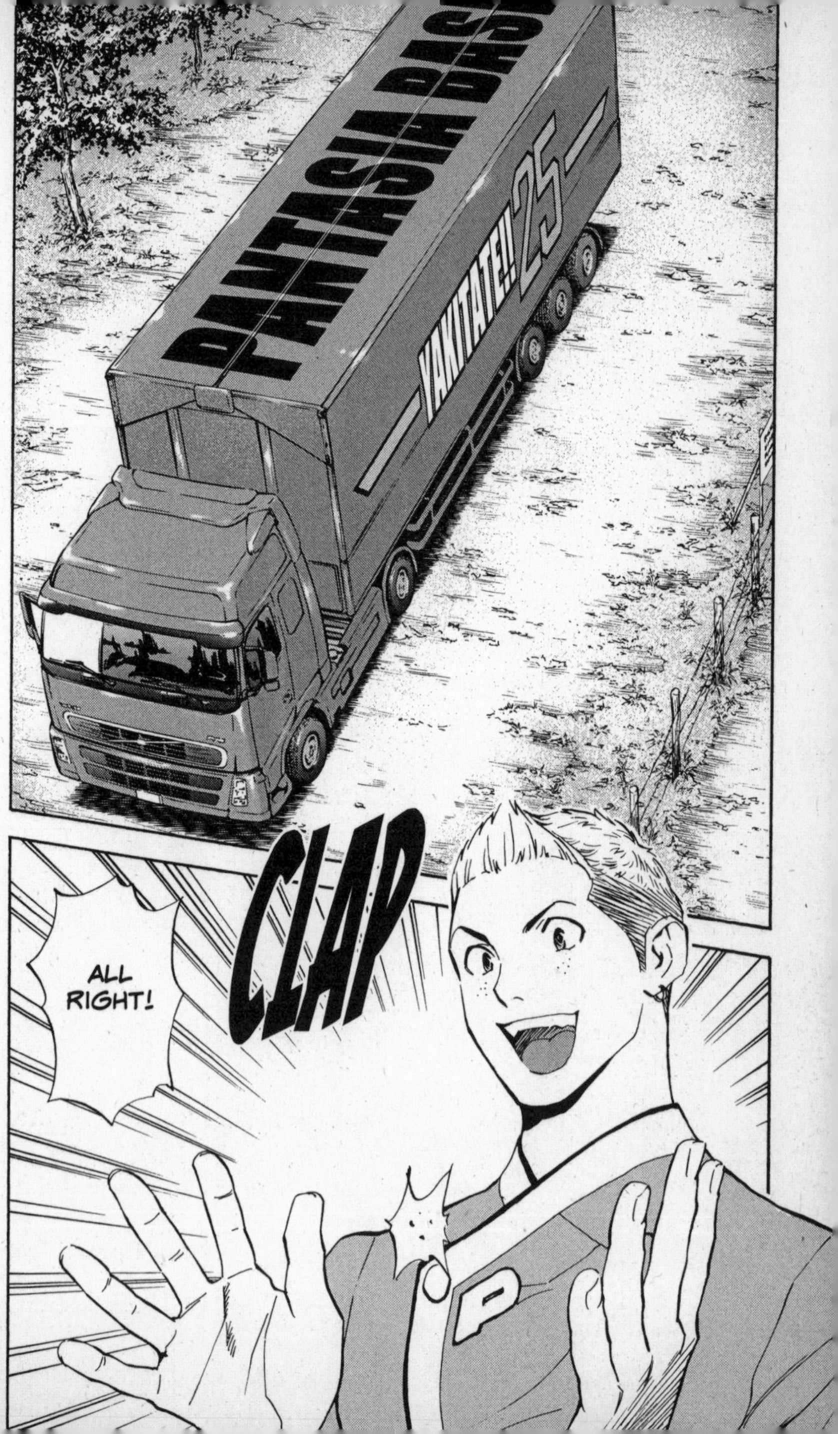
PANTASIA DAS
YAKITATE!! 25
CLAP
ALL RIGHT!

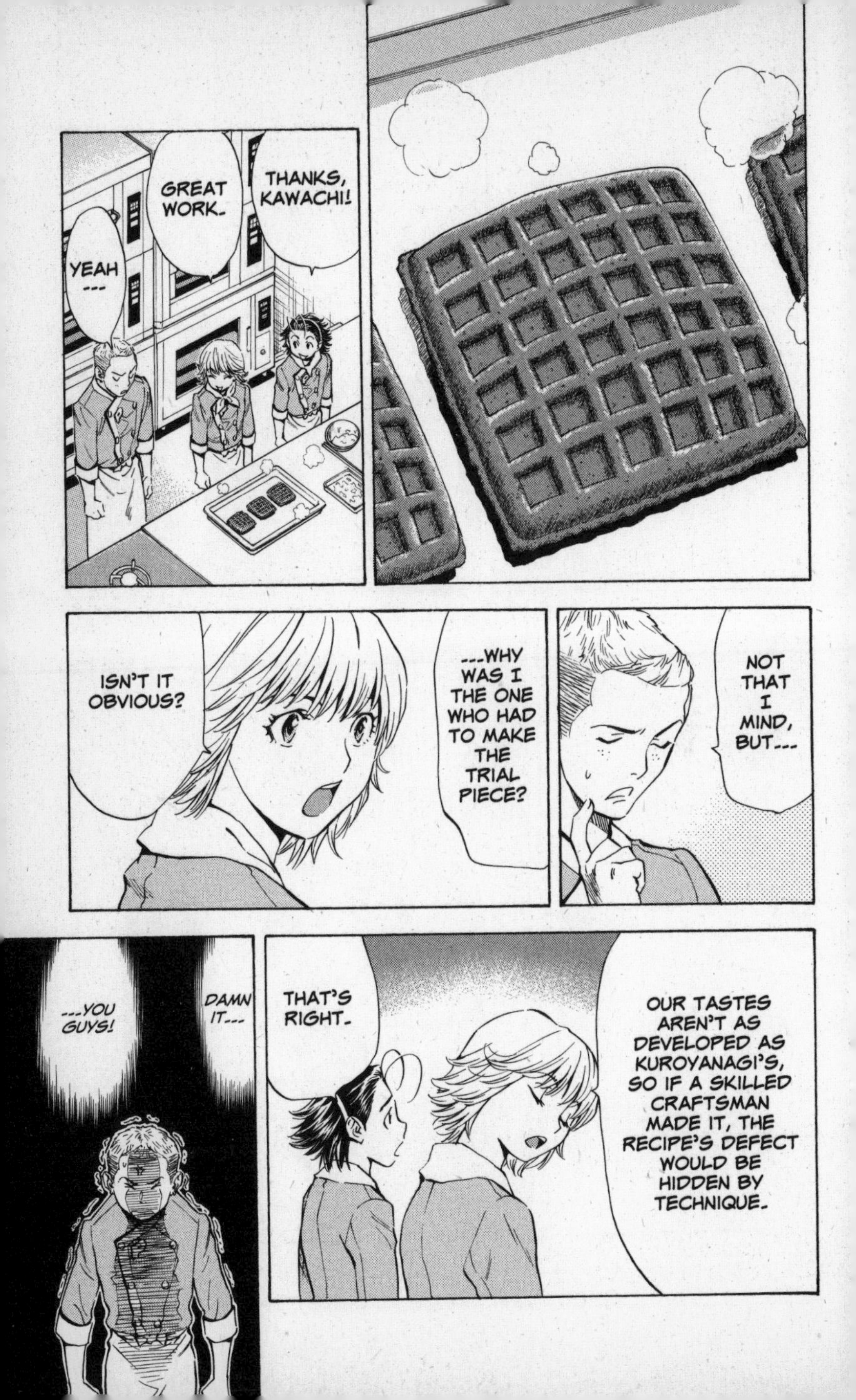
THANKS, KAWACHI!
GREAT WORK.
YEAH...
NOT THAT I MIND, BUT...
...WHY WAS I THE ONE WHO HAD TO MAKE THE TRIAL PIECE?
ISN'T IT OBVIOUS?
OUR TASTES AREN'T AS DEVELOPED AS KUROYANAGI'S, SO IF A SKILLED CRAFTSMAN MADE IT, THE RECIPE'S DEFECT WOULD BE HIDDEN BY TECHNIQUE.
THAT'S RIGHT.
DAMN IT...
...YOU GUYS!

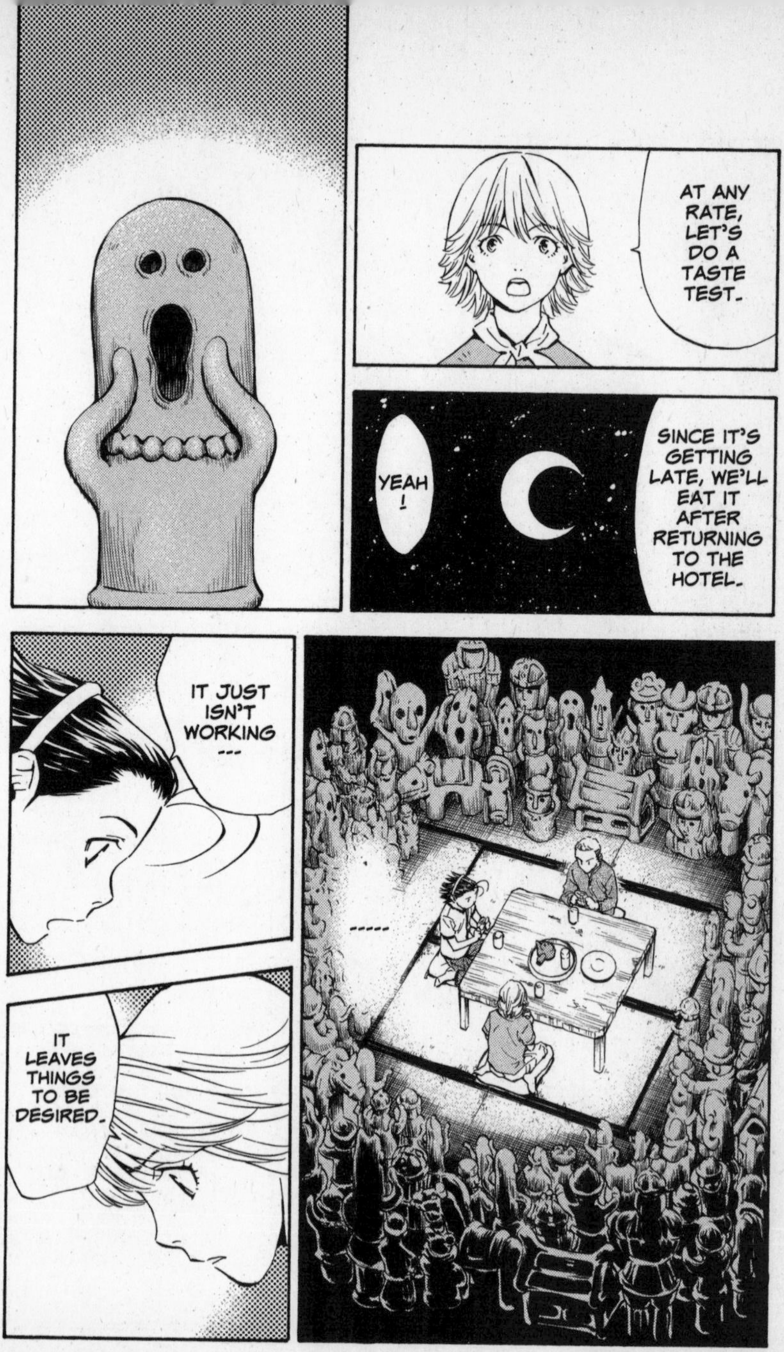
AT ANY RATE, LET'S DO A TASTE TEST.
SINCE IT'S GETTING LATE, WE'LL EAT IT AFTER RETURNING TO THE HOTEL.
YEAH!

IT JUST ISN'T WORKING ---
IT LEAVES THINGS TO BE DESIRED.

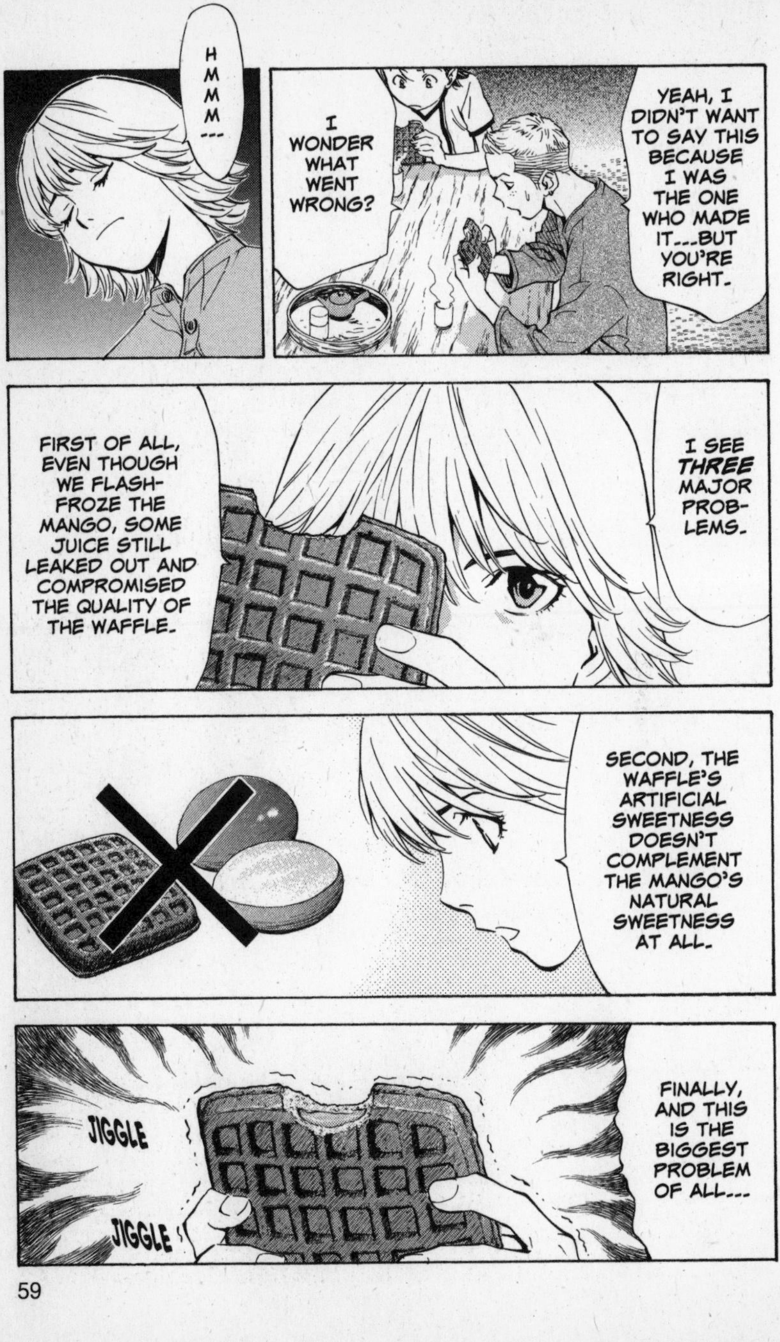
YEAH, I DIDN'T WANT TO SAY THIS BECAUSE I WAS THE ONE WHO MADE IT...BUT YOU'RE RIGHT.
I WONDER WHAT WENT WRONG?
HMMM---
I SEE *THREE* MAJOR PROBLEMS.
FIRST OF ALL, EVEN THOUGH WE FLASH-FROZE THE MANGO, SOME JUICE STILL LEAKED OUT AND COMPROMISED THE QUALITY OF THE WAFFLE.
SECOND, THE WAFFLE'S ARTIFICIAL SWEETNESS DOESN'T COMPLEMENT THE MANGO'S NATURAL SWEETNESS AT ALL.
FINALLY, AND THIS IS THE BIGGEST PROBLEM OF ALL...
JIGGLE
JIGGLE

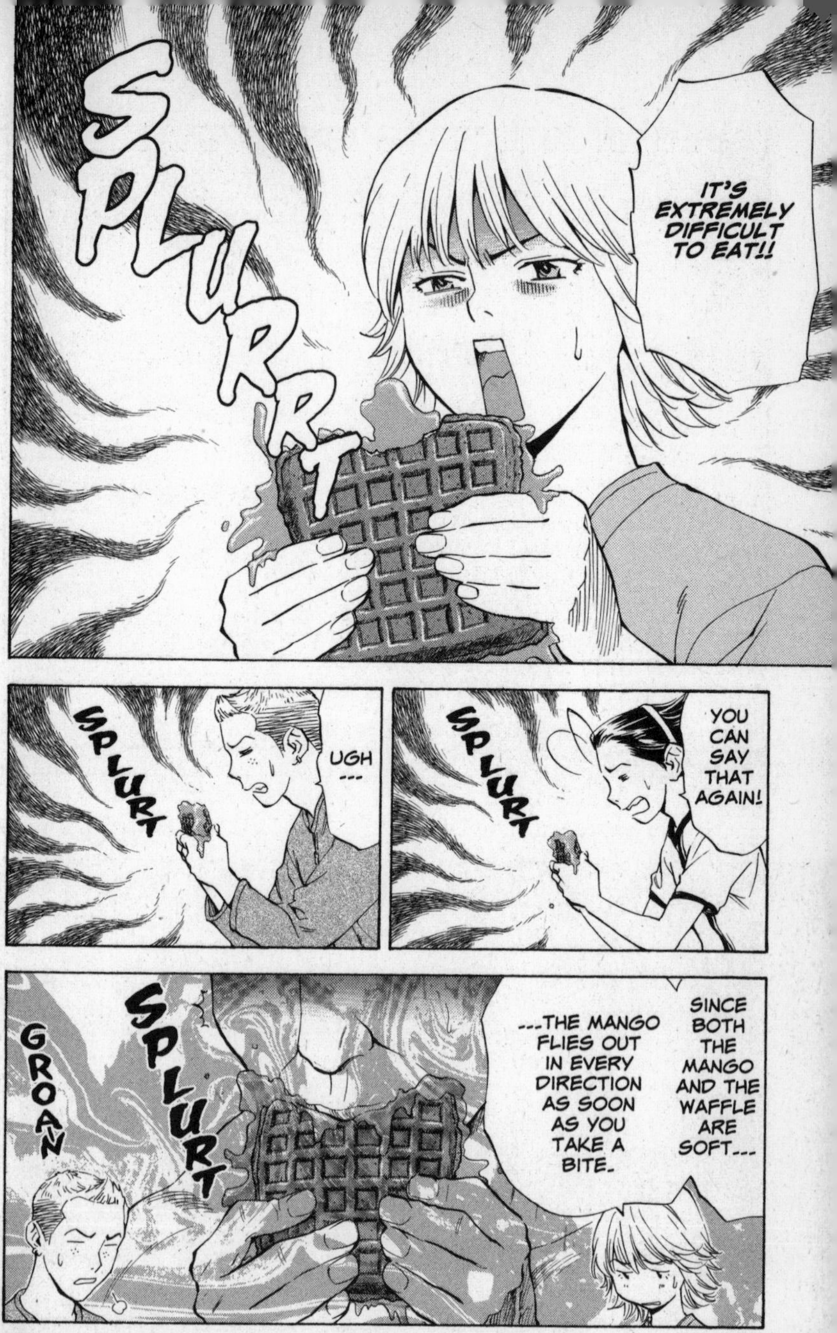
IT'S EXTREMELY DIFFICULT TO EAT!!
SPLURRT
YOU CAN SAY THAT AGAIN!
SPLURT
UGH...
SPLURT
SINCE BOTH THE MANGO AND THE WAFFLE ARE SOFT...
...THE MANGO FLIES OUT IN EVERY DIRECTION AS SOON AS YOU TAKE A BITE.
SPLURT
GROAN

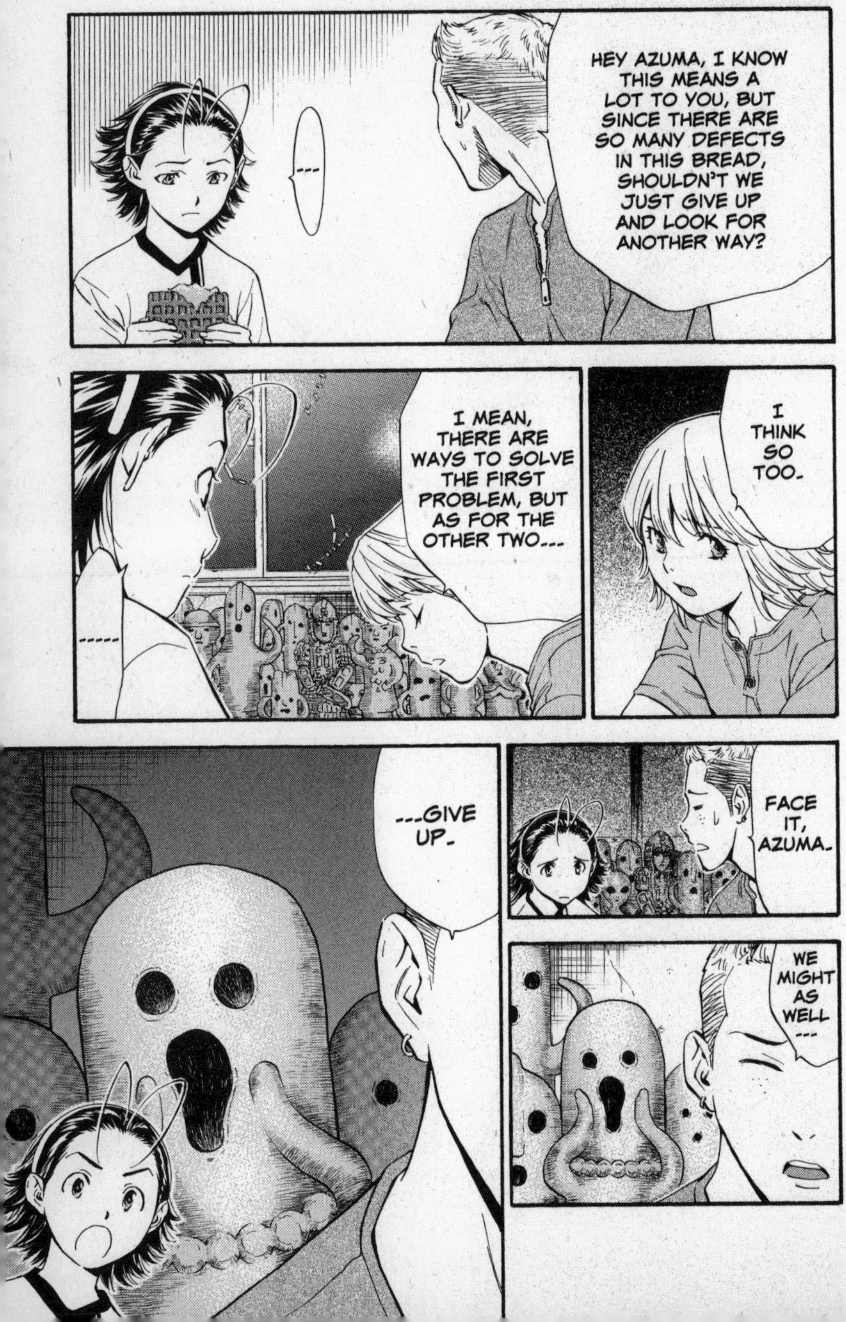
HEY AZUMA, I KNOW THIS MEANS A LOT TO YOU, BUT SINCE THERE ARE SO MANY DEFECTS IN THIS BREAD, SHOULDN'T WE JUST GIVE UP AND LOOK FOR ANOTHER WAY?
...
I THINK SO TOO.
I MEAN, THERE ARE WAYS TO SOLVE THE FIRST PROBLEM, BUT AS FOR THE OTHER TWO...
.....
FACE IT, AZUMA.
WE MIGHT AS WELL...
...GIVE UP.

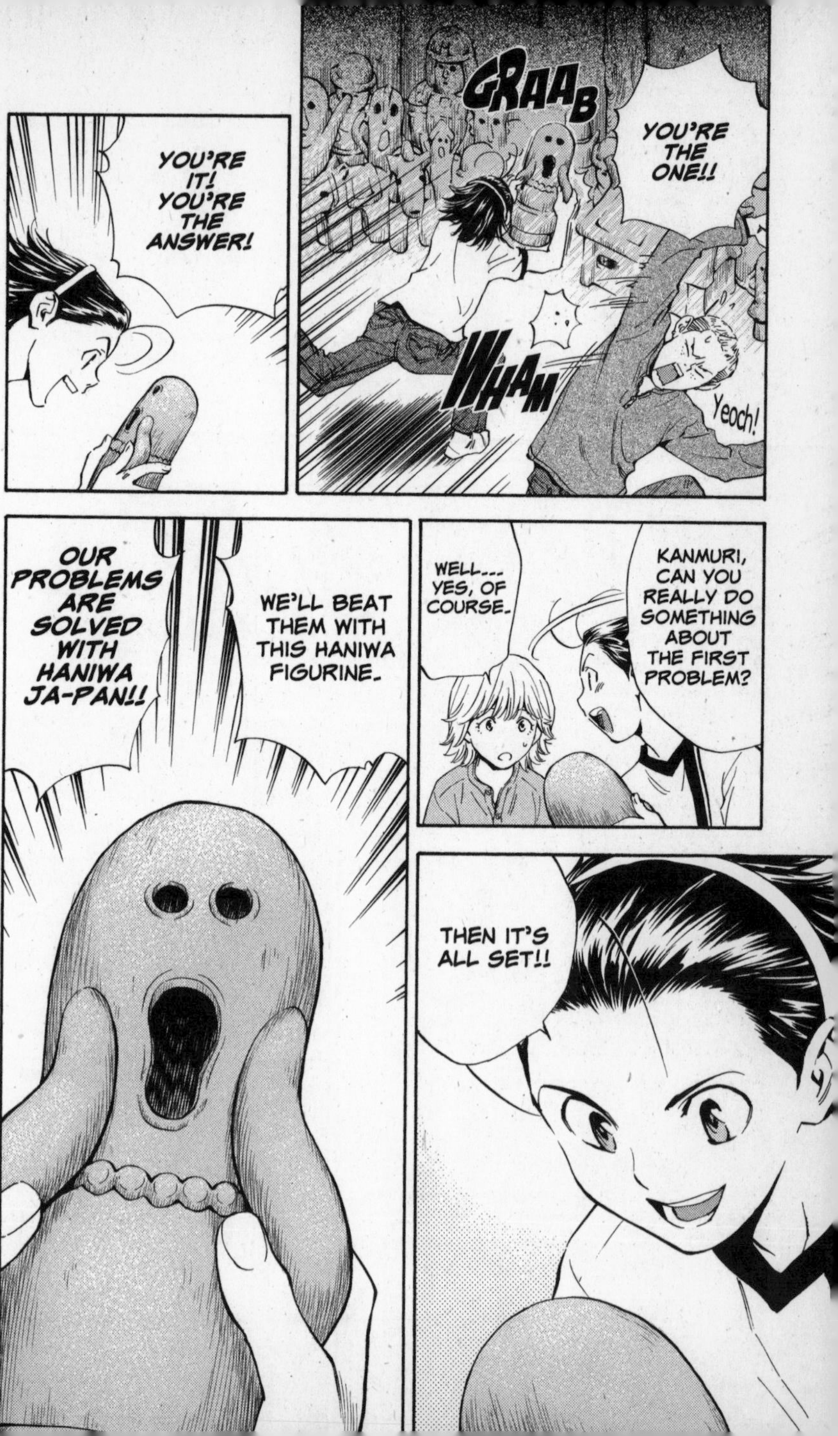
GRAAB
YOU'RE THE ONE!!
WHAM
Yeoch!
YOU'RE IT! YOU'RE THE ANSWER!
KANMURI, CAN YOU REALLY DO SOMETHING ABOUT THE FIRST PROBLEM?
WELL... YES, OF COURSE.
THEN IT'S ALL SET!!
WE'LL BEAT THEM WITH THIS HANIWA FIGURINE.
OUR PROBLEMS ARE SOLVED WITH HANIWA JA-PAN!!

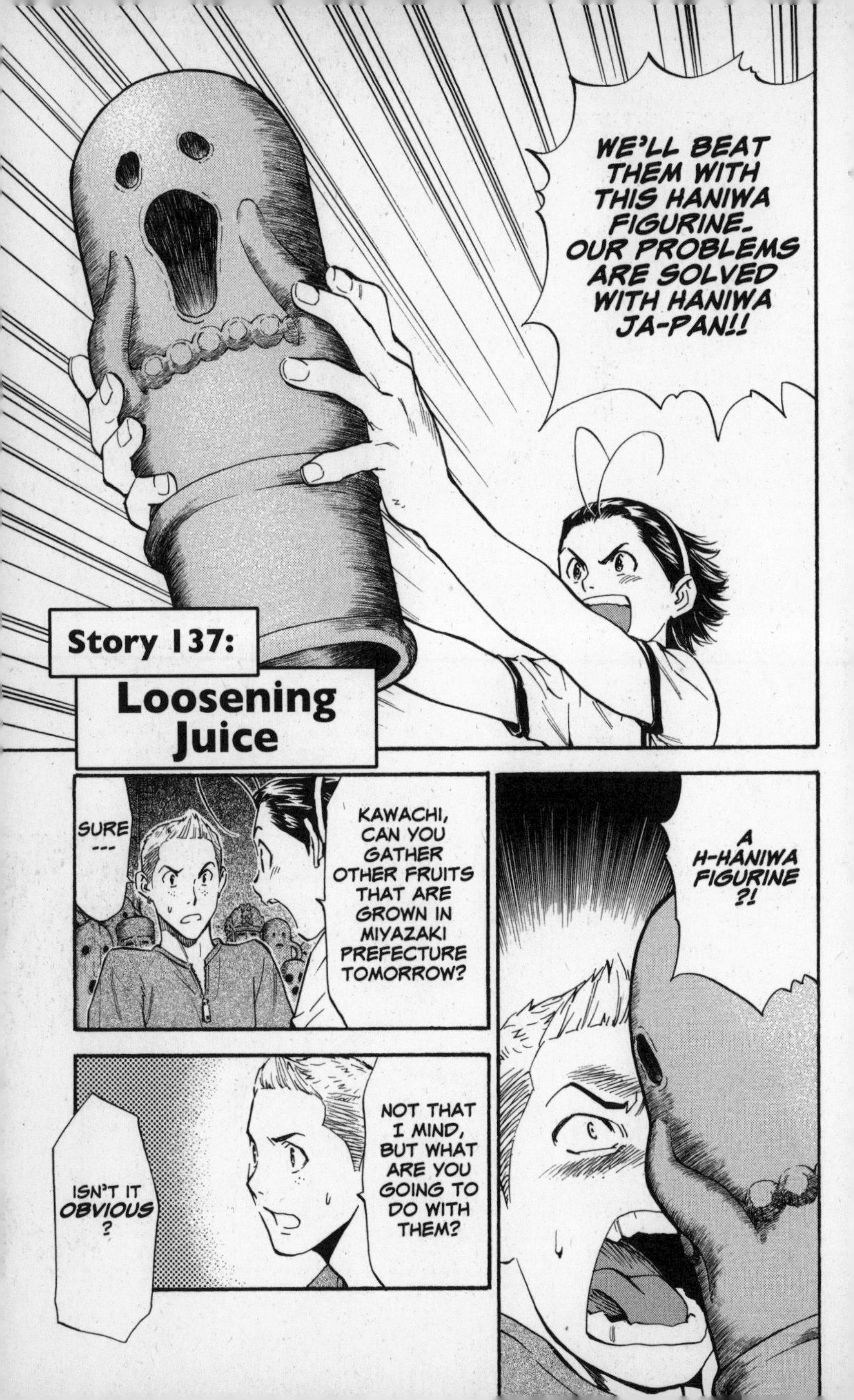
WE'LL BEAT THEM WITH THIS HANIWA FIGURINE- OUR PROBLEMS ARE SOLVED WITH HANIWA JA-PAN!!
Story 137:
Loosening Juice
A H-HANIWA FIGURINE?!
KAWACHI, CAN YOU GATHER OTHER FRUITS THAT ARE GROWN IN MIYAZAKI PREFECTURE TOMORROW?
SURE---
NOT THAT I MIND, BUT WHAT ARE YOU GOING TO DO WITH THEM?
ISN'T IT OBVIOUS?

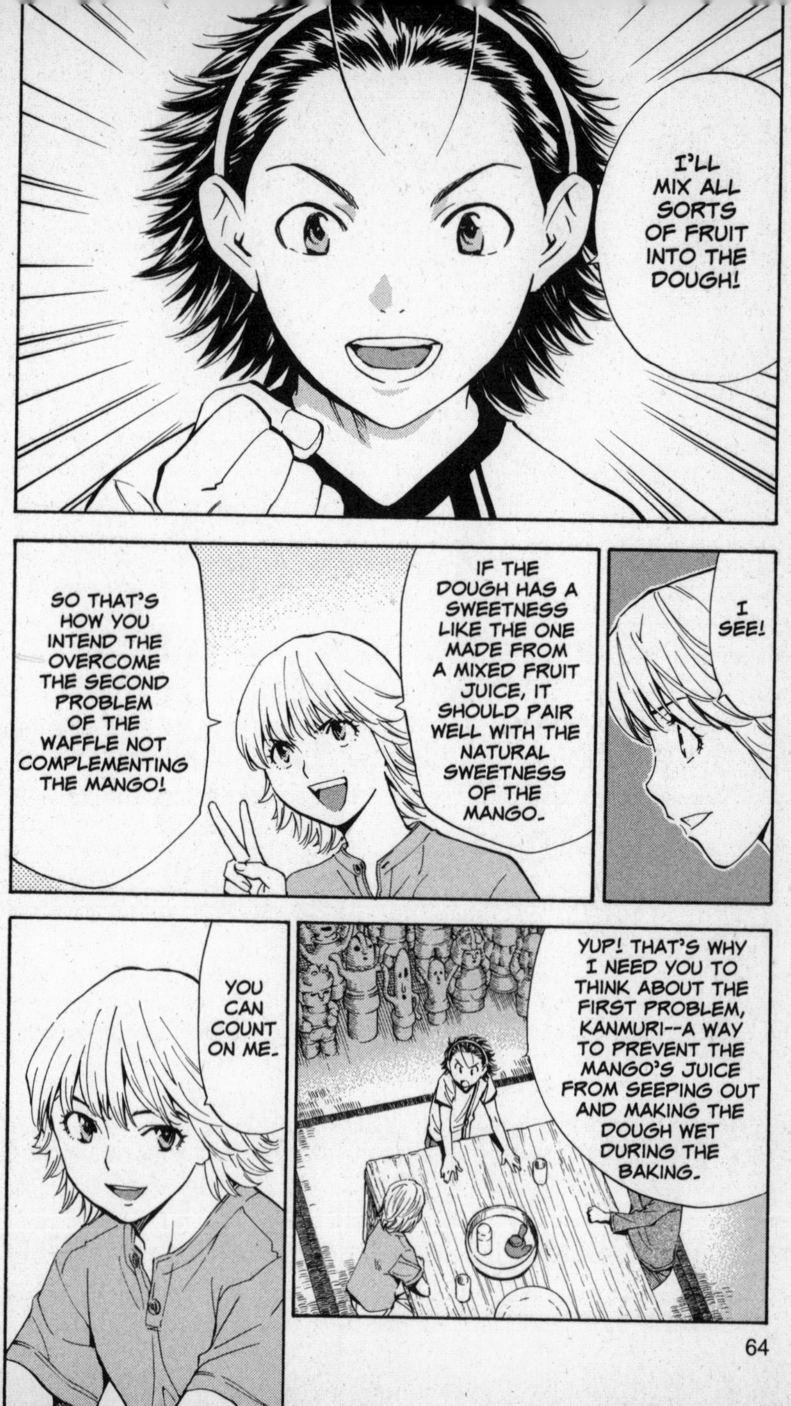
I'LL MIX ALL SORTS OF FRUIT INTO THE DOUGH!
I SEE!
IF THE DOUGH HAS A SWEETNESS LIKE THE ONE MADE FROM A MIXED FRUIT JUICE, IT SHOULD PAIR WELL WITH THE NATURAL SWEETNESS OF THE MANGO.
SO THAT'S HOW YOU INTEND THE OVERCOME THE SECOND PROBLEM OF THE WAFFLE NOT COMPLEMENTING THE MANGO!
YUP! THAT'S WHY I NEED YOU TO THINK ABOUT THE FIRST PROBLEM, KANMURI--A WAY TO PREVENT THE MANGO'S JUICE FROM SEEPING OUT AND MAKING THE DOUGH WET DURING THE BAKING.
YOU CAN COUNT ON ME.

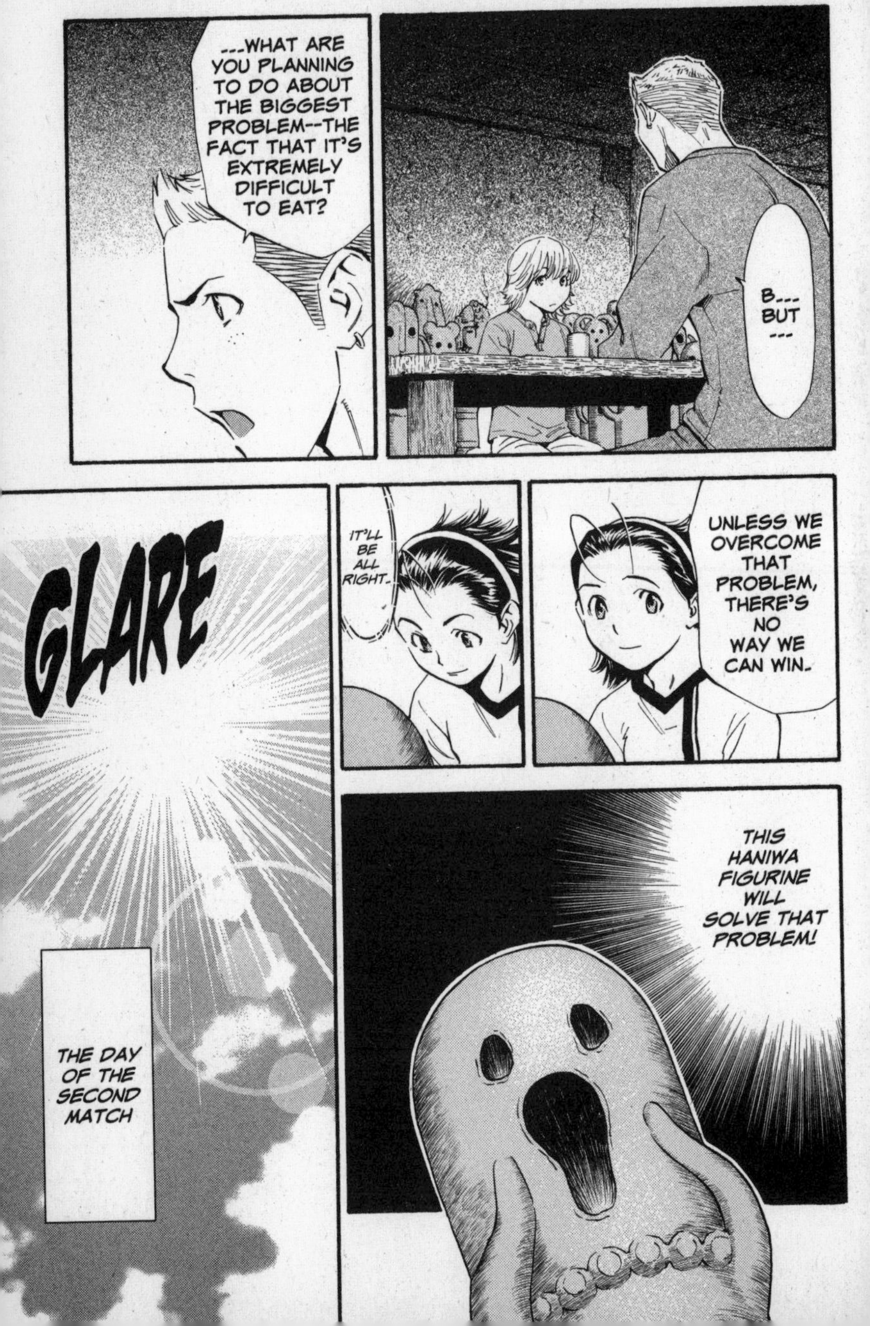
B... BUT ...
...WHAT ARE YOU PLANNING TO DO ABOUT THE BIGGEST PROBLEM--THE FACT THAT IT'S EXTREMELY DIFFICULT TO EAT?
UNLESS WE OVERCOME THAT PROBLEM, THERE'S NO WAY WE CAN WIN.
IT'LL BE ALL RIGHT.
THIS HANIWA FIGURINE WILL SOLVE THAT PROBLEM!
GLARE
THE DAY OF THE SECOND MATCH

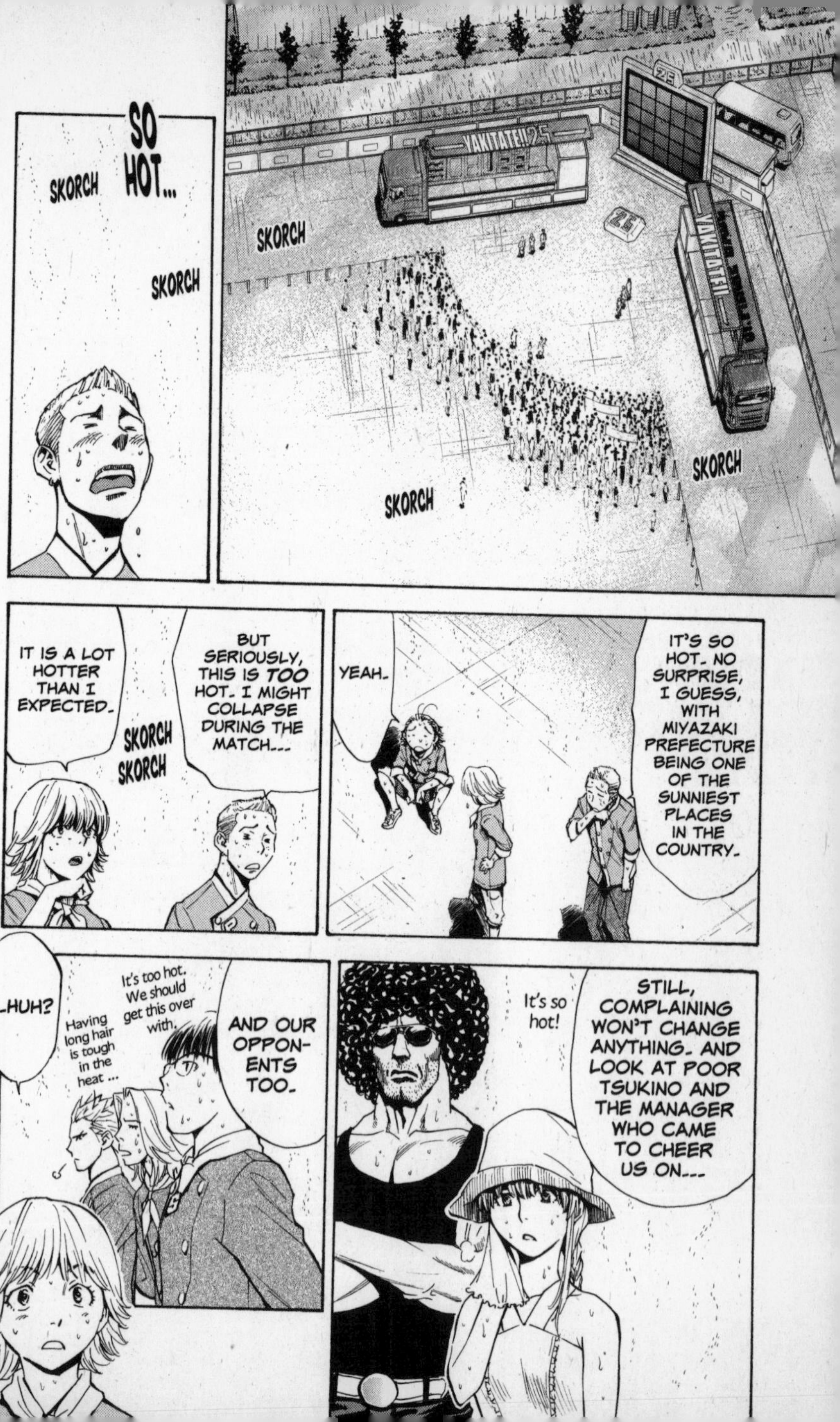
SKORCH
SKORCH
SKORCH
SKORCH
SO HOT...
SKORCH
SKORCH
IT'S SO HOT. NO SURPRISE, I GUESS, WITH MIYAZAKI PREFECTURE BEING ONE OF THE SUNNIEST PLACES IN THE COUNTRY.
YEAH.
BUT SERIOUSLY, THIS IS *TOO* HOT. I MIGHT COLLAPSE DURING THE MATCH...
SKORCH SKORCH
IT IS A LOT HOTTER THAN I EXPECTED.
STILL, COMPLAINING WON'T CHANGE ANYTHING. AND LOOK AT POOR TSUKINO AND THE MANAGER WHO CAME TO CHEER US ON...
It's so hot!
AND OUR OPPONENTS TOO.
It's too hot. We should get this over with.
Having long hair is tough in the heat ...
...HUH?

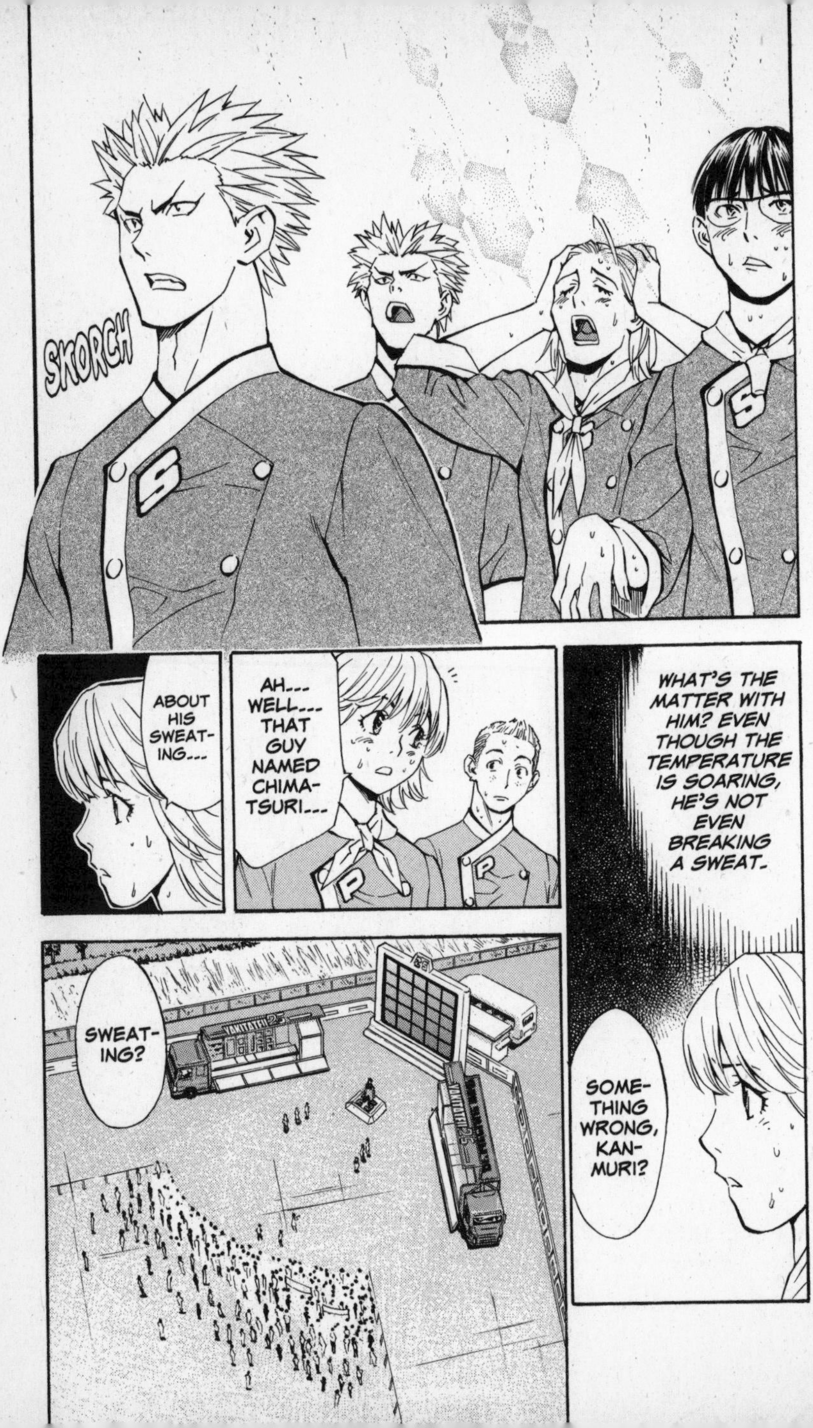
SKORCH
WHAT'S THE MATTER WITH HIM? EVEN THOUGH THE TEMPERATURE IS SOARING, HE'S NOT EVEN BREAKING A SWEAT.
SOME-THING WRONG, KAN-MURI?
AH... WELL... THAT GUY NAMED CHIMA-TSURI...
ABOUT HIS SWEAT-ING...
SWEAT-ING?

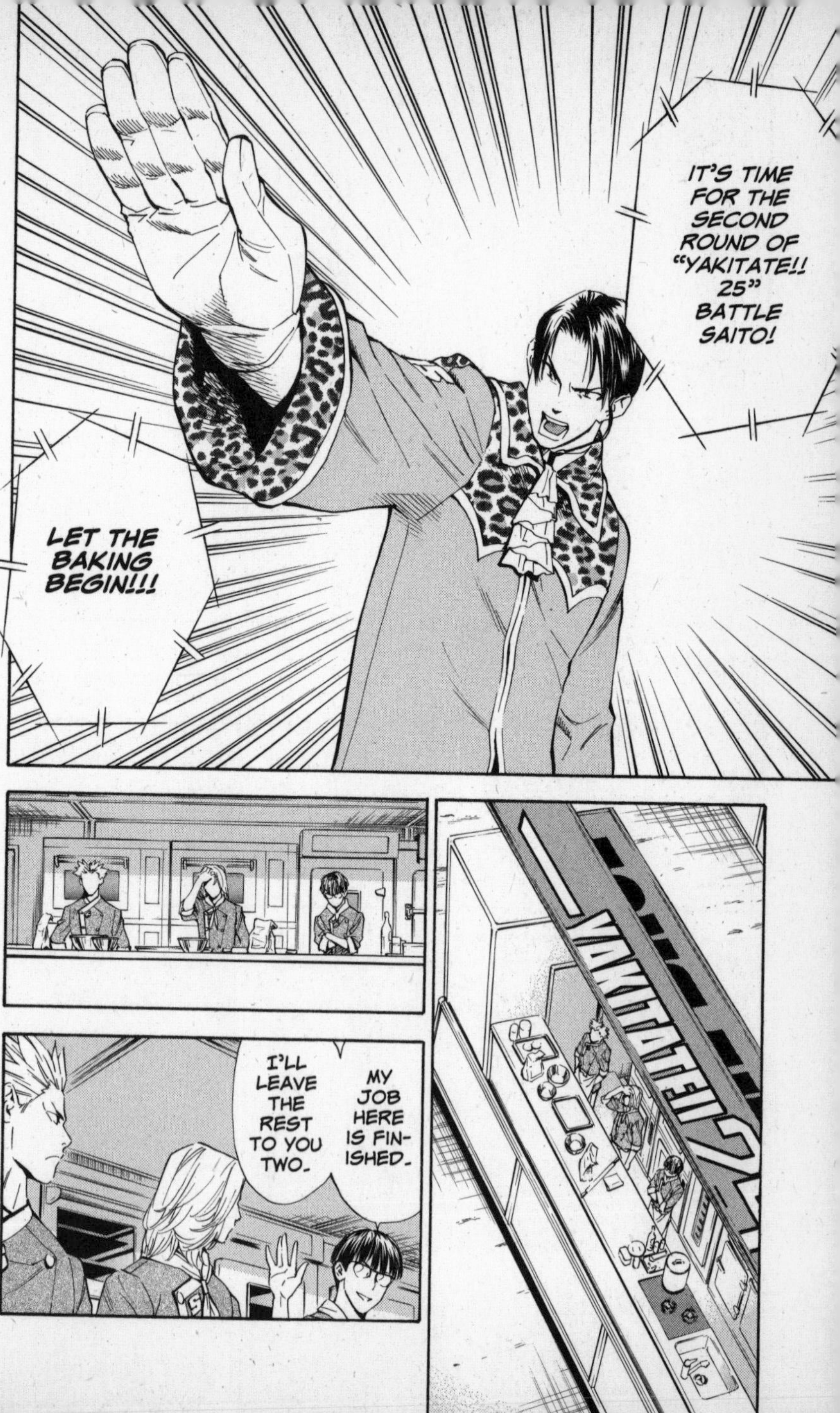
IT'S TIME FOR THE SECOND ROUND OF "YAKITATE!! 25" BATTLE SAITO!
LET THE BAKING BEGIN!!!
YAKITATE!!
MY JOB HERE IS FIN-ISHED.
I'LL LEAVE THE REST TO YOU TWO.

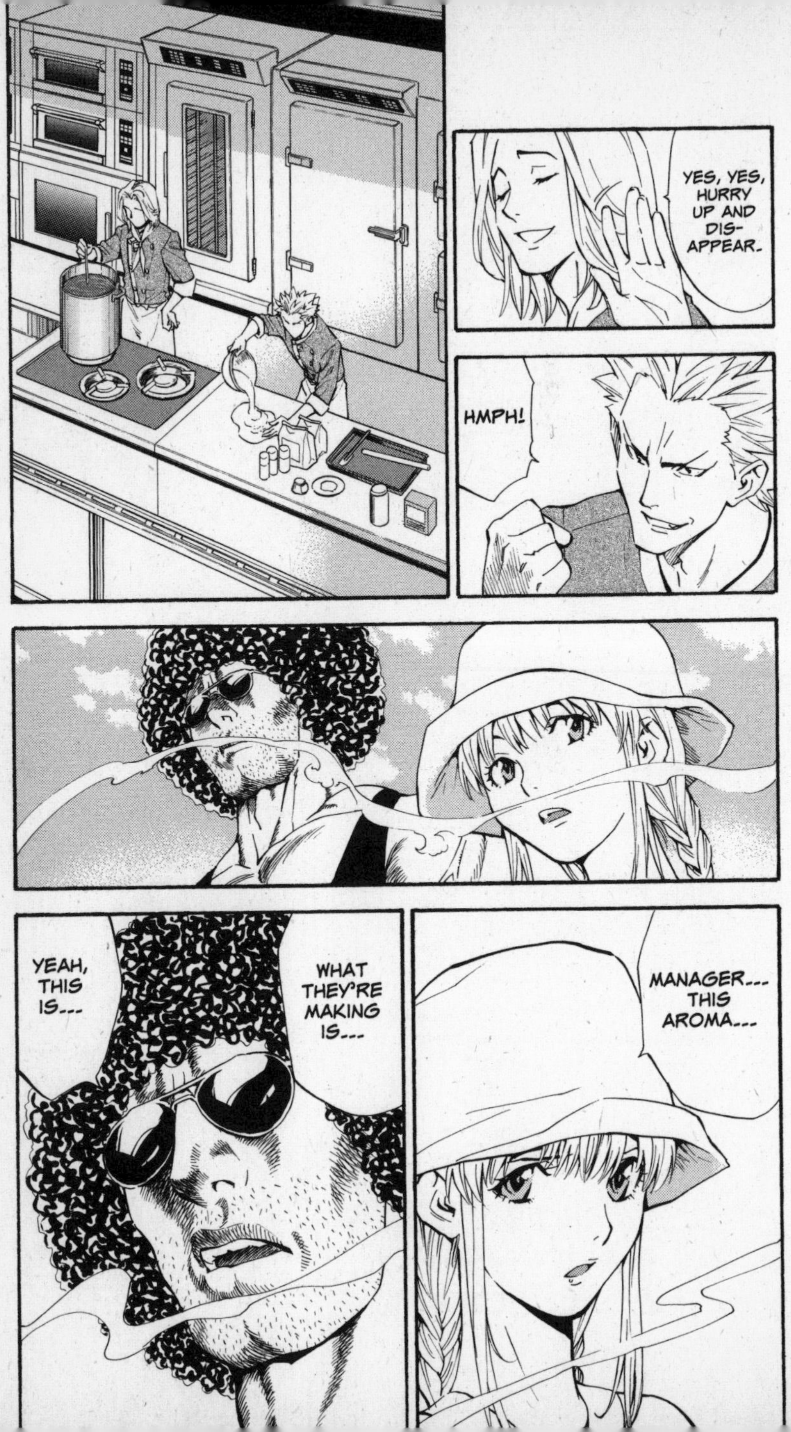
YES, YES, HURRY UP AND DIS-APPEAR.
HMPH!
MANAGER... THIS AROMA...
WHAT THEY'RE MAKING IS...
YEAH, THIS IS...

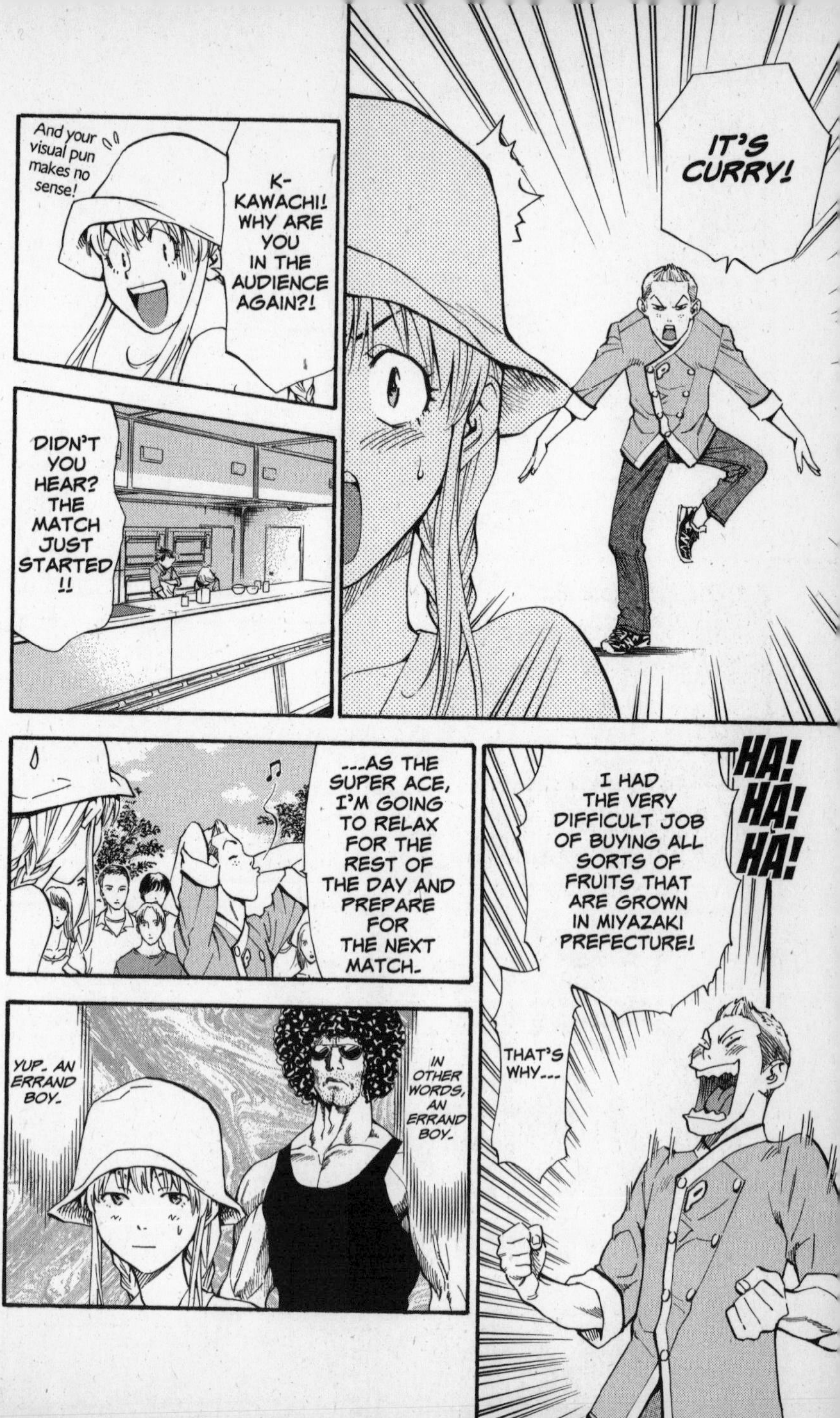
IT'S CURRY!
K-KAWACHI! WHY ARE YOU IN THE AUDIENCE AGAIN?!
And your visual pun makes no sense!
DIDN'T YOU HEAR? THE MATCH JUST STARTED!!
HA! HA! HA!
I HAD THE VERY DIFFICULT JOB OF BUYING ALL SORTS OF FRUITS THAT ARE GROWN IN MIYAZAKI PREFECTURE!
THAT'S WHY...
...AS THE SUPER ACE, I'M GOING TO RELAX FOR THE REST OF THE DAY AND PREPARE FOR THE NEXT MATCH.
IN OTHER WORDS, AN ERRAND BOY.
YUP. AN ERRAND BOY.

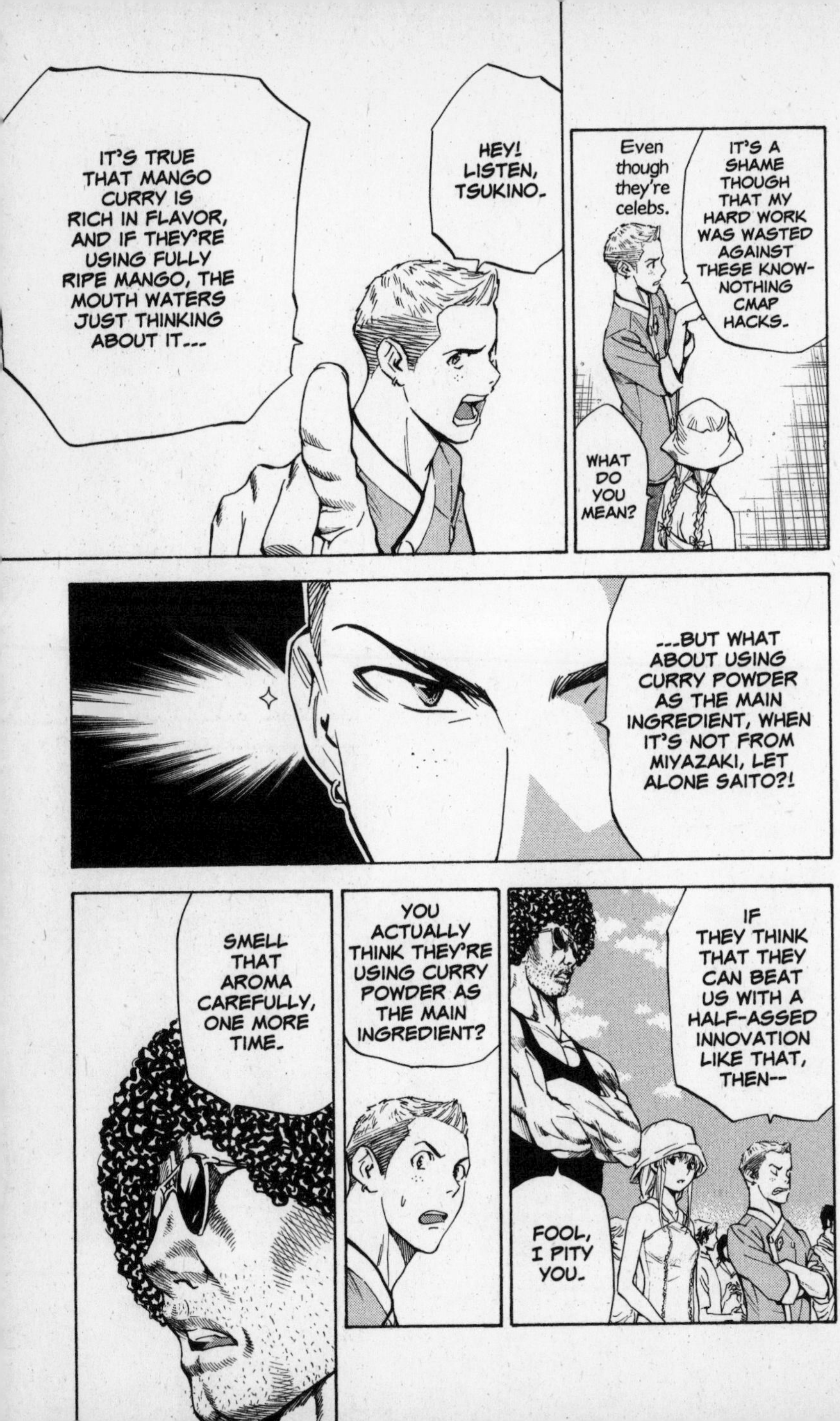
IT'S A SHAME THOUGH THAT MY HARD WORK WAS WASTED AGAINST THESE KNOW-NOTHING CMAP HACKS.
Even though they're celebs.
WHAT DO YOU MEAN?
HEY! LISTEN, TSUKINO.
IT'S TRUE THAT MANGO CURRY IS RICH IN FLAVOR, AND IF THEY'RE USING FULLY RIPE MANGO, THE MOUTH WATERS JUST THINKING ABOUT IT...
...BUT WHAT ABOUT USING CURRY POWDER AS THE MAIN INGREDIENT, WHEN IT'S NOT FROM MIYAZAKI, LET ALONE SAITO?!
IF THEY THINK THAT THEY CAN BEAT US WITH A HALF-ASSED INNOVATION LIKE THAT, THEN--
FOOL, I PITY YOU.
YOU ACTUALLY THINK THEY'RE USING CURRY POWDER AS THE MAIN INGREDIENT?
SMELL THAT AROMA CAREFULLY, ONE MORE TIME.

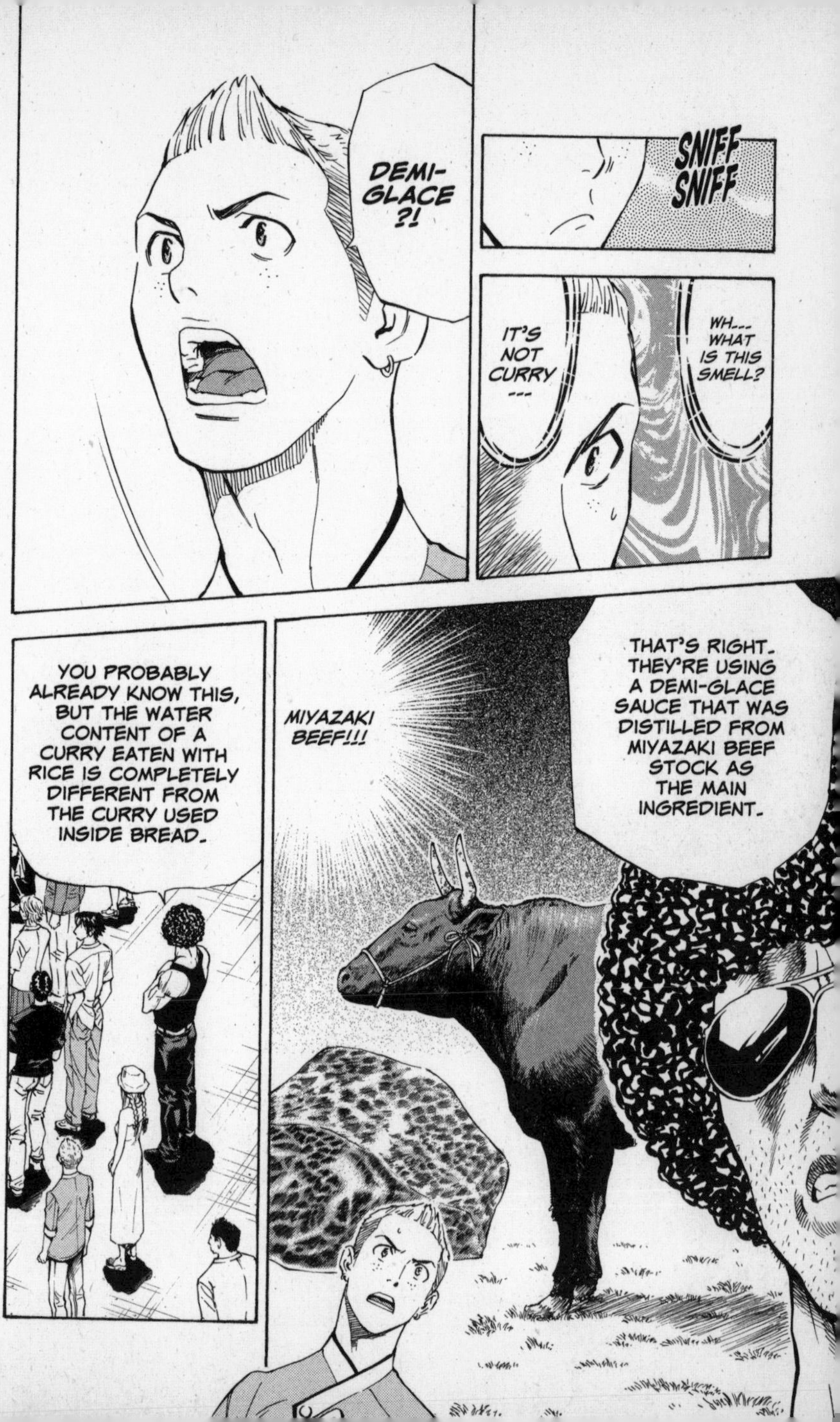
SNIFF SNIFF
WH... WHAT IS THIS SMELL?
IT'S NOT CURRY...
DEMI-GLACE ?!
THAT'S RIGHT. THEY'RE USING A DEMI-GLACE SAUCE THAT WAS DISTILLED FROM MIYAZAKI BEEF STOCK AS THE MAIN INGREDIENT.
MIYAZAKI BEEF!!!
YOU PROBABLY ALREADY KNOW THIS, BUT THE WATER CONTENT OF A CURRY EATEN WITH RICE IS COMPLETELY DIFFERENT FROM THE CURRY USED INSIDE BREAD.

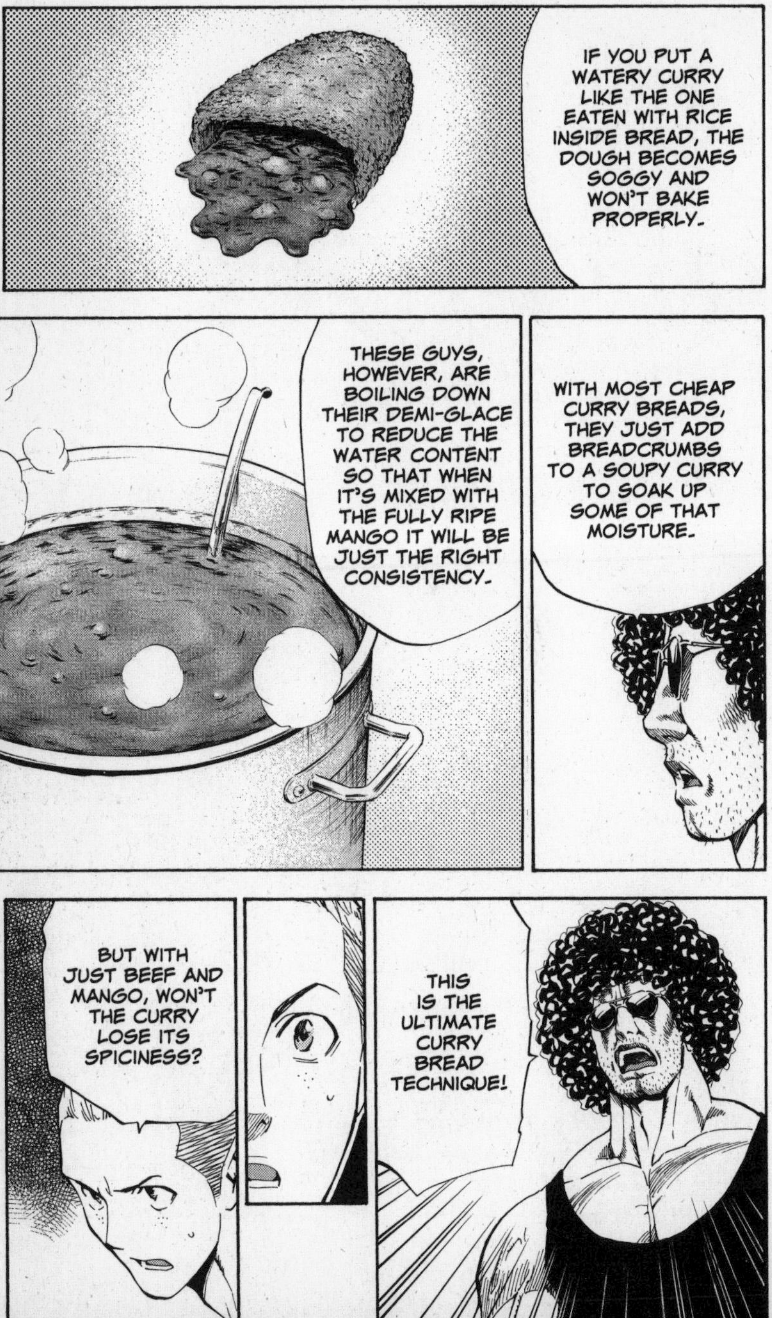
IF YOU PUT A WATERY CURRY LIKE THE ONE EATEN WITH RICE INSIDE BREAD, THE DOUGH BECOMES SOGGY AND WON'T BAKE PROPERLY.
WITH MOST CHEAP CURRY BREADS, THEY JUST ADD BREADCRUMBS TO A SOUPY CURRY TO SOAK UP SOME OF THAT MOISTURE.
THESE GUYS, HOWEVER, ARE BOILING DOWN THEIR DEMI-GLACE TO REDUCE THE WATER CONTENT SO THAT WHEN IT'S MIXED WITH THE FULLY RIPE MANGO IT WILL BE JUST THE RIGHT CONSISTENCY.
THIS IS THE ULTIMATE CURRY BREAD TECHNIQUE!
BUT WITH JUST BEEF AND MANGO, WON'T THE CURRY LOSE ITS SPICINESS?

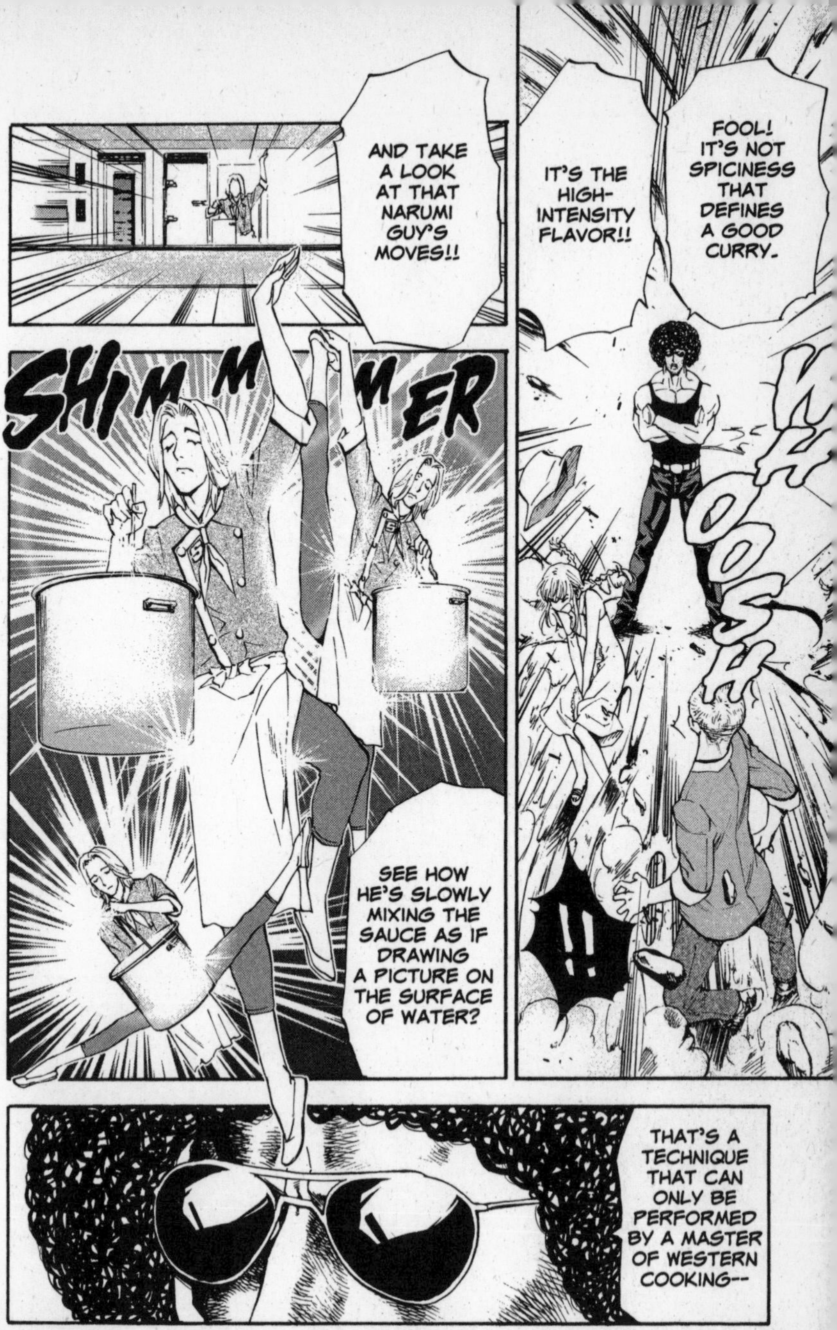
FOOL! IT'S NOT SPICINESS THAT DEFINES A GOOD CURRY.
IT'S THE HIGH-INTENSITY FLAVOR!!
WHOOSH
!!
AND TAKE A LOOK AT THAT NARUMI GUY'S MOVES!!
SHIMMMMER
SEE HOW HE'S SLOWLY MIXING THE SAUCE AS IF DRAWING A PICTURE ON THE SURFACE OF WATER?
THAT'S A TECHNIQUE THAT CAN ONLY BE PERFORMED BY A MASTER OF WESTERN COOKING--

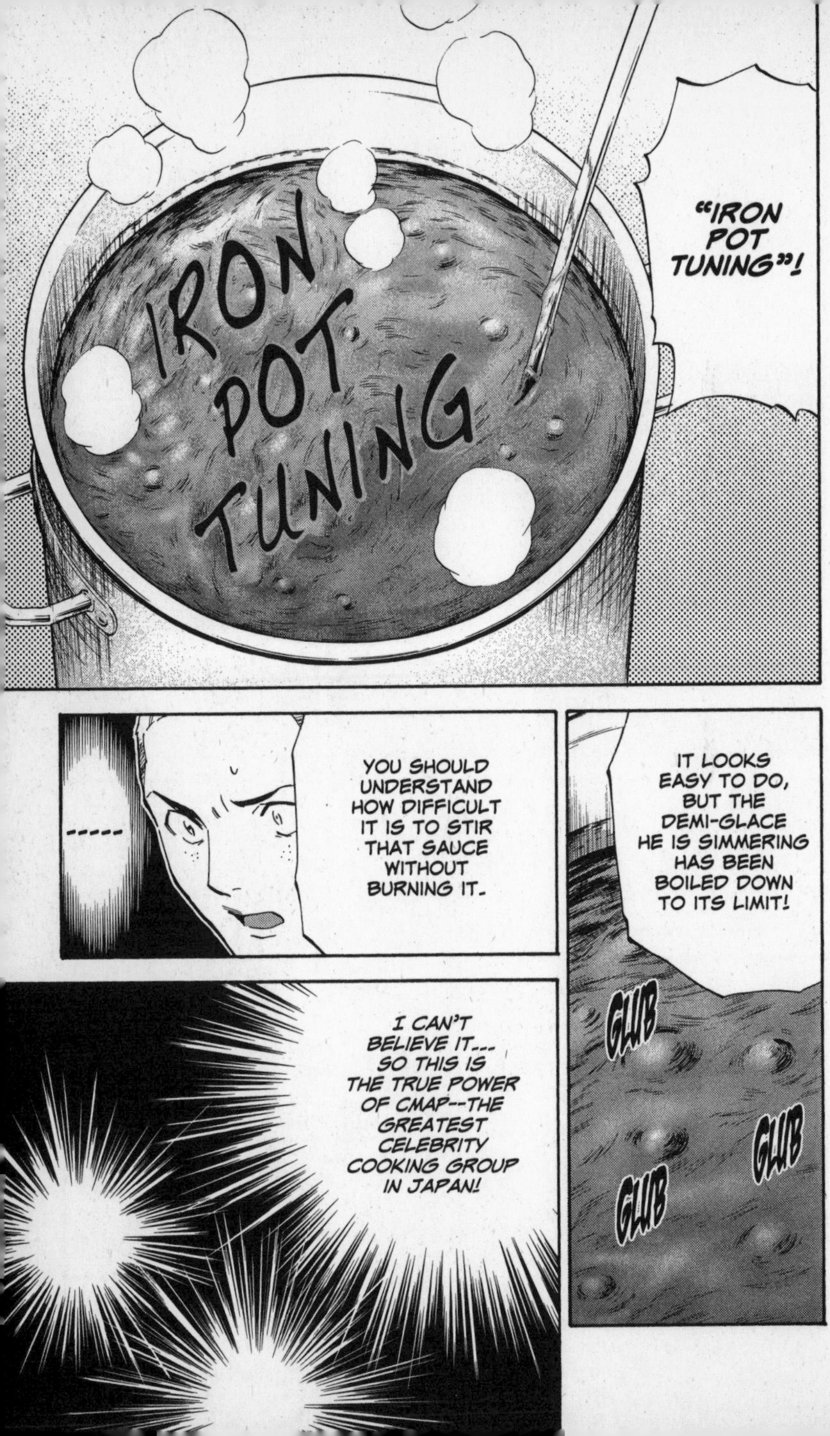
"IRON POT TUNING"!
IRON POT TUNING
IT LOOKS EASY TO DO, BUT THE DEMI-GLACE HE IS SIMMERING HAS BEEN BOILED DOWN TO ITS LIMIT!
GLUB
GLUB
GLUB
YOU SHOULD UNDERSTAND HOW DIFFICULT IT IS TO STIR THAT SAUCE WITHOUT BURNING IT.

I CAN'T BELIEVE IT... SO THIS IS THE TRUE POWER OF CMAP--THE GREATEST CELEBRITY COOKING GROUP IN JAPAN!

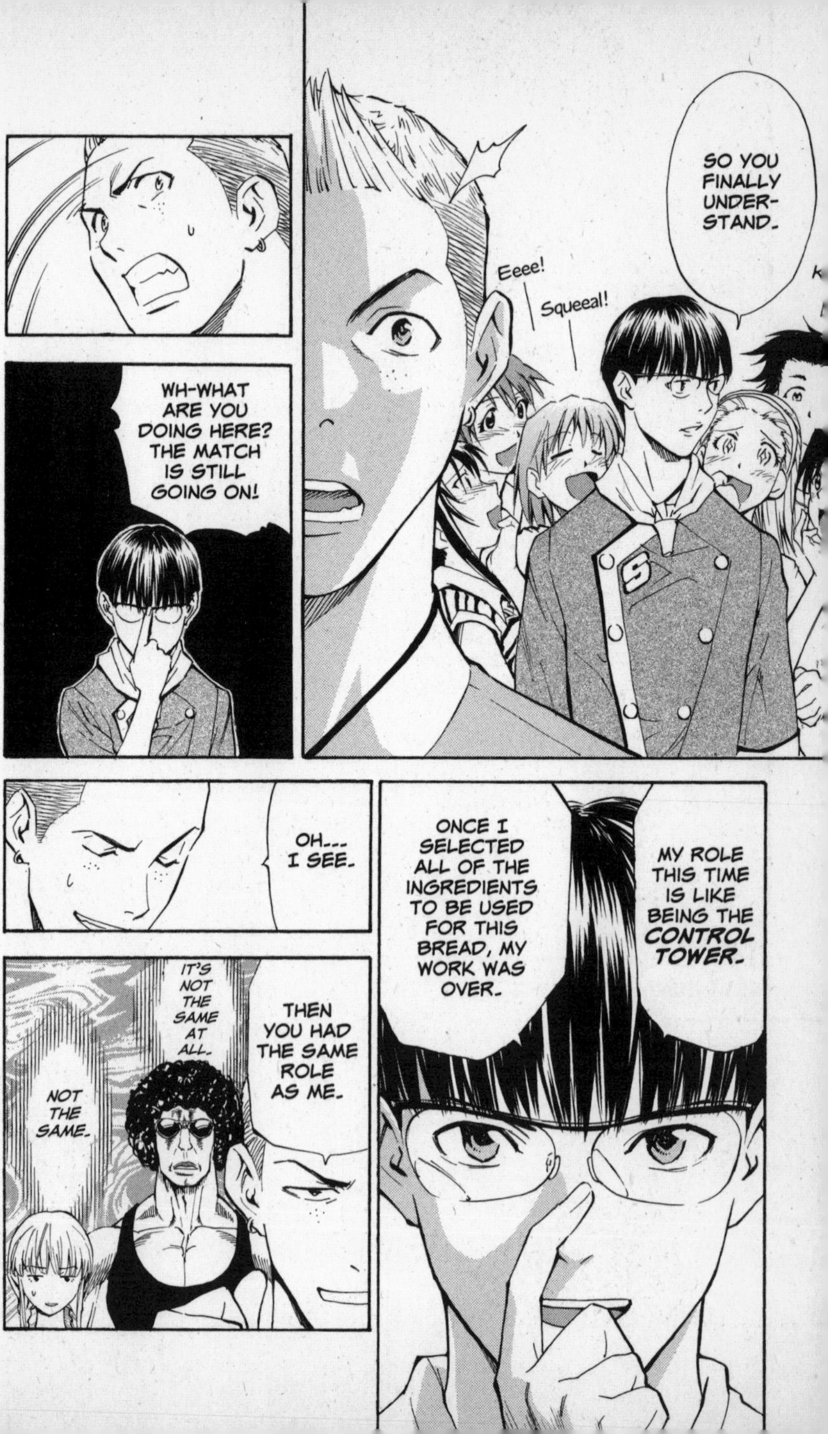
SO YOU FINALLY UNDER-STAND.
Eeee!
Squeeal!
WH-WHAT ARE YOU DOING HERE? THE MATCH IS STILL GOING ON!
MY ROLE THIS TIME IS LIKE BEING THE CONTROL TOWER.
ONCE I SELECTED ALL OF THE INGREDIENTS TO BE USED FOR THIS BREAD, MY WORK WAS OVER.
OH... I SEE.
THEN YOU HAD THE SAME ROLE AS ME.
IT'S NOT THE SAME AT ALL.
NOT THE SAME.

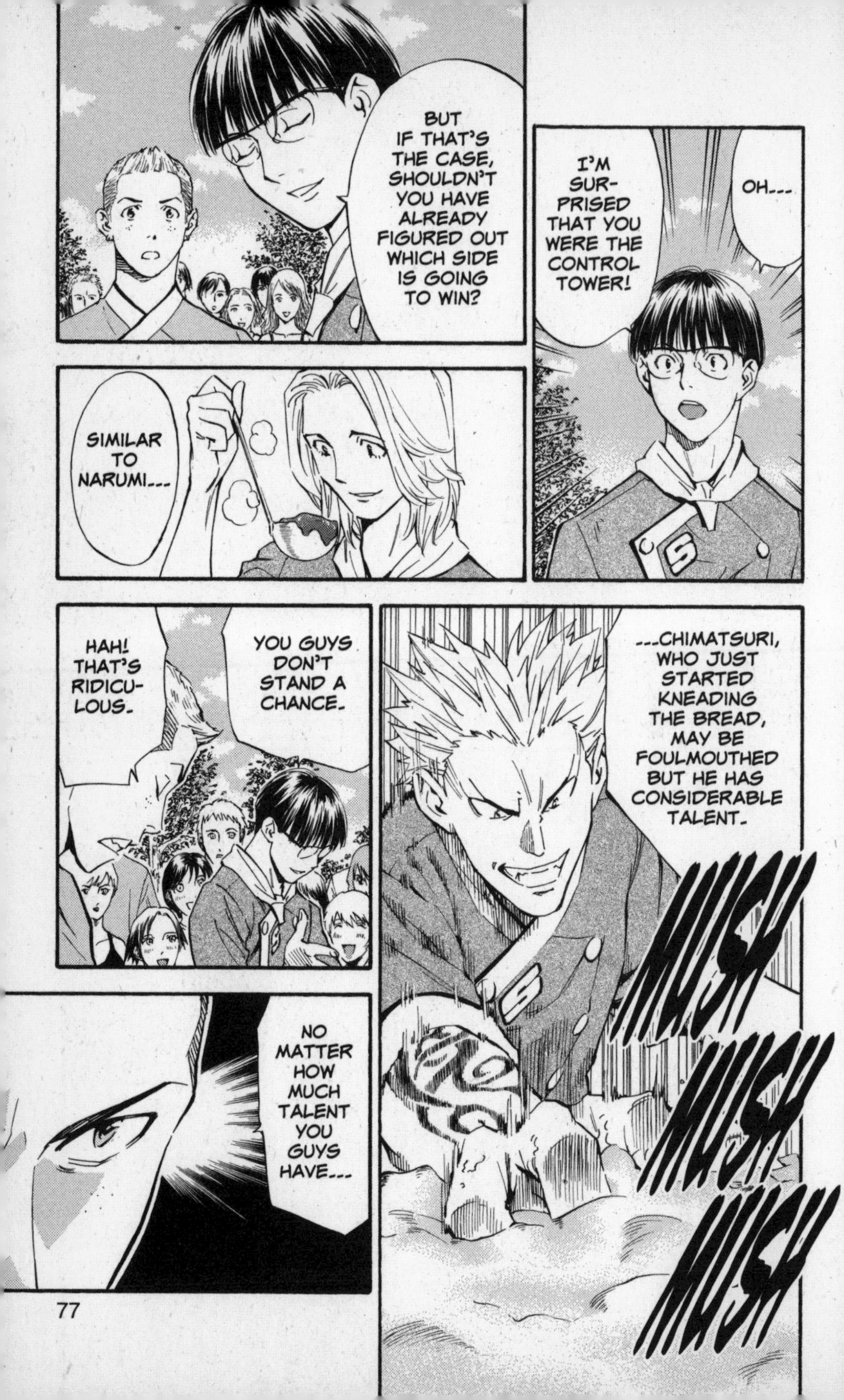
OH...
I'M SUR-PRISED THAT YOU WERE THE CONTROL TOWER!
BUT IF THAT'S THE CASE, SHOULDN'T YOU HAVE ALREADY FIGURED OUT WHICH SIDE IS GOING TO WIN?
SIMILAR TO NARUMI...
...CHIMATSURI, WHO JUST STARTED KNEADING THE BREAD, MAY BE FOULMOUTHED BUT HE HAS CONSIDERABLE TALENT.
MUSH
MUSH
MUSH
YOU GUYS DON'T STAND A CHANCE.
HAH! THAT'S RIDICU-LOUS.
NO MATTER HOW MUCH TALENT YOU GUYS HAVE...

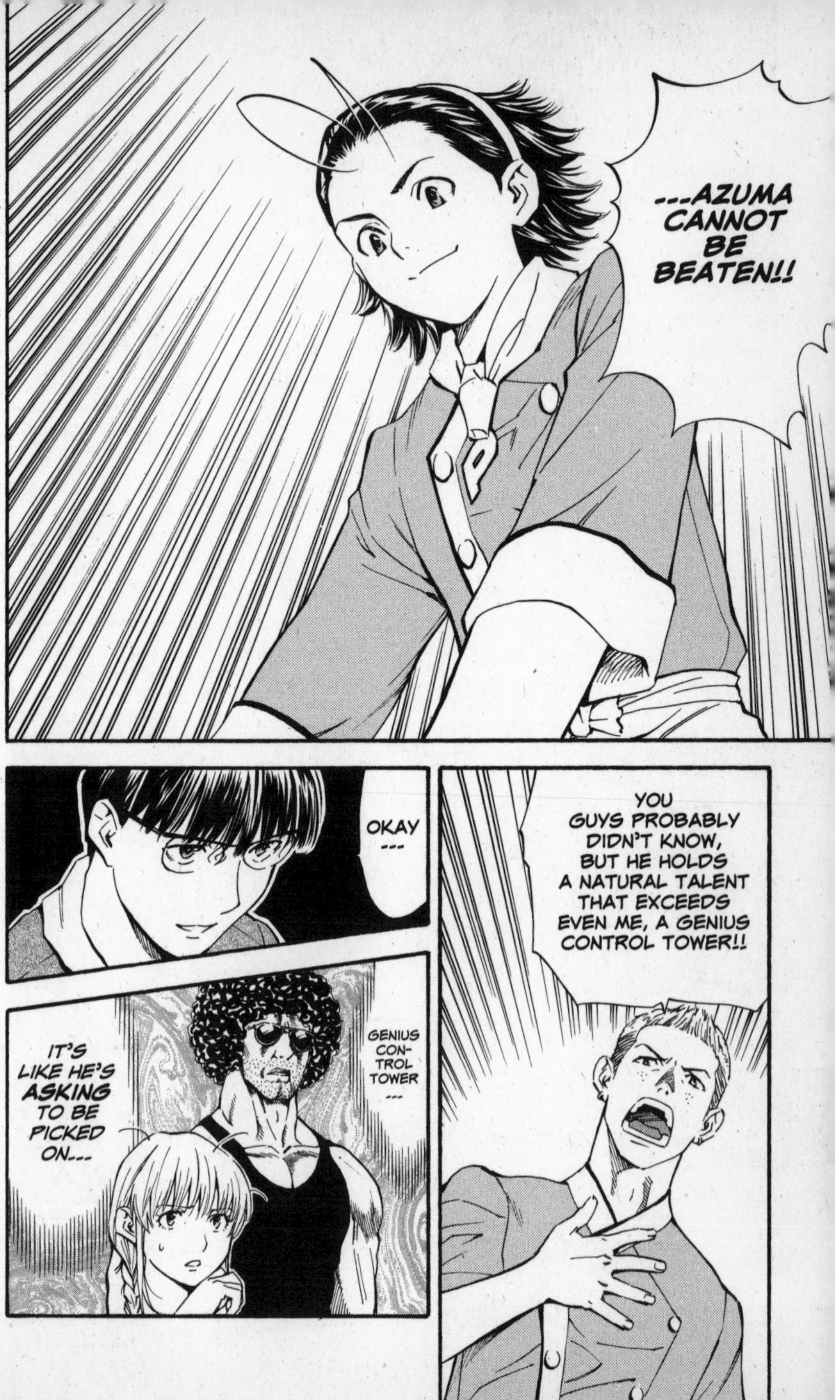
---AZUMA CANNOT BE BEATEN!!
YOU GUYS PROBABLY DIDN'T KNOW, BUT HE HOLDS A NATURAL TALENT THAT EXCEEDS EVEN ME, A GENIUS CONTROL TOWER!!
OKAY---
GENIUS CON-TROL TOWER---
IT'S LIKE HE'S ASKING TO BE PICKED ON---

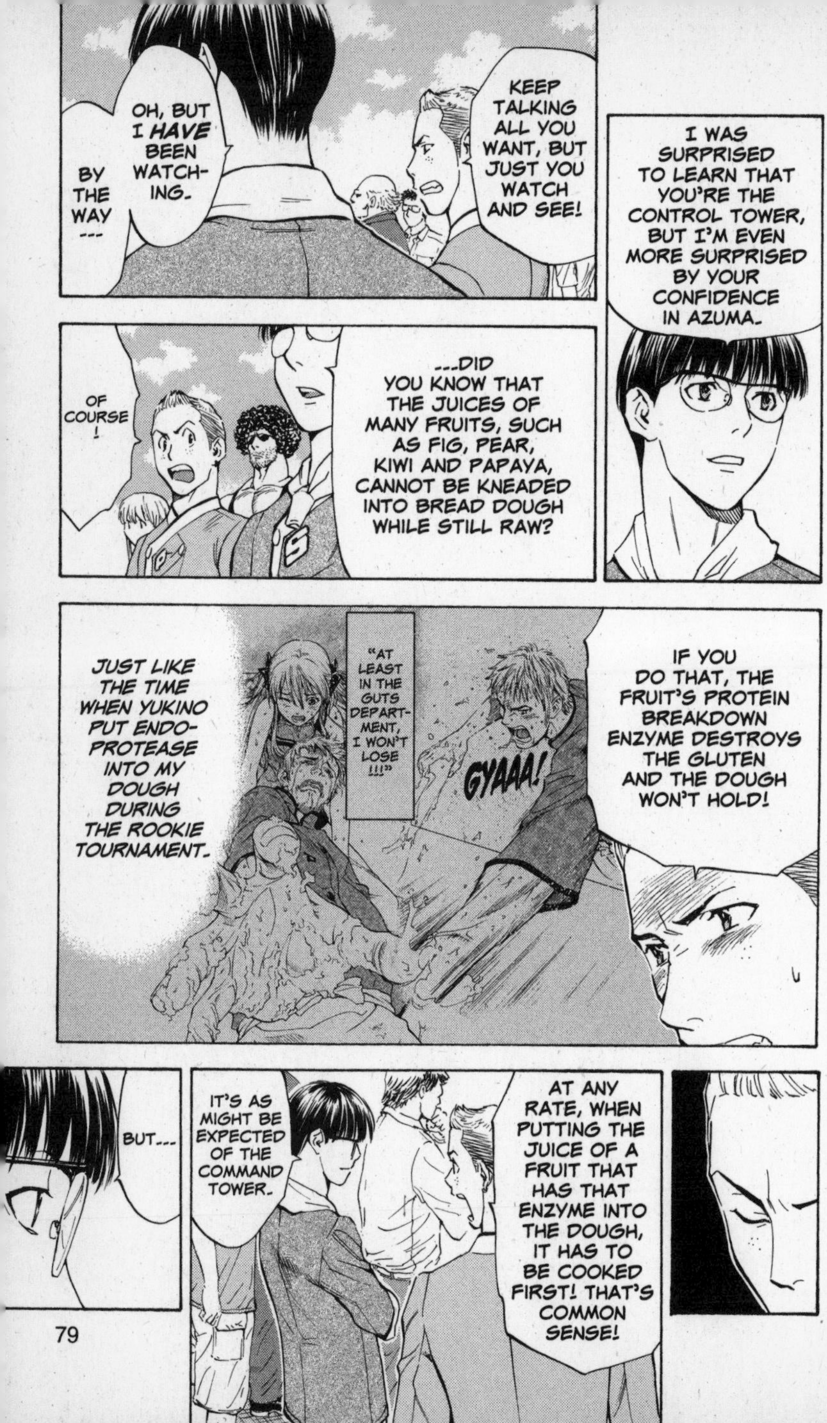

I WAS SURPRISED TO LEARN THAT YOU'RE THE CONTROL TOWER, BUT I'M EVEN MORE SURPRISED BY YOUR CONFIDENCE IN AZUMA.
KEEP TALKING ALL YOU WANT, BUT JUST YOU WATCH AND SEE!
OH, BUT I *HAVE* BEEN WATCHING.
BY THE WAY ---
---DID YOU KNOW THAT THE JUICES OF MANY FRUITS, SUCH AS FIG, PEAR, KIWI AND PAPAYA, CANNOT BE KNEADED INTO BREAD DOUGH WHILE STILL RAW?
OF COURSE!
IF YOU DO THAT, THE FRUIT'S PROTEIN BREAKDOWN ENZYME DESTROYS THE GLUTEN AND THE DOUGH WON'T HOLD!
"AT LEAST IN THE GUTS DEPARTMENT, I WON'T LOSE!!!"
GYAAA!
JUST LIKE THE TIME WHEN YUKINO PUT ENDOPROTEASE INTO MY DOUGH DURING THE ROOKIE TOURNAMENT.
AT ANY RATE, WHEN PUTTING THE JUICE OF A FRUIT THAT HAS THAT ENZYME INTO THE DOUGH, IT HAS TO BE COOKED FIRST! THAT'S COMMON SENSE!
IT'S AS MIGHT BE EXPECTED OF THE COMMAND TOWER.
BUT---

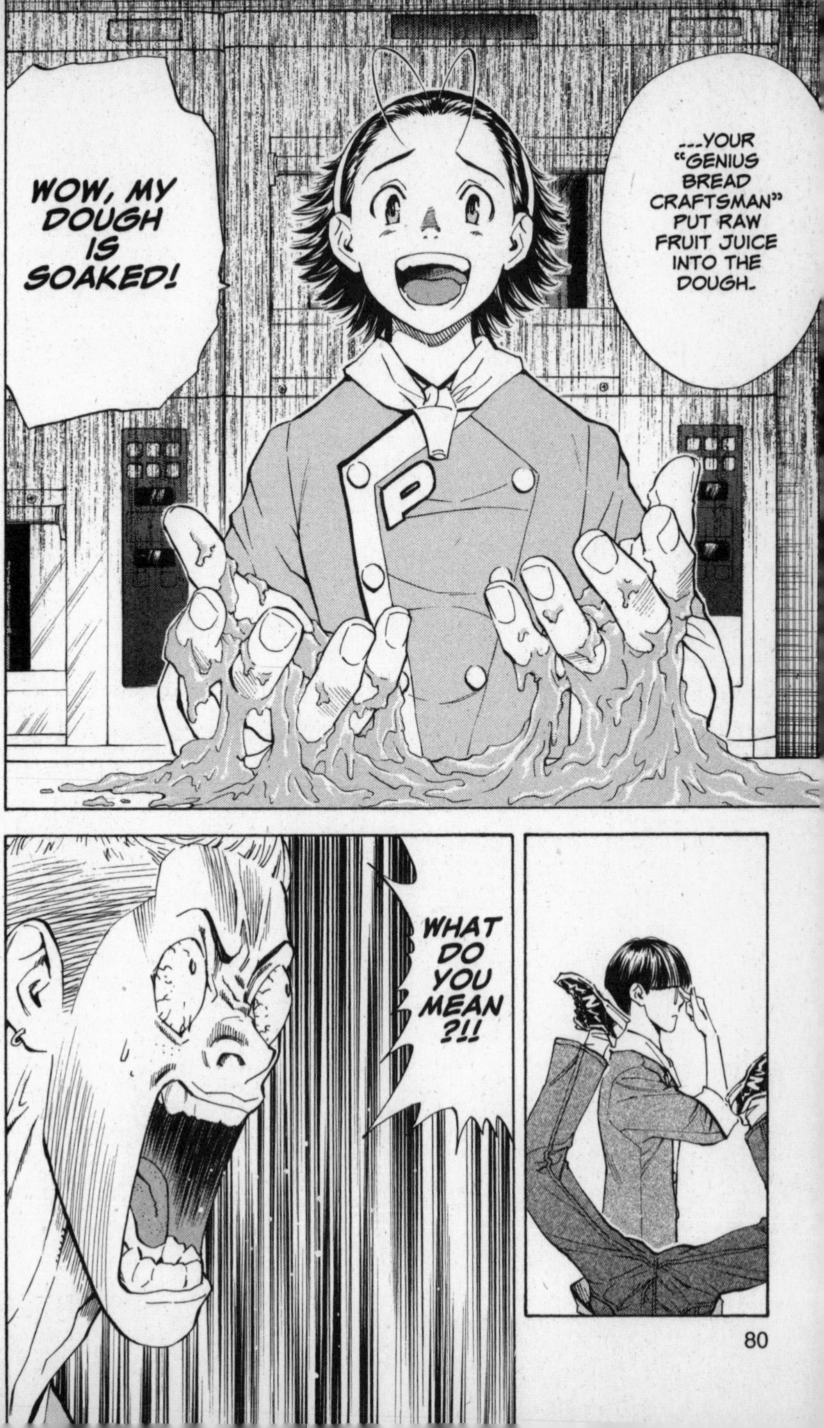
...YOUR "GENIUS BREAD CRAFTSMAN" PUT RAW FRUIT JUICE INTO THE DOUGH.
WOW, MY DOUGH IS SOAKED!
WHAT DO YOU MEAN ?!!

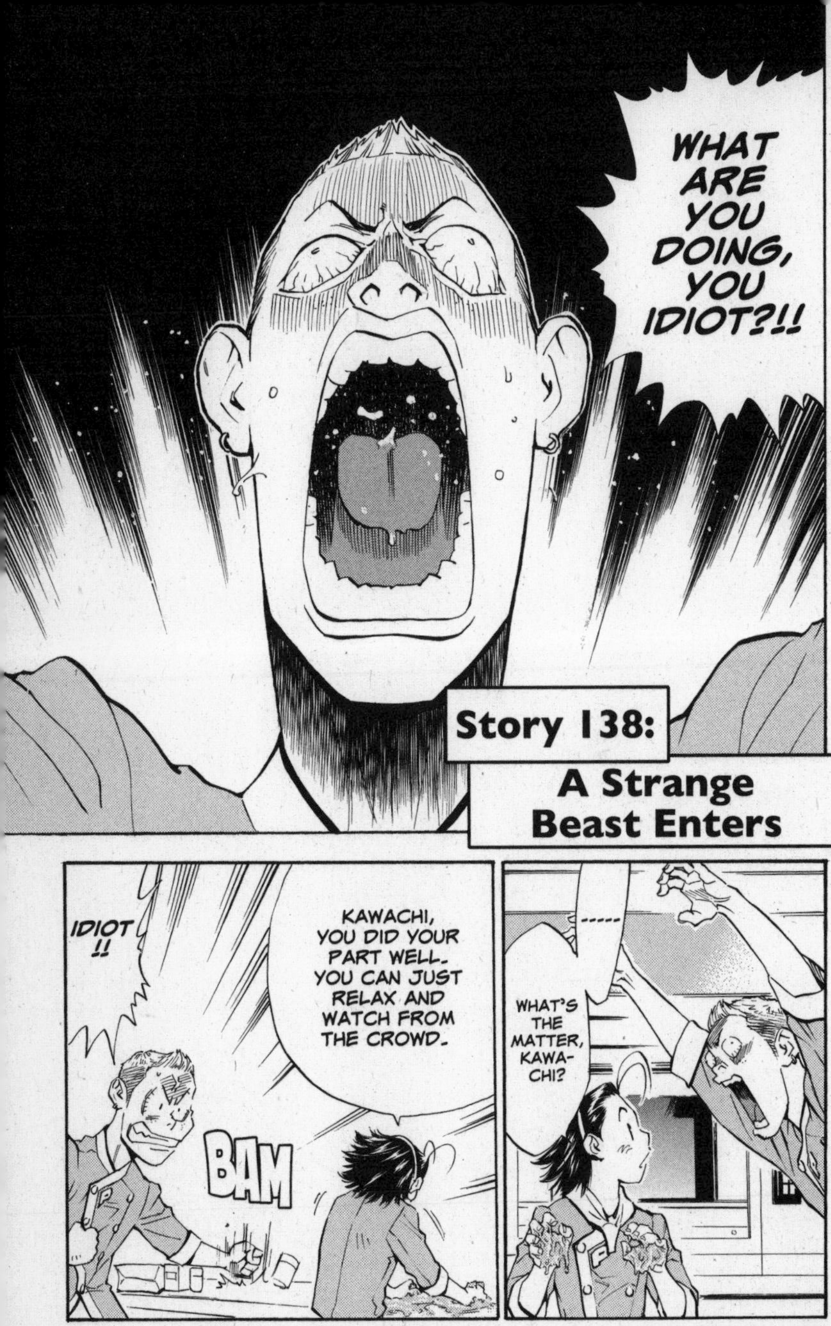
WHAT ARE YOU DOING, YOU IDIOT?!!
Story 138:
A Strange Beast Enters

WHAT'S THE MATTER, KAWACHI?
KAWACHI, YOU DID YOUR PART WELL. YOU CAN JUST RELAX AND WATCH FROM THE CROWD.
IDIOT!!
BAM

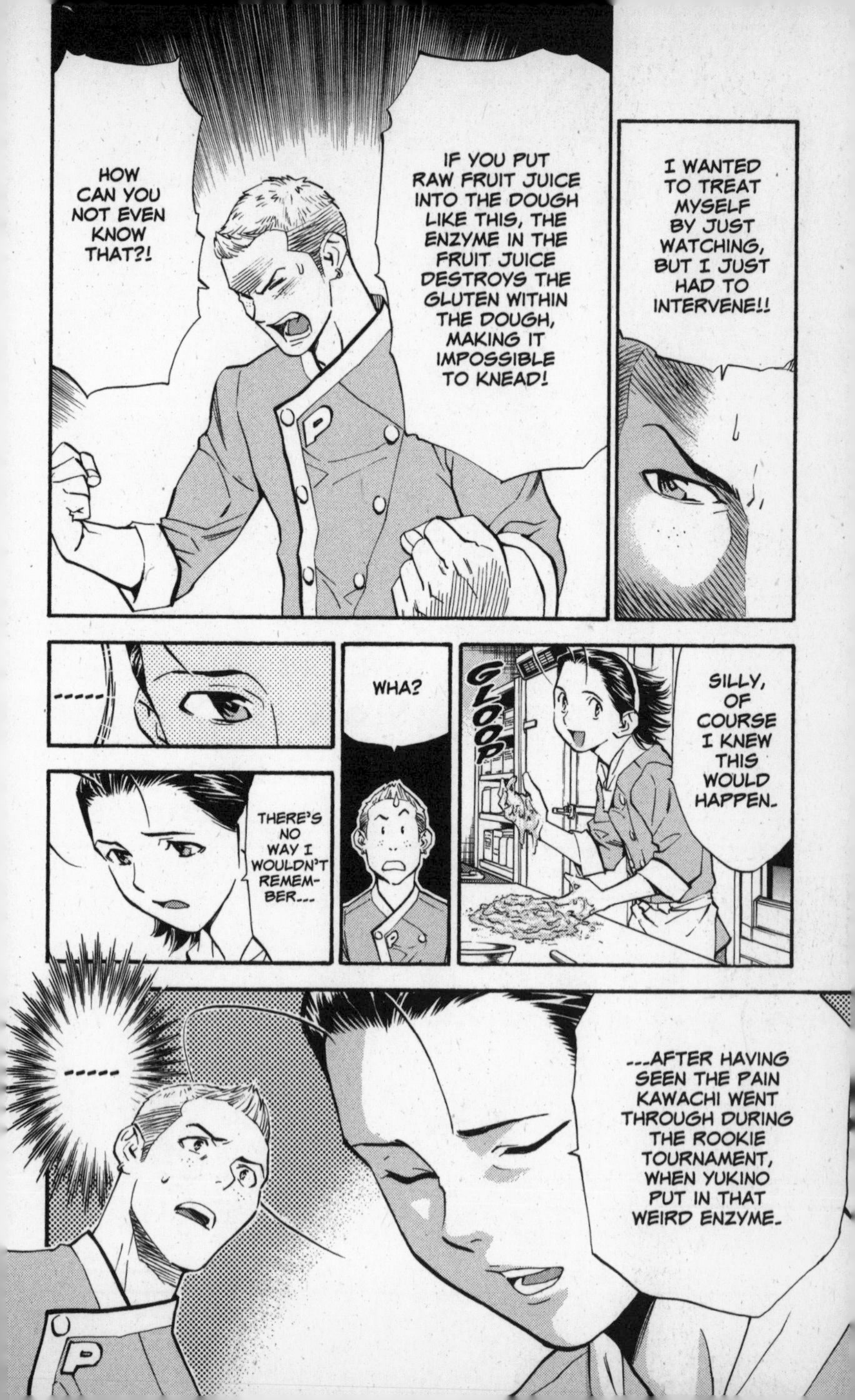
I WANTED TO TREAT MYSELF BY JUST WATCHING, BUT I JUST HAD TO INTERVENE!!
IF YOU PUT RAW FRUIT JUICE INTO THE DOUGH LIKE THIS, THE ENZYME IN THE FRUIT JUICE DESTROYS THE GLUTEN WITHIN THE DOUGH, MAKING IT IMPOSSIBLE TO KNEAD!
HOW CAN YOU NOT EVEN KNOW THAT?!
SILLY, OF COURSE I KNEW THIS WOULD HAPPEN...
GLOOP
WHA?

THERE'S NO WAY I WOULDN'T REMEMBER...
...AFTER HAVING SEEN THE PAIN KAWACHI WENT THROUGH DURING THE ROOKIE TOURNAMENT, WHEN YUKINO PUT IN THAT WEIRD ENZYME...

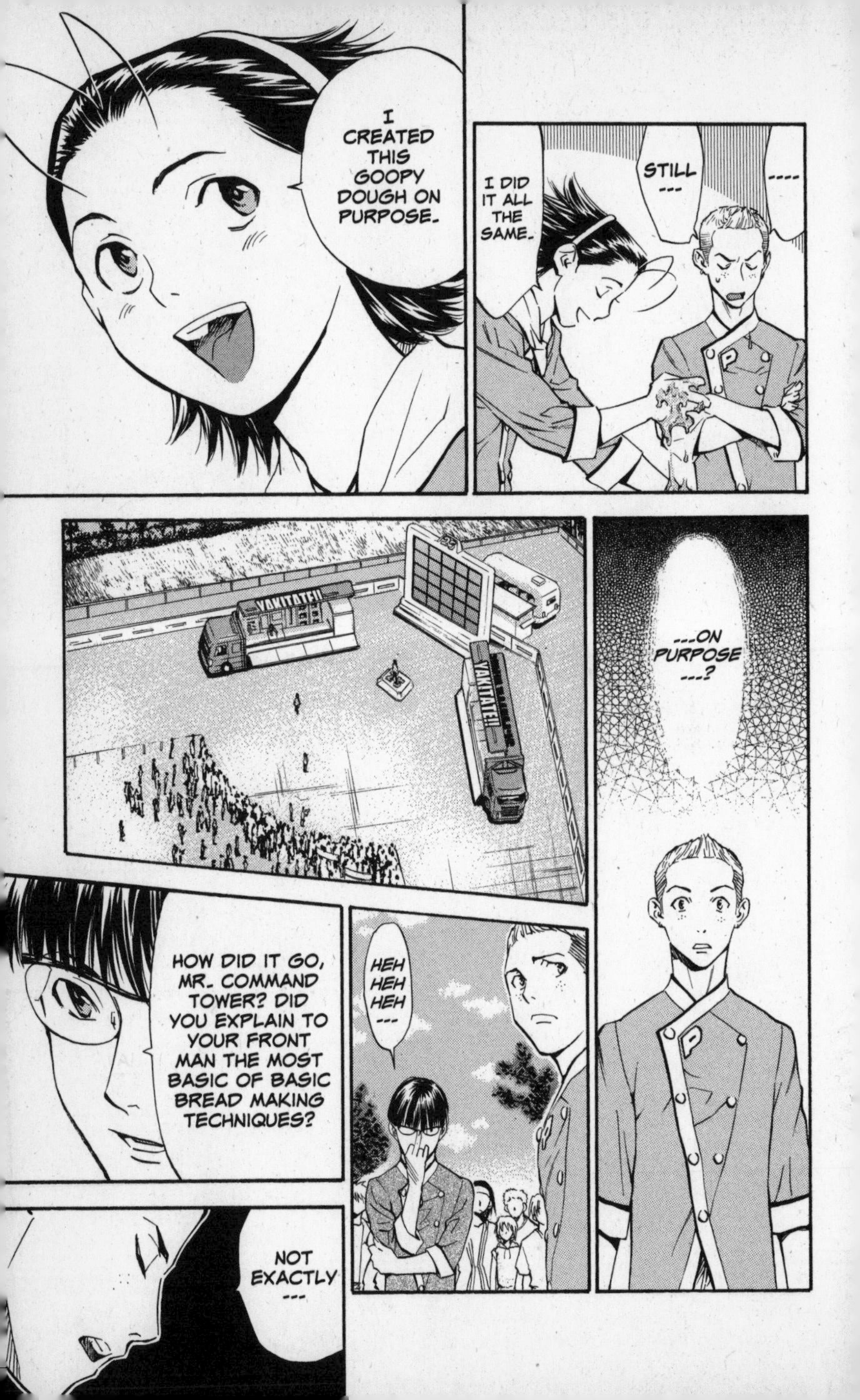

STILL ---
I DID IT ALL THE SAME.
I CREATED THIS GOOPY DOUGH ON PURPOSE.
...ON PURPOSE ...?
YAKITATE!!
YAKITATE!!
HEH HEH HEH ---
HOW DID IT GO, MR. COMMAND TOWER? DID YOU EXPLAIN TO YOUR FRONT MAN THE MOST BASIC OF BASIC BREAD MAKING TECHNIQUES?
NOT EXACTLY ---

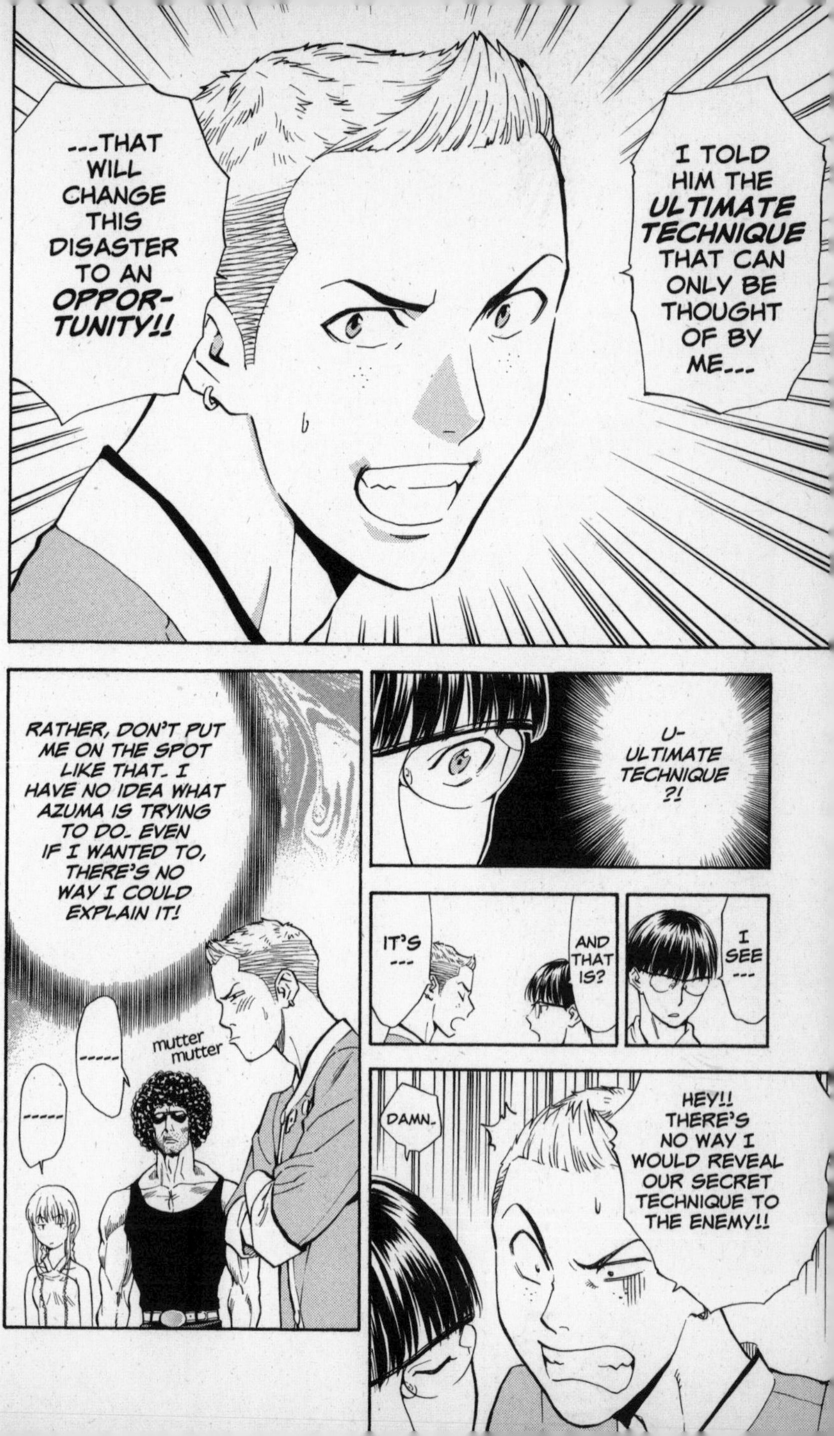
I TOLD HIM THE ULTIMATE TECHNIQUE THAT CAN ONLY BE THOUGHT OF BY ME...
...THAT WILL CHANGE THIS DISASTER TO AN OPPORTUNITY!!
U-ULTIMATE TECHNIQUE?!
I SEE...
AND THAT IS?
IT'S...
HEY!! THERE'S NO WAY I WOULD REVEAL OUR SECRET TECHNIQUE TO THE ENEMY!!
DAMN.
RATHER, DON'T PUT ME ON THE SPOT LIKE THAT. I HAVE NO IDEA WHAT AZUMA IS TRYING TO DO. EVEN IF I WANTED TO, THERE'S NO WAY I COULD EXPLAIN IT!
mutter mutter
.....
.....

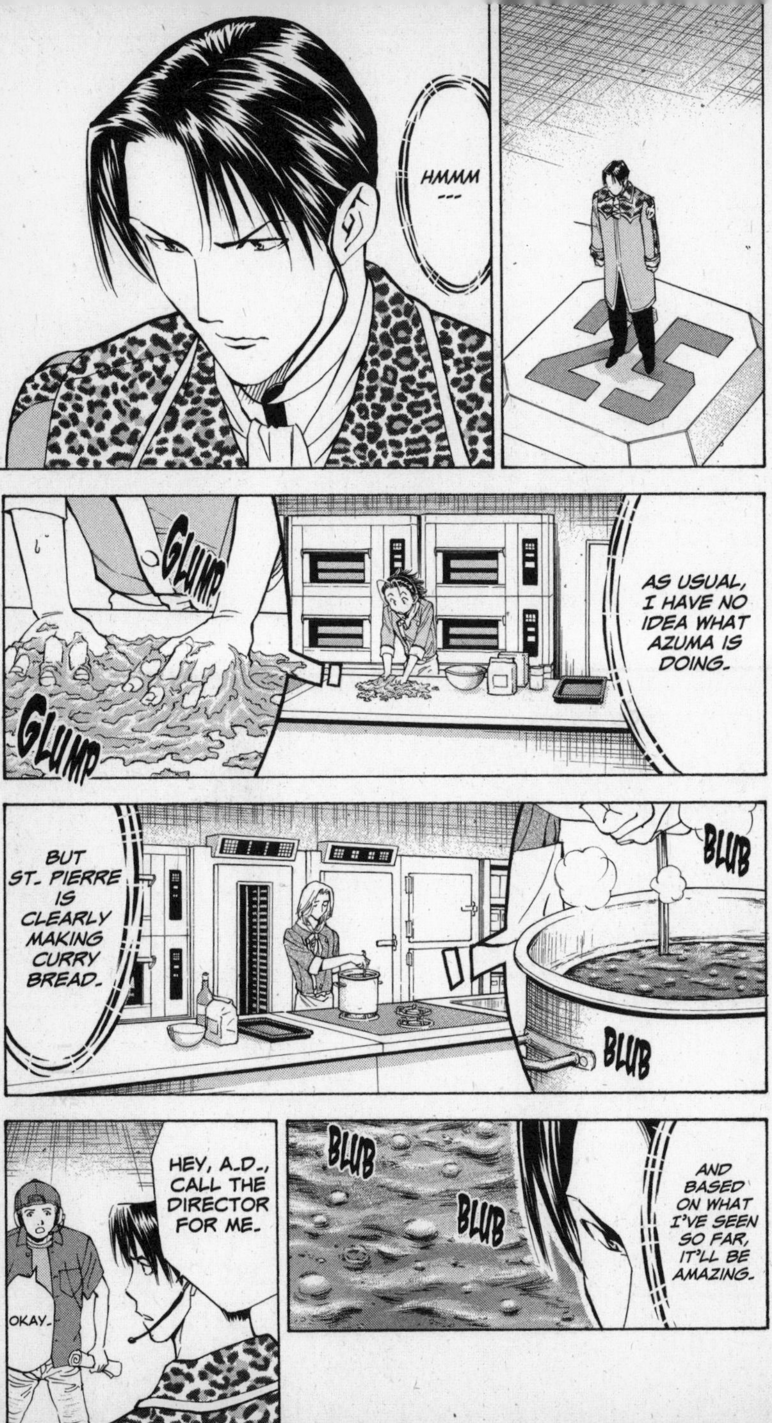
HMMM---
AS USUAL, I HAVE NO IDEA WHAT AZUMA IS DOING.
GLUMP
GLUMP
BLUB
BLUB
BUT ST. PIERRE IS CLEARLY MAKING CURRY BREAD.
AND BASED ON WHAT I'VE SEEN SO FAR, IT'LL BE AMAZING.
BLUB
BLUB
HEY, A.D., CALL THE DIRECTOR FOR ME.
OKAY.

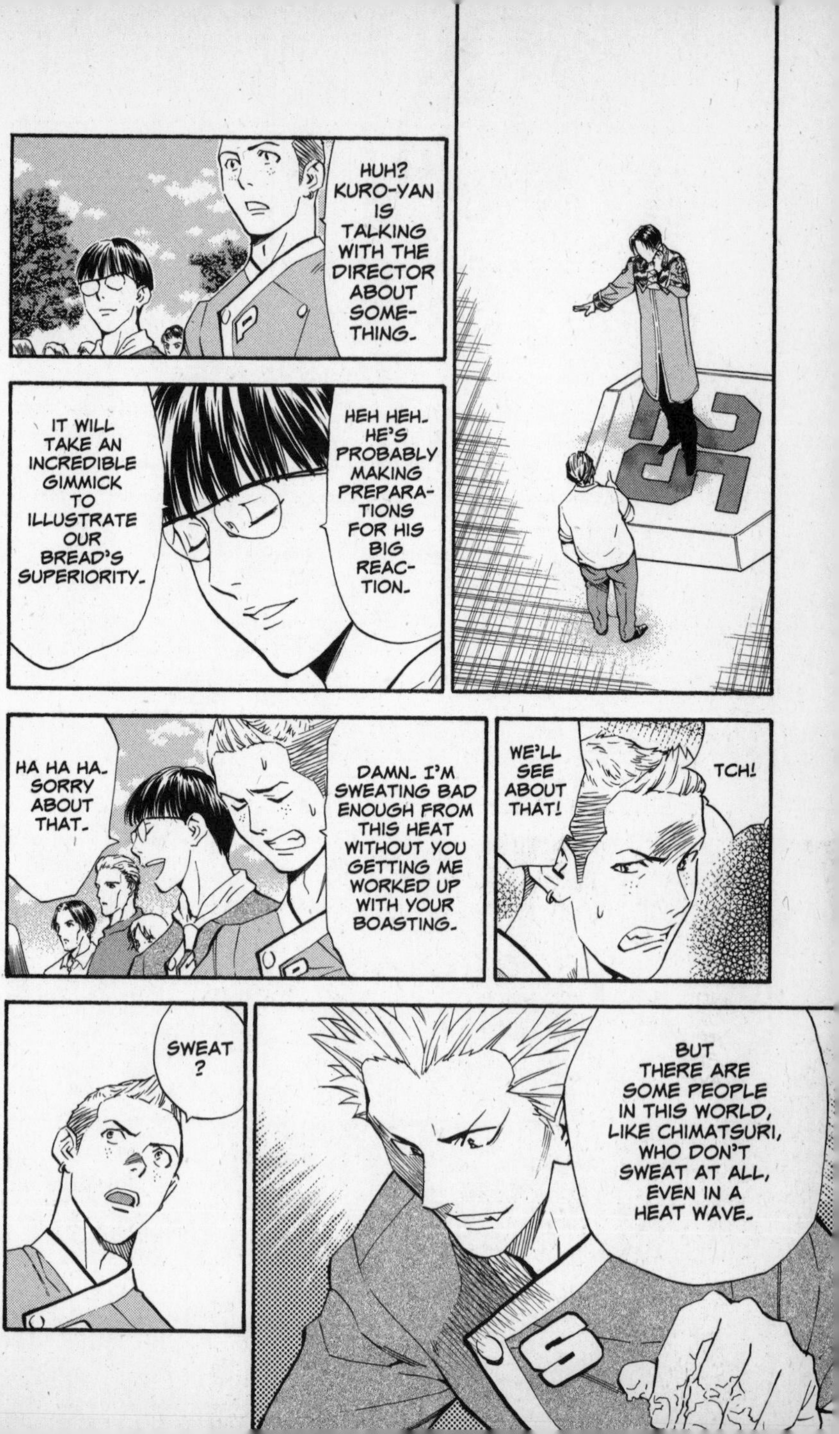
HUH? KURO-YAN IS TALKING WITH THE DIRECTOR ABOUT SOME-THING...
HEH HEH... HE'S PROBABLY MAKING PREPARA-TIONS FOR HIS BIG REAC-TION...
IT WILL TAKE AN INCREDIBLE GIMMICK TO ILLUSTRATE OUR BREAD'S SUPERIORITY...
TCH!
WE'LL SEE ABOUT THAT!
DAMN... I'M SWEATING BAD ENOUGH FROM THIS HEAT WITHOUT YOU GETTING ME WORKED UP WITH YOUR BOASTING...
HA HA HA... SORRY ABOUT THAT...
BUT THERE ARE SOME PEOPLE IN THIS WORLD, LIKE CHIMATSURI, WHO DON'T SWEAT AT ALL, EVEN IN A HEAT WAVE...
SWEAT?

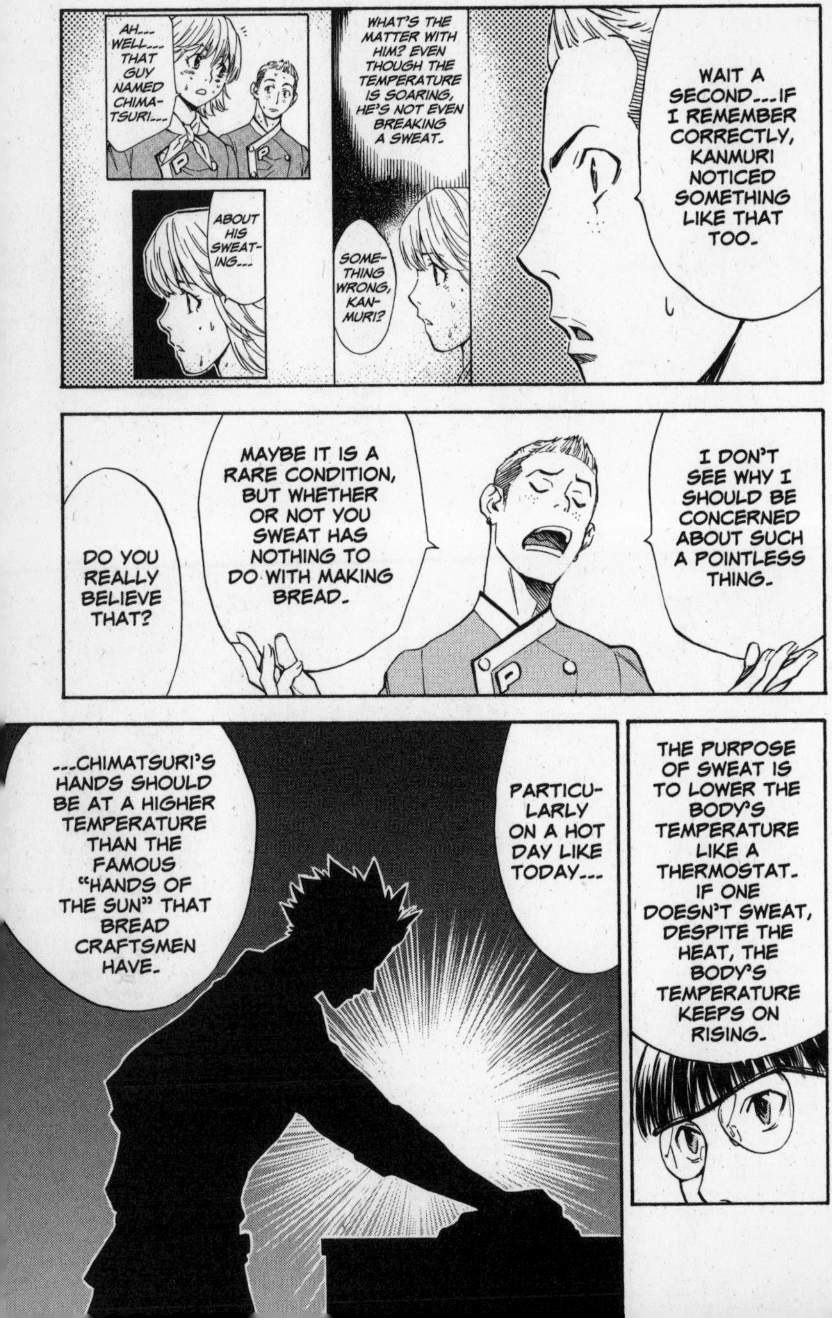
WAIT A SECOND... IF I REMEMBER CORRECTLY, KANMURI NOTICED SOMETHING LIKE THAT TOO.
WHAT'S THE MATTER WITH HIM? EVEN THOUGH THE TEMPERATURE IS SOARING, HE'S NOT EVEN BREAKING A SWEAT.
SOMETHING WRONG, KANMURI?
AH... WELL... THAT GUY NAMED CHIMATSURI...
ABOUT HIS SWEATING...
I DON'T SEE WHY I SHOULD BE CONCERNED ABOUT SUCH A POINTLESS THING.
MAYBE IT IS A RARE CONDITION, BUT WHETHER OR NOT YOU SWEAT HAS NOTHING TO DO WITH MAKING BREAD.
DO YOU REALLY BELIEVE THAT?
THE PURPOSE OF SWEAT IS TO LOWER THE BODY'S TEMPERATURE LIKE A THERMOSTAT. IF ONE DOESN'T SWEAT, DESPITE THE HEAT, THE BODY'S TEMPERATURE KEEPS ON RISING.
PARTICULARLY ON A HOT DAY LIKE TODAY...
...CHIMATSURI'S HANDS SHOULD BE AT A HIGHER TEMPERATURE THAN THE FAMOUS "HANDS OF THE SUN" THAT BREAD CRAFTSMEN HAVE.

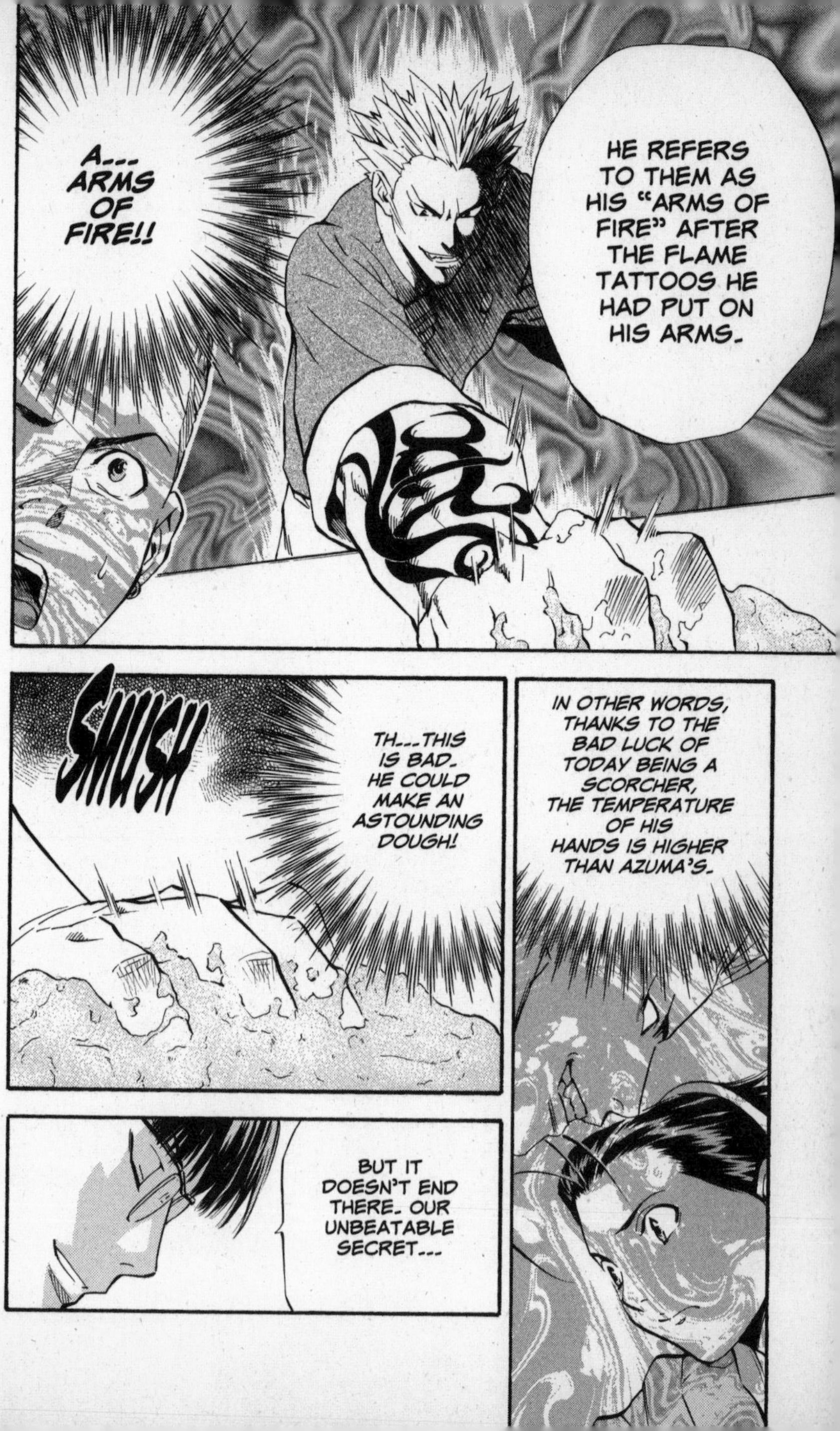
HE REFERS TO THEM AS HIS "ARMS OF FIRE" AFTER THE FLAME TATTOOS HE HAD PUT ON HIS ARMS.
A... ARMS OF FIRE!!
IN OTHER WORDS, THANKS TO THE BAD LUCK OF TODAY BEING A SCORCHER, THE TEMPERATURE OF HIS HANDS IS HIGHER THAN AZUMA'S.
SMUSH
TH...THIS IS BAD. HE COULD MAKE AN ASTOUNDING DOUGH!
BUT IT DOESN'T END THERE. OUR UNBEATABLE SECRET...

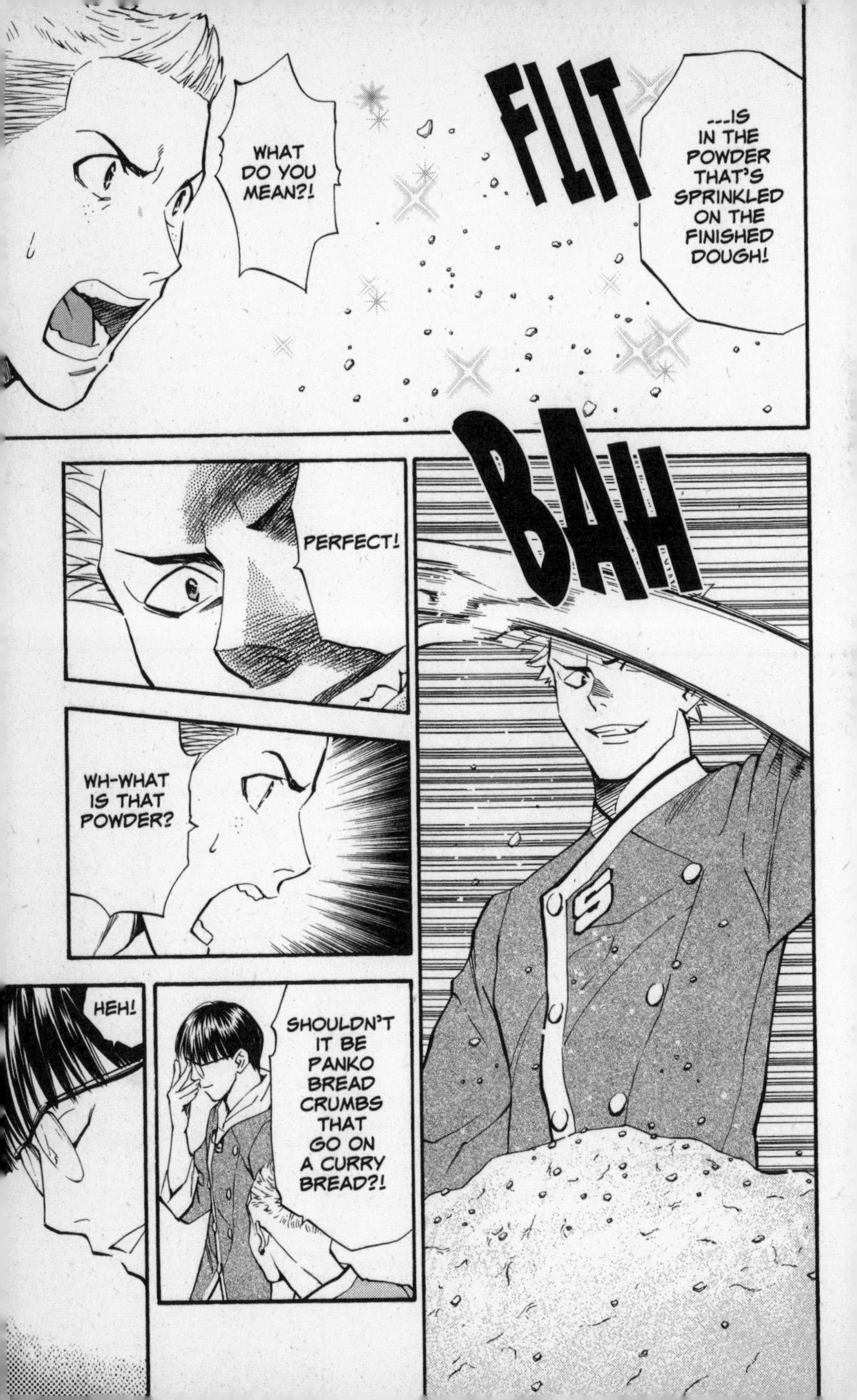
...IS IN THE POWDER THAT'S SPRINKLED ON THE FINISHED DOUGH!
FLIT
WHAT DO YOU MEAN?!
BAH
PERFECT!
WH-WHAT IS THAT POWDER?
SHOULDN'T IT BE PANKO BREAD CRUMBS THAT GO ON A CURRY BREAD?!
HEH!

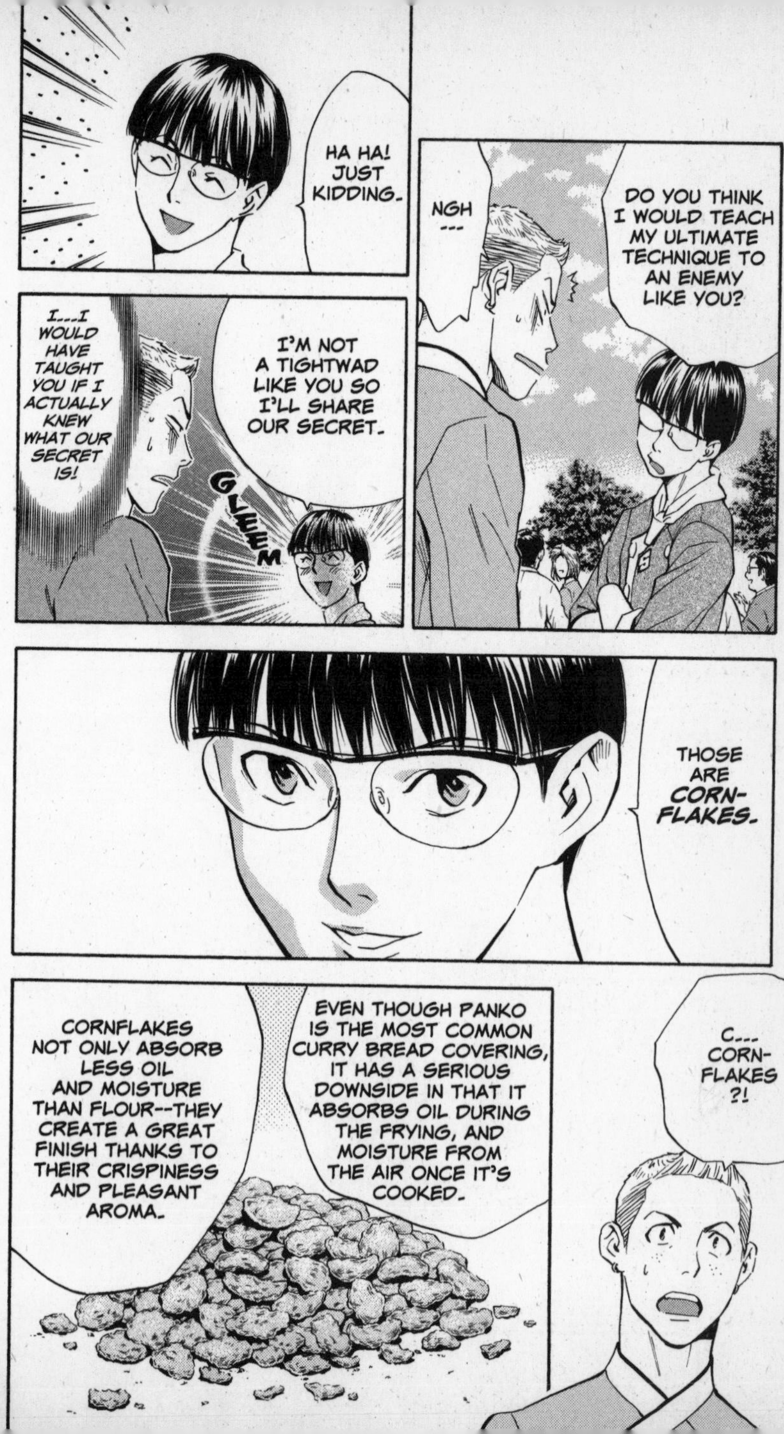
DO YOU THINK I WOULD TEACH MY ULTIMATE TECHNIQUE TO AN ENEMY LIKE YOU?
NGH ---
HA HA! JUST KIDDING.
I'M NOT A TIGHTWAD LIKE YOU SO I'LL SHARE OUR SECRET.
GLEEEM
I...I WOULD HAVE TAUGHT YOU IF I ACTUALLY KNEW WHAT OUR SECRET IS!
THOSE ARE CORN-FLAKES.
C... CORN-FLAKES?!
EVEN THOUGH PANKO IS THE MOST COMMON CURRY BREAD COVERING, IT HAS A SERIOUS DOWNSIDE IN THAT IT ABSORBS OIL DURING THE FRYING, AND MOISTURE FROM THE AIR ONCE IT'S COOKED.
CORNFLAKES NOT ONLY ABSORB LESS OIL AND MOISTURE THAN FLOUR--THEY CREATE A GREAT FINISH THANKS TO THEIR CRISPINESS AND PLEASANT AROMA.

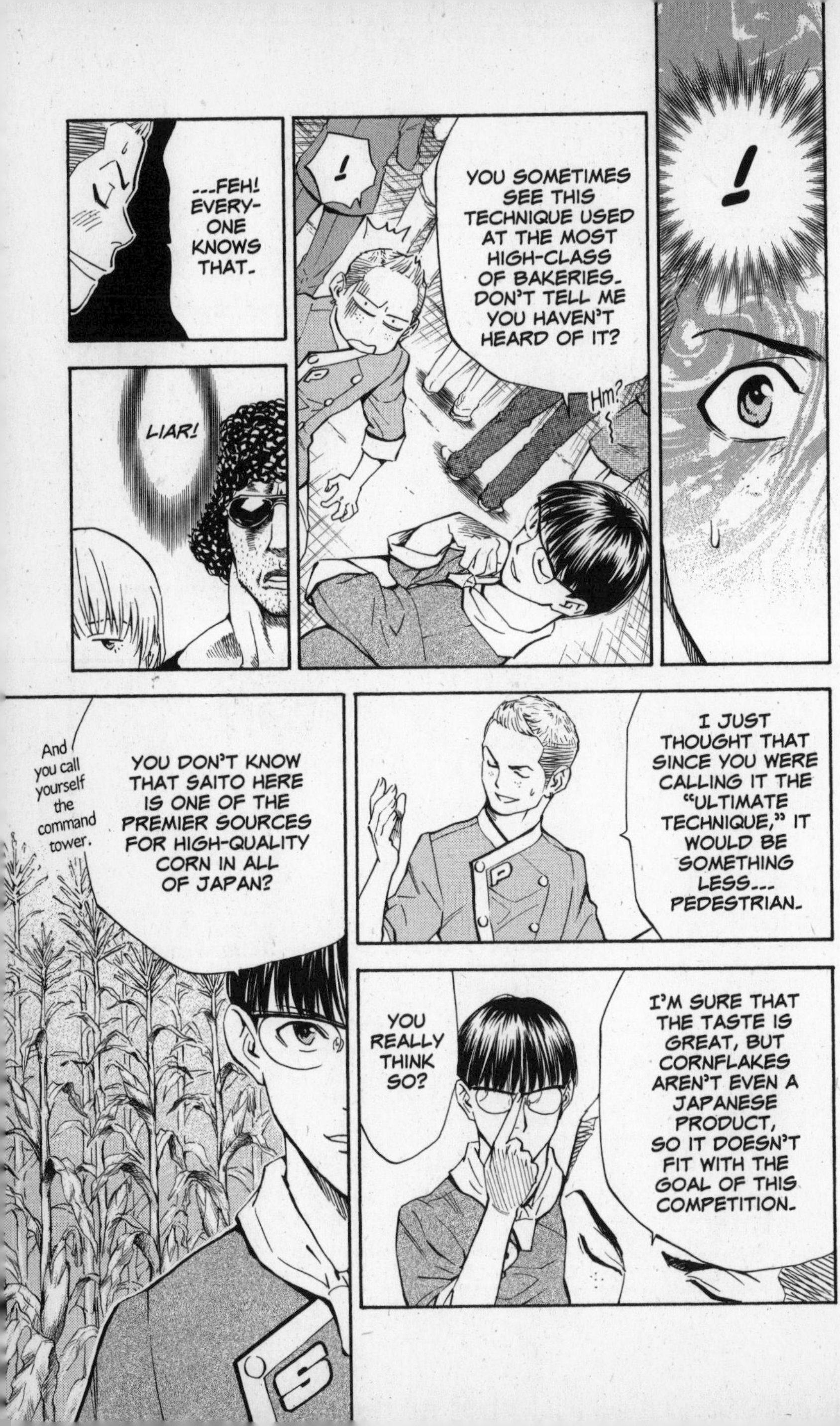
!
YOU SOMETIMES SEE THIS TECHNIQUE USED AT THE MOST HIGH-CLASS OF BAKERIES. DON'T TELL ME YOU HAVEN'T HEARD OF IT?
!
Hm?
---FEH! EVERY-ONE KNOWS THAT.
LIAR!
I JUST THOUGHT THAT SINCE YOU WERE CALLING IT THE "ULTIMATE TECHNIQUE," IT WOULD BE SOMETHING LESS--- PEDESTRIAN.
I'M SURE THAT THE TASTE IS GREAT, BUT CORNFLAKES AREN'T EVEN A JAPANESE PRODUCT, SO IT DOESN'T FIT WITH THE GOAL OF THIS COMPETITION.
YOU REALLY THINK SO?
YOU DON'T KNOW THAT SAITO HERE IS ONE OF THE PREMIER SOURCES FOR HIGH-QUALITY CORN IN ALL OF JAPAN?
And you call yourself the command tower.

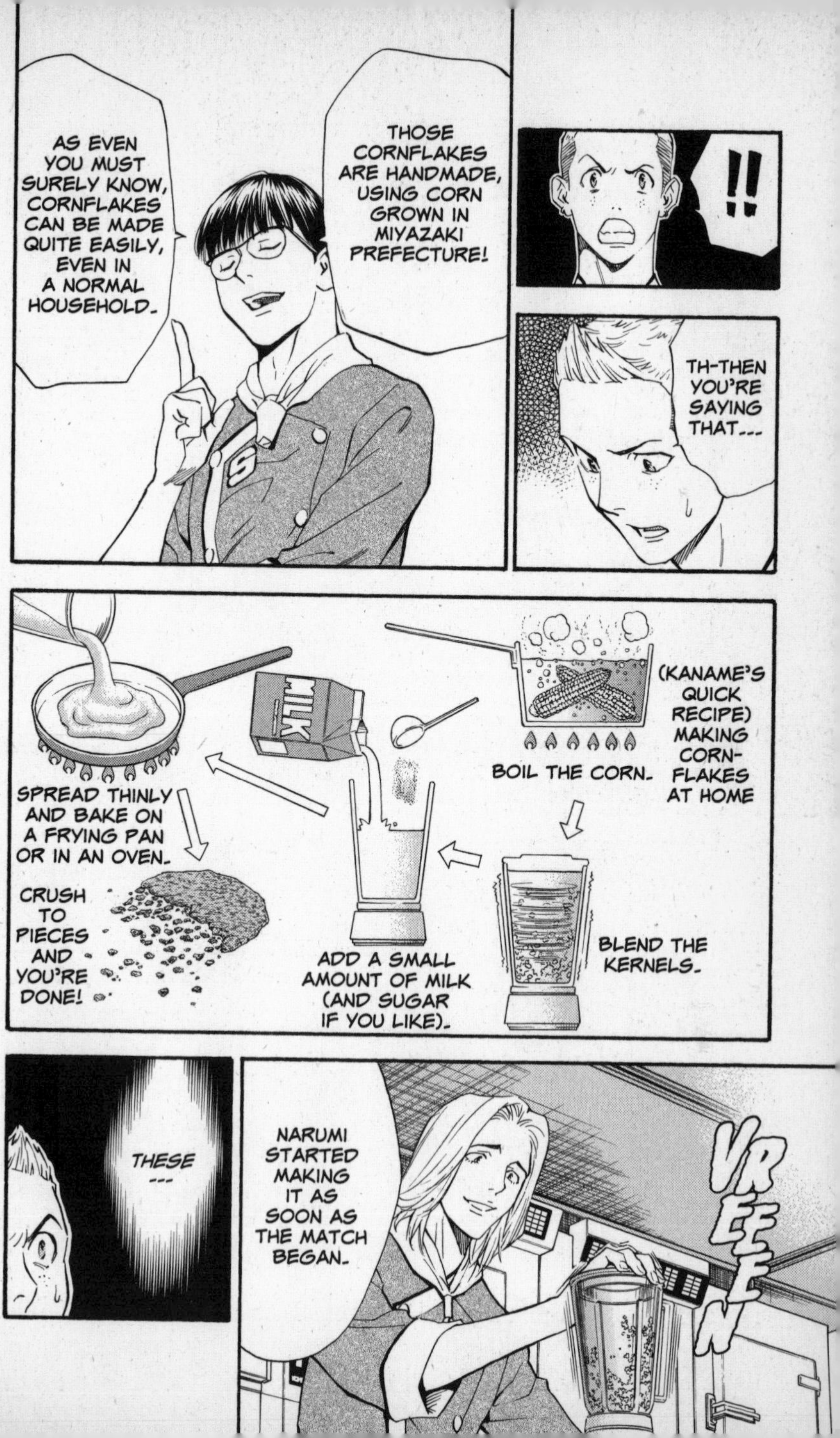
!!
TH-THEN YOU'RE SAYING THAT...
THOSE CORNFLAKES ARE HANDMADE, USING CORN GROWN IN MIYAZAKI PREFECTURE!
AS EVEN YOU MUST SURELY KNOW, CORNFLAKES CAN BE MADE QUITE EASILY, EVEN IN A NORMAL HOUSEHOLD.
(KANAME'S QUICK RECIPE) MAKING CORN-FLAKES AT HOME
BOIL THE CORN.
BLEND THE KERNELS.
MILK
ADD A SMALL AMOUNT OF MILK (AND SUGAR IF YOU LIKE).
SPREAD THINLY AND BAKE ON A FRYING PAN OR IN AN OVEN.
CRUSH TO PIECES AND YOU'RE DONE!
VREEEN
NARUMI STARTED MAKING IT AS SOON AS THE MATCH BEGAN.
THESE...

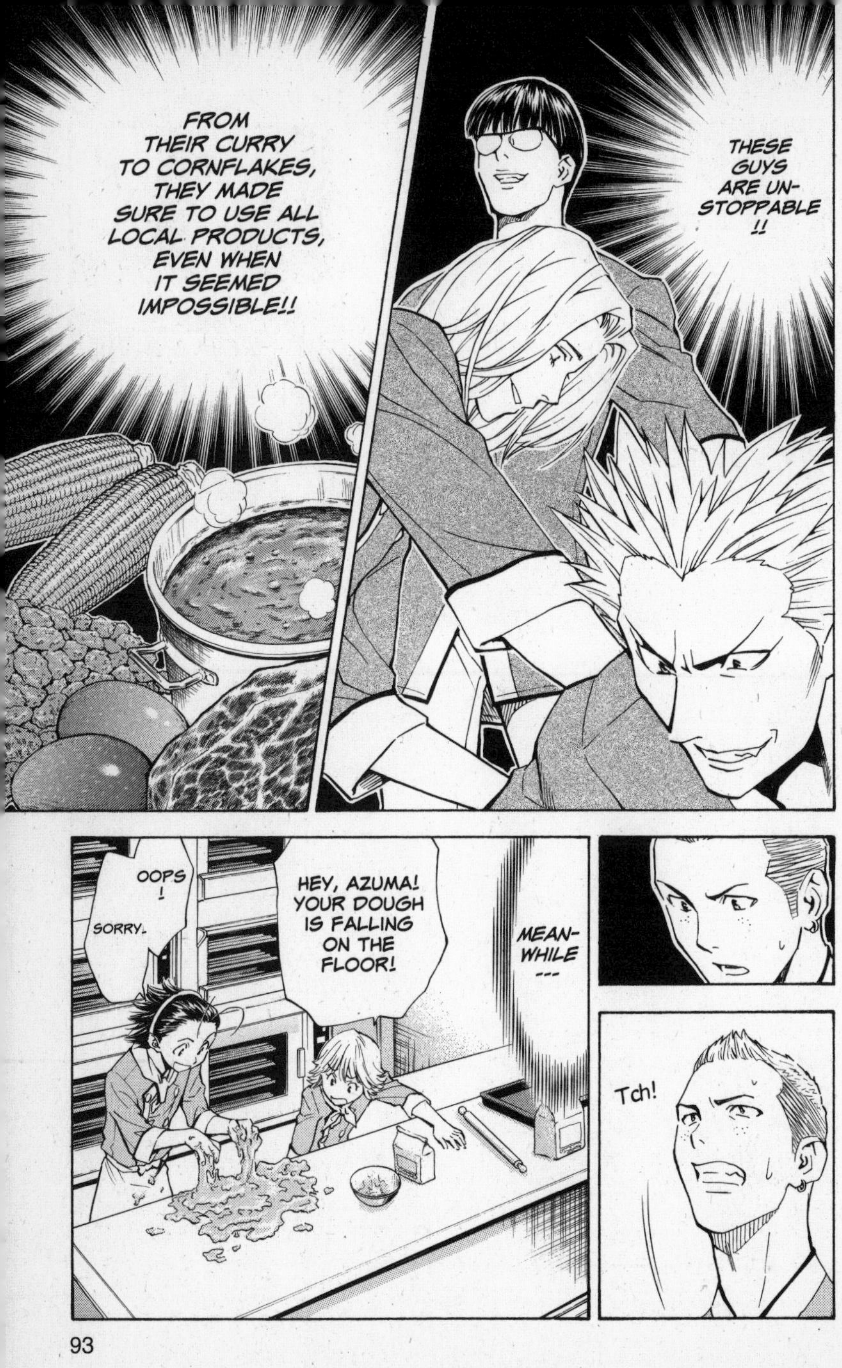
THESE GUYS ARE UN-STOPPABLE!!
FROM THEIR CURRY TO CORNFLAKES, THEY MADE SURE TO USE ALL LOCAL PRODUCTS, EVEN WHEN IT SEEMED IMPOSSIBLE!!
Tch!
MEAN-WHILE---
HEY, AZUMA! YOUR DOUGH IS FALLING ON THE FLOOR!
OOPS!
SORRY.

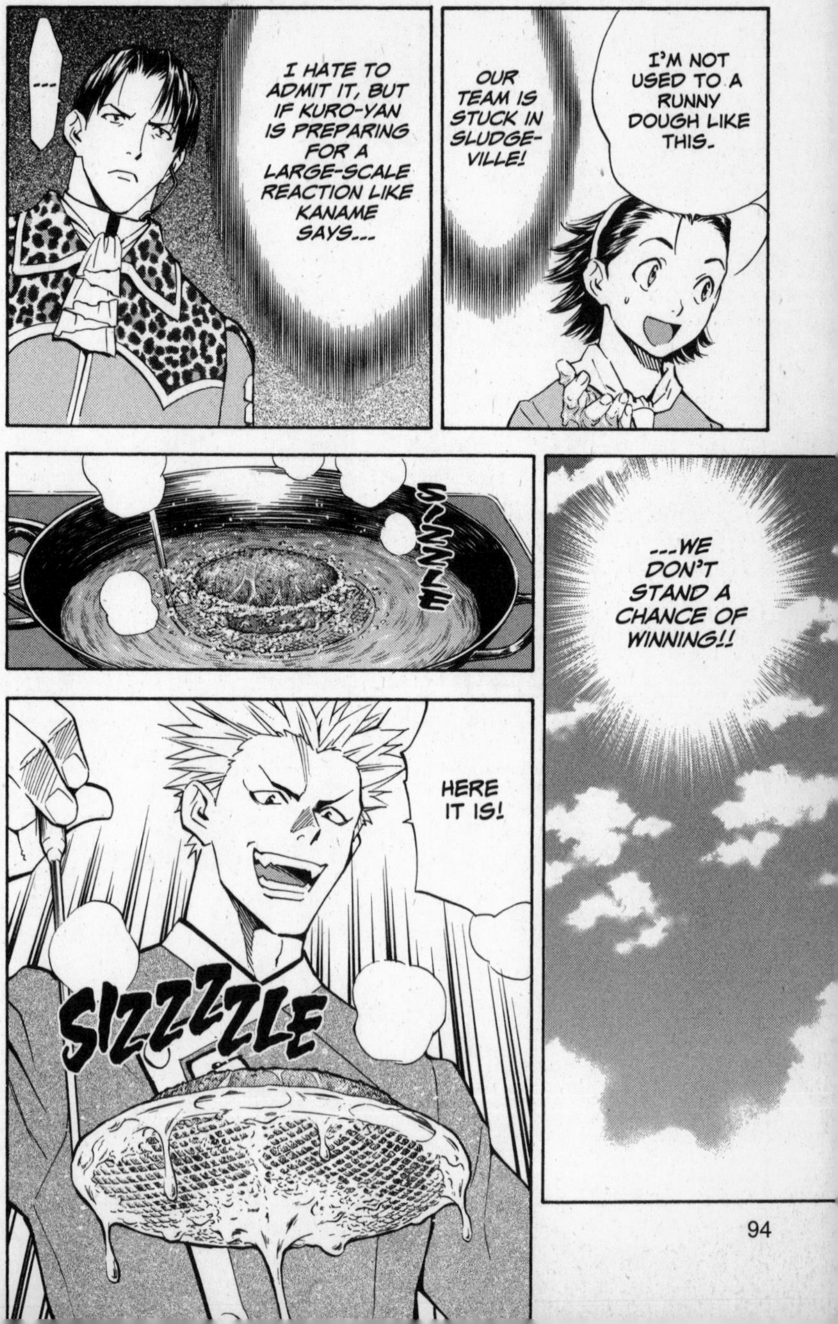
I'M NOT USED TO A RUNNY DOUGH LIKE THIS.
OUR TEAM IS STUCK IN SLUDGE-VILLE!
I HATE TO ADMIT IT, BUT IF KURO-YAN IS PREPARING FOR A LARGE-SCALE REACTION LIKE KANAME SAYS...
...
...WE DON'T STAND A CHANCE OF WINNING!!
SIZZZLE
HERE IT IS!
SIZZZZLE

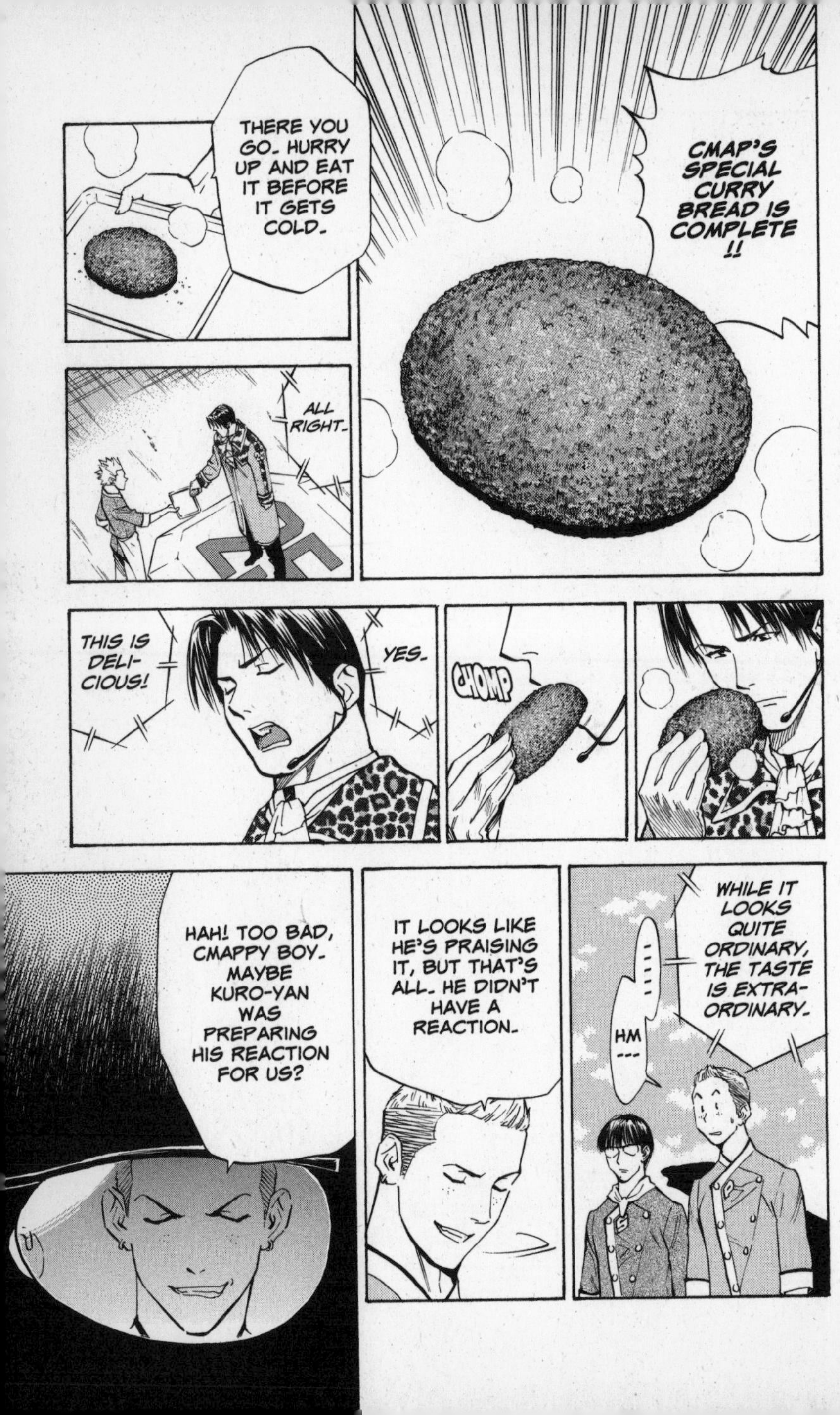
CMAP'S SPECIAL CURRY BREAD IS COMPLETE!!
THERE YOU GO. HURRY UP AND EAT IT BEFORE IT GETS COLD.
ALL RIGHT.
CHOMP
YES.
THIS IS DELICIOUS!
WHILE IT LOOKS QUITE ORDINARY, THE TASTE IS EXTRA-ORDINARY.
......
HM---
IT LOOKS LIKE HE'S PRAISING IT, BUT THAT'S ALL. HE DIDN'T HAVE A REACTION.
HAH! TOO BAD, CMAPPY BOY. MAYBE KURO-YAN WAS PREPARING HIS REACTION FOR US?

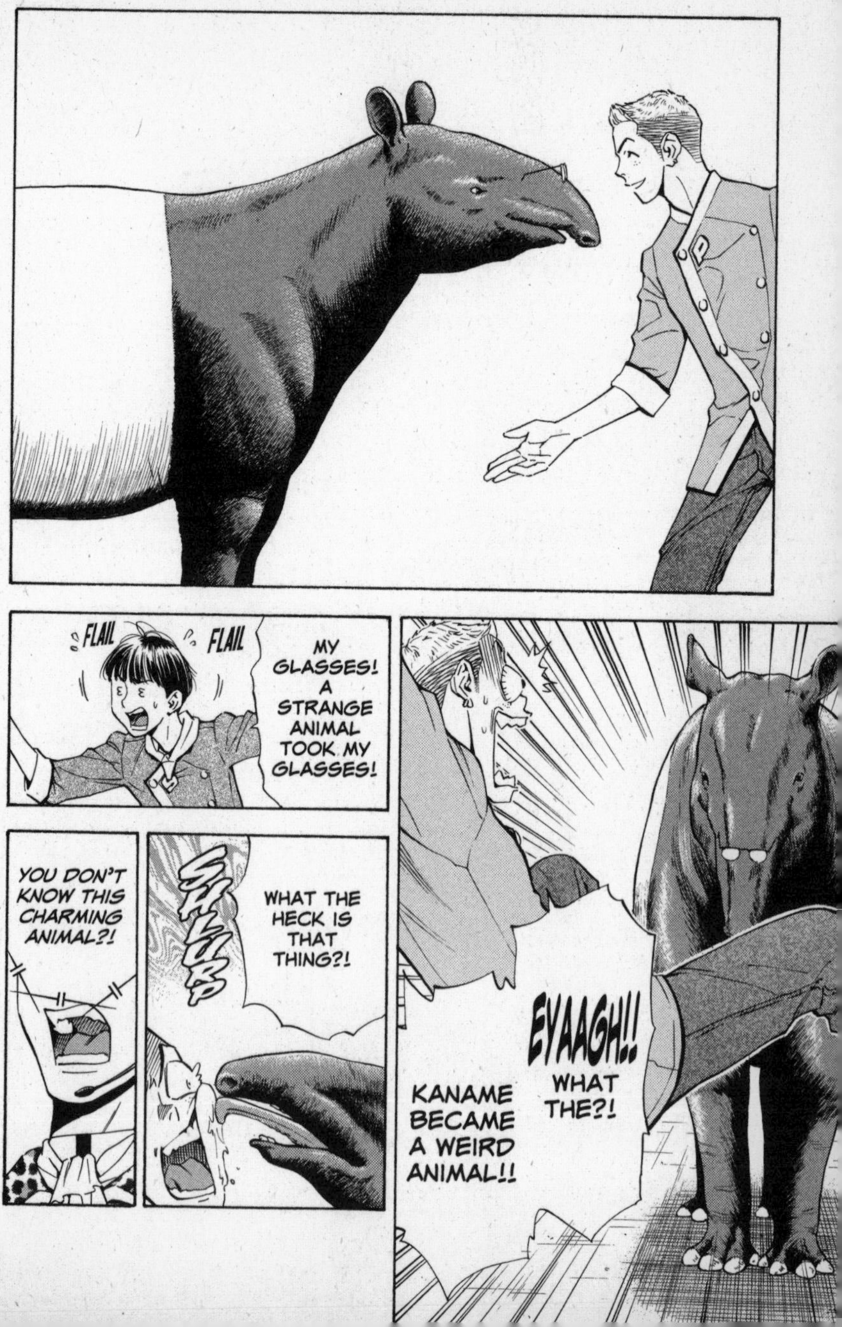
EYAAGH!!
WHAT THE?!
KANAME BECAME A WEIRD ANIMAL!!
FLAIL
FLAIL
MY GLASSES! A STRANGE ANIMAL TOOK MY GLASSES!
SHLURP
WHAT THE HECK IS THAT THING?!
YOU DON'T KNOW THIS CHARMING ANIMAL?!

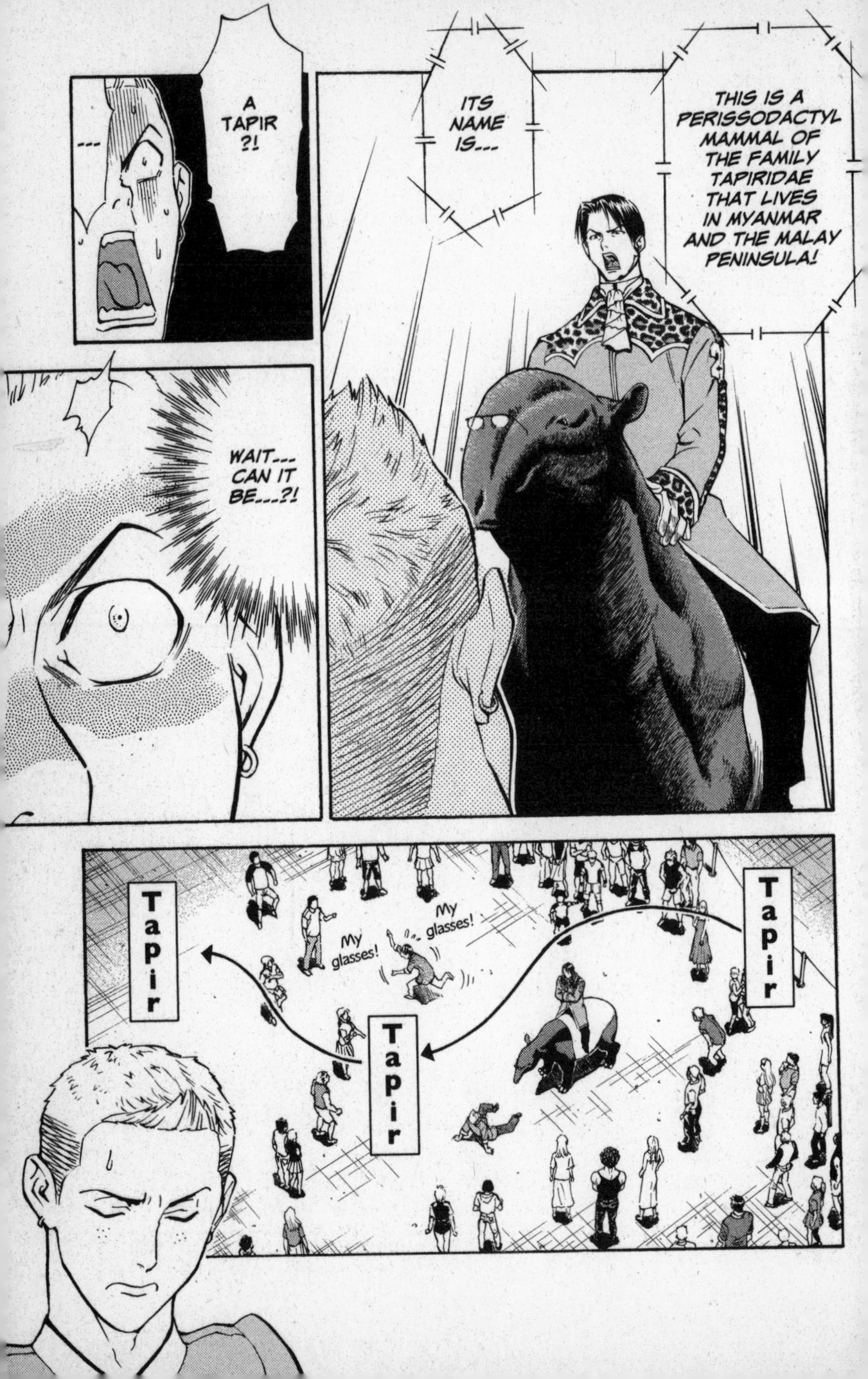
THIS IS A PERISSODACTYL MAMMAL OF THE FAMILY TAPIRIDAE THAT LIVES IN MYANMAR AND THE MALAY PENINSULA!
ITS NAME IS---
A TAPIR ?!

WAIT--- CAN IT BE---?!
Tapir
My glasses!
My glasses!
Tapir
Tapir

A CURRY BREAD THAT'S MORE THAN IT "TAPIRS" TO BE.
Malay Malay

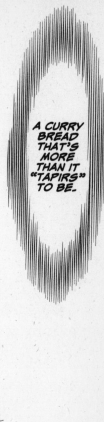

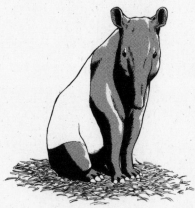

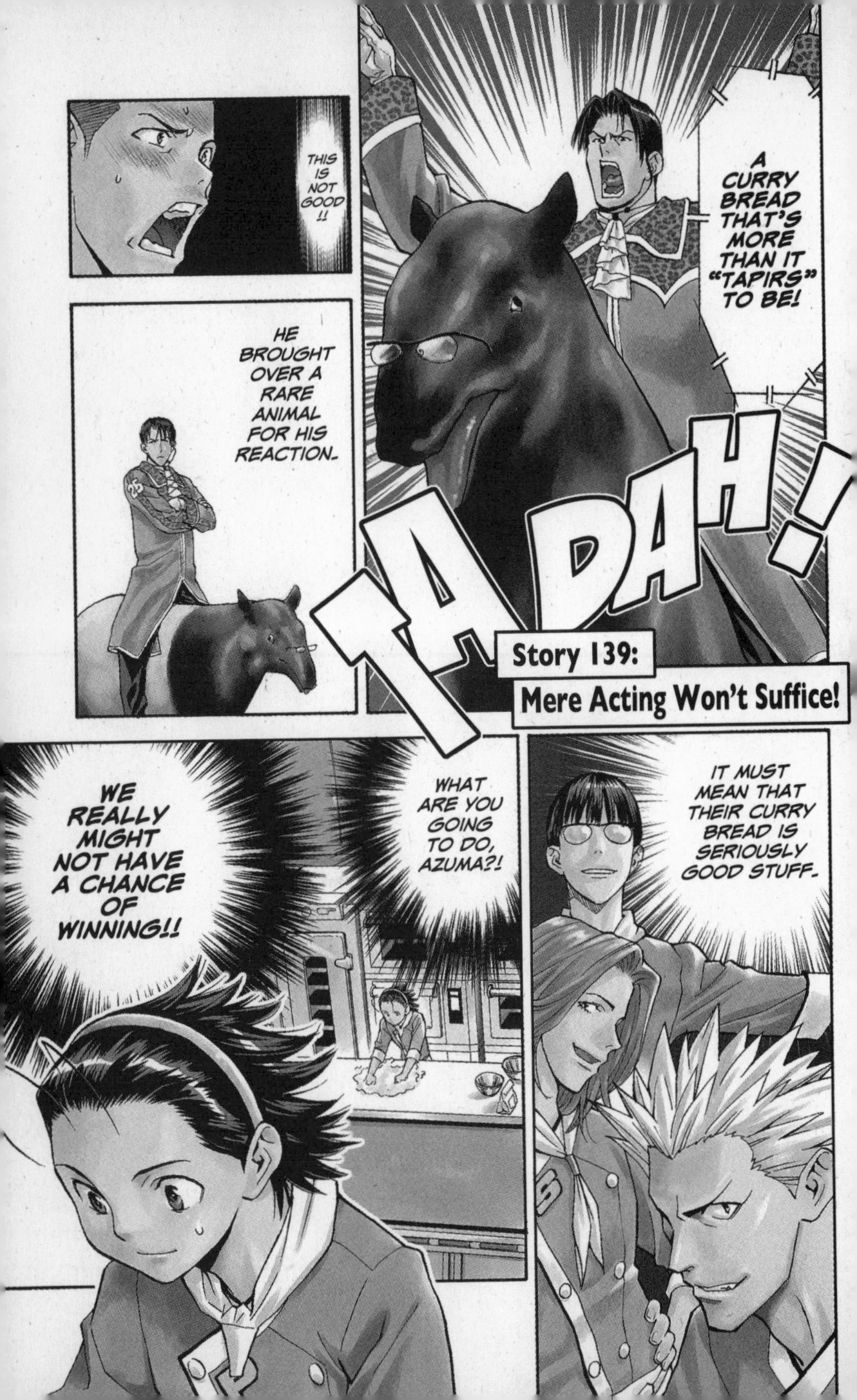
A CURRY BREAD THAT'S MORE THAN IT "TAPIRS" TO BE!
TA-DAH!!
Story 139:
Mere Acting Won't Suffice!
THIS IS NOT GOOD!!
HE BROUGHT OVER A RARE ANIMAL FOR HIS REACTION...
IT MUST MEAN THAT THEIR CURRY BREAD IS SERIOUSLY GOOD STUFF...
WHAT ARE YOU GOING TO DO, AZUMA?!
WE REALLY MIGHT NOT HAVE A CHANCE OF WINNING!!

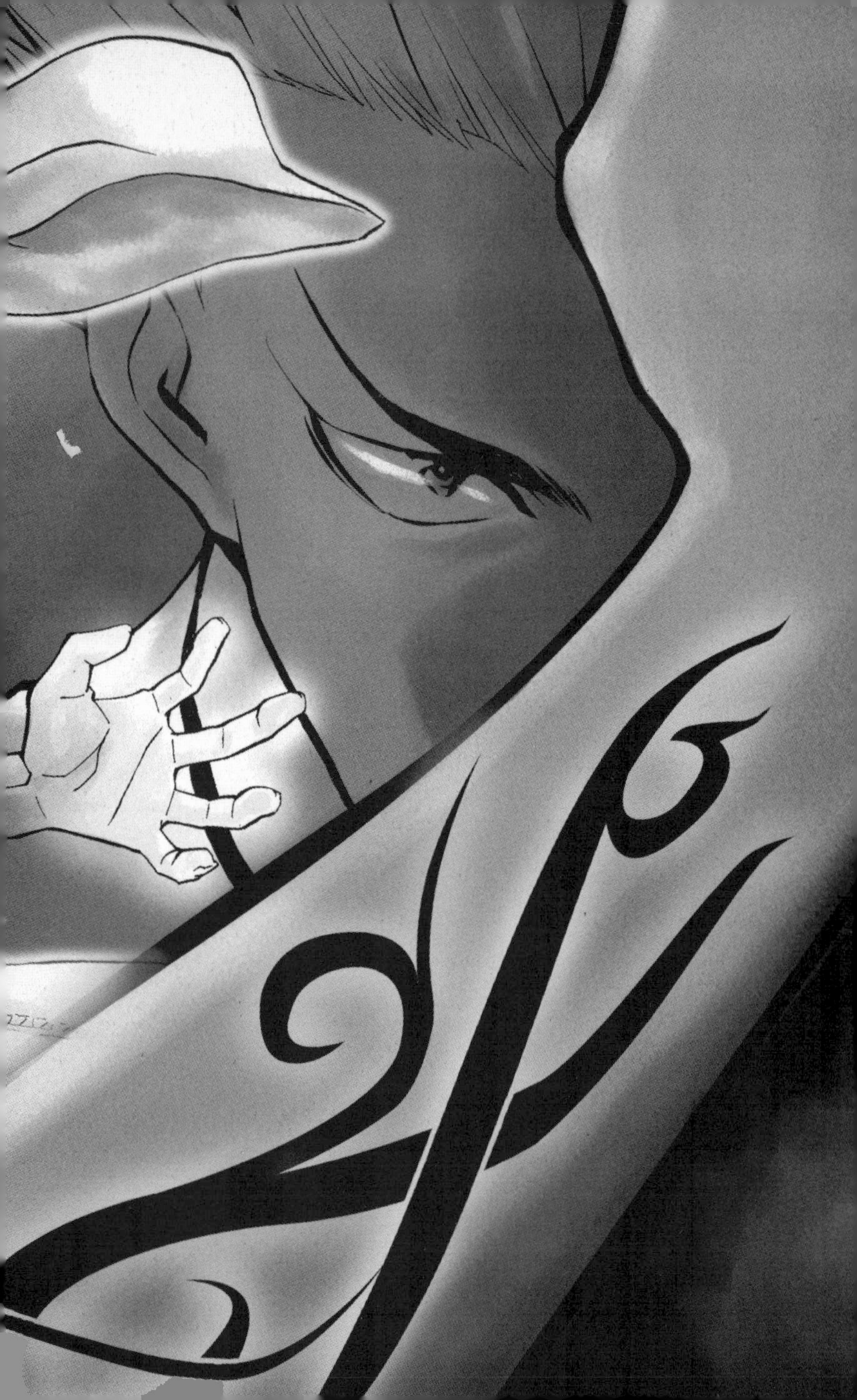

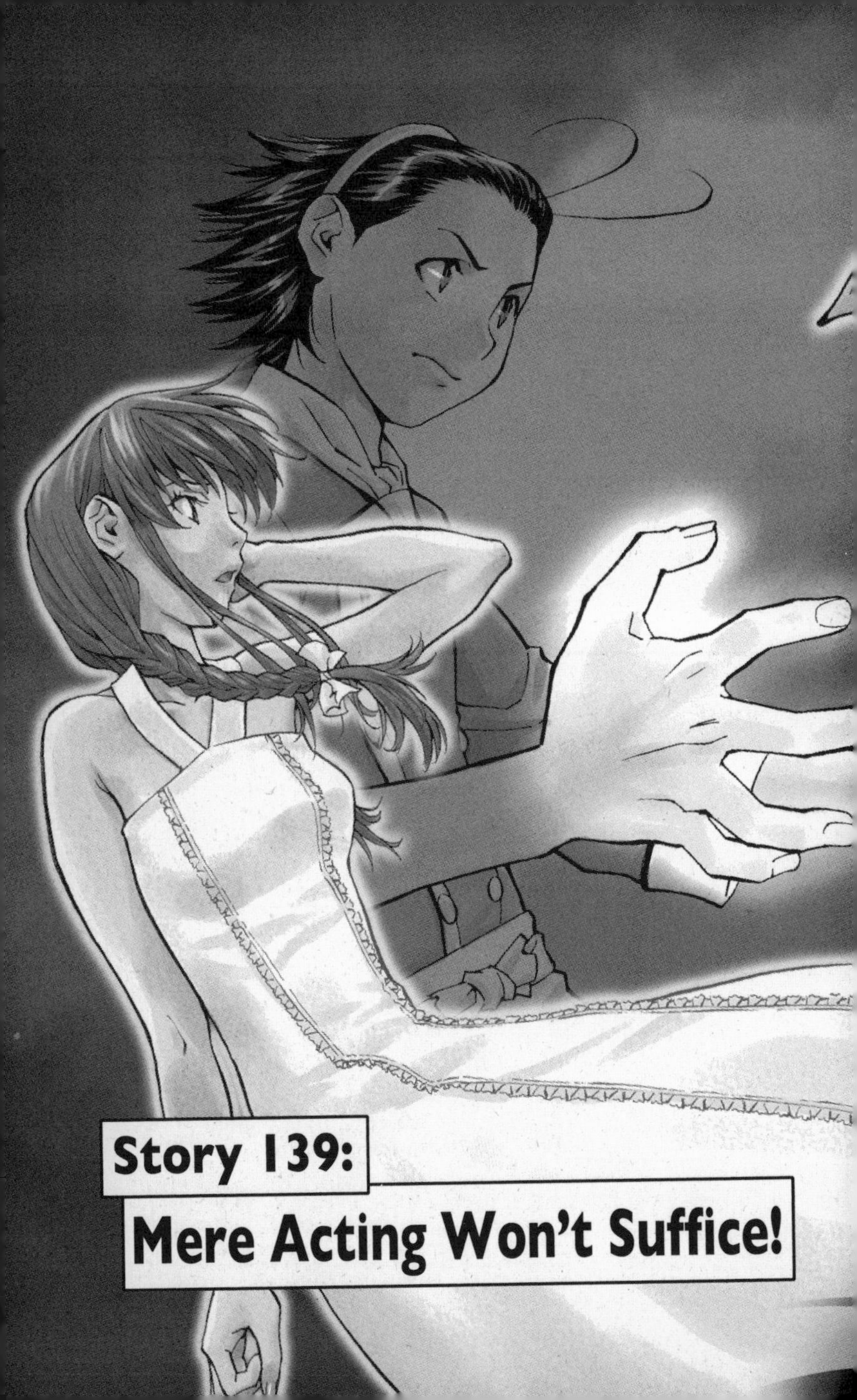
Story 139:
Mere Acting Won't Suffice!

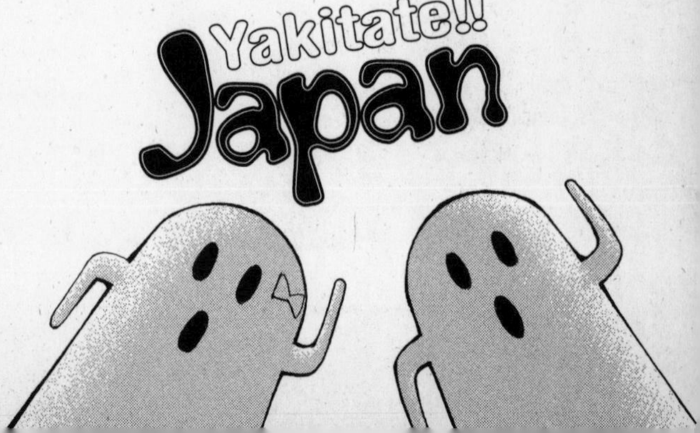
Yakitate!!
Japan

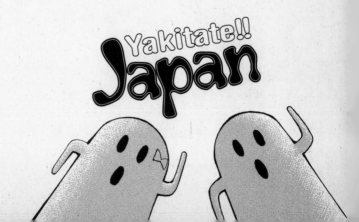

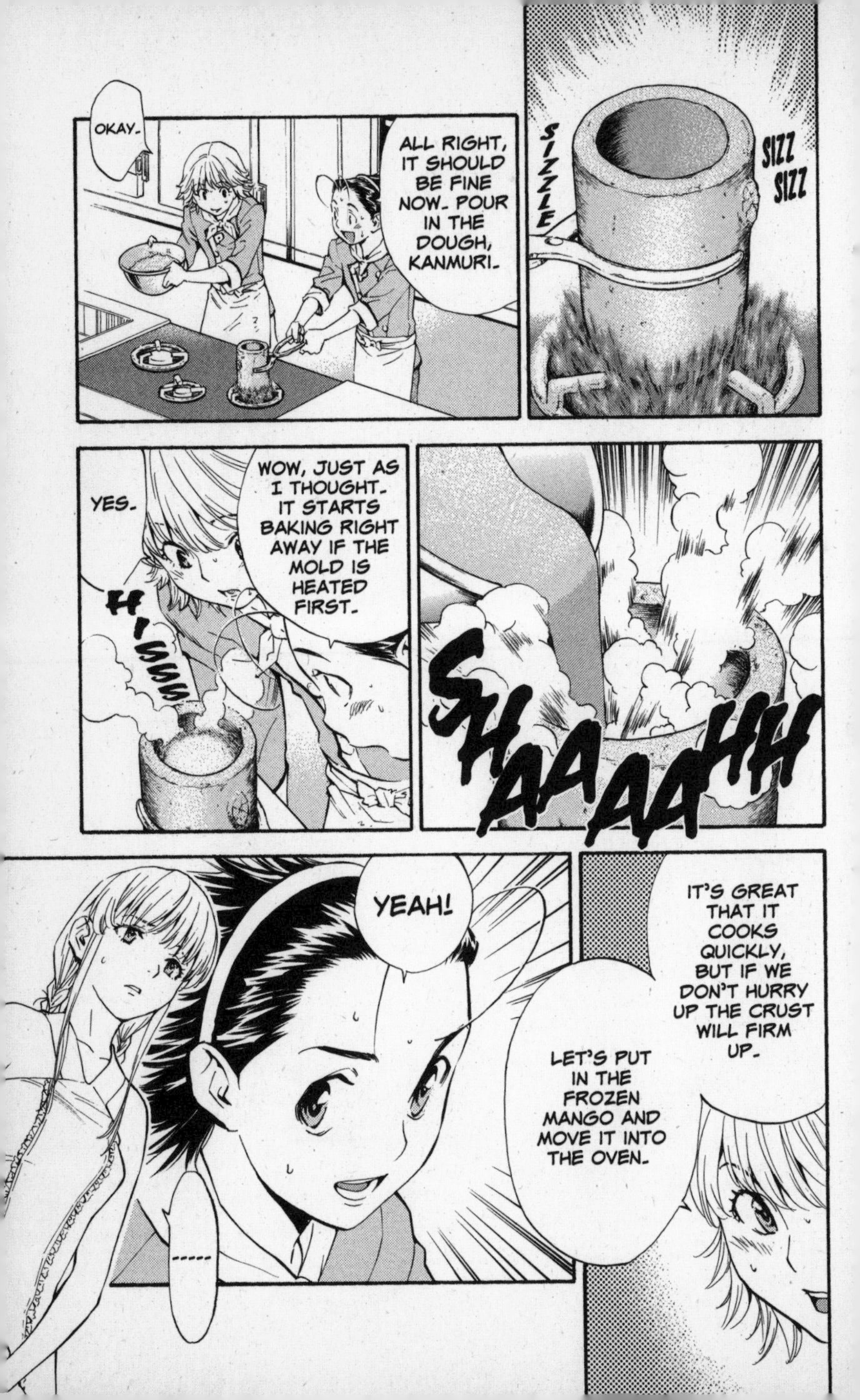
SIZZLE
SIZZ SIZZ
ALL RIGHT, IT SHOULD BE FINE NOW. POUR IN THE DOUGH, KANMURI.
OKAY.
SHAAAAHH
WOW, JUST AS I THOUGHT. IT STARTS BAKING RIGHT AWAY IF THE MOLD IS HEATED FIRST.
YES.
HISSSS
IT'S GREAT THAT IT COOKS QUICKLY, BUT IF WE DON'T HURRY UP THE CRUST WILL FIRM UP.
LET'S PUT IN THE FROZEN MANGO AND MOVE IT INTO THE OVEN.
YEAH!
.....

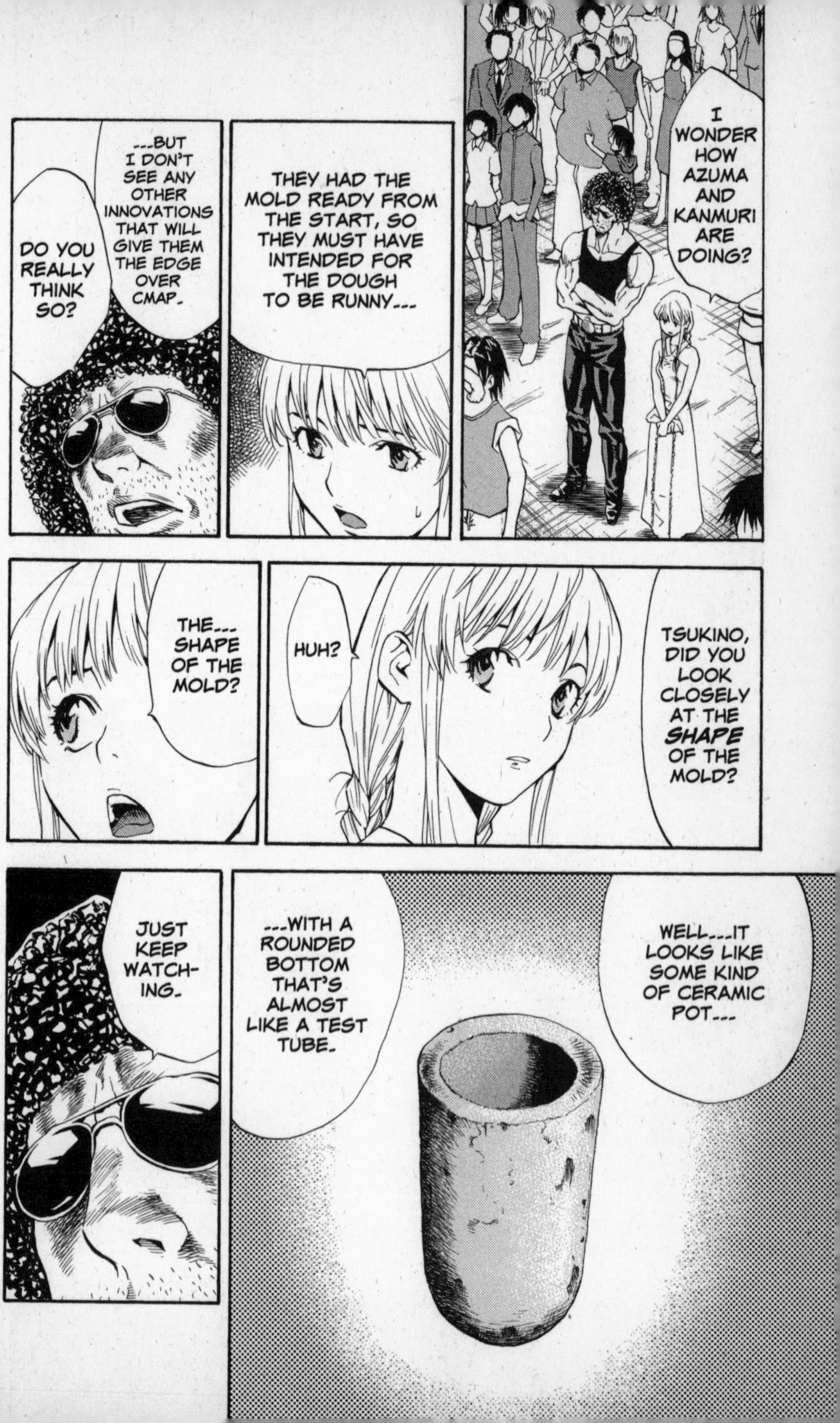

I WONDER HOW AZUMA AND KANMURI ARE DOING?
THEY HAD THE MOLD READY FROM THE START, SO THEY MUST HAVE INTENDED FOR THE DOUGH TO BE RUNNY...
...BUT I DON'T SEE ANY OTHER INNOVATIONS THAT WILL GIVE THEM THE EDGE OVER CMAP.
DO YOU REALLY THINK SO?
TSUKINO, DID YOU LOOK CLOSELY AT THE ***SHAPE*** OF THE MOLD?
HUH?
THE... SHAPE OF THE MOLD?
WELL...IT LOOKS LIKE SOME KIND OF CERAMIC POT...
...WITH A ROUNDED BOTTOM THAT'S ALMOST LIKE A TEST TUBE.
JUST KEEP WATCHING.

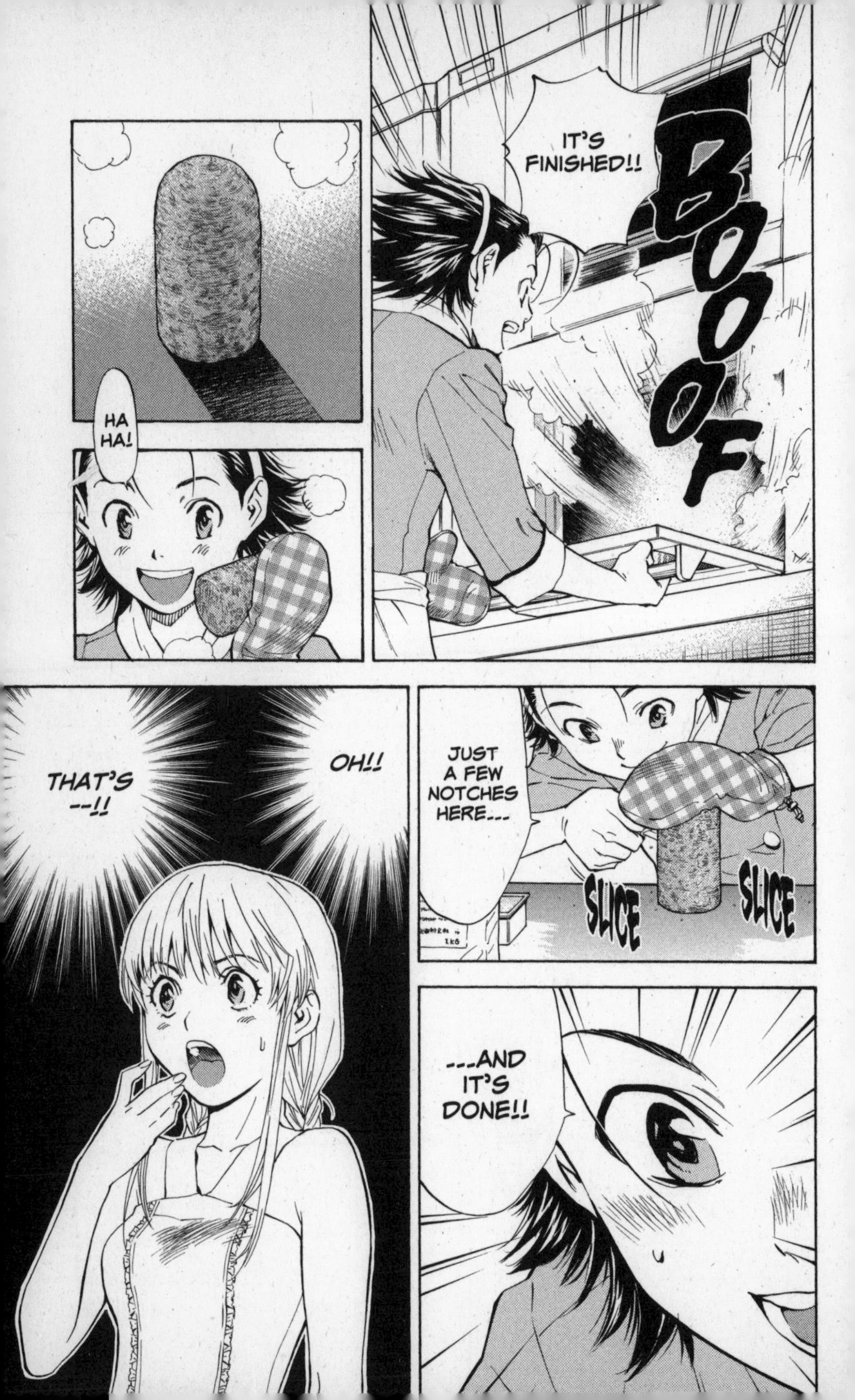
IT'S FINISHED!!
BOOOF
HA HA!
JUST A FEW NOTCHES HERE...
SLICE
SLICE
...AND IT'S DONE!!
OH!!
THAT'S --!!

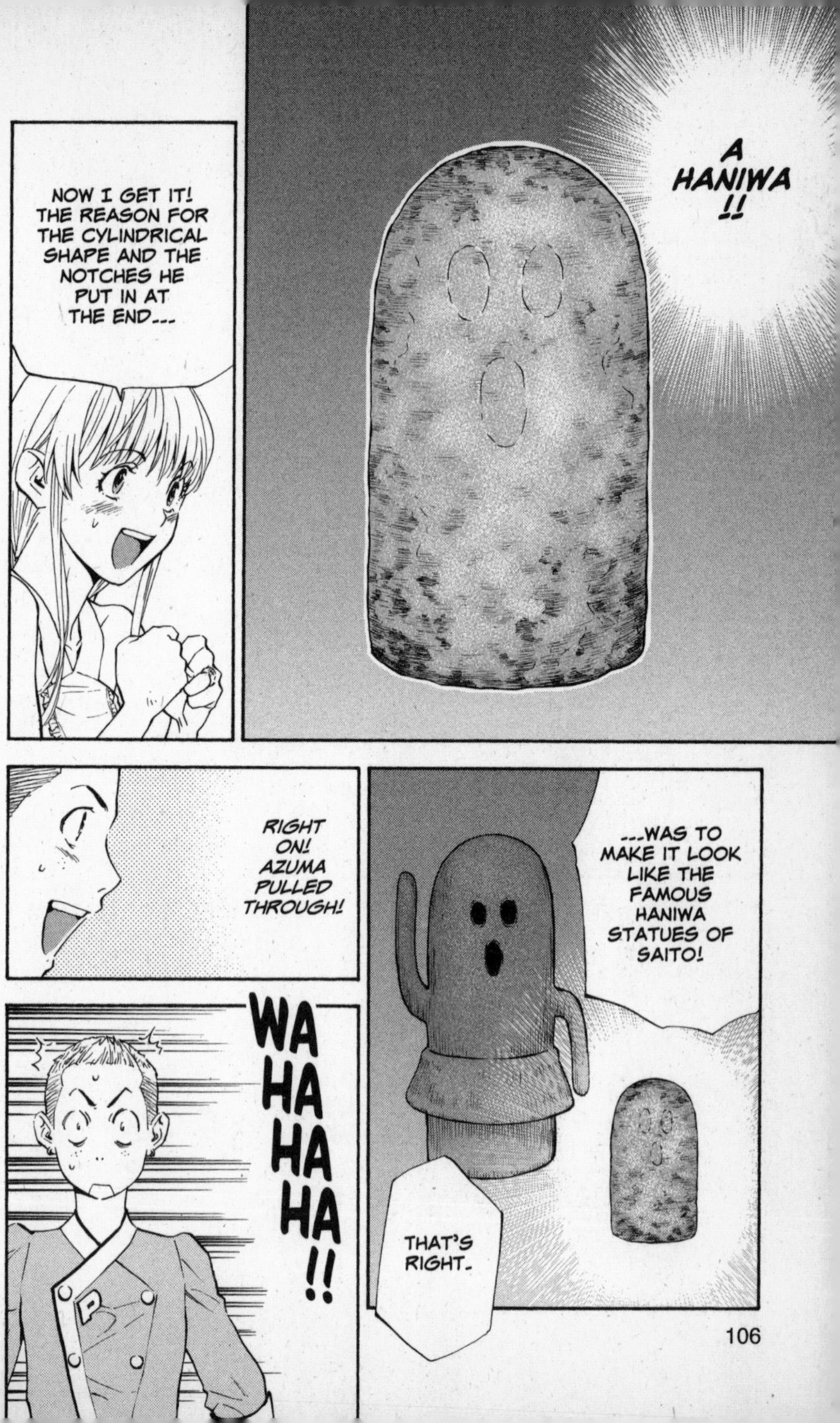
A HANIWA!!
NOW I GET IT! THE REASON FOR THE CYLINDRICAL SHAPE AND THE NOTCHES HE PUT IN AT THE END...
...WAS TO MAKE IT LOOK LIKE THE FAMOUS HANIWA STATUES OF SAITO!
THAT'S RIGHT.
RIGHT ON! AZUMA PULLED THROUGH!
WAHAHAHAHA!!

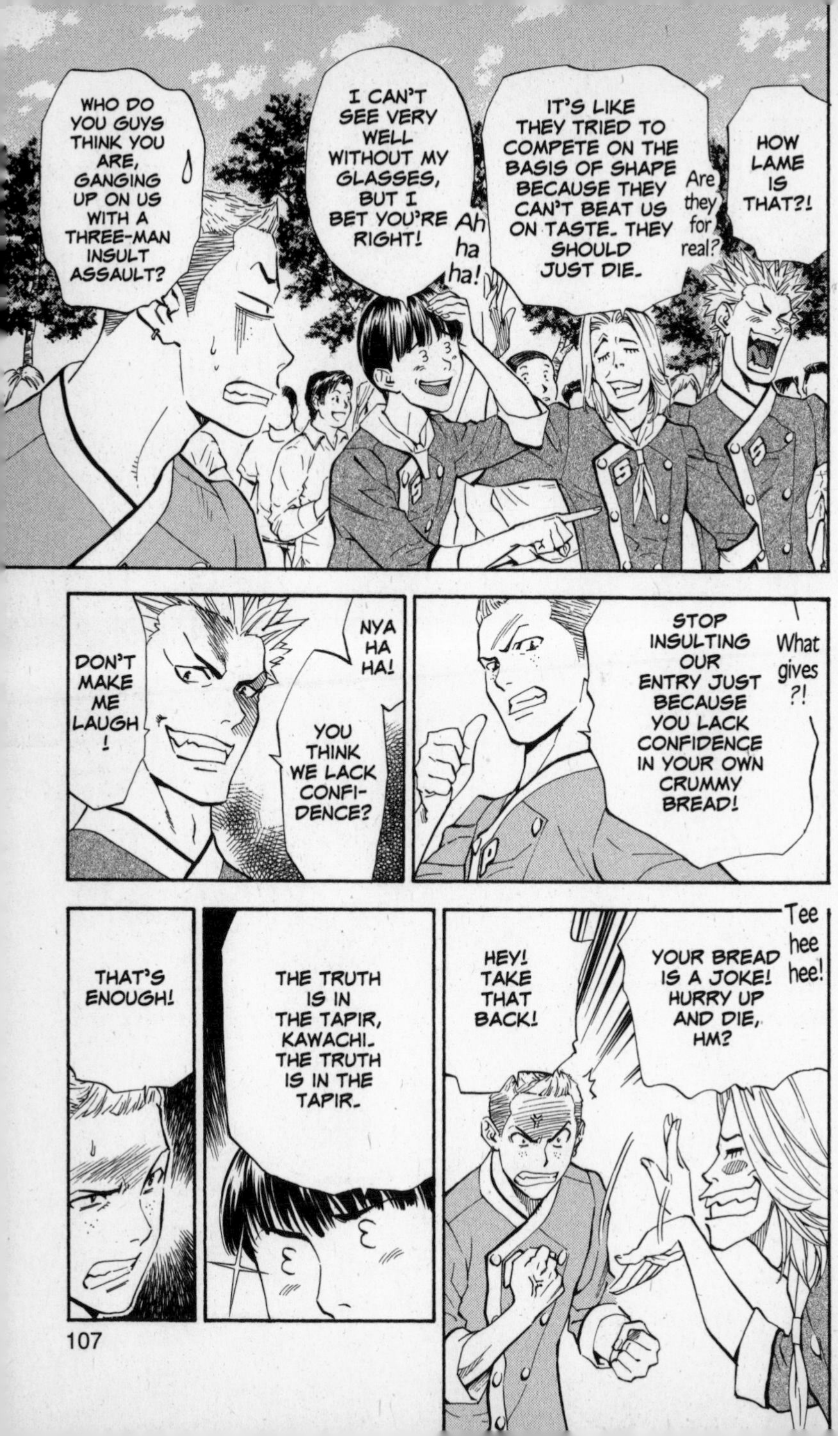
HOW LAME IS THAT?!
Are they for real?
IT'S LIKE THEY TRIED TO COMPETE ON THE BASIS OF SHAPE BECAUSE THEY CAN'T BEAT US ON TASTE. THEY SHOULD JUST DIE.
Ah ha ha!
I CAN'T SEE VERY WELL WITHOUT MY GLASSES, BUT I BET YOU'RE RIGHT!
WHO DO YOU GUYS THINK YOU ARE, GANGING UP ON US WITH A THREE-MAN INSULT ASSAULT?
What gives?!
STOP INSULTING OUR ENTRY JUST BECAUSE YOU LACK CONFIDENCE IN YOUR OWN CRUMMY BREAD!
NYA HA HA!
YOU THINK WE LACK CONFI-DENCE?
DON'T MAKE ME LAUGH!
Tee hee hee!
YOUR BREAD IS A JOKE! HURRY UP AND DIE, HM?
HEY! TAKE THAT BACK!
THE TRUTH IS IN THE TAPIR, KAWACHI. THE TRUTH IS IN THE TAPIR.
THAT'S ENOUGH!

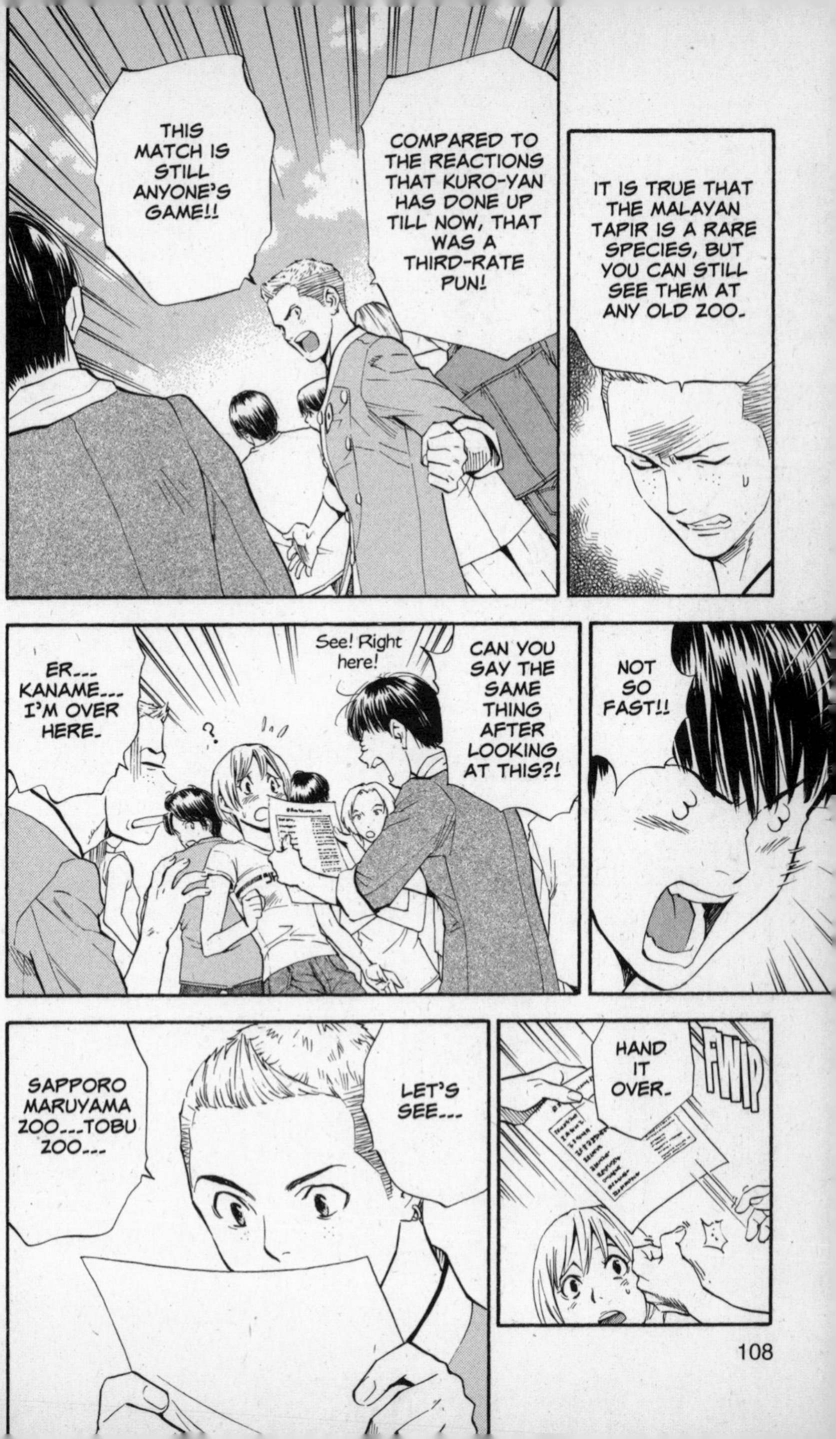
IT IS TRUE THAT THE MALAYAN TAPIR IS A RARE SPECIES, BUT YOU CAN STILL SEE THEM AT ANY OLD ZOO.
COMPARED TO THE REACTIONS THAT KURO-YAN HAS DONE UP TILL NOW, THAT WAS A THIRD-RATE PUN!
THIS MATCH IS STILL ANYONE'S GAME!!
NOT SO FAST!!
CAN YOU SAY THE SAME THING AFTER LOOKING AT THIS?!
See! Right here!
ER... KANAME... I'M OVER HERE.
HAND IT OVER.
FWIP
LET'S SEE...
SAPPORO MARUYAMA ZOO...TOBU ZOO...

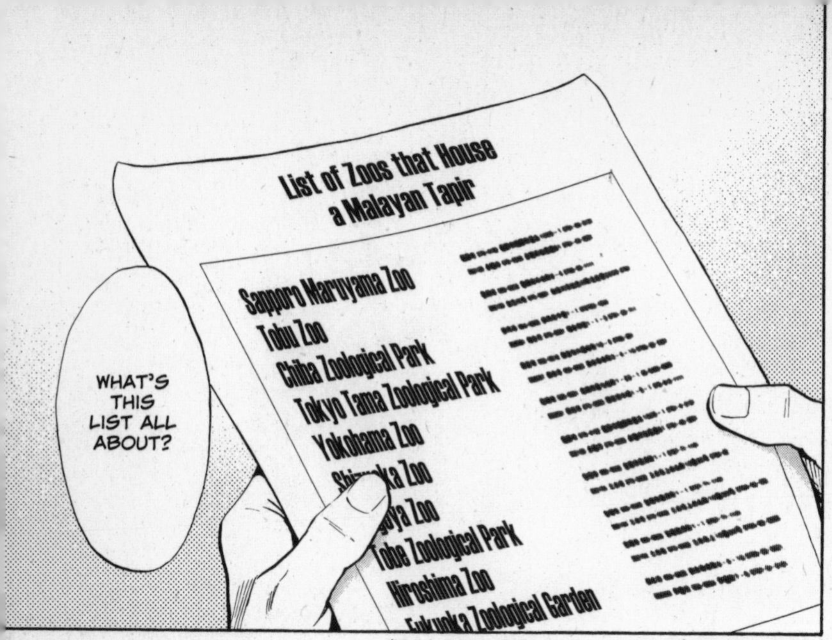
List of Zoos that House a Malayan Tapir
Sapporo Maruyama Zoo
Tobu Zoo
Chiba Zoological Park
Tokyo Tama Zoological Park
Yokohama Zoo
Tobe Zoological Park
Hiroshima Zoo
WHAT'S THIS LIST ALL ABOUT?

*THIS DATA IS FACTUAL AS OF SEPTEMBER 2004.

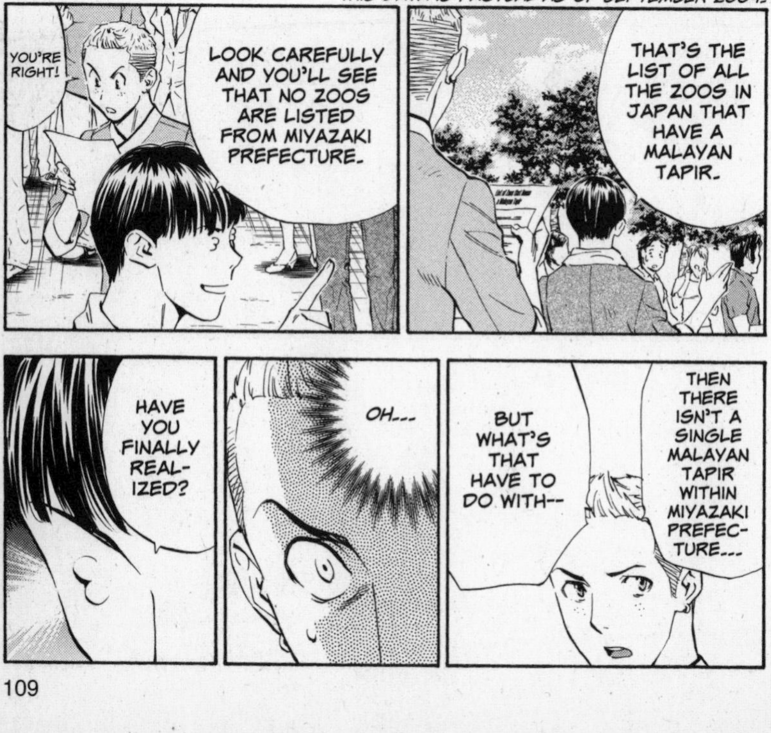
THAT'S THE LIST OF ALL THE ZOOS IN JAPAN THAT HAVE A MALAYAN TAPIR.
LOOK CAREFULLY AND YOU'LL SEE THAT NO ZOOS ARE LISTED FROM MIYAZAKI PREFECTURE.
YOU'RE RIGHT!
THEN THERE ISN'T A SINGLE MALAYAN TAPIR WITHIN MIYAZAKI PREFECTURE...
BUT WHAT'S THAT HAVE TO DO WITH--
OH...
HAVE YOU FINALLY REALIZED?

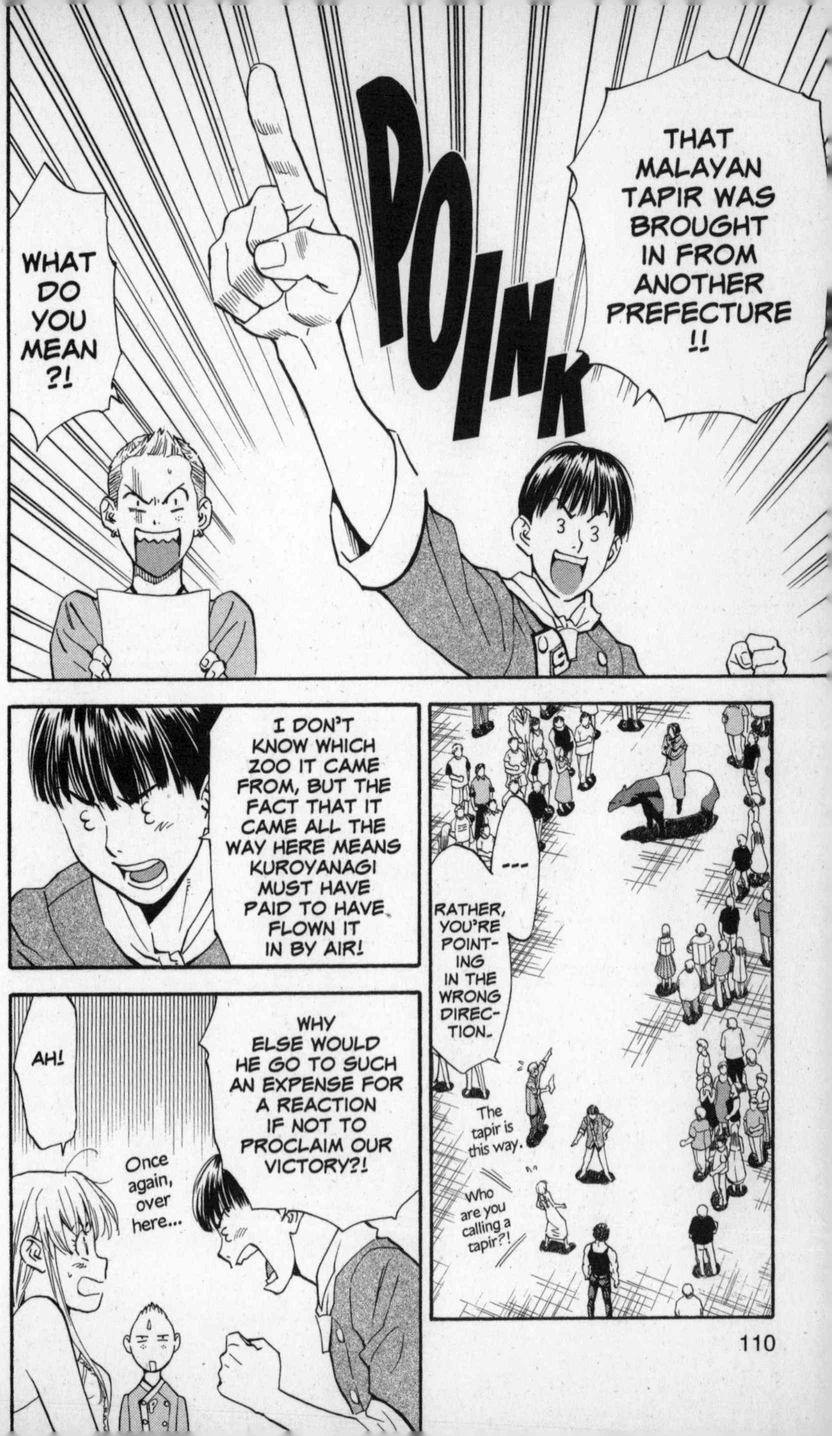
THAT MALAYAN TAPIR WAS BROUGHT IN FROM ANOTHER PREFECTURE !!
POINK
WHAT DO YOU MEAN ?!

RATHER, YOU'RE POINT-ING IN THE WRONG DIREC-TION.
The tapir is this way.
Who are you calling a tapir?!
I DON'T KNOW WHICH ZOO IT CAME FROM, BUT THE FACT THAT IT CAME ALL THE WAY HERE MEANS KUROYANAGI MUST HAVE PAID TO HAVE FLOWN IT IN BY AIR!
WHY ELSE WOULD HE GO TO SUCH AN EXPENSE FOR A REACTION IF NOT TO PROCLAIM OUR VICTORY?!
AH!
Once again, over here...

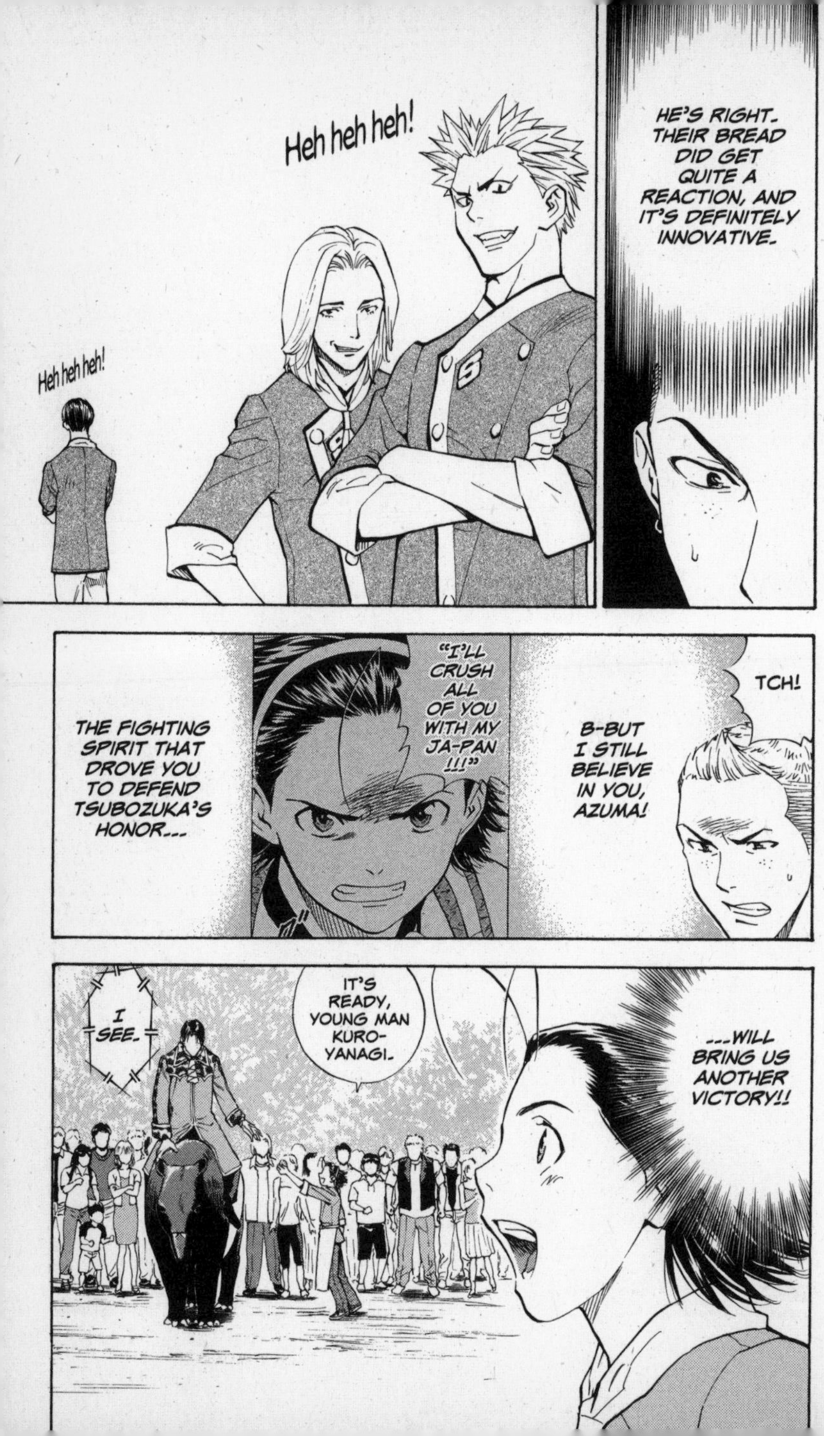
HE'S RIGHT. THEIR BREAD DID GET QUITE A REACTION, AND IT'S DEFINITELY INNOVATIVE.
Heh heh heh!
Heh heh heh!
TCH!
B-BUT I STILL BELIEVE IN YOU, AZUMA!
"I'LL CRUSH ALL OF YOU WITH MY JA-PAN!!!"
THE FIGHTING SPIRIT THAT DROVE YOU TO DEFEND TSUBOZUKA'S HONOR...
...WILL BRING US ANOTHER VICTORY!!
IT'S READY, YOUNG MAN KURO-YANAGI.
I SEE.

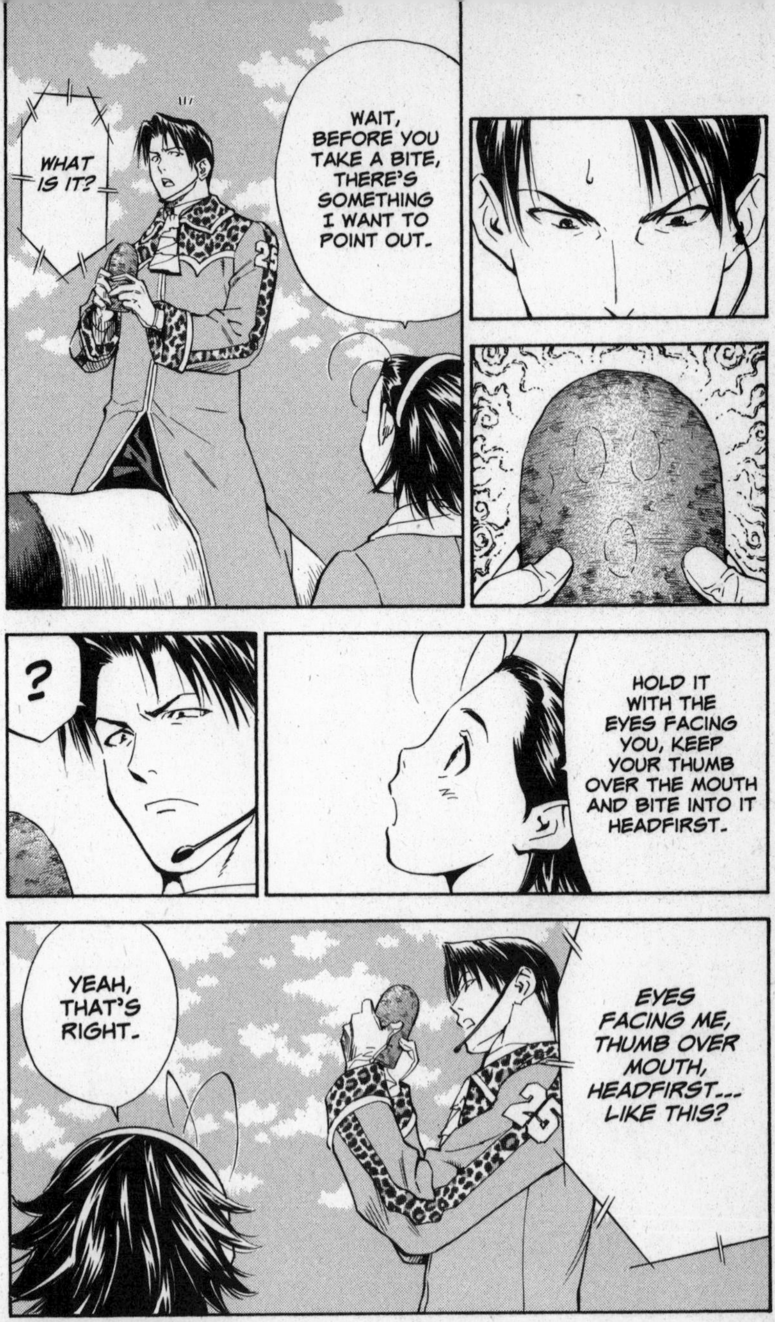
WAIT, BEFORE YOU TAKE A BITE, THERE'S SOMETHING I WANT TO POINT OUT.
WHAT IS IT?
HOLD IT WITH THE EYES FACING YOU, KEEP YOUR THUMB OVER THE MOUTH AND BITE INTO IT HEADFIRST.
?
EYES FACING ME, THUMB OVER MOUTH, HEADFIRST... LIKE THIS?
YEAH, THAT'S RIGHT.

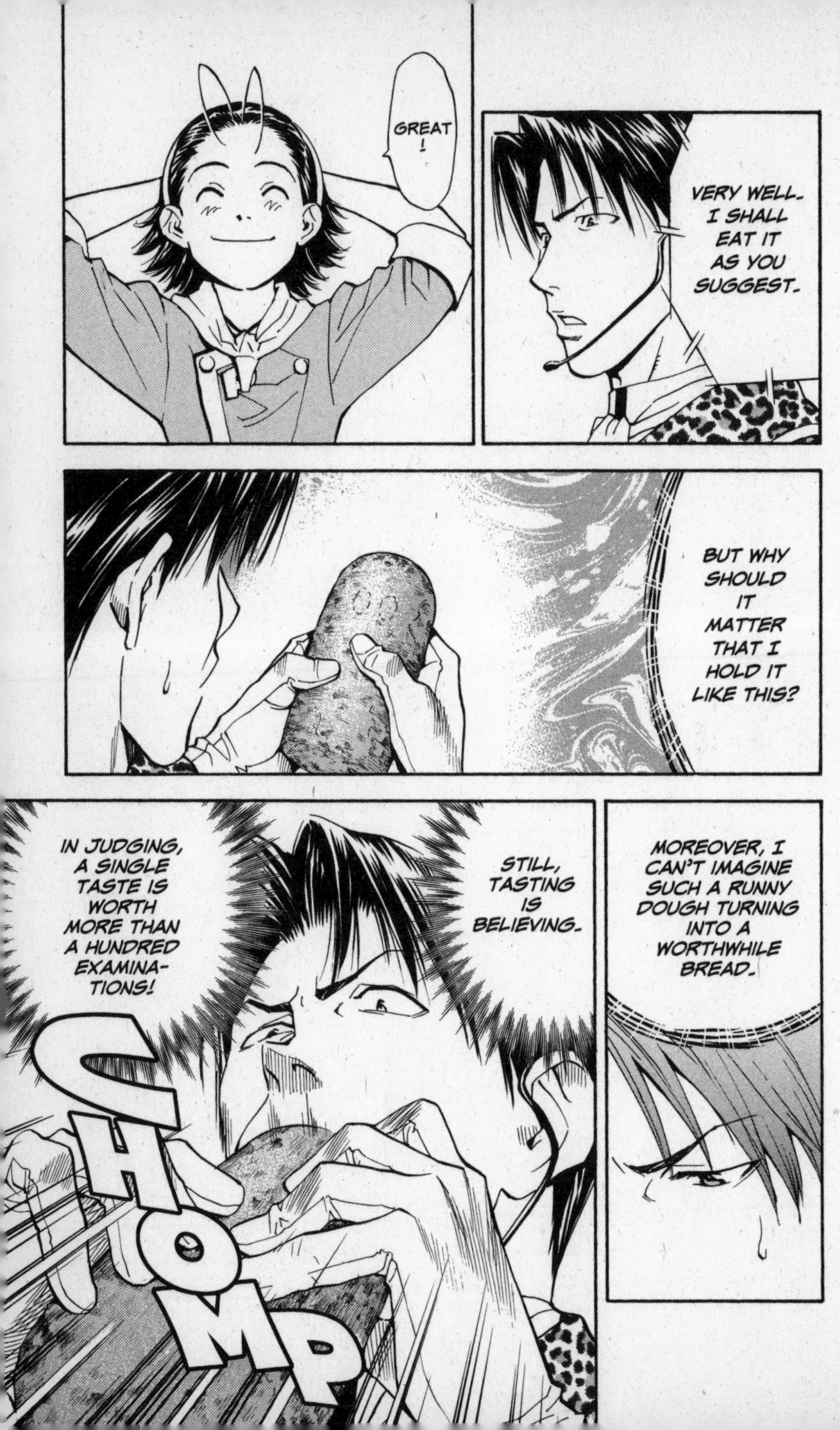
VERY WELL. I SHALL EAT IT AS YOU SUGGEST.
GREAT!
BUT WHY SHOULD IT MATTER THAT I HOLD IT LIKE THIS?
MOREOVER, I CAN'T IMAGINE SUCH A RUNNY DOUGH TURNING INTO A WORTHWHILE BREAD.
STILL, TASTING IS BELIEVING.
IN JUDGING, A SINGLE TASTE IS WORTH MORE THAN A HUNDRED EXAMINATIONS!
CHOMP

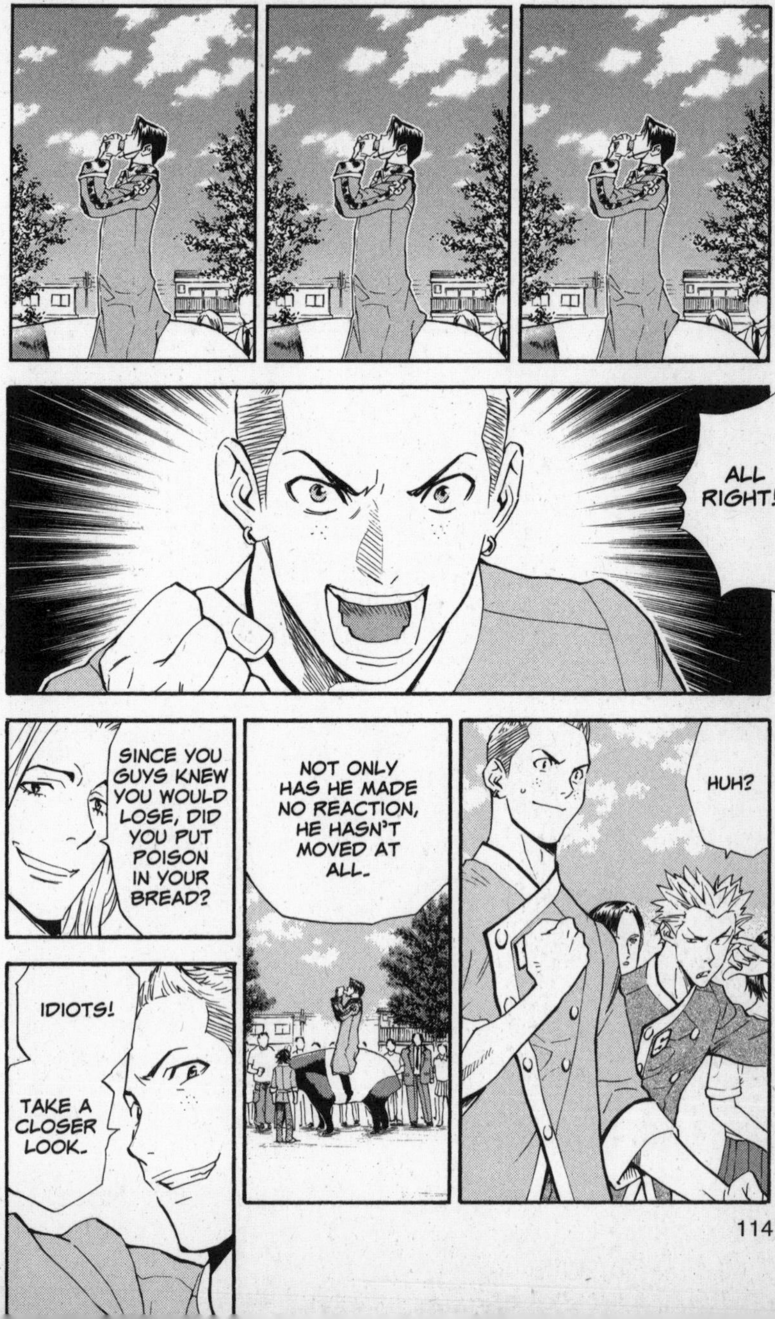
ALL RIGHT!!
HUH?
NOT ONLY HAS HE MADE NO REACTION, HE HASN'T MOVED AT ALL.
SINCE YOU GUYS KNEW YOU WOULD LOSE, DID YOU PUT POISON IN YOUR BREAD?
IDIOTS!
TAKE A CLOSER LOOK.

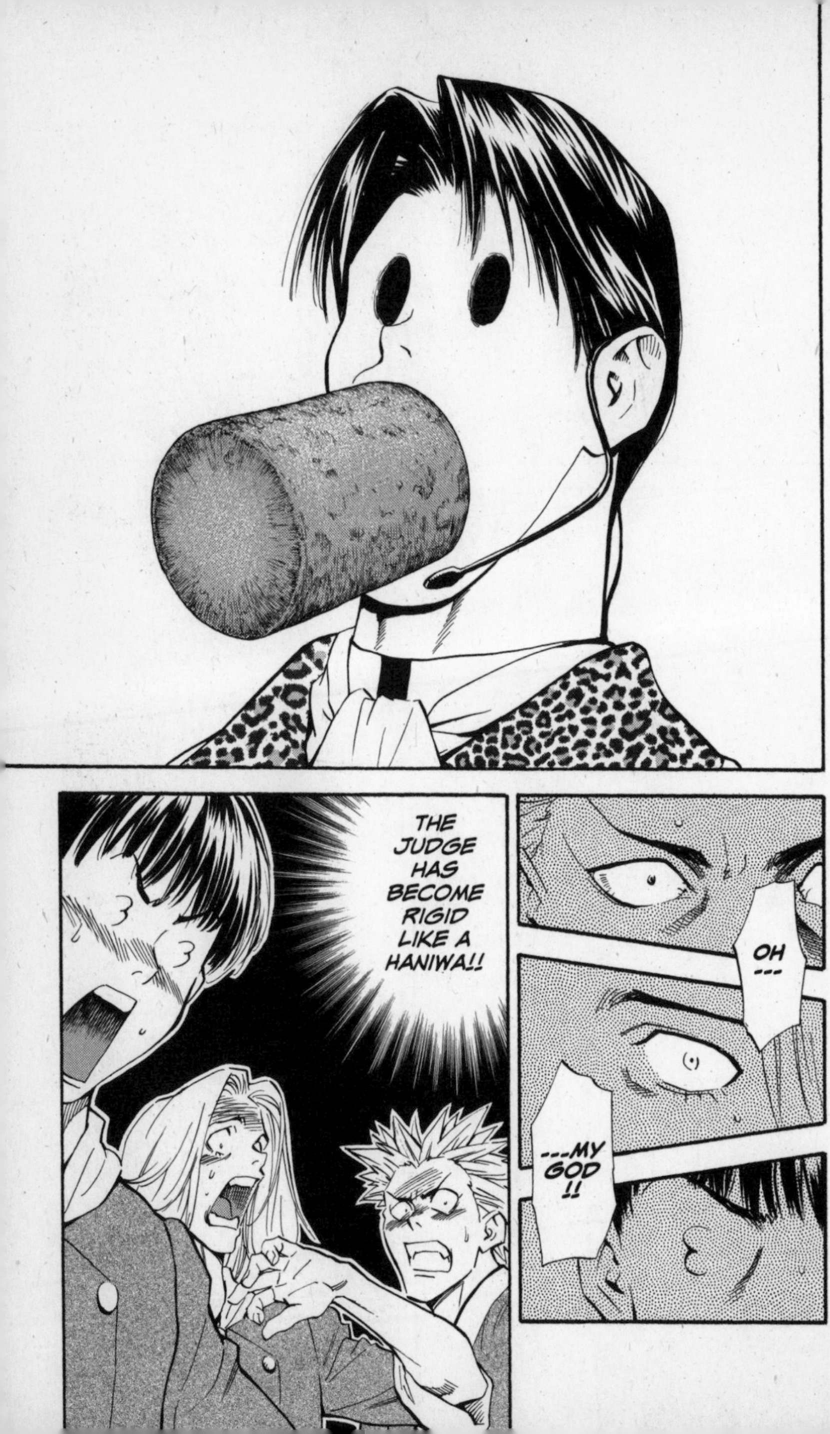
OH ---
---MY GOD!!
THE JUDGE HAS BECOME RIGID LIKE A HANIWA!!

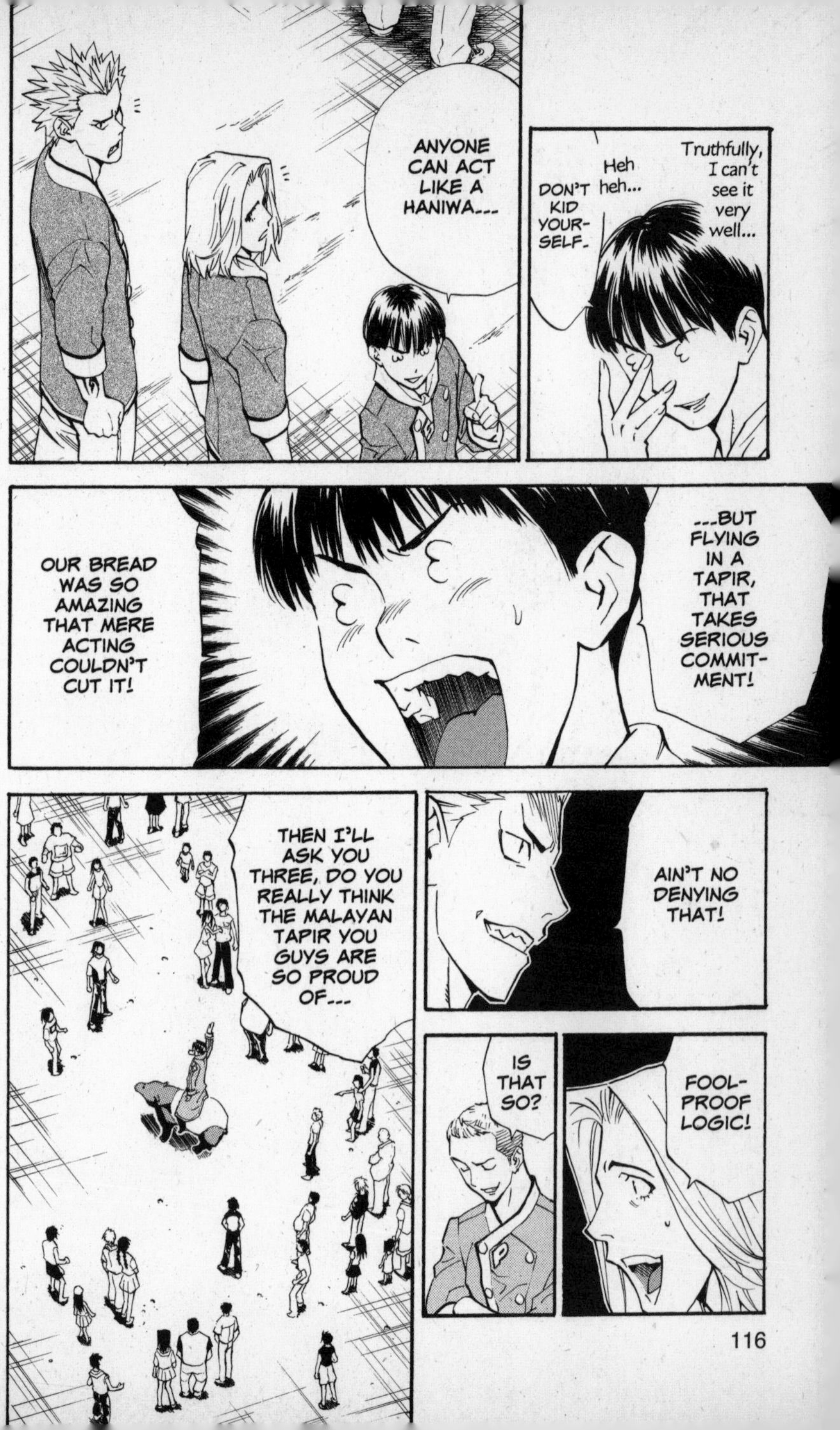
Truthfully, I can't see it very well...
Heh heh...
DON'T KID YOURSELF.
ANYONE CAN ACT LIKE A HANIWA...
...BUT FLYING IN A TAPIR, THAT TAKES SERIOUS COMMITMENT!
OUR BREAD WAS SO AMAZING THAT MERE ACTING COULDN'T CUT IT!
AIN'T NO DENYING THAT!
FOOL-PROOF LOGIC!
IS THAT SO?
THEN I'LL ASK YOU THREE, DO YOU REALLY THINK THE MALAYAN TAPIR YOU GUYS ARE SO PROUD OF...

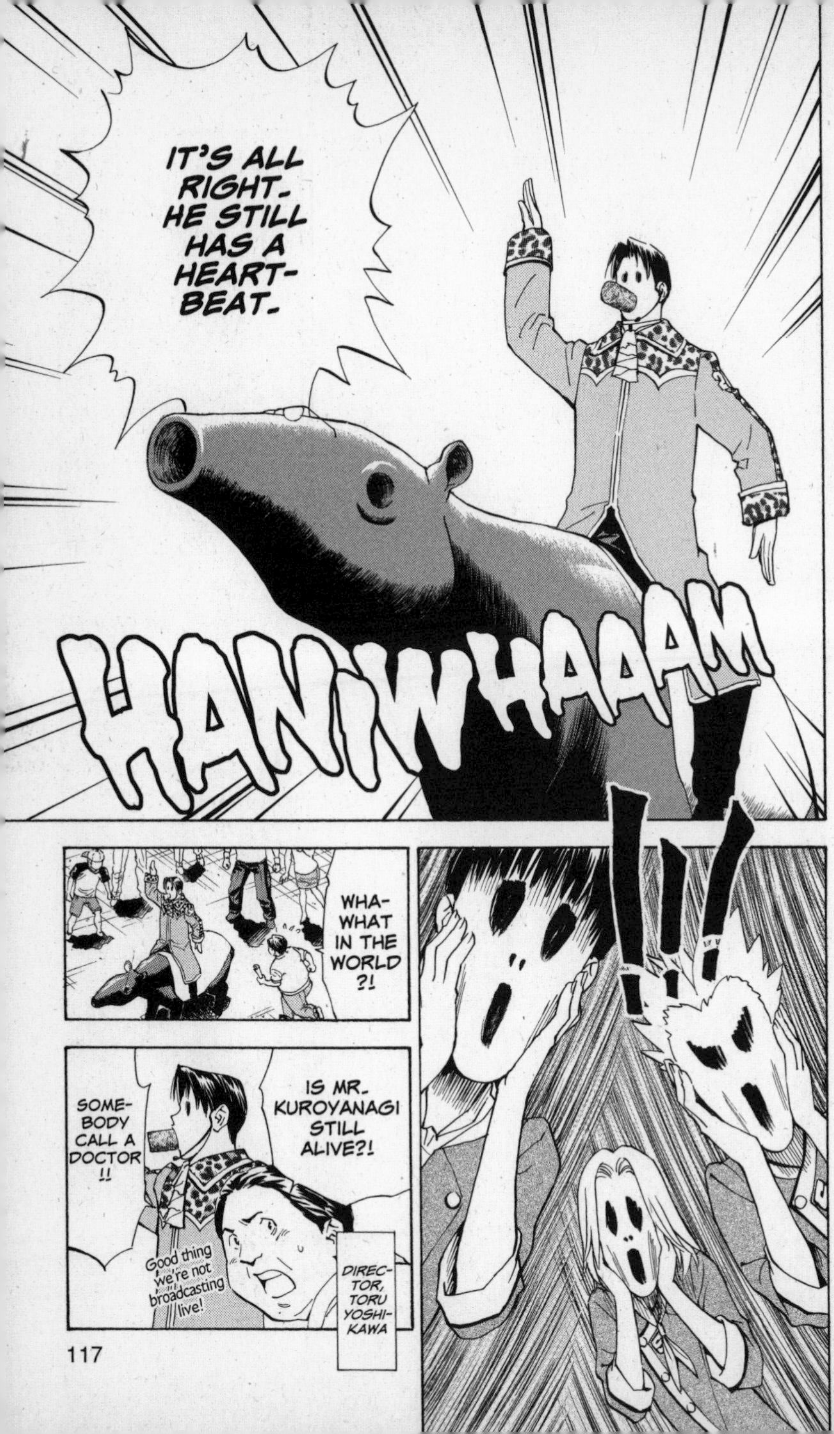
IT'S ALL RIGHT. HE STILL HAS A HEART-BEAT.
HAMWHAAAM
!!
WHA-WHAT IN THE WORLD?!
IS MR. KUROYANAGI STILL ALIVE?!
SOME-BODY CALL A DOCTOR!!
DIREC-TOR, TORU YOSHI-KAWA
Good thing we're not broadcasting live!

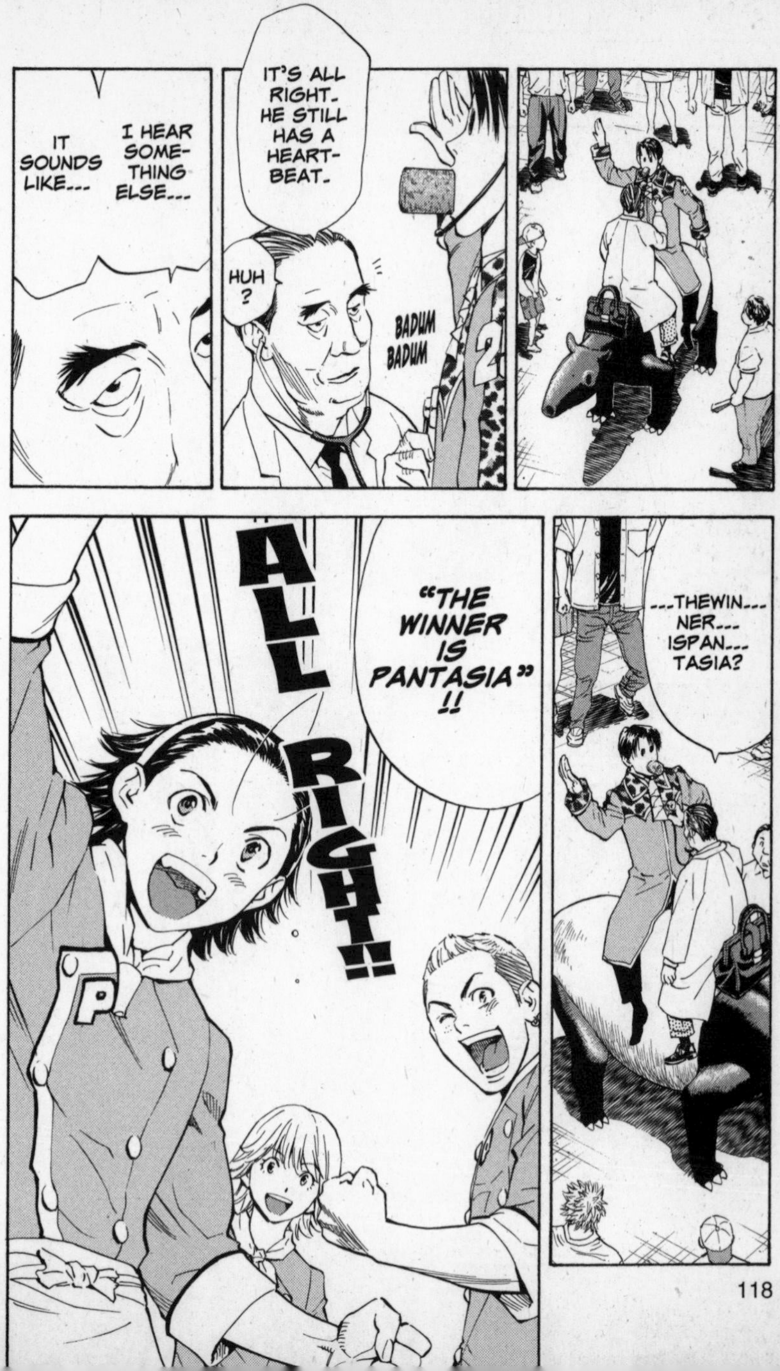
IT'S ALL RIGHT. HE STILL HAS A HEARTBEAT.
HUH?
BADUM BADUM
I HEAR SOME-THING ELSE...
IT SOUNDS LIKE...
...THEWIN... NER... ISPAN... TASIA?
"THE WINNER IS PANTASIA"!!
ALL RIGHT!!

Story 140: Rapport with the Haniwas

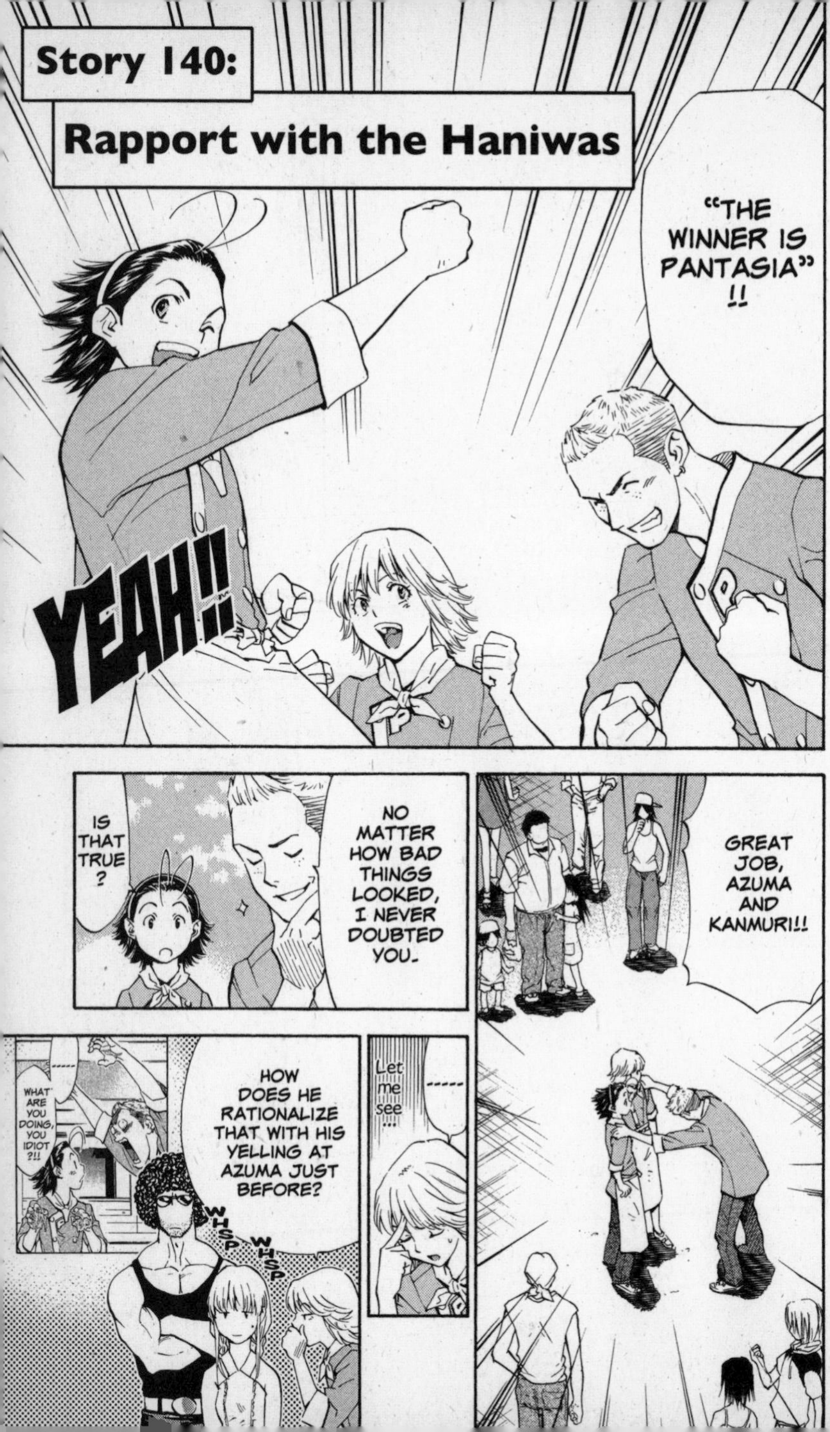
"THE WINNER IS PANTASIA" !!
YEAH!!
GREAT JOB, AZUMA AND KANMURI!!
NO MATTER HOW BAD THINGS LOOKED, I NEVER DOUBTED YOU.
IS THAT TRUE?

Let me see...
HOW DOES HE RATIONALIZE THAT WITH HIS YELLING AT AZUMA JUST BEFORE?
WHSP WHSP

WHAT ARE YOU DOING, YOU IDIOT?!!

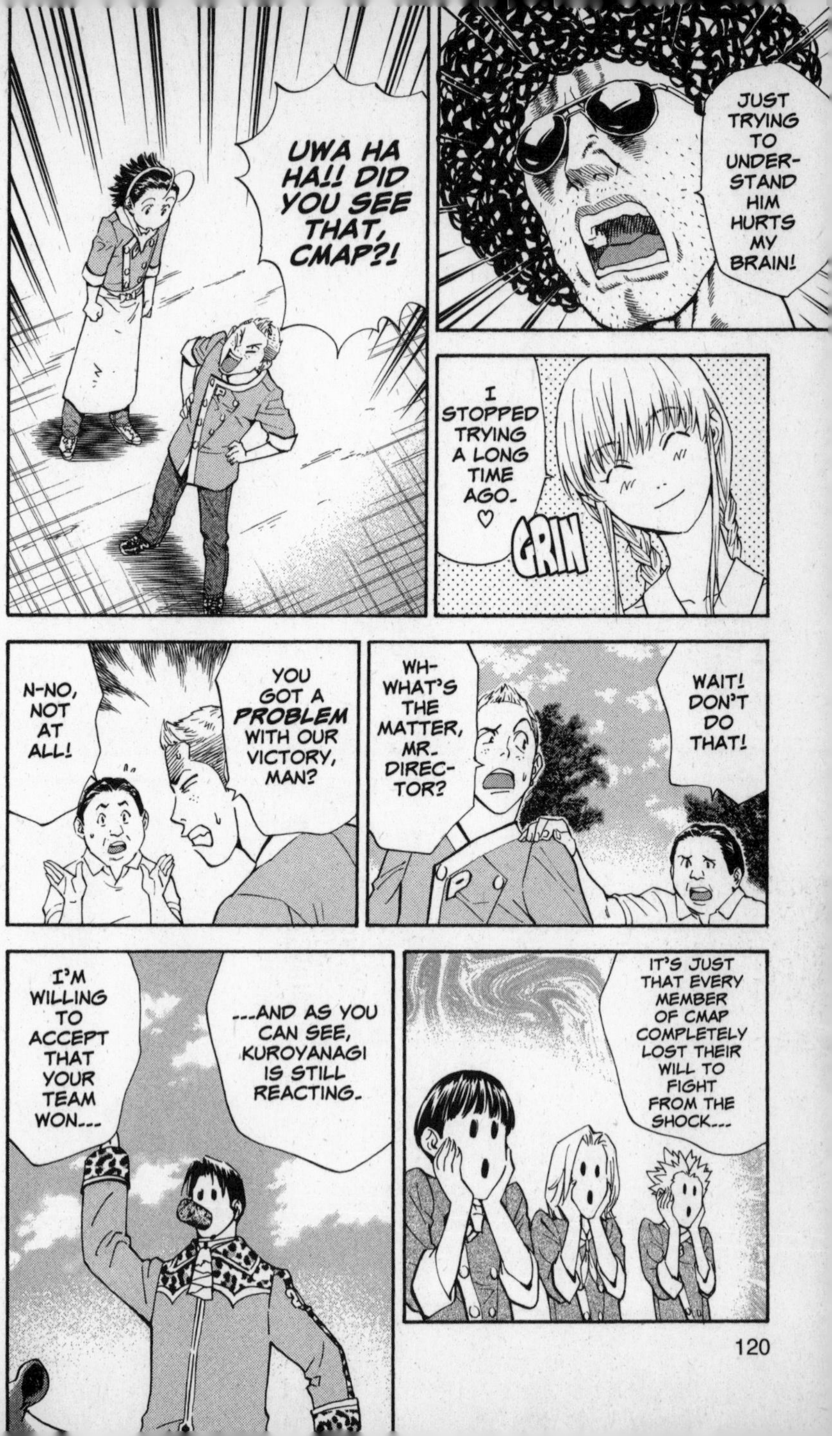
JUST TRYING TO UNDER-STAND HIM HURTS MY BRAIN!
I STOPPED TRYING A LONG TIME AGO. ♡
GRIN
UWA HA HA!! DID YOU SEE THAT, CMAP?!
WAIT! DON'T DO THAT!
WH- WHAT'S THE MATTER, MR. DIRECTOR?
YOU GOT A PROBLEM WITH OUR VICTORY, MAN?
N-NO, NOT AT ALL!
IT'S JUST THAT EVERY MEMBER OF CMAP COMPLETELY LOST THEIR WILL TO FIGHT FROM THE SHOCK...
...AND AS YOU CAN SEE, KUROYANAGI IS STILL REACTING.
I'M WILLING TO ACCEPT THAT YOUR TEAM WON...

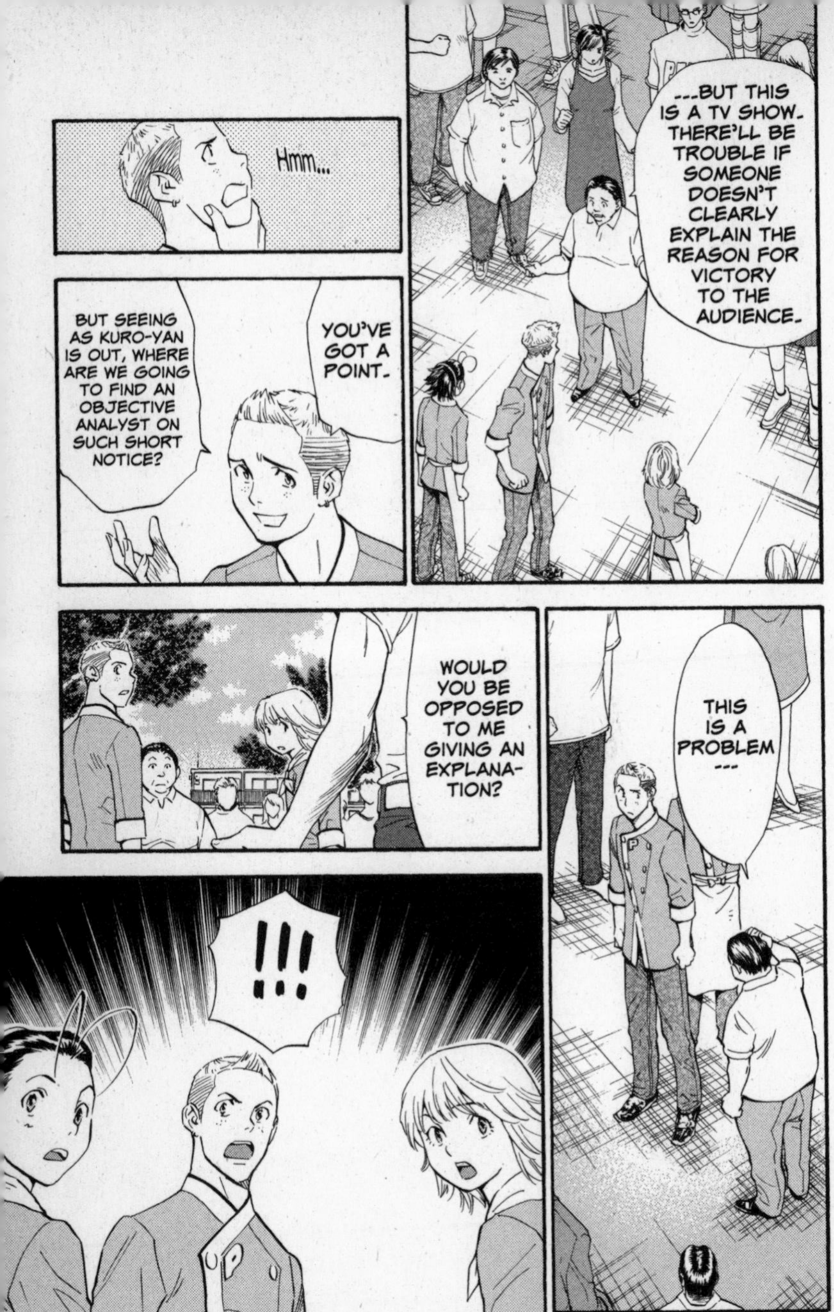
---BUT THIS IS A TV SHOW. THERE'LL BE TROUBLE IF SOMEONE DOESN'T CLEARLY EXPLAIN THE REASON FOR VICTORY TO THE AUDIENCE.
Hmm...
YOU'VE GOT A POINT.
BUT SEEING AS KURO-YAN IS OUT, WHERE ARE WE GOING TO FIND AN OBJECTIVE ANALYST ON SUCH SHORT NOTICE?
THIS IS A PROBLEM ---
WOULD YOU BE OPPOSED TO ME GIVING AN EXPLANATION?
!!!

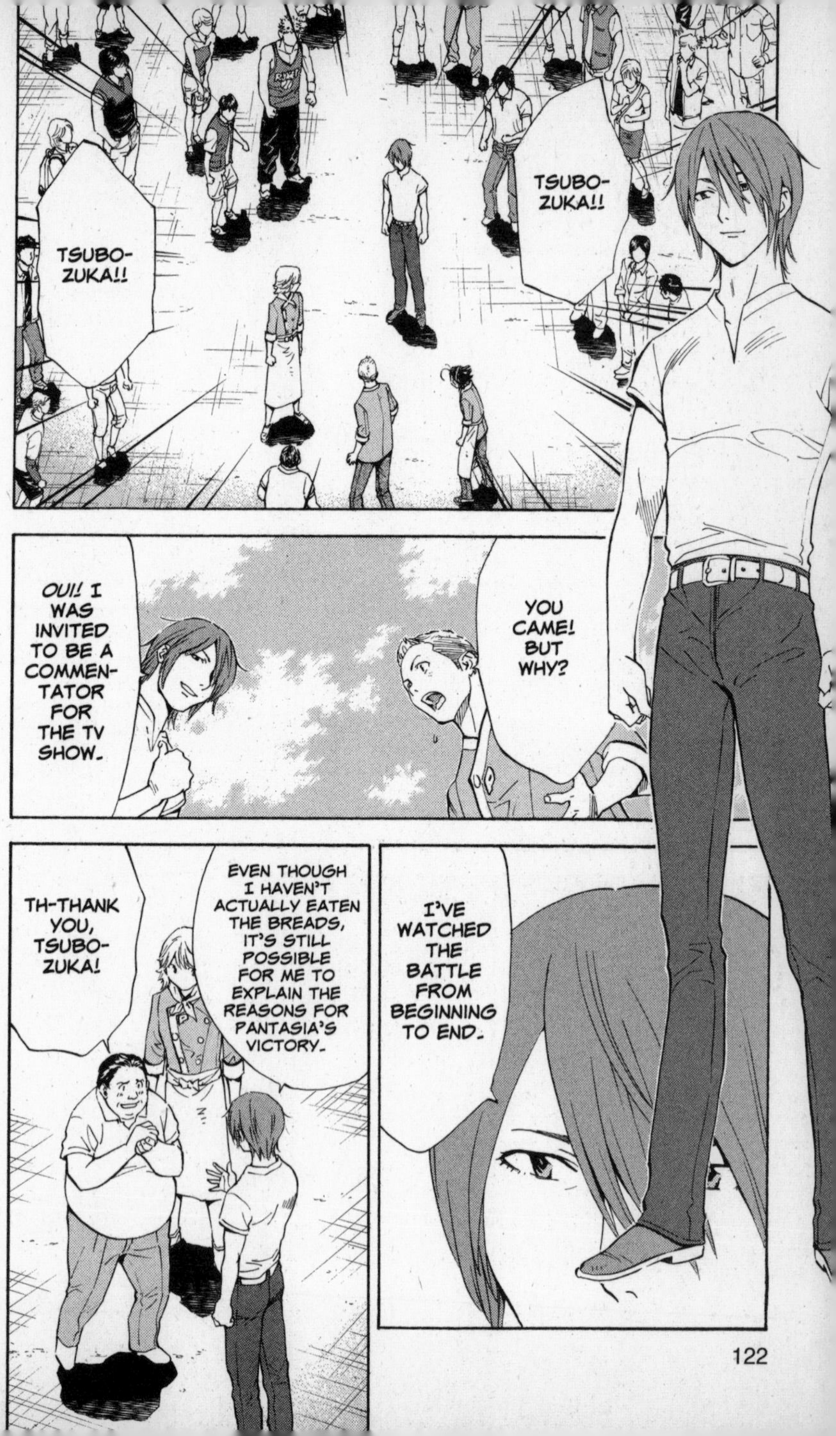
TSUBO-ZUKA!!
TSUBO-ZUKA!!
YOU CAME! BUT WHY?
OUI! I WAS INVITED TO BE A COMMENTATOR FOR THE TV SHOW...
I'VE WATCHED THE BATTLE FROM BEGINNING TO END...
EVEN THOUGH I HAVEN'T ACTUALLY EATEN THE BREADS, IT'S STILL POSSIBLE FOR ME TO EXPLAIN THE REASONS FOR PANTASIA'S VICTORY...
TH-THANK YOU, TSUBO-ZUKA!

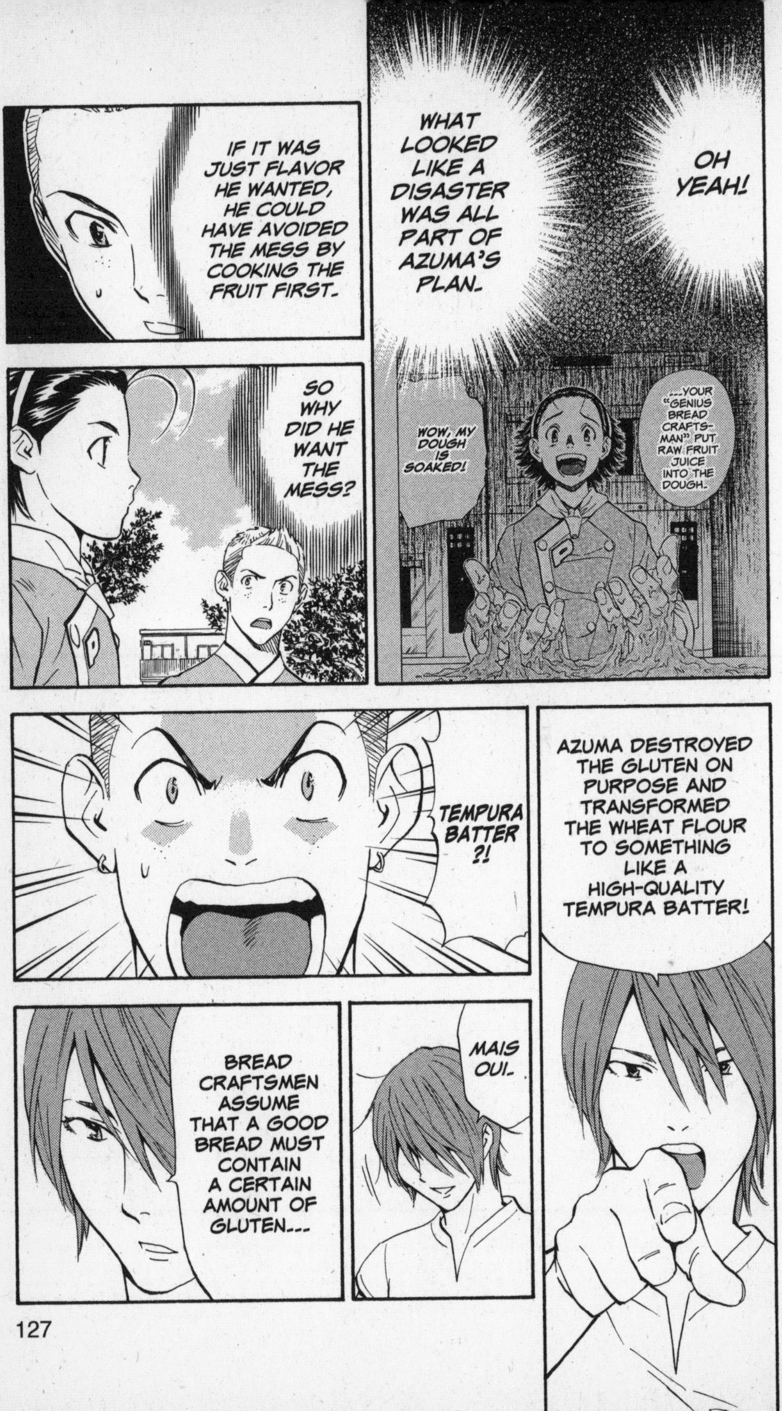
OH YEAH!
WHAT LOOKED LIKE A DISASTER WAS ALL PART OF AZUMA'S PLAN.
...YOUR "GENIUS BREAD CRAFTSMAN" PUT RAW FRUIT JUICE INTO THE DOUGH.
WOW, MY DOUGH IS SOAKED!
IF IT WAS JUST FLAVOR HE WANTED, HE COULD HAVE AVOIDED THE MESS BY COOKING THE FRUIT FIRST.
SO WHY DID HE WANT THE MESS?
AZUMA DESTROYED THE GLUTEN ON PURPOSE AND TRANSFORMED THE WHEAT FLOUR TO SOMETHING LIKE A HIGH-QUALITY TEMPURA BATTER!
TEMPURA BATTER?!
MAIS OUI.
BREAD CRAFTSMEN ASSUME THAT A GOOD BREAD MUST CONTAIN A CERTAIN AMOUNT OF GLUTEN...

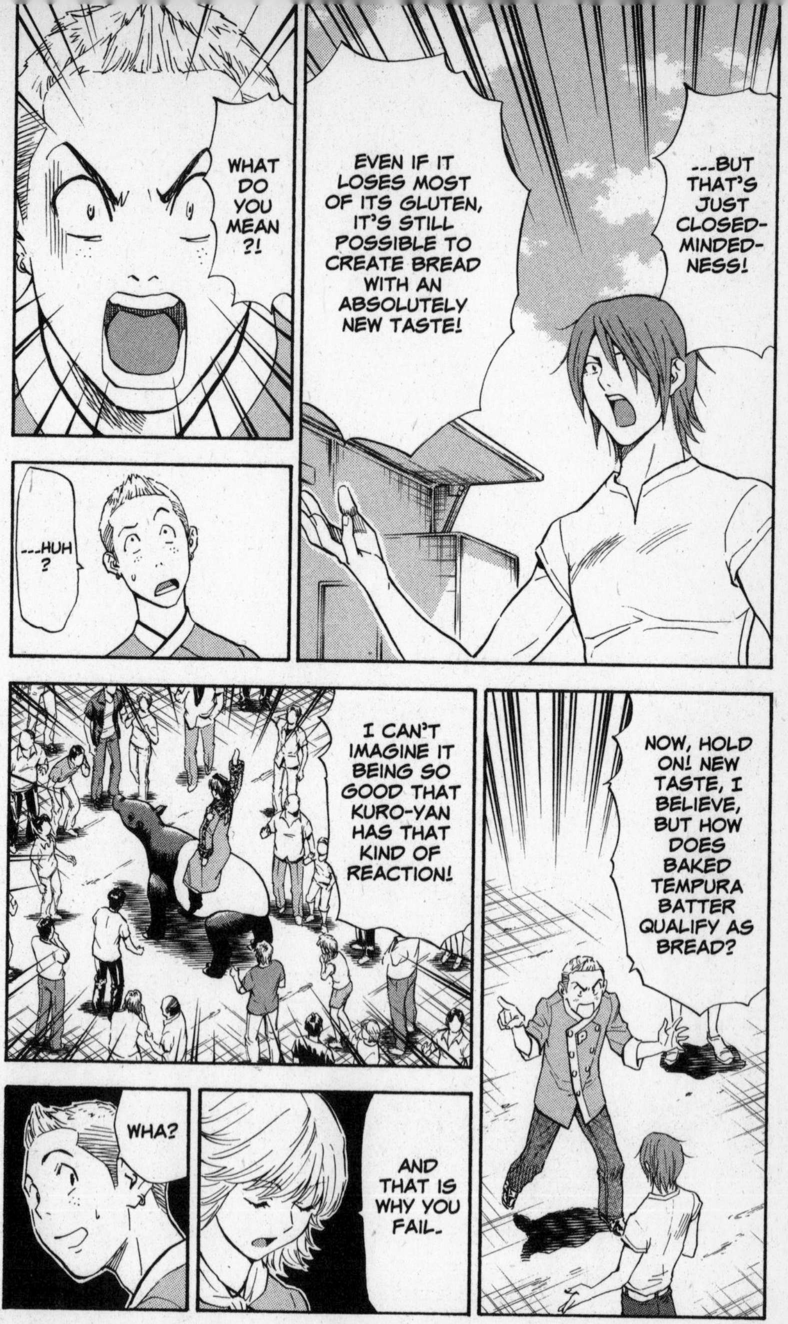
---BUT THAT'S JUST CLOSED-MINDEDNESS!
EVEN IF IT LOSES MOST OF ITS GLUTEN, IT'S STILL POSSIBLE TO CREATE BREAD WITH AN ABSOLUTELY NEW TASTE!
WHAT DO YOU MEAN ?!
---HUH ?
NOW, HOLD ON! NEW TASTE, I BELIEVE, BUT HOW DOES BAKED TEMPURA BATTER QUALIFY AS BREAD?
I CAN'T IMAGINE IT BEING SO GOOD THAT KURO-YAN HAS THAT KIND OF REACTION!
AND THAT IS WHY YOU FAIL.
WHA?

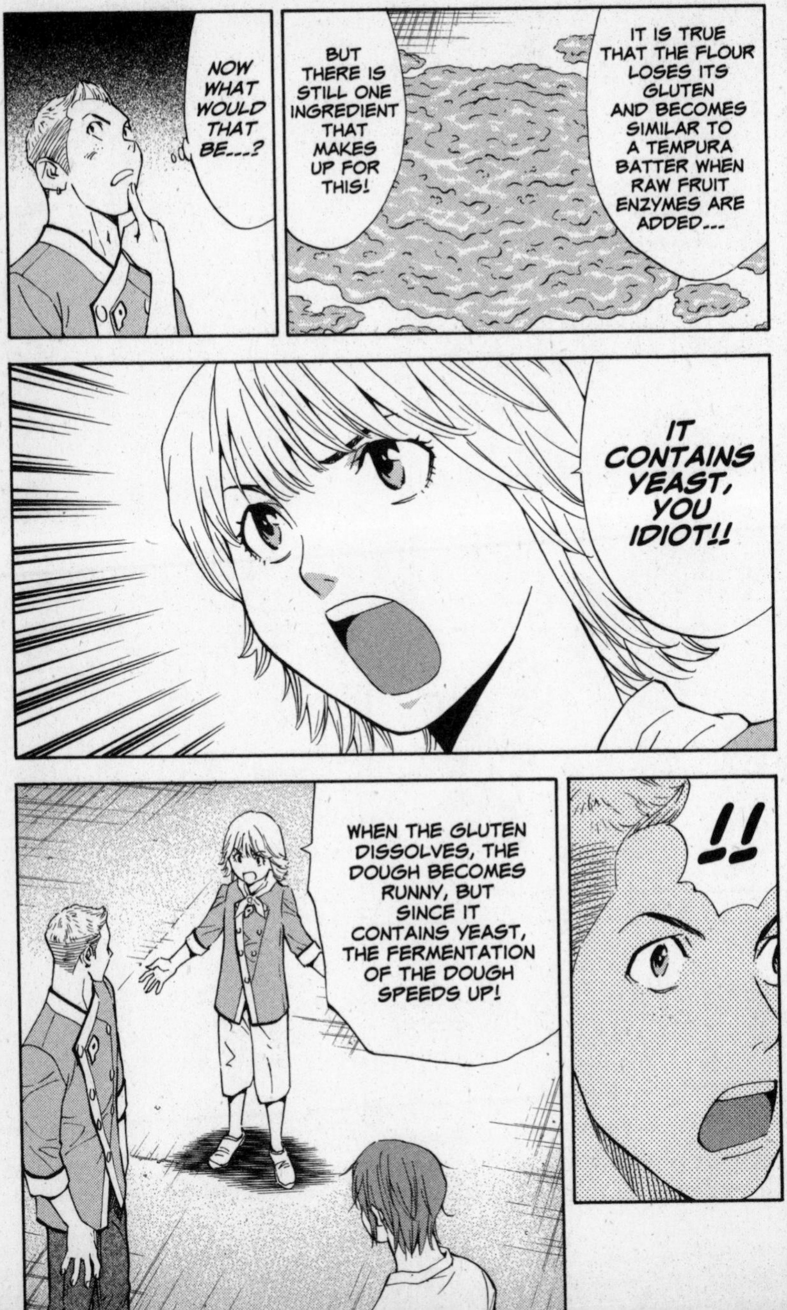
IT IS TRUE THAT THE FLOUR LOSES ITS GLUTEN AND BECOMES SIMILAR TO A TEMPURA BATTER WHEN RAW FRUIT ENZYMES ARE ADDED...
BUT THERE IS STILL ONE INGREDIENT THAT MAKES UP FOR THIS!
NOW WHAT WOULD THAT BE...?
IT CONTAINS YEAST, YOU IDIOT!!
!!
WHEN THE GLUTEN DISSOLVES, THE DOUGH BECOMES RUNNY, BUT SINCE IT CONTAINS YEAST, THE FERMENTATION OF THE DOUGH SPEEDS UP!

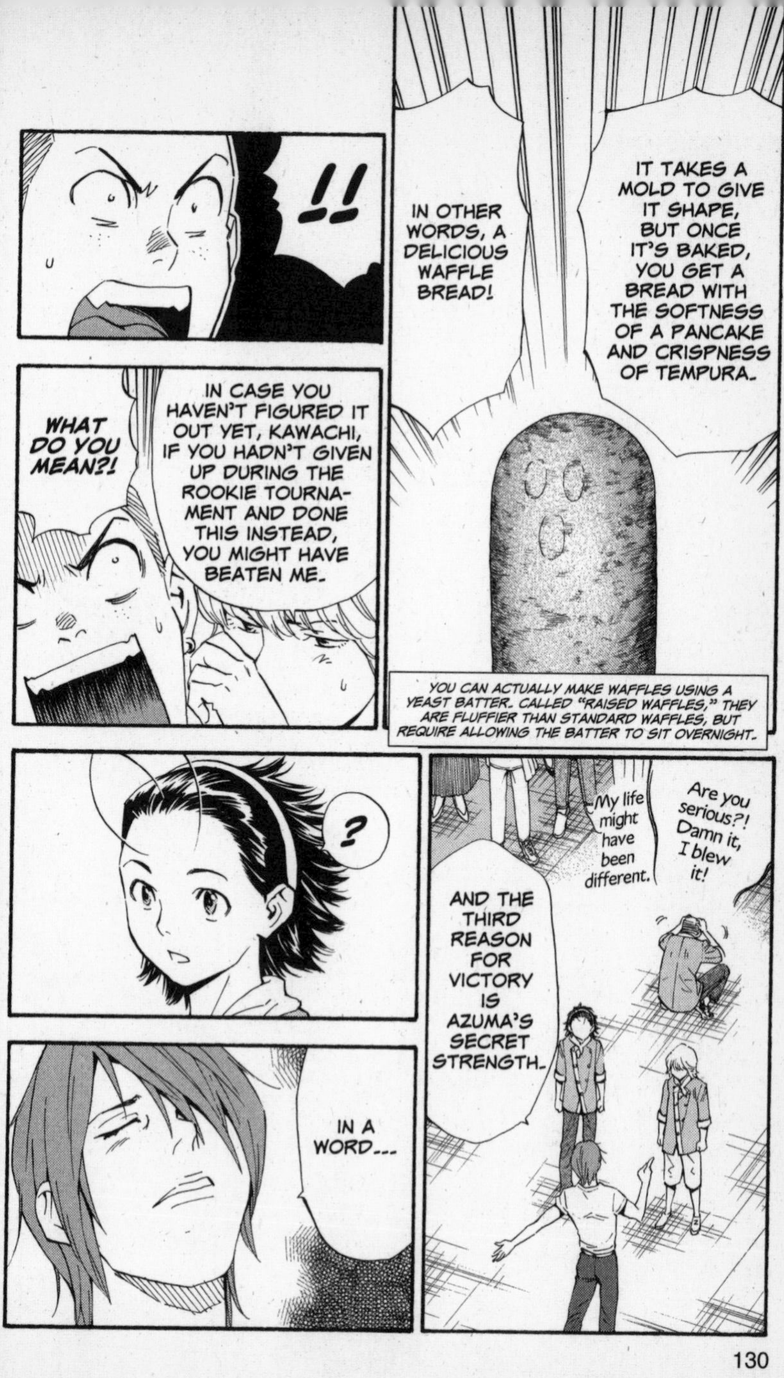
IT TAKES A MOLD TO GIVE IT SHAPE, BUT ONCE IT'S BAKED, YOU GET A BREAD WITH THE SOFTNESS OF A PANCAKE AND CRISPNESS OF TEMPURA.
IN OTHER WORDS, A DELICIOUS WAFFLE BREAD!
YOU CAN ACTUALLY MAKE WAFFLES USING A YEAST BATTER. CALLED "RAISED WAFFLES," THEY ARE FLUFFIER THAN STANDARD WAFFLES, BUT REQUIRE ALLOWING THE BATTER TO SIT OVERNIGHT.
!!
IN CASE YOU HAVEN'T FIGURED IT OUT YET, KAWACHI, IF YOU HADN'T GIVEN UP DURING THE ROOKIE TOURNAMENT AND DONE THIS INSTEAD, YOU MIGHT HAVE BEATEN ME.
WHAT DO YOU MEAN?!
Are you serious?! Damn it, I blew it!
My life might have been different.
AND THE THIRD REASON FOR VICTORY IS AZUMA'S SECRET STRENGTH.
?
IN A WORD...

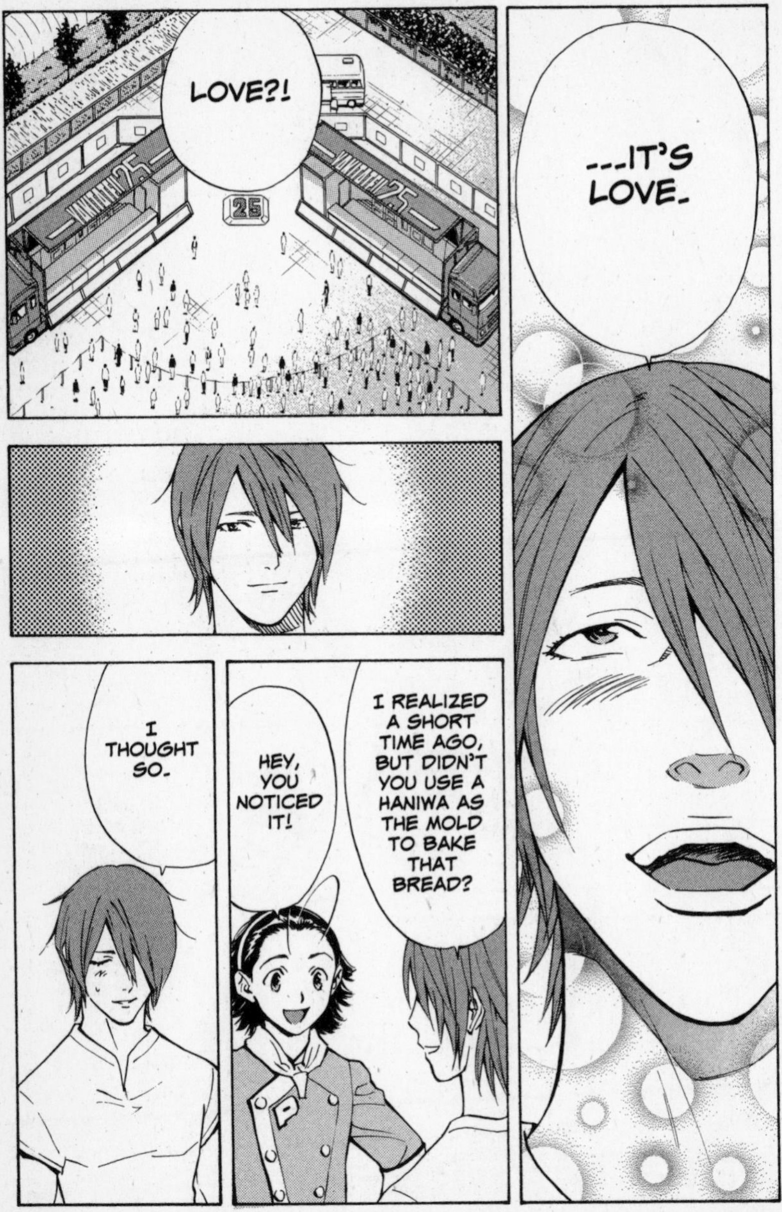
...IT'S LOVE.
LOVE?!
I REALIZED A SHORT TIME AGO, BUT DIDN'T YOU USE A HANIWA AS THE MOLD TO BAKE THAT BREAD?
HEY, YOU NOTICED IT!
I THOUGHT SO.

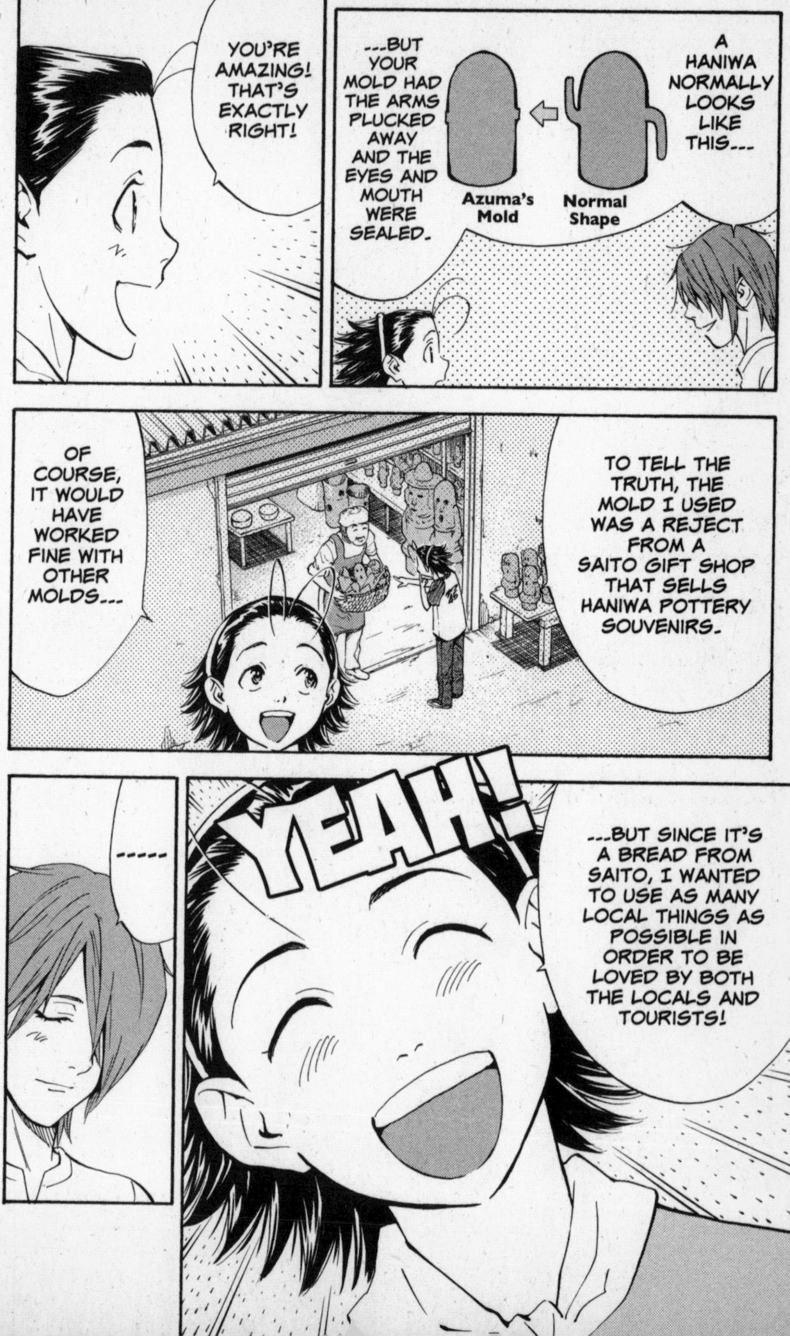
A HANIWA NORMALLY LOOKS LIKE THIS...
Normal Shape
Azuma's Mold
...BUT YOUR MOLD HAD THE ARMS PLUCKED AWAY AND THE EYES AND MOUTH WERE SEALED.
YOU'RE AMAZING! THAT'S EXACTLY RIGHT!
TO TELL THE TRUTH, THE MOLD I USED WAS A REJECT FROM A SAITO GIFT SHOP THAT SELLS HANIWA POTTERY SOUVENIRS.
OF COURSE, IT WOULD HAVE WORKED FINE WITH OTHER MOLDS...
...BUT SINCE IT'S A BREAD FROM SAITO, I WANTED TO USE AS MANY LOCAL THINGS AS POSSIBLE IN ORDER TO BE LOVED BY BOTH THE LOCALS AND TOURISTS!
YEAH!!
.....

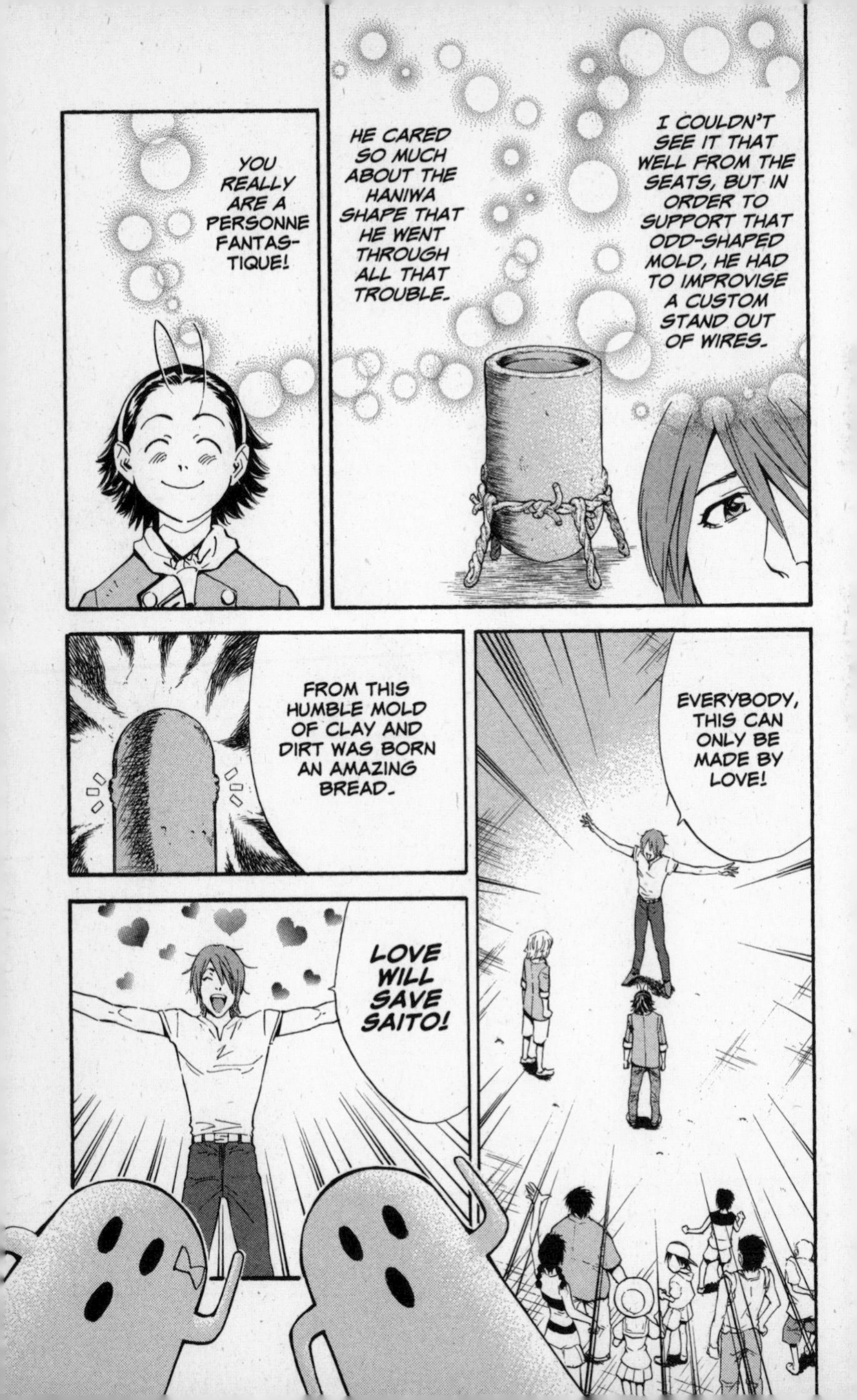
I COULDN'T SEE IT THAT WELL FROM THE SEATS, BUT IN ORDER TO SUPPORT THAT ODD-SHAPED MOLD, HE HAD TO IMPROVISE A CUSTOM STAND OUT OF WIRES.
HE CARED SO MUCH ABOUT THE HANIWA SHAPE THAT HE WENT THROUGH ALL THAT TROUBLE.
YOU REALLY ARE A PERSONNE FANTAS-TIQUE!
EVERYBODY, THIS CAN ONLY BE MADE BY LOVE!
FROM THIS HUMBLE MOLD OF CLAY AND DIRT WAS BORN AN AMAZING BREAD.
LOVE WILL SAVE SAITO!

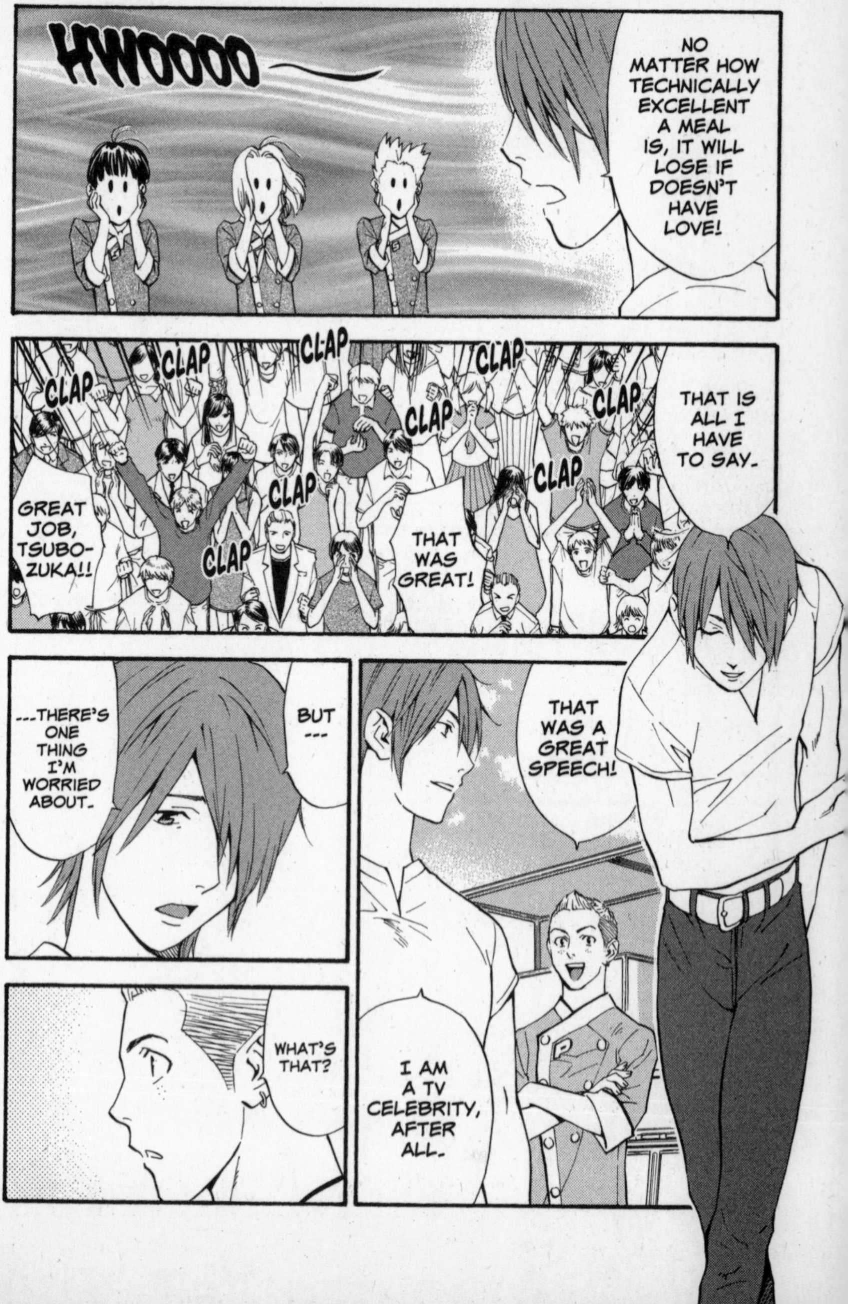
NO MATTER HOW TECHNICALLY EXCELLENT A MEAL IS, IT WILL LOSE IF DOESN'T HAVE LOVE!
HWOOOO—
THAT IS ALL I HAVE TO SAY.
CLAP
CLAP
CLAP
CLAP
CLAP
CLAP
CLAP
CLAP
THAT WAS GREAT!
GREAT JOB, TSUBO-ZUKA!!
THAT WAS A GREAT SPEECH!
I AM A TV CELEBRITY, AFTER ALL.
BUT---
---THERE'S ONE THING I'M WORRIED ABOUT.
WHAT'S THAT?

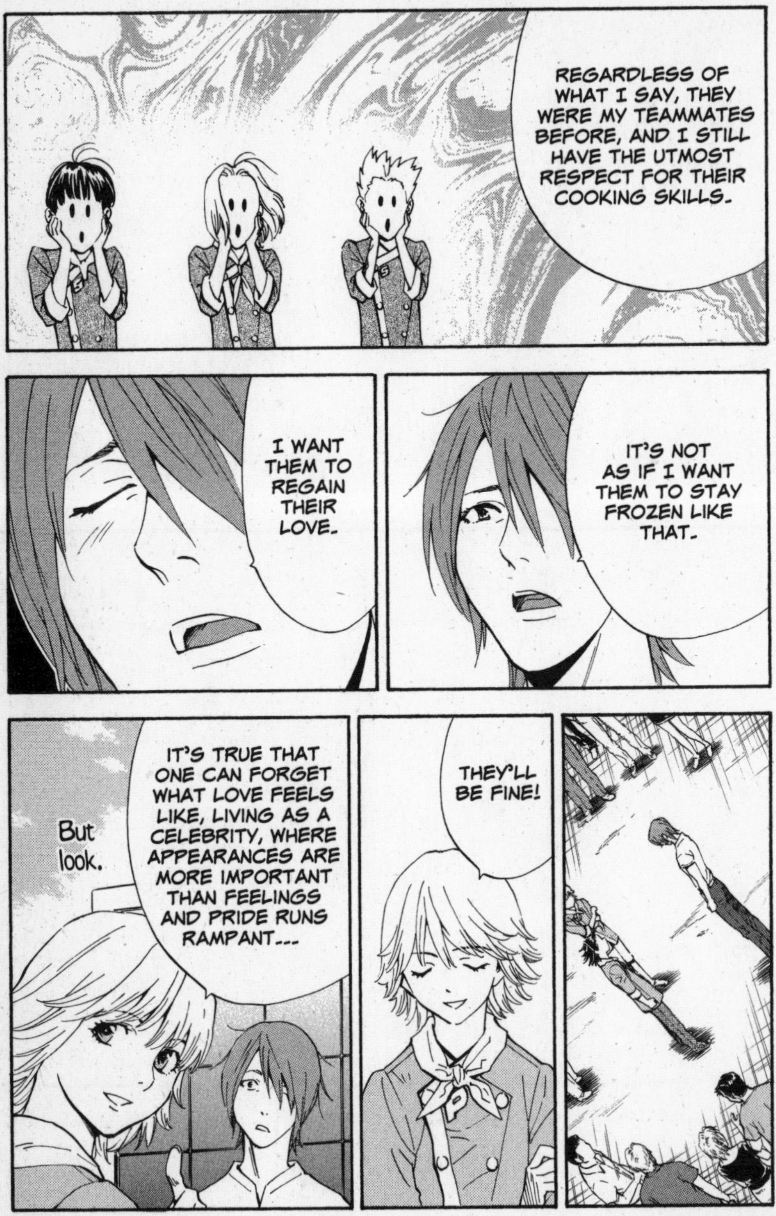
REGARDLESS OF WHAT I SAY, THEY WERE MY TEAMMATES BEFORE, AND I STILL HAVE THE UTMOST RESPECT FOR THEIR COOKING SKILLS.
IT'S NOT AS IF I WANT THEM TO STAY FROZEN LIKE THAT.
I WANT THEM TO REGAIN THEIR LOVE.
THEY'LL BE FINE!
IT'S TRUE THAT ONE CAN FORGET WHAT LOVE FEELS LIKE, LIVING AS A CELEBRITY, WHERE APPEARANCES ARE MORE IMPORTANT THAN FEELINGS AND PRIDE RUNS RAMPANT...
But look.

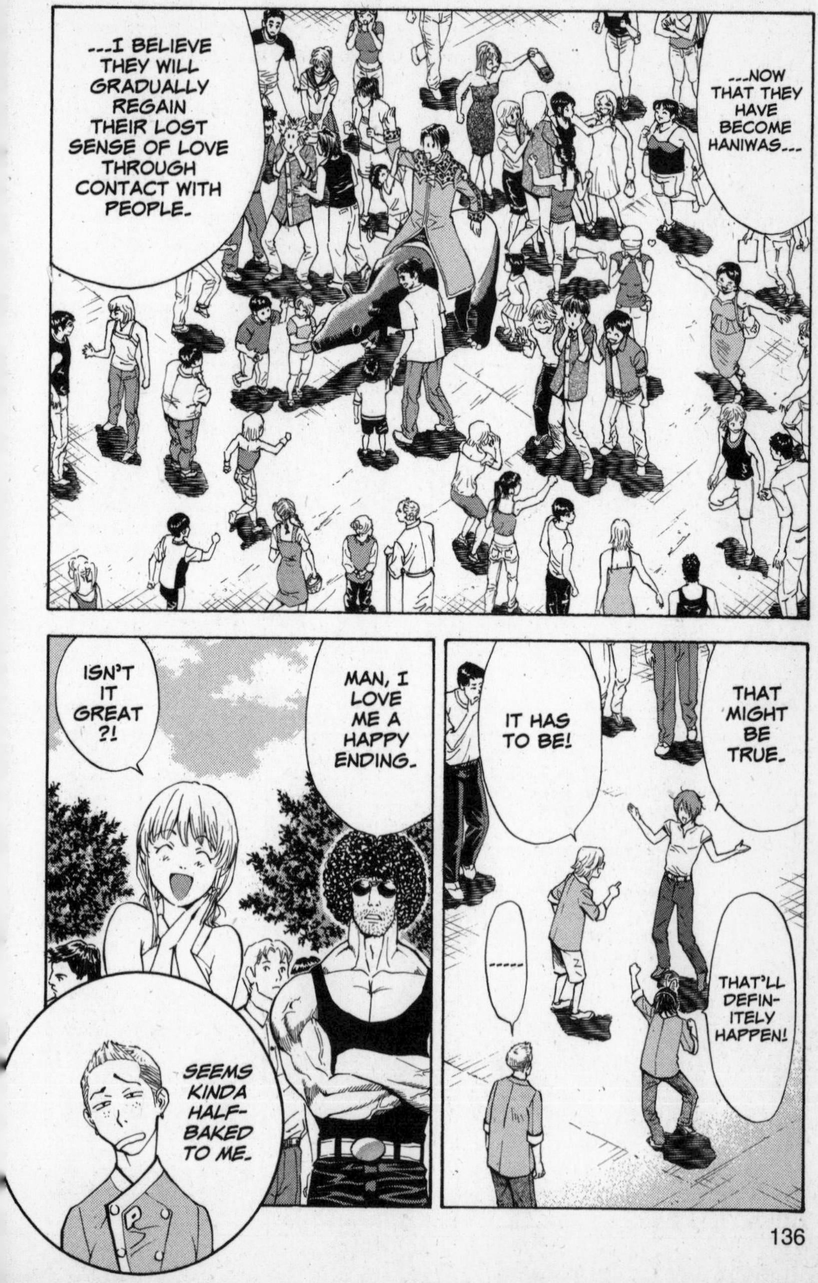
...NOW THAT THEY HAVE BECOME HANIWAS...
...I BELIEVE THEY WILL GRADUALLY REGAIN THEIR LOST SENSE OF LOVE THROUGH CONTACT WITH PEOPLE.
THAT MIGHT BE TRUE.
IT HAS TO BE!
THAT'LL DEFINITELY HAPPEN!
.....
MAN, I LOVE ME A HAPPY ENDING.
ISN'T IT GREAT?!
SEEMS KINDA HALF-BAKED TO ME.

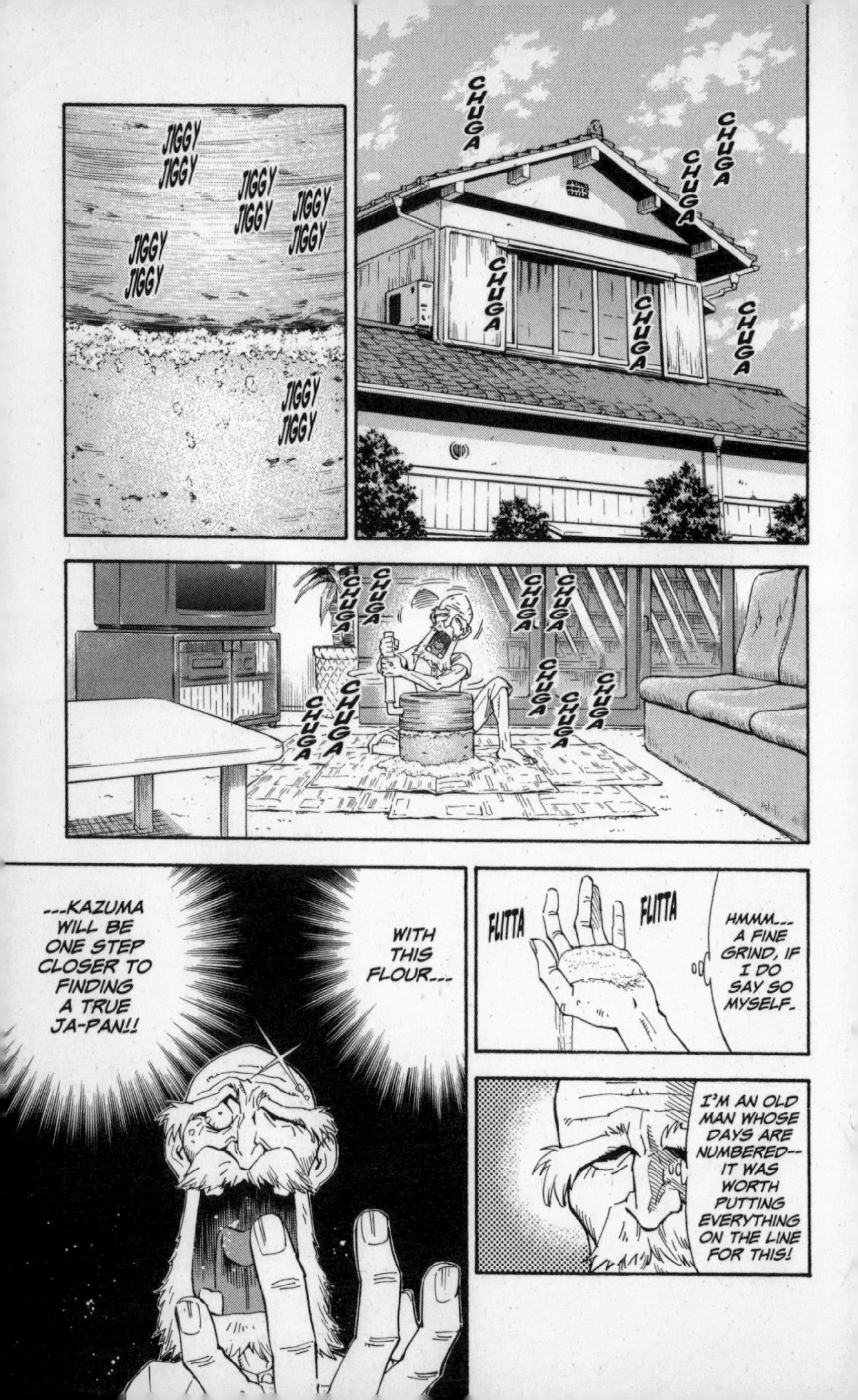
CHUGA
CHUGA
CHUGA
CHUGA
CHUGA
CHUGA
JIGGY JIGGY
JIGGY JIGGY
JIGGY JIGGY
JIGGY JIGGY
JIGGY JIGGY
CHUGA
CHUGA
CHUGA
CHUGA
CHUGA
CHUGA
CHUGA
CHUGA
CHUGA
CHUGA
HMMM... A FINE GRIND, IF I DO SAY SO MYSELF.
FLITTA
FLITTA
I'M AN OLD MAN WHOSE DAYS ARE NUMBERED-- IT WAS WORTH PUTTING EVERYTHING ON THE LINE FOR THIS!
WITH THIS FLOUR...
...KAZUMA WILL BE ONE STEP CLOSER TO FINDING A TRUE JA-PAN!!

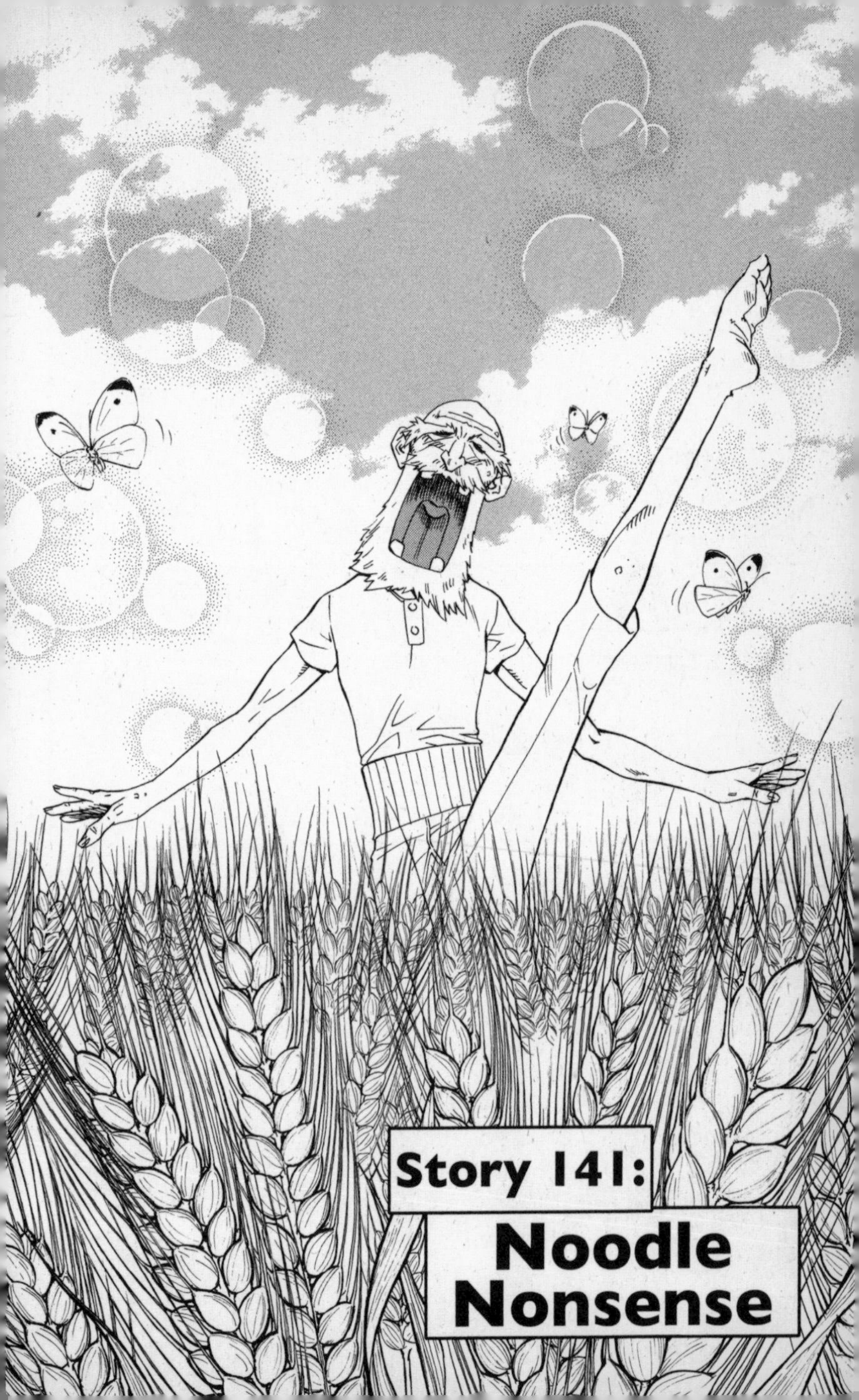
Story 141:
Noodle Nonsense

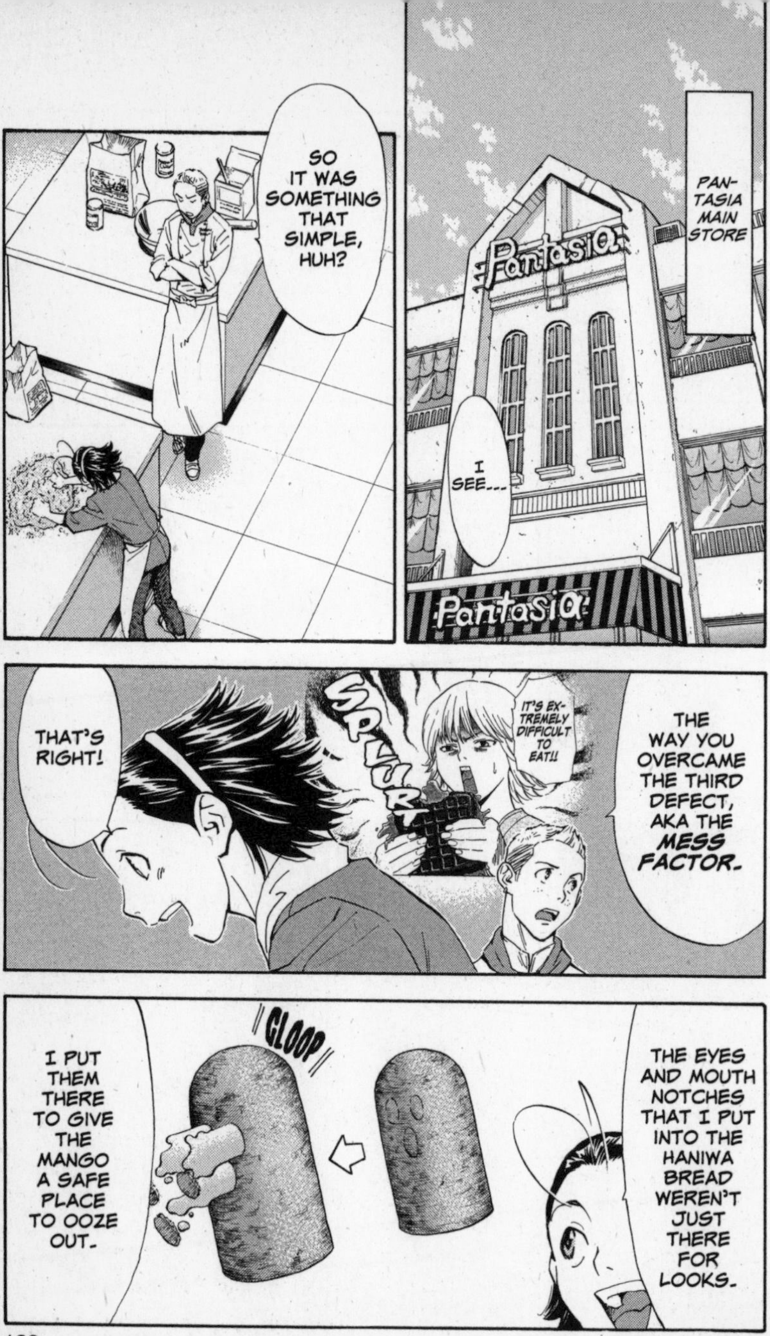
PANTASIA MAIN STORE
Pantasia
I SEE...
Pantasia
SO IT WAS SOMETHING THAT SIMPLE, HUH?
THE WAY YOU OVERCAME THE THIRD DEFECT, AKA THE *MESS FACTOR*.
IT'S EXTREMELY DIFFICULT TO EAT!!
SPLURT
THAT'S RIGHT!
THE EYES AND MOUTH NOTCHES THAT I PUT INTO THE HANIWA BREAD WEREN'T JUST THERE FOR LOOKS.
GLOOP
I PUT THEM THERE TO GIVE THE MANGO A SAFE PLACE TO OOZE OUT.

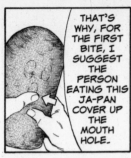

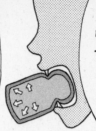

IT'S THE FIRST BITE IN PARTICULAR THAT CAUSES MANGO TO SQUIRT OUT IN EVERY DIRECTION...
...BECAUSE WHEN THE FORCE OF THE BITE IS APPLIED TO THE BREAD, THE MANGO INSIDE DOESN'T HAVE ANYWHERE TO ESCAPE.
THAT'S WHY, FOR THE FIRST BITE, I SUGGEST THE PERSON EATING THIS JA-PAN COVER UP THE MOUTH HOLE.
IN THAT WAY, THE NOTCHES FOR THE EYES POP OPEN AND THE MANGO WILL GUSH INTO THE MOUTH WITHOUT SPILLING ALL OVER THE PERSON'S HANDS.
Part going into the mouth.
Normal bite
Large bite
WHEN A PERSON WANTS TO TAKE A BIGGER BITE, THEY CAN GO ALL THE WAY DOWN OVER THE MOUTH ON THE HANIWA!
...NOW I GET IT.
THAT'S RIGHT.
IN SHORT, AS LONG AS THE PERSON EATING IT CAN GET PAST THE FIRST BITE WITHOUT MAKING A MESS, THEY'RE HOME FREE.
.....
BY THE WAY, WHAT ARE YOU KNEADING OVER THERE?
GLUMP GLUMP

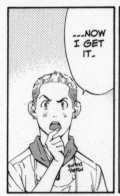

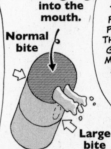

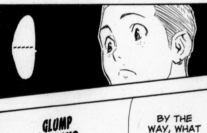

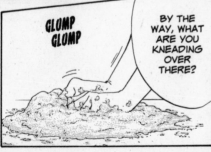

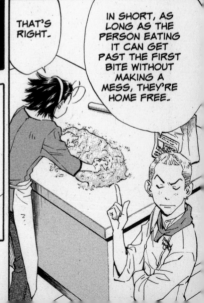

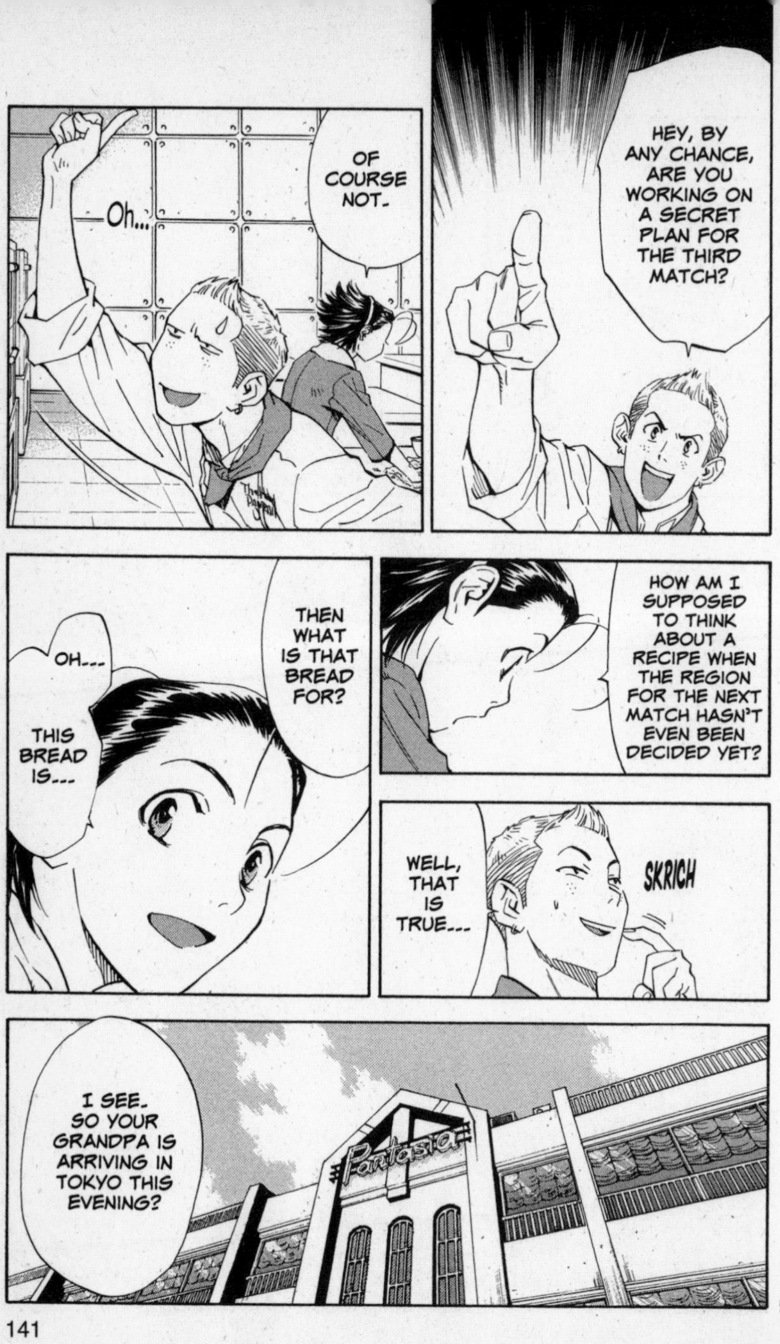
HEY, BY ANY CHANCE, ARE YOU WORKING ON A SECRET PLAN FOR THE THIRD MATCH?
OF COURSE NOT.
Oh...
HOW AM I SUPPOSED TO THINK ABOUT A RECIPE WHEN THE REGION FOR THE NEXT MATCH HASN'T EVEN BEEN DECIDED YET?
SKRICH
WELL, THAT IS TRUE...
THEN WHAT IS THAT BREAD FOR?
OH...
THIS BREAD IS...
I SEE. SO YOUR GRANDPA IS ARRIVING IN TOKYO THIS EVENING?
Pantasia

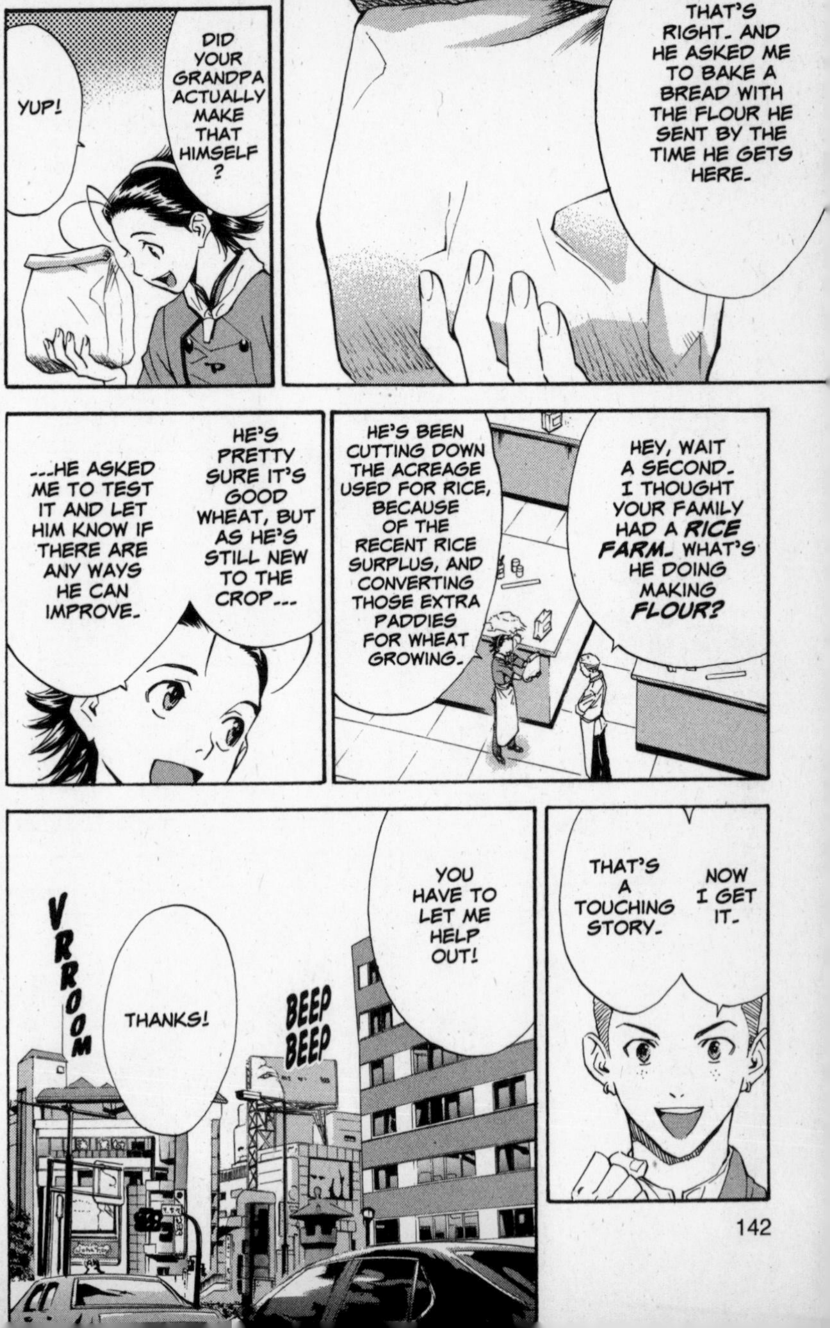
THAT'S RIGHT. AND HE ASKED ME TO BAKE A BREAD WITH THE FLOUR HE SENT BY THE TIME HE GETS HERE.
DID YOUR GRANDPA ACTUALLY MAKE THAT HIMSELF?
YUP!
HEY, WAIT A SECOND. I THOUGHT YOUR FAMILY HAD A *RICE FARM.* WHAT'S HE DOING MAKING *FLOUR?*
HE'S BEEN CUTTING DOWN THE ACREAGE USED FOR RICE, BECAUSE OF THE RECENT RICE SURPLUS, AND CONVERTING THOSE EXTRA PADDIES FOR WHEAT GROWING.
HE'S PRETTY SURE IT'S GOOD WHEAT, BUT AS HE'S STILL NEW TO THE CROP...
...HE ASKED ME TO TEST IT AND LET HIM KNOW IF THERE ARE ANY WAYS HE CAN IMPROVE.
NOW I GET IT.
THAT'S A TOUCHING STORY.
YOU HAVE TO LET ME HELP OUT!
BEEP BEEP
THANKS!
VRROOM

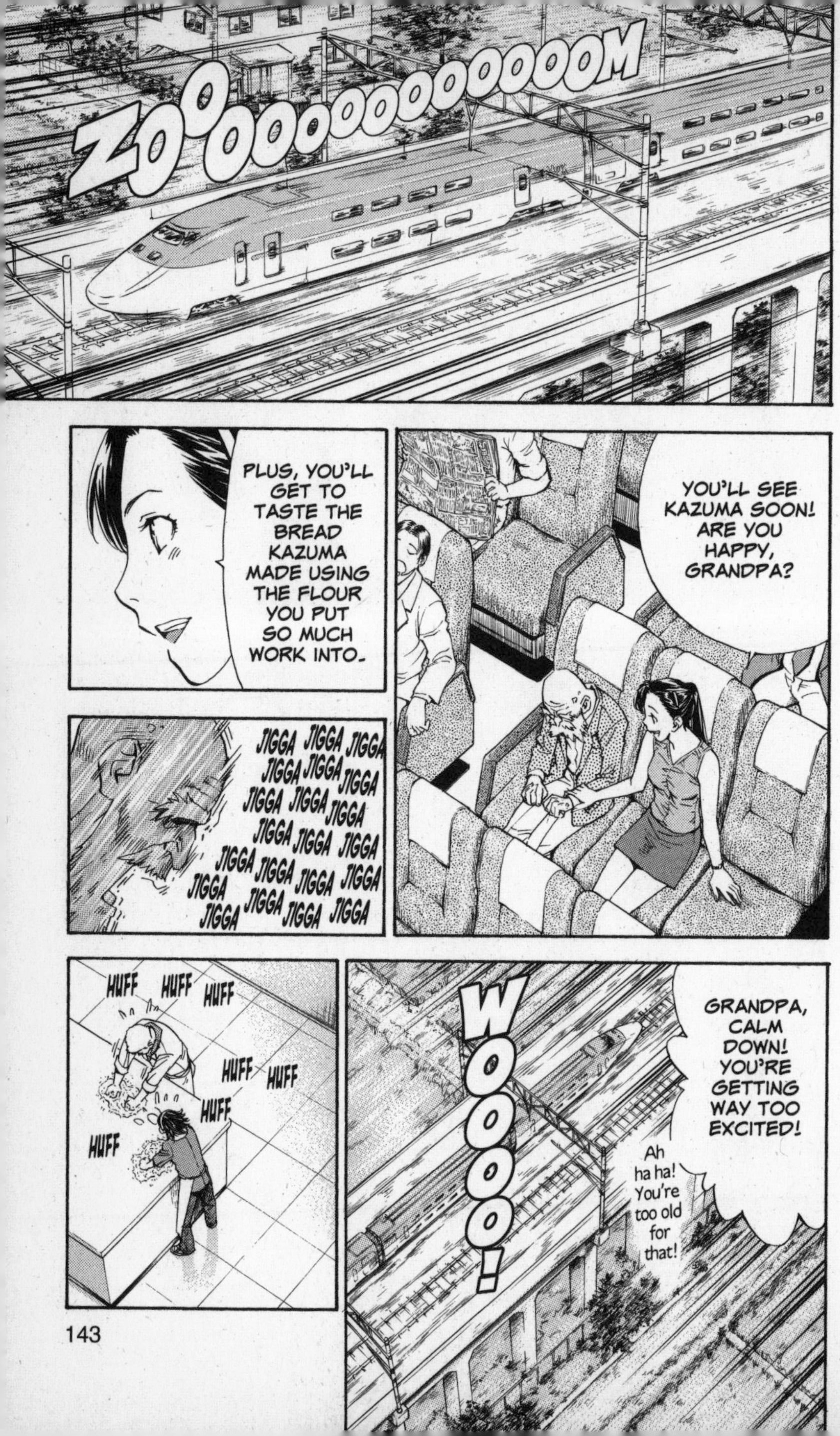
ZOOOOOOOOOOOOM
YOU'LL SEE KAZUMA SOON! ARE YOU HAPPY, GRANDPA?
PLUS, YOU'LL GET TO TASTE THE BREAD KAZUMA MADE USING THE FLOUR YOU PUT SO MUCH WORK INTO...
JIGGA JIGGA
GRANDPA, CALM DOWN! YOU'RE GETTING WAY TOO EXCITED!
WOOOOO!
Ah ha ha! You're too old for that!
HUFF HUFF HUFF
HUFF HUFF
HUFF
HUFF

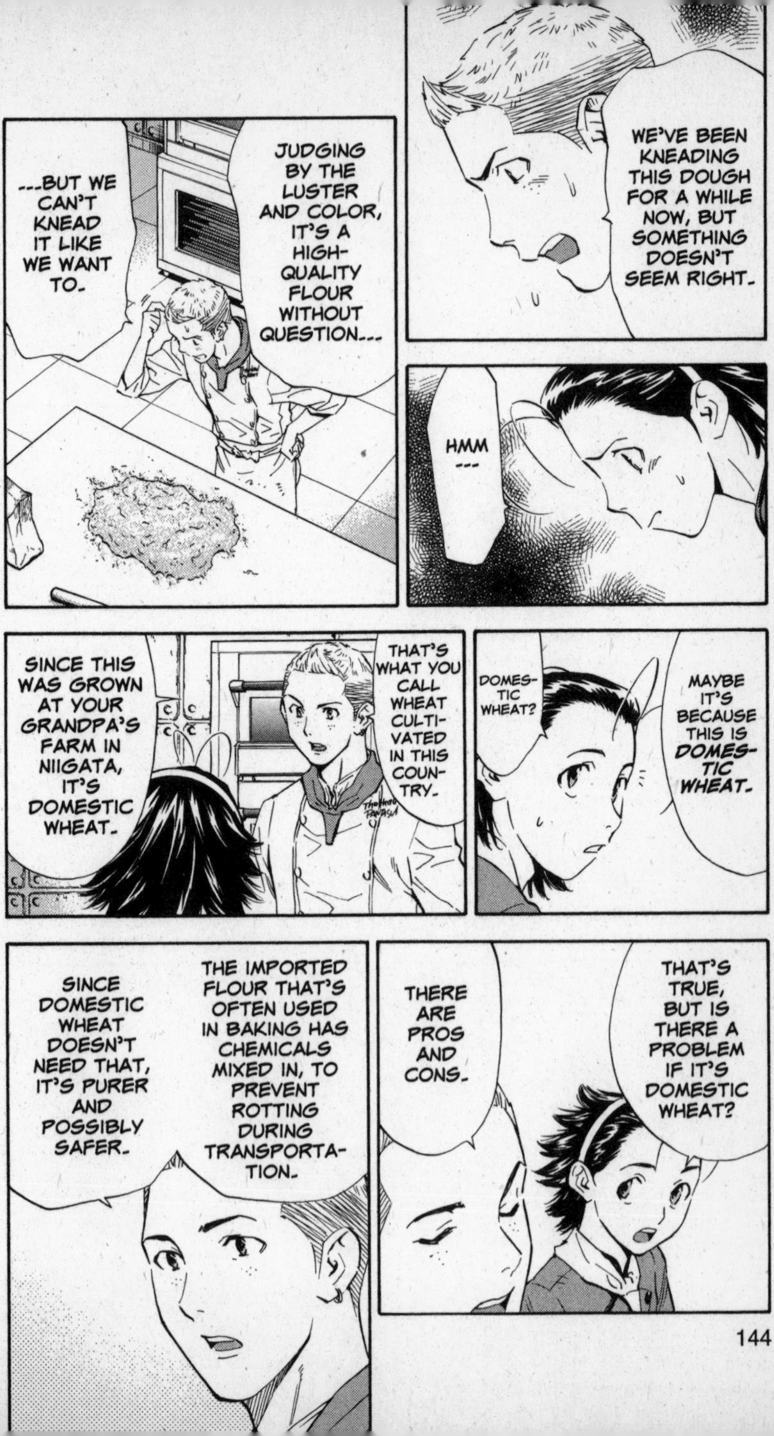
WE'VE BEEN KNEADING THIS DOUGH FOR A WHILE NOW, BUT SOMETHING DOESN'T SEEM RIGHT.
HMM...
JUDGING BY THE LUSTER AND COLOR, IT'S A HIGH-QUALITY FLOUR WITHOUT QUESTION...
...BUT WE CAN'T KNEAD IT LIKE WE WANT TO.
MAYBE IT'S BECAUSE THIS IS *DOMESTIC WHEAT*.
DOMESTIC WHEAT?
THAT'S WHAT YOU CALL WHEAT CULTIVATED IN THIS COUNTRY.
SINCE THIS WAS GROWN AT YOUR GRANDPA'S FARM IN NIIGATA, IT'S DOMESTIC WHEAT.
THAT'S TRUE, BUT IS THERE A PROBLEM IF IT'S DOMESTIC WHEAT?
THERE ARE PROS AND CONS.
THE IMPORTED FLOUR THAT'S OFTEN USED IN BAKING HAS CHEMICALS MIXED IN, TO PREVENT ROTTING DURING TRANSPORTATION.
SINCE DOMESTIC WHEAT DOESN'T NEED THAT, IT'S PURER AND POSSIBLY SAFER.

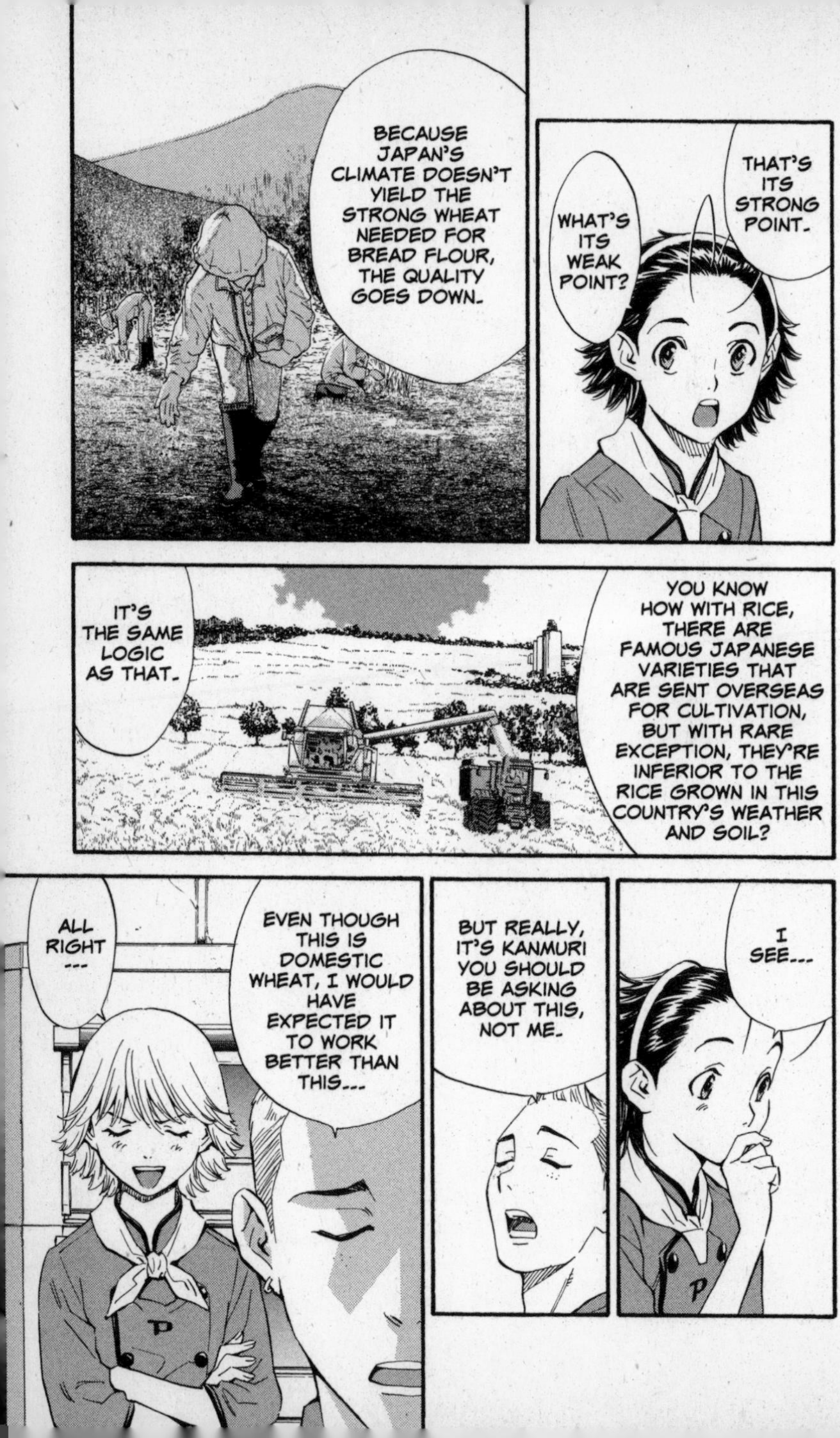
THAT'S ITS STRONG POINT.
WHAT'S ITS WEAK POINT?
BECAUSE JAPAN'S CLIMATE DOESN'T YIELD THE STRONG WHEAT NEEDED FOR BREAD FLOUR, THE QUALITY GOES DOWN.
YOU KNOW HOW WITH RICE, THERE ARE FAMOUS JAPANESE VARIETIES THAT ARE SENT OVERSEAS FOR CULTIVATION, BUT WITH RARE EXCEPTION, THEY'RE INFERIOR TO THE RICE GROWN IN THIS COUNTRY'S WEATHER AND SOIL?
IT'S THE SAME LOGIC AS THAT.
I SEE...
BUT REALLY, IT'S KANMURI YOU SHOULD BE ASKING ABOUT THIS, NOT ME.
EVEN THOUGH THIS IS DOMESTIC WHEAT, I WOULD HAVE EXPECTED IT TO WORK BETTER THAN THIS...
ALL RIGHT...

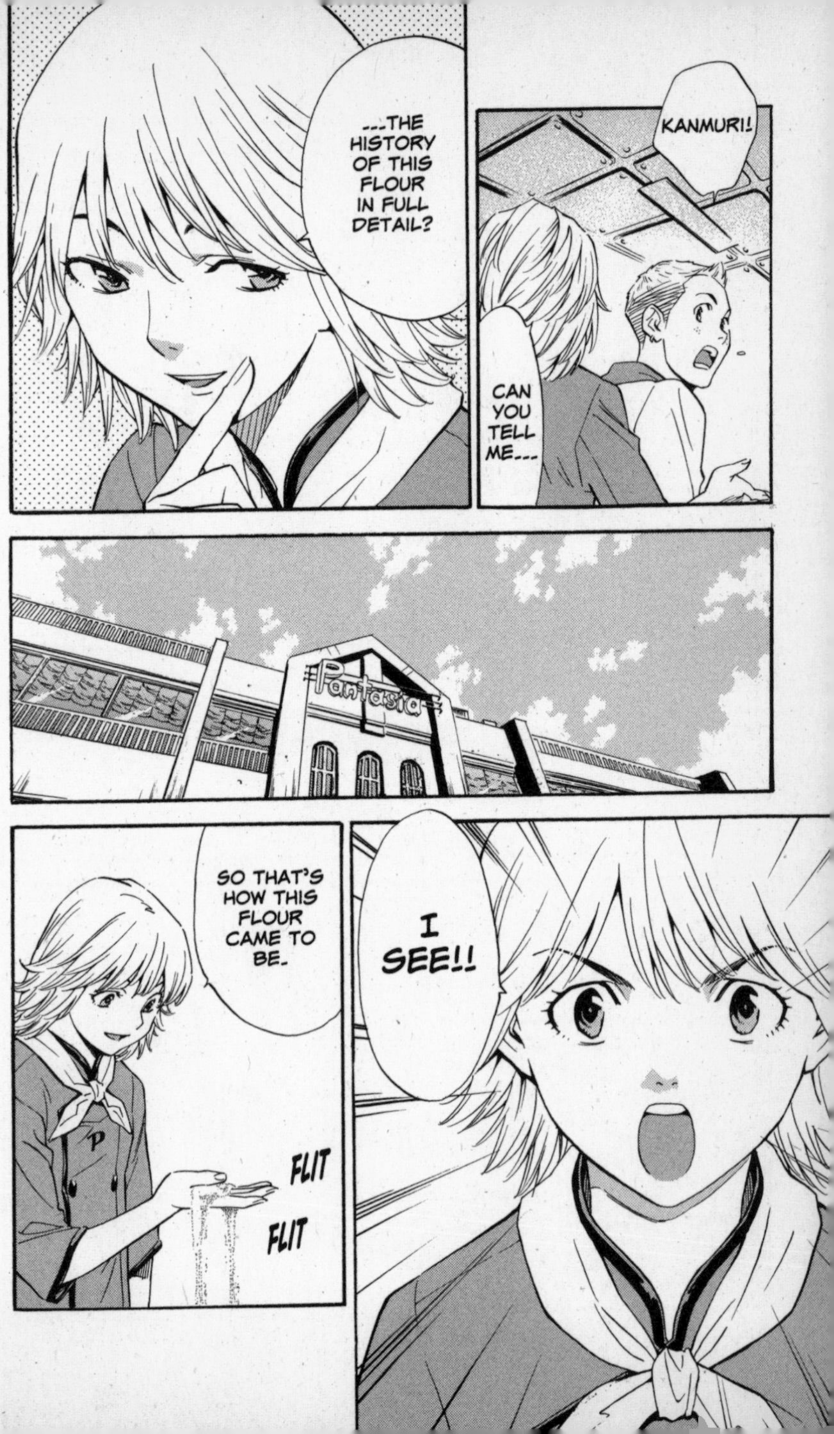
KANMURI!
CAN YOU TELL ME...
...THE HISTORY OF THIS FLOUR IN FULL DETAIL?
Pantasia
I SEE!!
SO THAT'S HOW THIS FLOUR CAME TO BE.
FLIT
FLIT

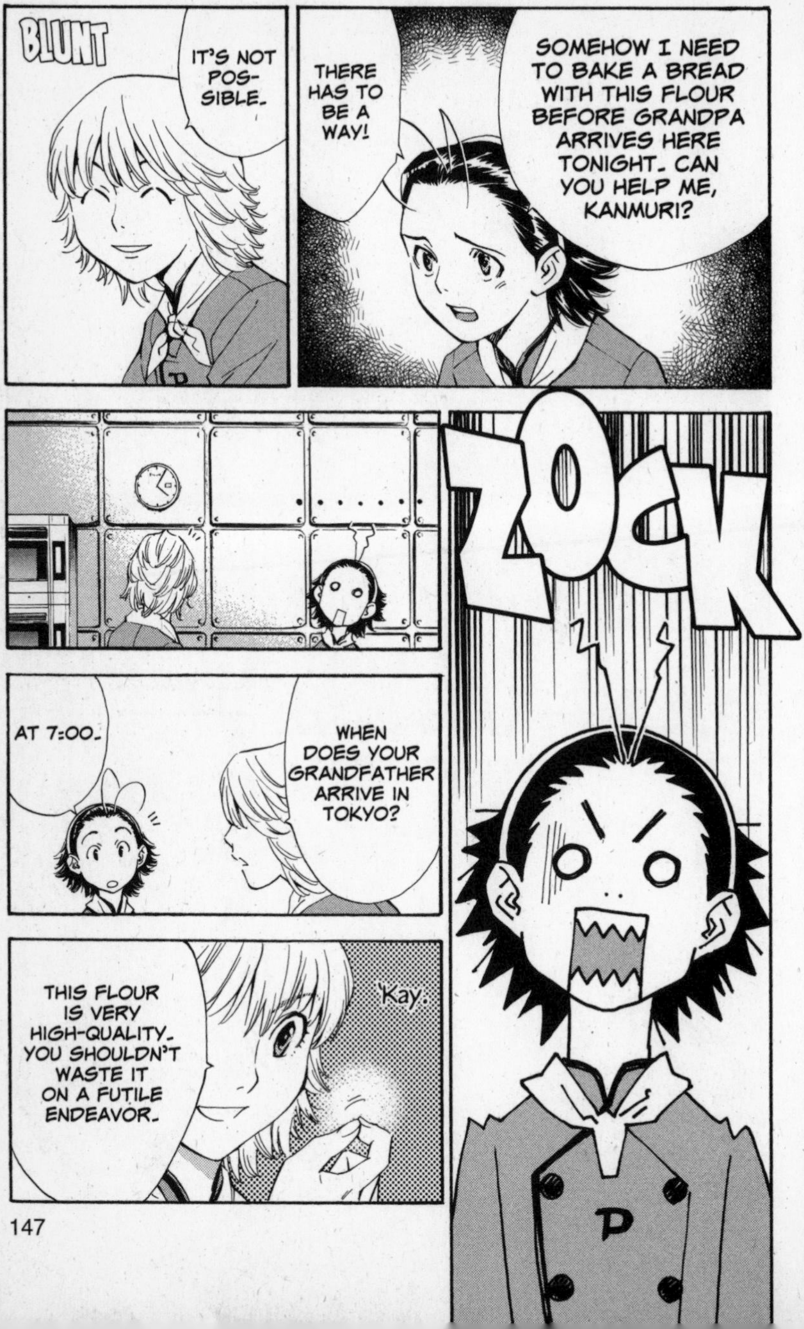
SOMEHOW I NEED TO BAKE A BREAD WITH THIS FLOUR BEFORE GRANDPA ARRIVES HERE TONIGHT. CAN YOU HELP ME, KANMURI?
THERE HAS TO BE A WAY!
BLUNT
IT'S NOT POS-SIBLE.
ZOCK
......
WHEN DOES YOUR GRANDFATHER ARRIVE IN TOKYO?
AT 7:00.
'Kay.
THIS FLOUR IS VERY HIGH-QUALITY. YOU SHOULDN'T WASTE IT ON A FUTILE ENDEAVOR.

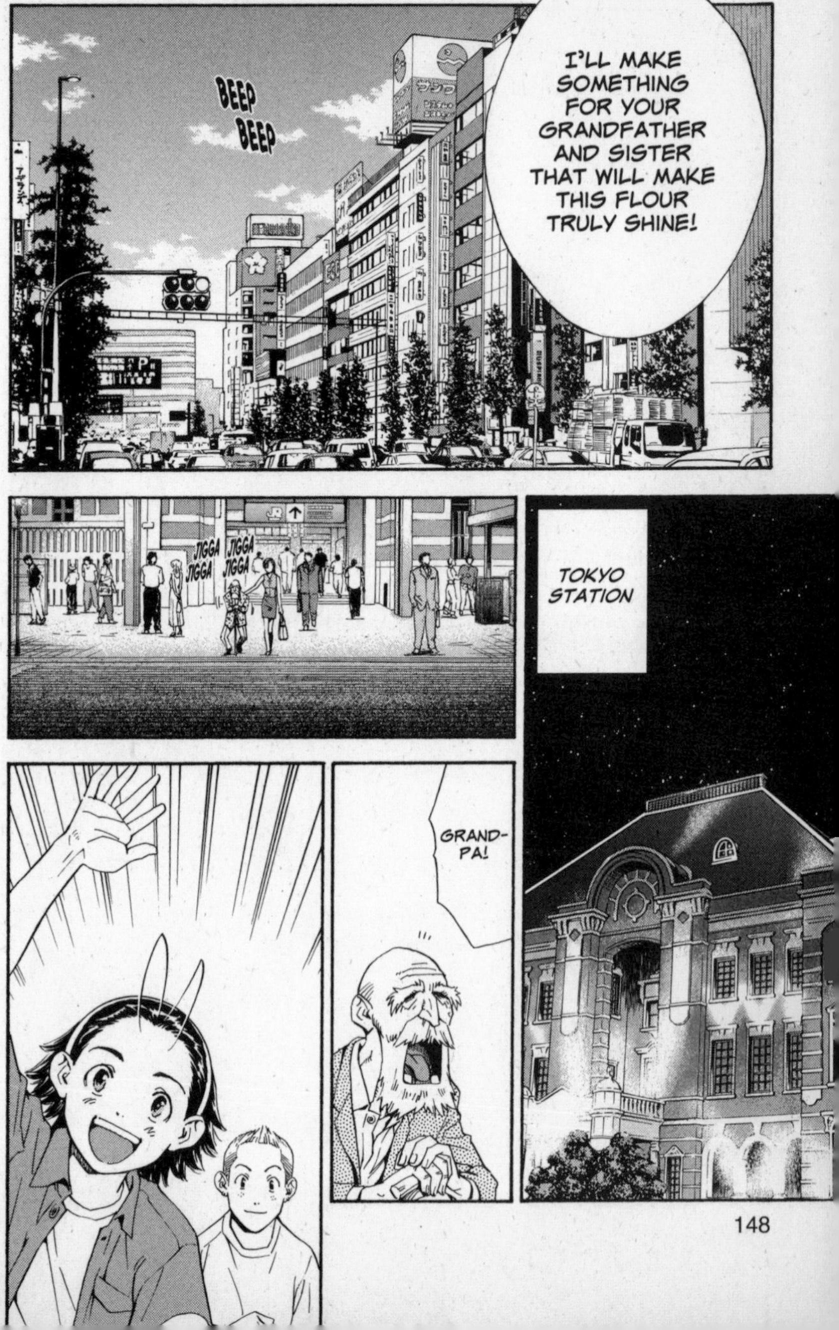
I'LL MAKE SOMETHING FOR YOUR GRANDFATHER AND SISTER THAT WILL MAKE THIS FLOUR TRULY SHINE!
BEEP BEEP
TOKYO STATION
JIGGA JIGGA
JIGGA JIGGA
GRAND-PA!

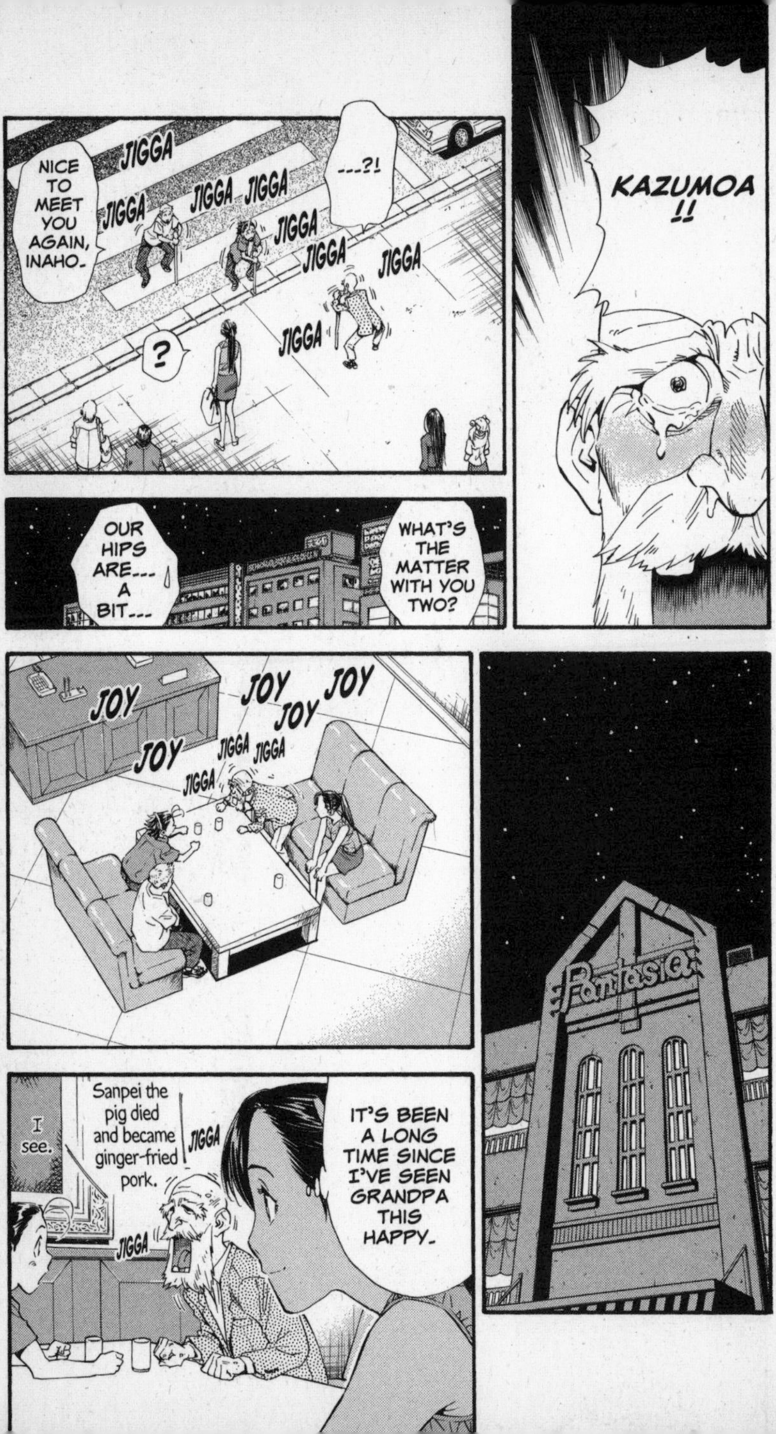
KAZUMOA !!
---?!
NICE TO MEET YOU AGAIN, INAHO.
JIGGA
JIGGA
JIGGA
JIGGA
JIGGA
JIGGA
JIGGA
JIGGA
?
WHAT'S THE MATTER WITH YOU TWO?
OUR HIPS ARE... A BIT...
Fantasia
JOY
JOY
JOY
JOY
JOY
JIGGA
JIGGA
JIGGA
IT'S BEEN A LONG TIME SINCE I'VE SEEN GRANDPA THIS HAPPY.
JIGGA
Sanpei the pig died and became ginger-fried pork.
JIGGA
I see.

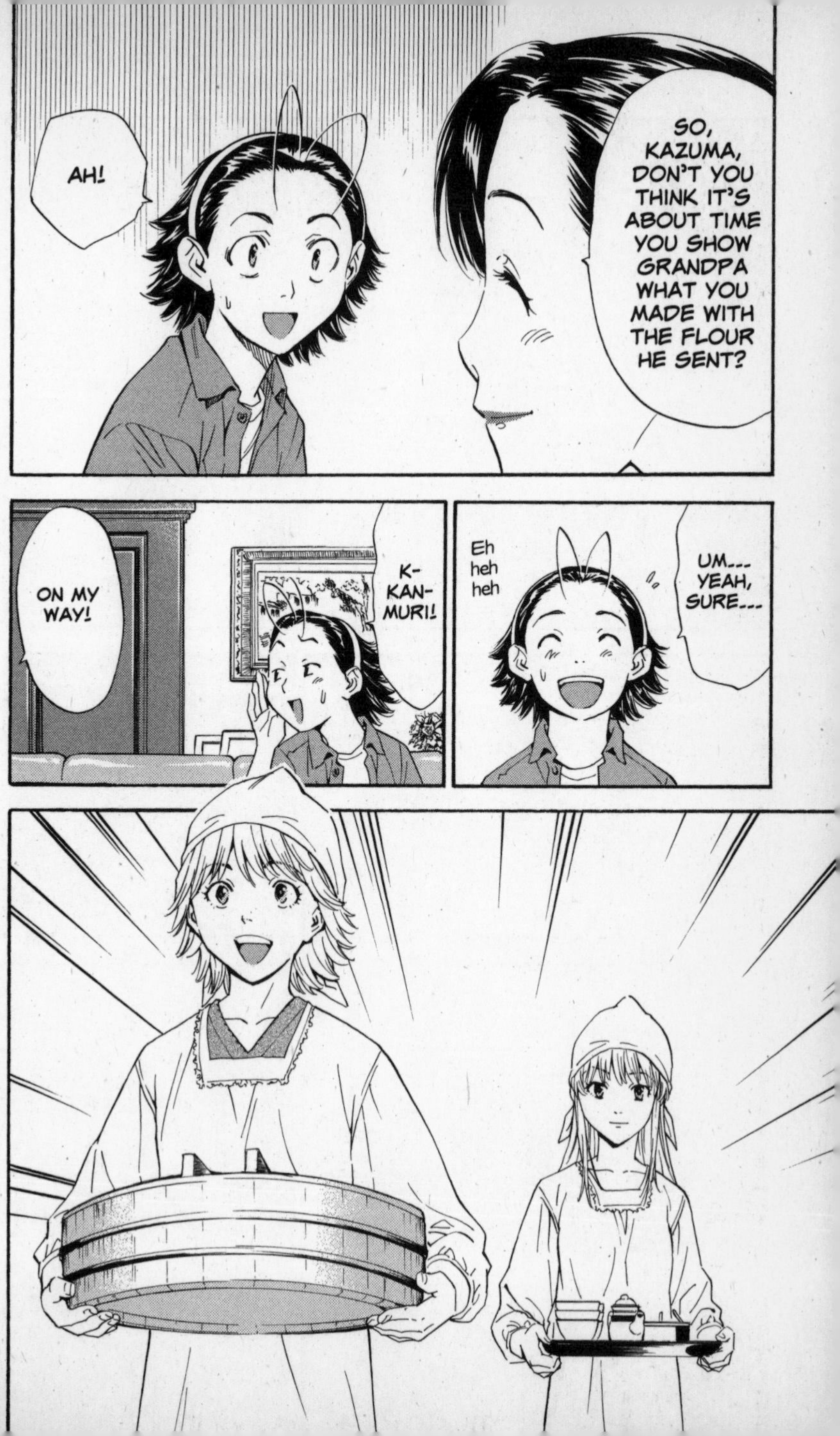
SO, KAZUMA, DON'T YOU THINK IT'S ABOUT TIME YOU SHOW GRANDPA WHAT YOU MADE WITH THE FLOUR HE SENT?
AH!
UM... YEAH, SURE...
Eh heh heh
K-KAN-MURI!
ON MY WAY!

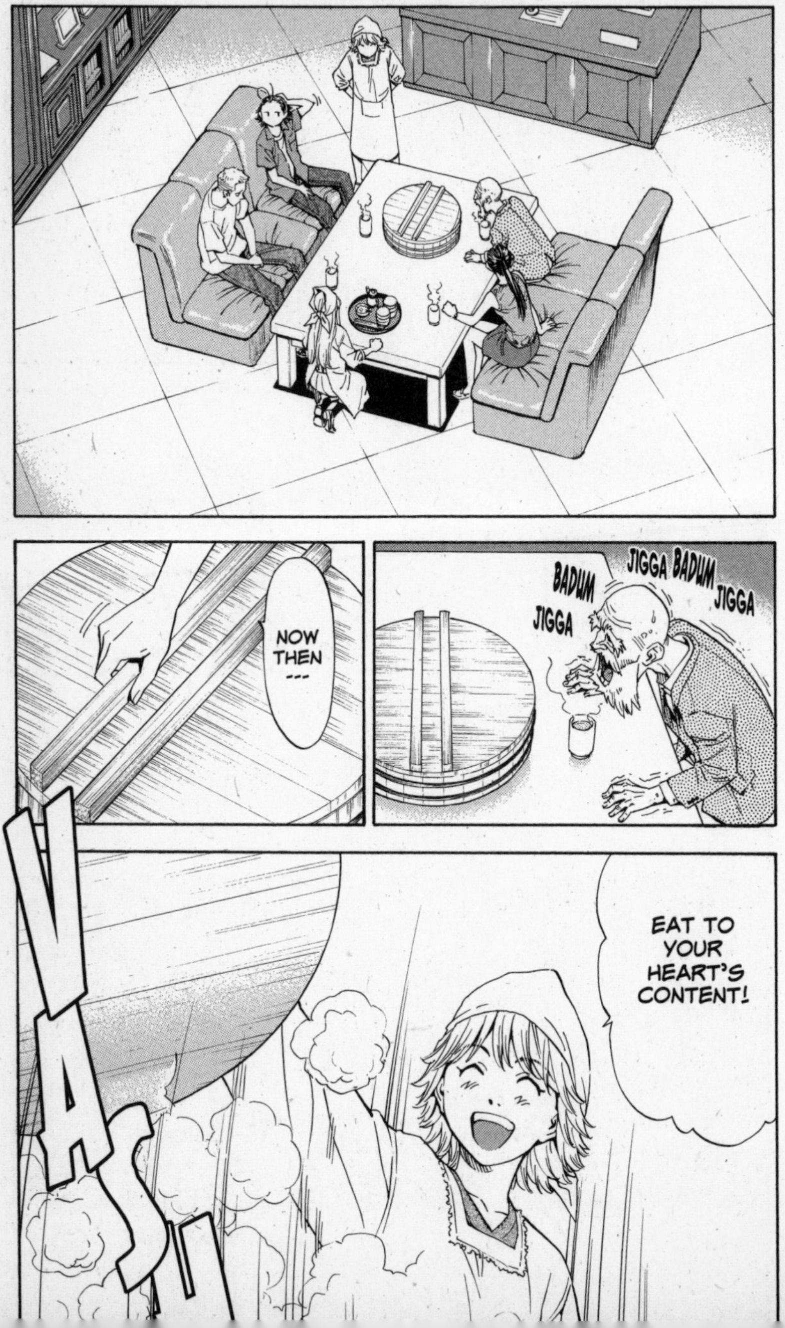
JIGGA BADUM JIGGA
BADUM JIGGA
NOW THEN ---
EAT TO YOUR HEART'S CONTENT!
VAS

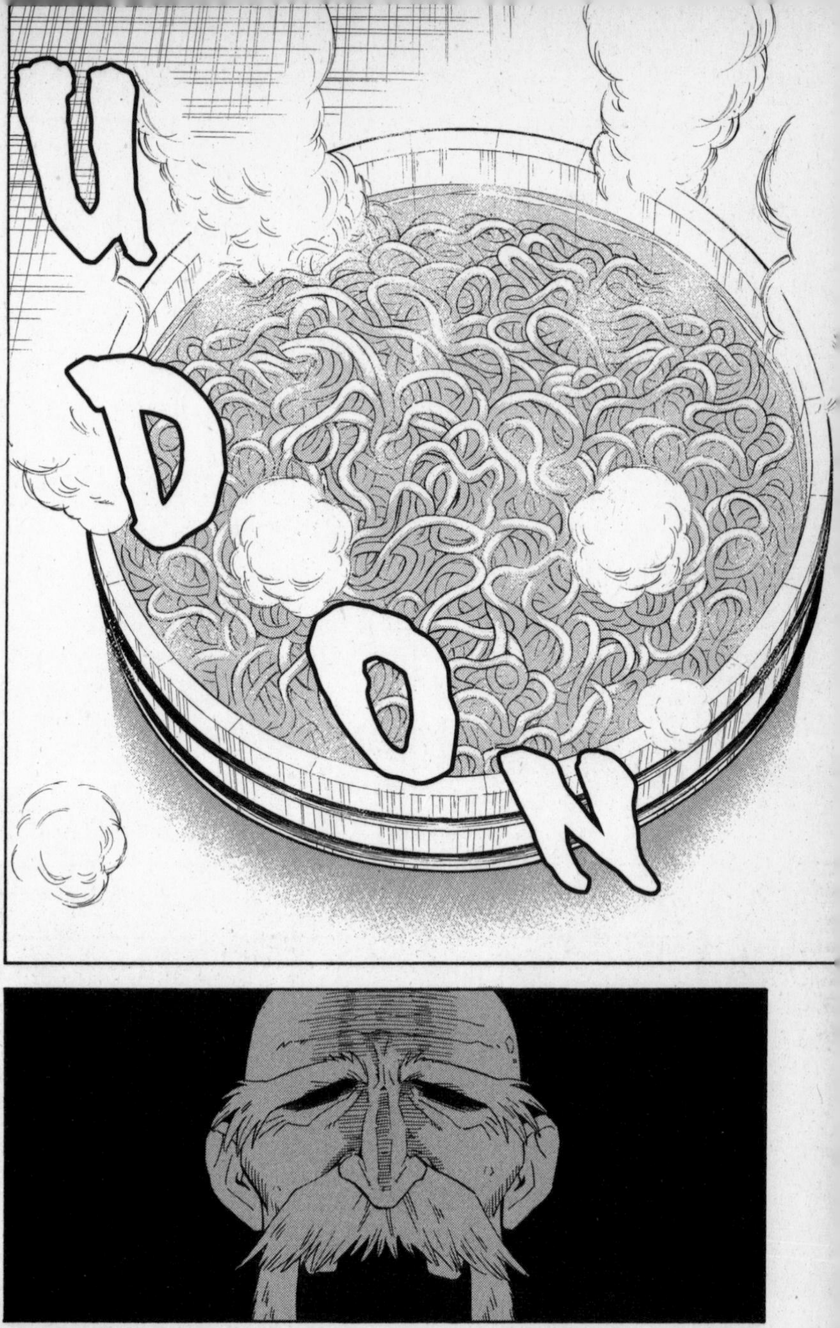
UDON

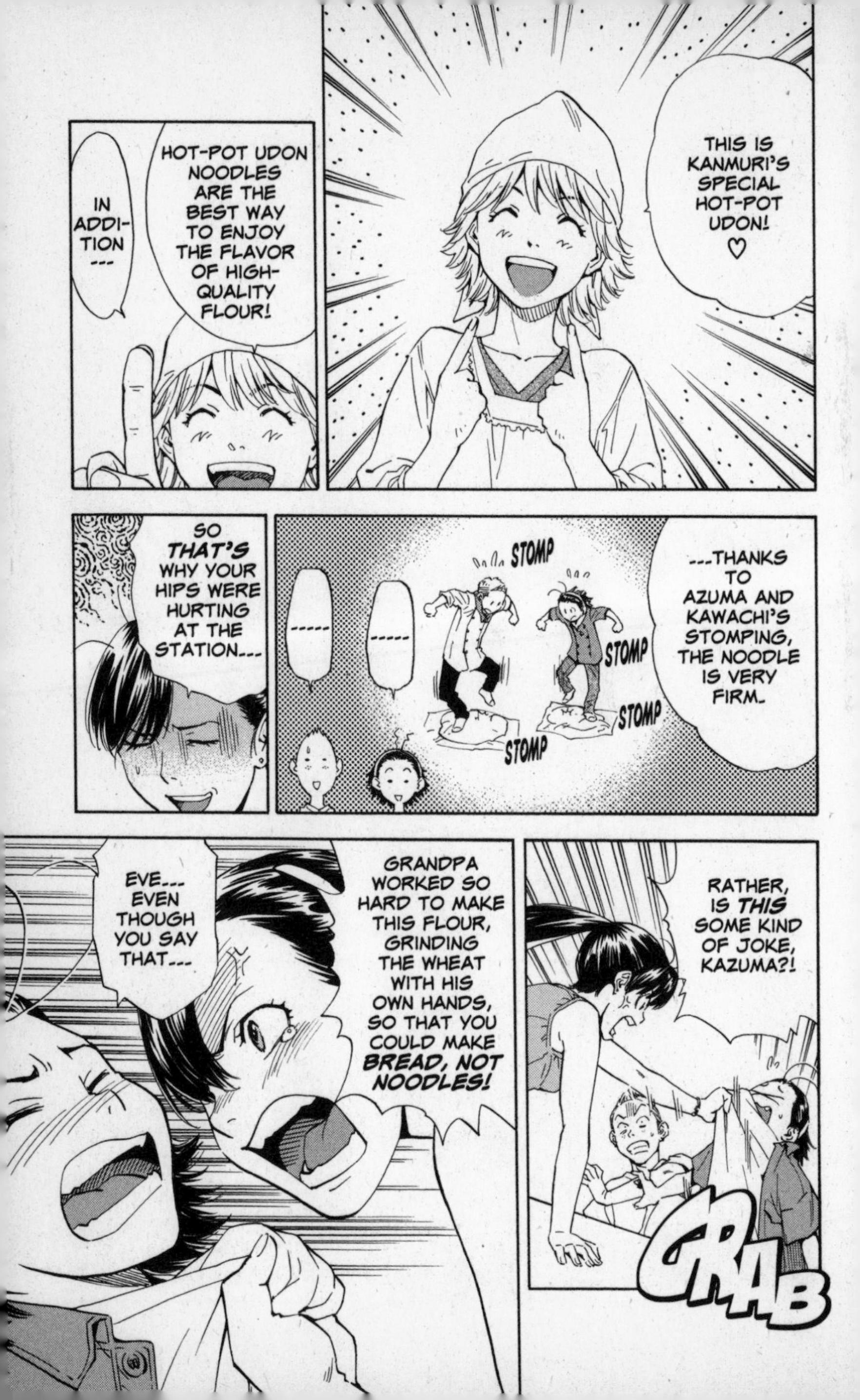
THIS IS KANMURI'S SPECIAL HOT-POT UDON! ♡
HOT-POT UDON NOODLES ARE THE BEST WAY TO ENJOY THE FLAVOR OF HIGH-QUALITY FLOUR!
IN ADDITION---
---THANKS TO AZUMA AND KAWACHI'S STOMPING, THE NOODLE IS VERY FIRM.
STOMP
STOMP
STOMP
STOMP

SO *THAT'S* WHY YOUR HIPS WERE HURTING AT THE STATION---
RATHER, IS *THIS* SOME KIND OF JOKE, KAZUMA?!
GRAB
GRANDPA WORKED SO HARD TO MAKE THIS FLOUR, GRINDING THE WHEAT WITH HIS OWN HANDS, SO THAT YOU COULD MAKE ***BREAD, NOT NOODLES!***
EVE--- EVEN THOUGH YOU SAY THAT---

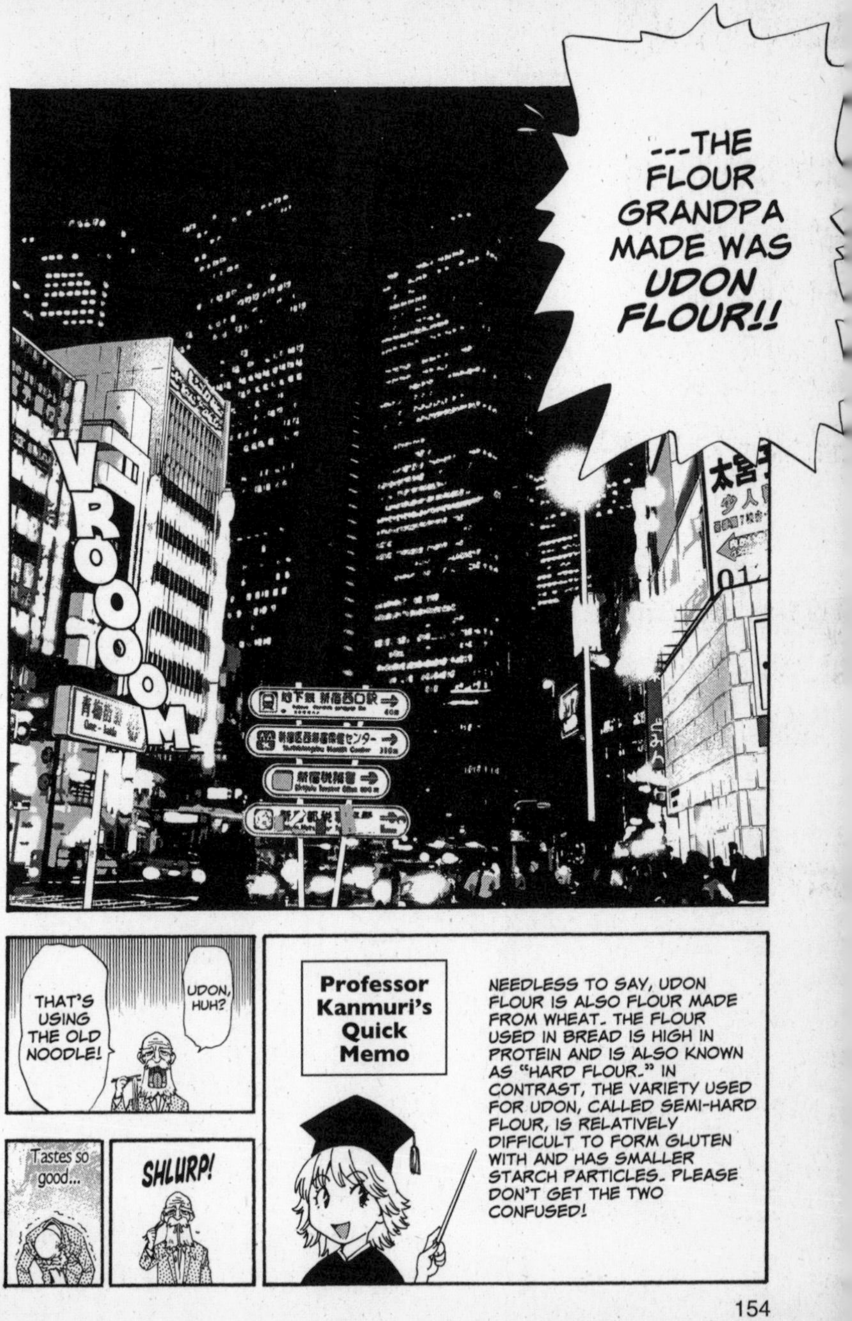
---THE FLOUR GRANDPA MADE WAS UDON FLOUR!!
VROOOOM
Professor Kanmuri's Quick Memo
NEEDLESS TO SAY, UDON FLOUR IS ALSO FLOUR MADE FROM WHEAT. THE FLOUR USED IN BREAD IS HIGH IN PROTEIN AND IS ALSO KNOWN AS "HARD FLOUR." IN CONTRAST, THE VARIETY USED FOR UDON, CALLED SEMI-HARD FLOUR, IS RELATIVELY DIFFICULT TO FORM GLUTEN WITH AND HAS SMALLER STARCH PARTICLES. PLEASE DON'T GET THE TWO CONFUSED!
UDON, HUH?
THAT'S USING THE OLD NOODLE!
SHLURP!
Tastes so good...

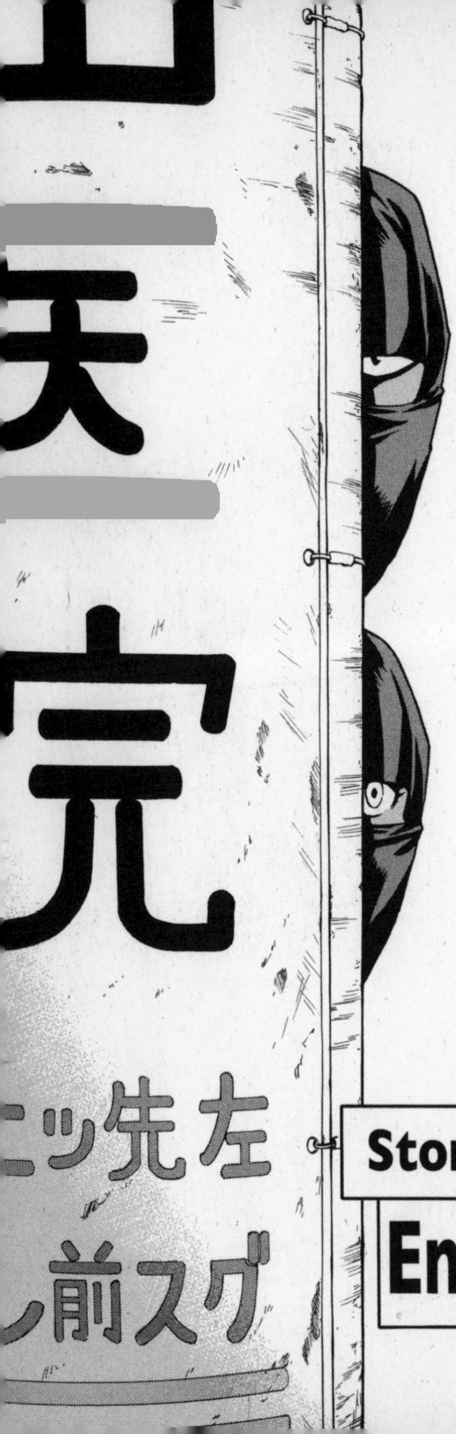

Story 142:

Enter the Ninja!

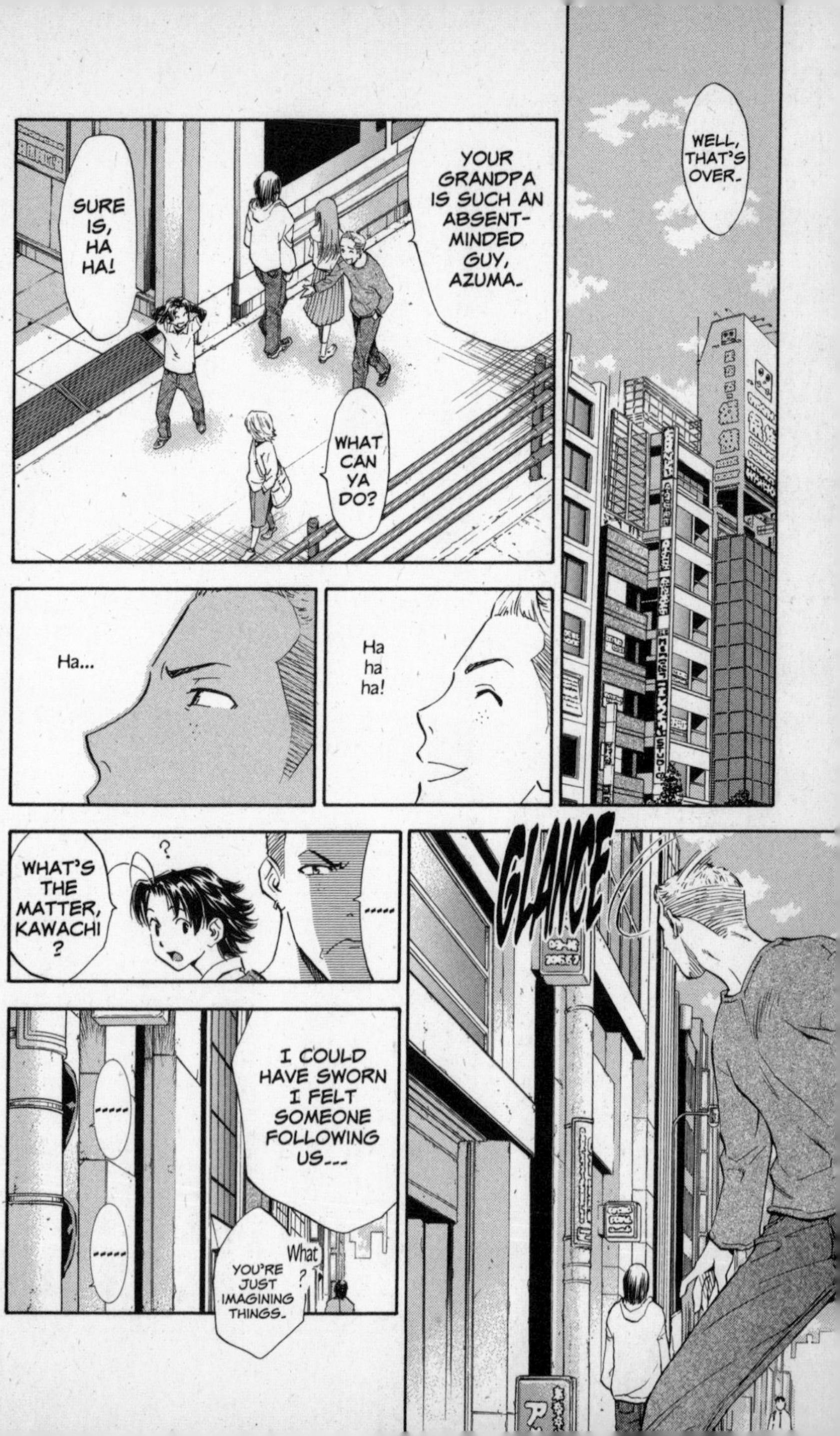
WELL, THAT'S OVER.
YOUR GRANDPA IS SUCH AN ABSENT-MINDED GUY, AZUMA.
SURE IS, HA HA!
WHAT CAN YA DO?
Ha ha ha!
Ha...
GLANCE
.....
?
WHAT'S THE MATTER, KAWACHI?
I COULD HAVE SWORN I FELT SOMEONE FOLLOWING US...
.....
.....
What?
YOU'RE JUST IMAGINING THINGS.

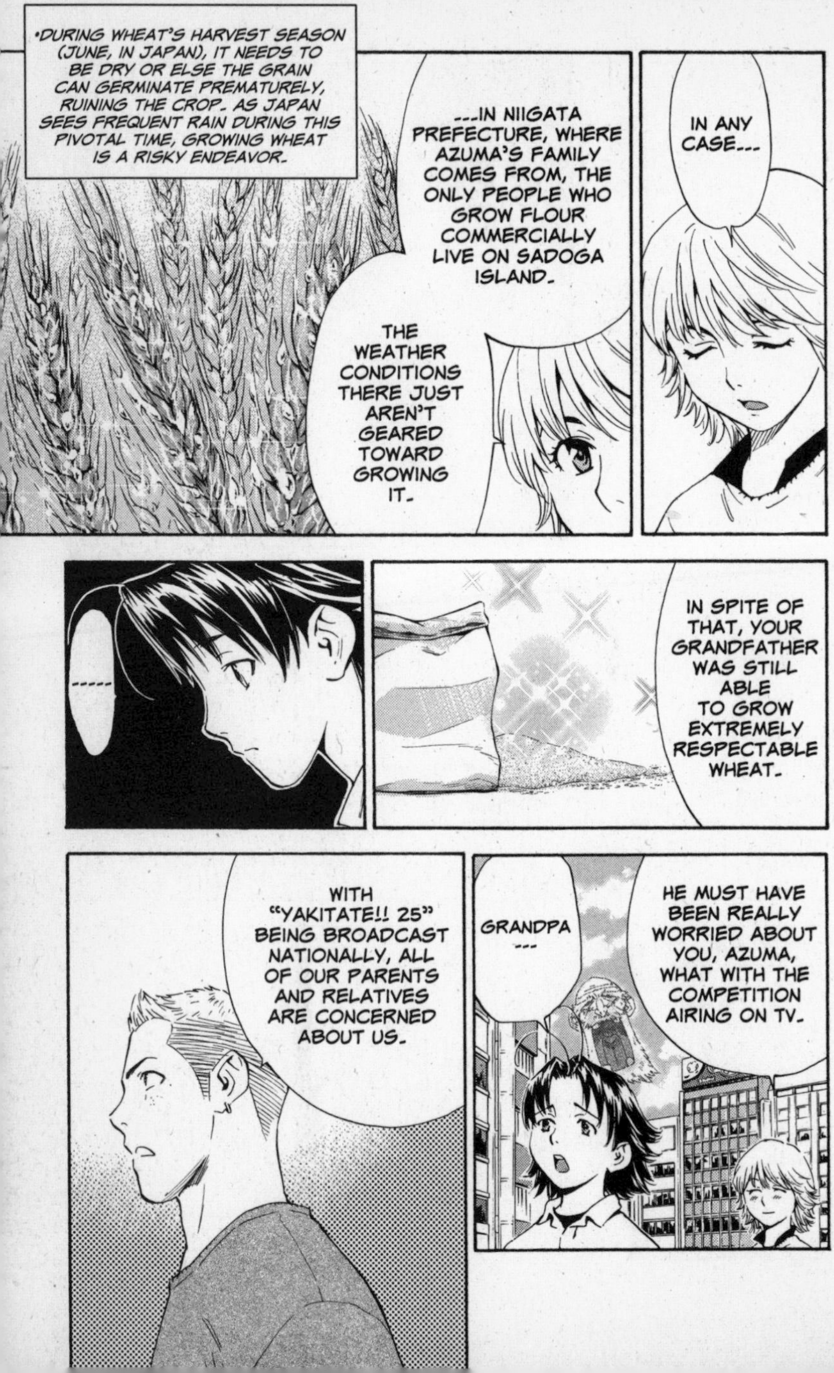
IN ANY CASE...
...IN NIIGATA PREFECTURE, WHERE AZUMA'S FAMILY COMES FROM, THE ONLY PEOPLE WHO GROW FLOUR COMMERCIALLY LIVE ON SADOGA ISLAND.
THE WEATHER CONDITIONS THERE JUST AREN'T GEARED TOWARD GROWING IT.
•DURING WHEAT'S HARVEST SEASON (JUNE, IN JAPAN), IT NEEDS TO BE DRY OR ELSE THE GRAIN CAN GERMINATE PREMATURELY, RUINING THE CROP. AS JAPAN SEES FREQUENT RAIN DURING THIS PIVOTAL TIME, GROWING WHEAT IS A RISKY ENDEAVOR.
IN SPITE OF THAT, YOUR GRANDFATHER WAS STILL ABLE TO GROW EXTREMELY RESPECTABLE WHEAT.
.....
HE MUST HAVE BEEN REALLY WORRIED ABOUT YOU, AZUMA, WHAT WITH THE COMPETITION AIRING ON TV.
GRANDPA...
WITH "YAKITATE!! 25" BEING BROADCAST NATIONALLY, ALL OF OUR PARENTS AND RELATIVES ARE CONCERNED ABOUT US.

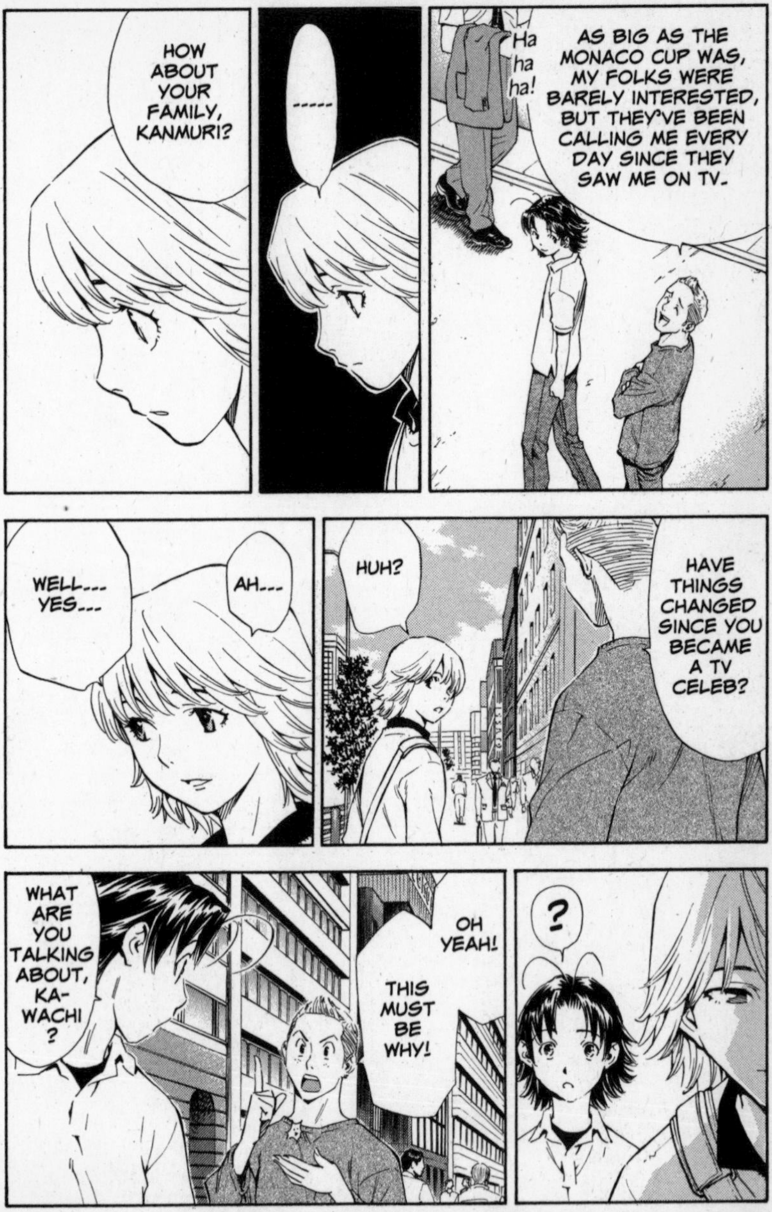
AS BIG AS THE MONACO CUP WAS, MY FOLKS WERE BARELY INTERESTED, BUT THEY'VE BEEN CALLING ME EVERY DAY SINCE THEY SAW ME ON TV...
Ha ha ha!

HOW ABOUT YOUR FAMILY, KANMURI?
HAVE THINGS CHANGED SINCE YOU BECAME A TV CELEB?
HUH?
AH...
WELL... YES...
?
OH YEAH!
THIS MUST BE WHY!
WHAT ARE YOU TALKING ABOUT, KA-WACHI?

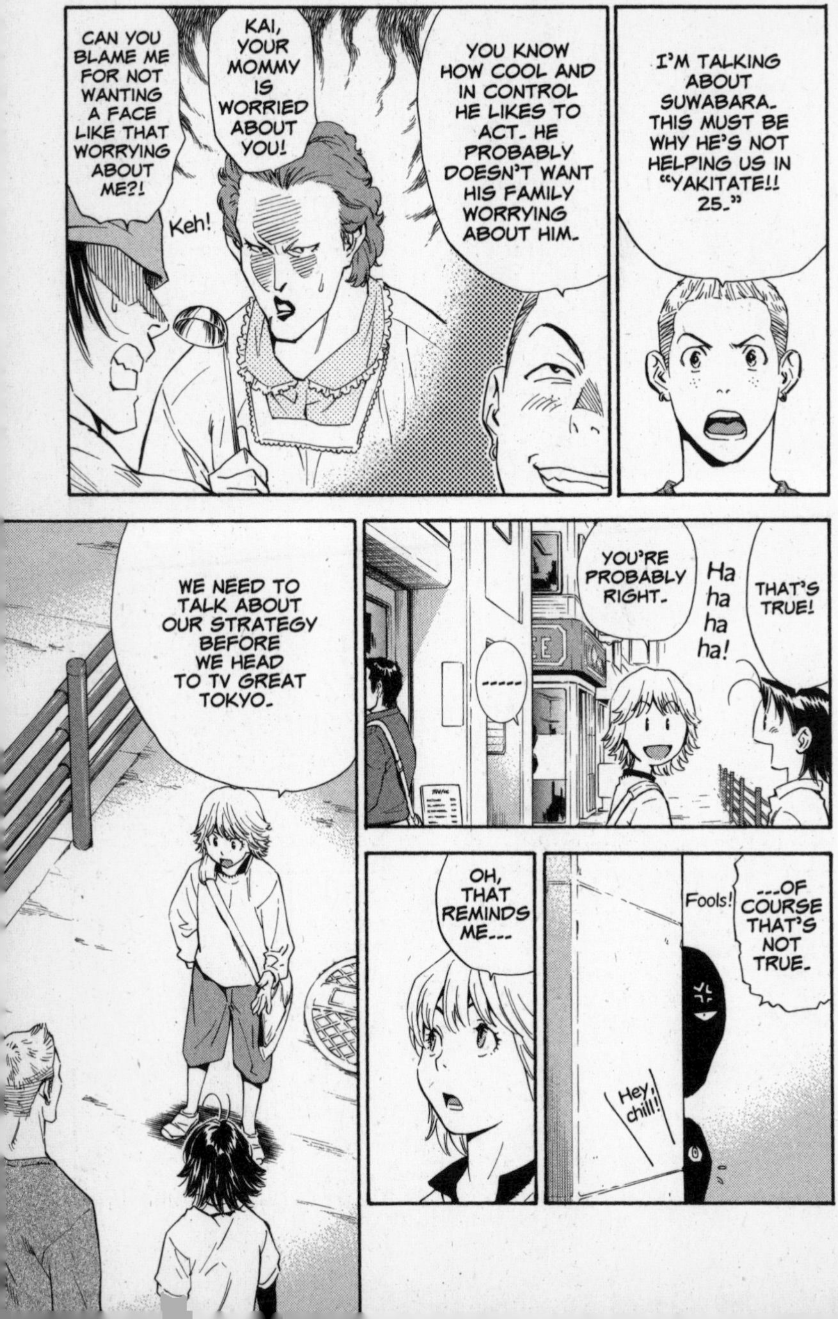

I'M TALKING ABOUT SUWABARA. THIS MUST BE WHY HE'S NOT HELPING US IN "YAKITATE!! 25."
YOU KNOW HOW COOL AND IN CONTROL HE LIKES TO ACT. HE PROBABLY DOESN'T WANT HIS FAMILY WORRYING ABOUT HIM.
KAI, YOUR MOMMY IS WORRIED ABOUT YOU!
CAN YOU BLAME ME FOR NOT WANTING A FACE LIKE THAT WORRYING ABOUT ME?!
Keh!
THAT'S TRUE!
Ha ha ha ha!
YOU'RE PROBABLY RIGHT.

...OF COURSE THAT'S NOT TRUE.
Fools!
Hey, chill!
OH, THAT REMINDS ME...
WE NEED TO TALK ABOUT OUR STRATEGY BEFORE WE HEAD TO TV GREAT TOKYO.

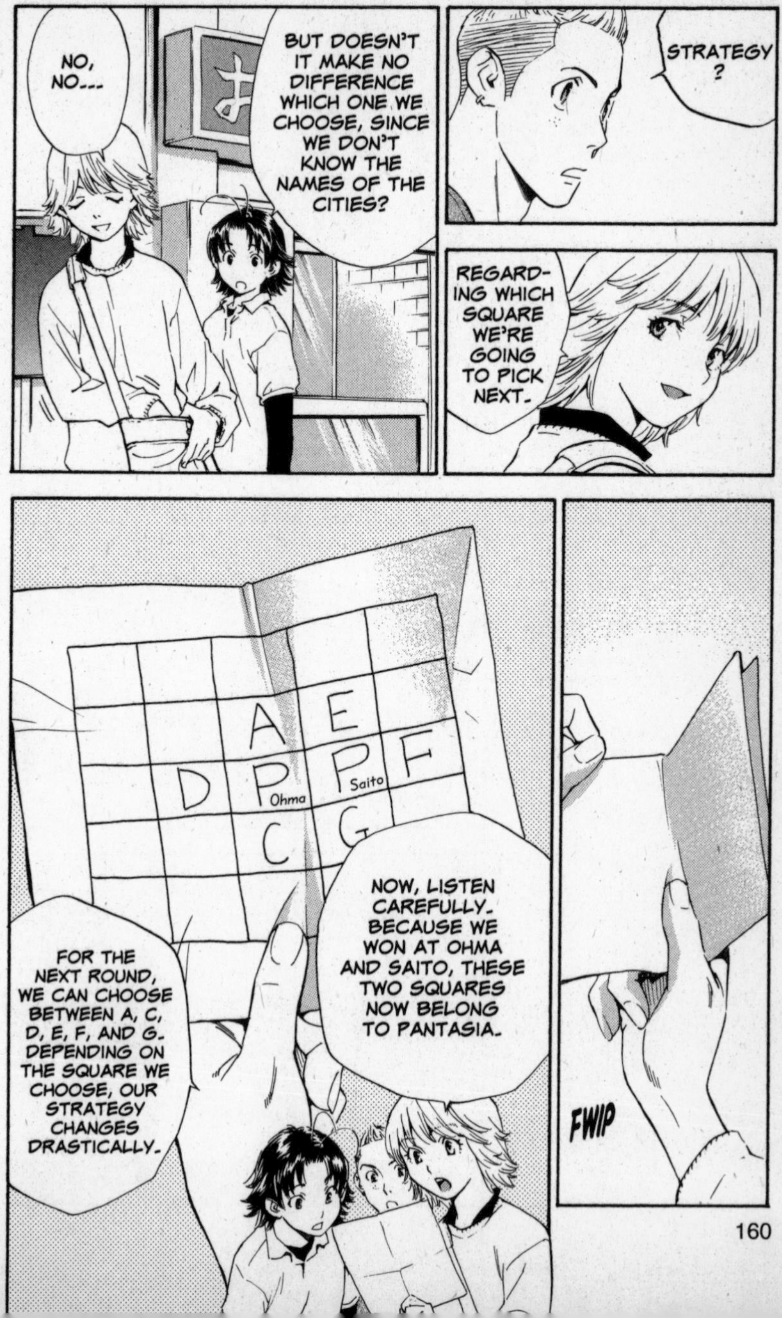
STRATEGY?
REGARDING WHICH SQUARE WE'RE GOING TO PICK NEXT.
BUT DOESN'T IT MAKE NO DIFFERENCE WHICH ONE WE CHOOSE, SINCE WE DON'T KNOW THE NAMES OF THE CITIES?
NO, NO...
FWIP
A E
D P P F
Ohma Saito
C G
NOW, LISTEN CAREFULLY. BECAUSE WE WON AT OHMA AND SAITO, THESE TWO SQUARES NOW BELONG TO PANTASIA.
FOR THE NEXT ROUND, WE CAN CHOOSE BETWEEN A, C, D, E, F, AND G. DEPENDING ON THE SQUARE WE CHOOSE, OUR STRATEGY CHANGES DRASTICALLY.

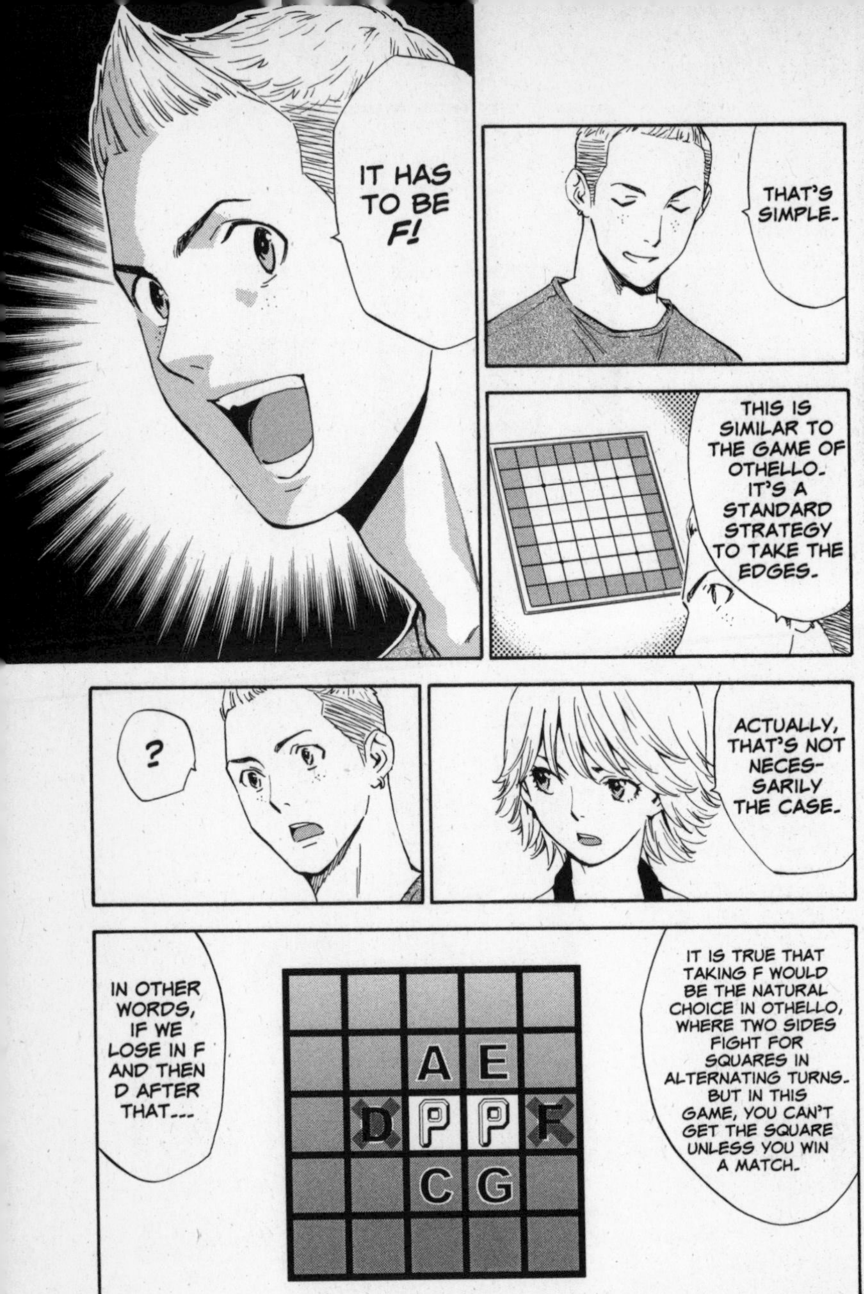
THAT'S SIMPLE.
THIS IS SIMILAR TO THE GAME OF OTHELLO. IT'S A STANDARD STRATEGY TO TAKE THE EDGES.
IT HAS TO BE *F!*
ACTUALLY, THAT'S NOT NECES-SARILY THE CASE.
?
IT IS TRUE THAT TAKING F WOULD BE THE NATURAL CHOICE IN OTHELLO, WHERE TWO SIDES FIGHT FOR SQUARES IN ALTERNATING TURNS. BUT IN THIS GAME, YOU CAN'T GET THE SQUARE UNLESS YOU WIN A MATCH.
A E
D P P F
C G
IN OTHER WORDS, IF WE LOSE IN F AND THEN D AFTER THAT...

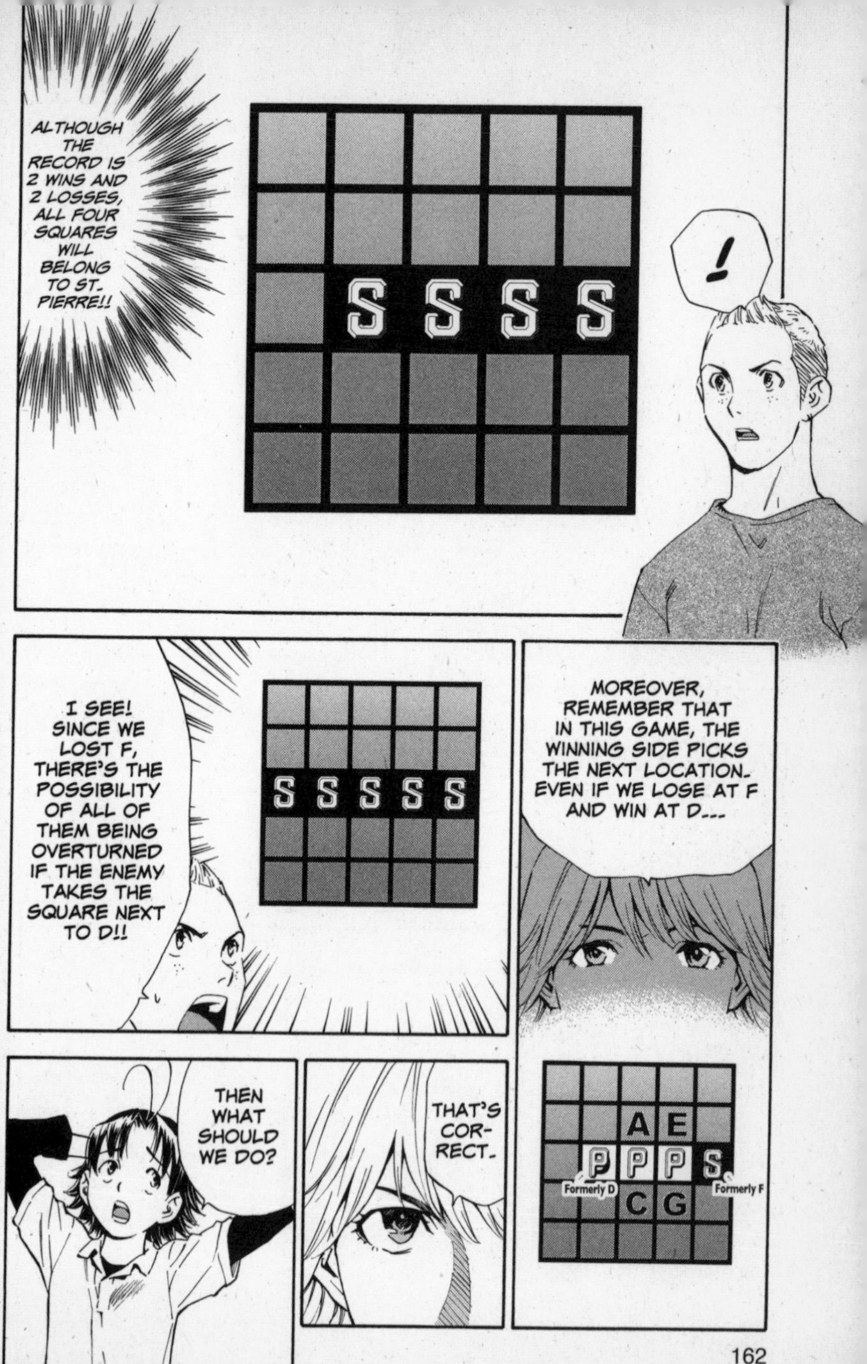
!
ALTHOUGH THE RECORD IS 2 WINS AND 2 LOSSES, ALL FOUR SQUARES WILL BELONG TO ST. PIERRE!!
S S S S
MOREOVER, REMEMBER THAT IN THIS GAME, THE WINNING SIDE PICKS THE NEXT LOCATION. EVEN IF WE LOSE AT F AND WIN AT D...
A E
P P P S
Formerly D
Formerly F
C G
I SEE! SINCE WE LOST F, THERE'S THE POSSIBILITY OF ALL OF THEM BEING OVERTURNED IF THE ENEMY TAKES THE SQUARE NEXT TO D!!
S S S S S
THAT'S CORRECT.
THEN WHAT SHOULD WE DO?

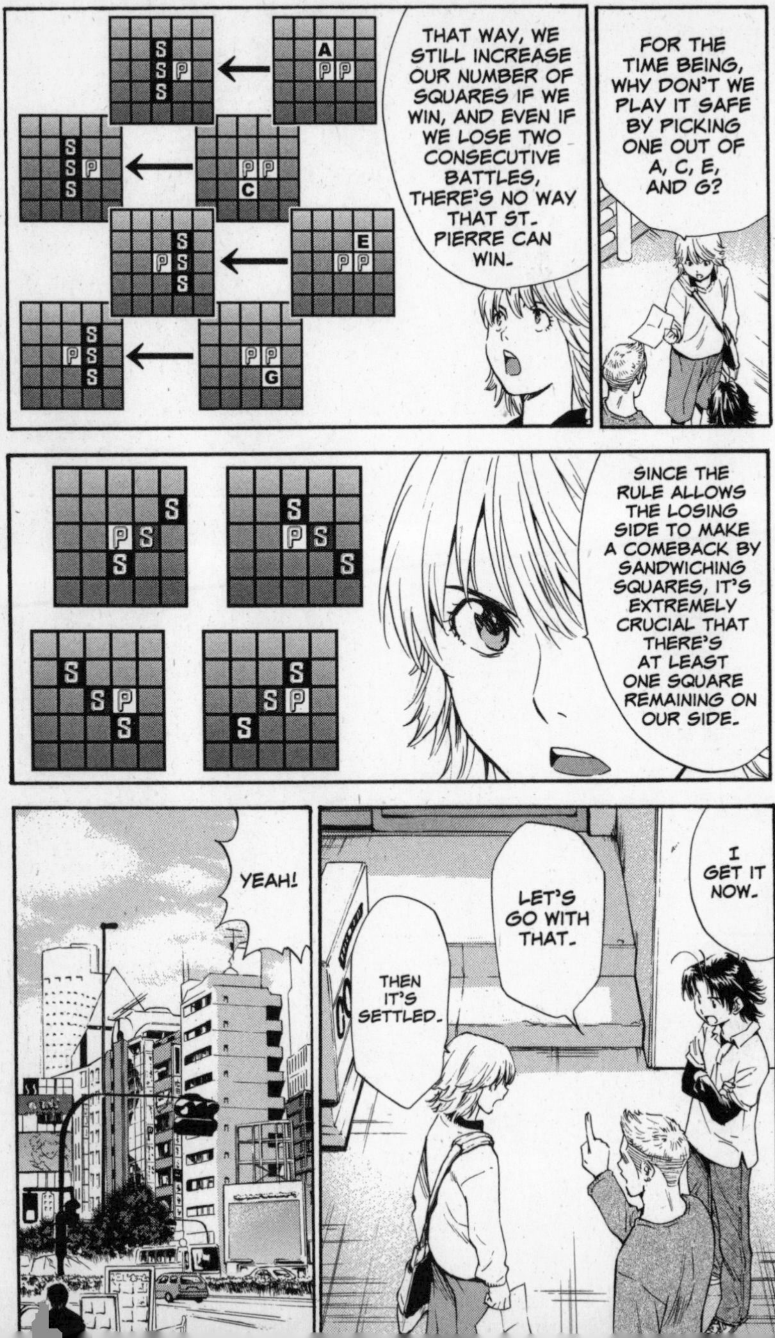
FOR THE TIME BEING, WHY DON'T WE PLAY IT SAFE BY PICKING ONE OUT OF A, C, E, AND G?
THAT WAY, WE STILL INCREASE OUR NUMBER OF SQUARES IF WE WIN, AND EVEN IF WE LOSE TWO CONSECUTIVE BATTLES, THERE'S NO WAY THAT ST. PIERRE CAN WIN.
SINCE THE RULE ALLOWS THE LOSING SIDE TO MAKE A COMEBACK BY SANDWICHING SQUARES, IT'S EXTREMELY CRUCIAL THAT THERE'S AT LEAST ONE SQUARE REMAINING ON OUR SIDE.
I GET IT NOW.
LET'S GO WITH THAT.
THEN IT'S SETTLED.
YEAH!

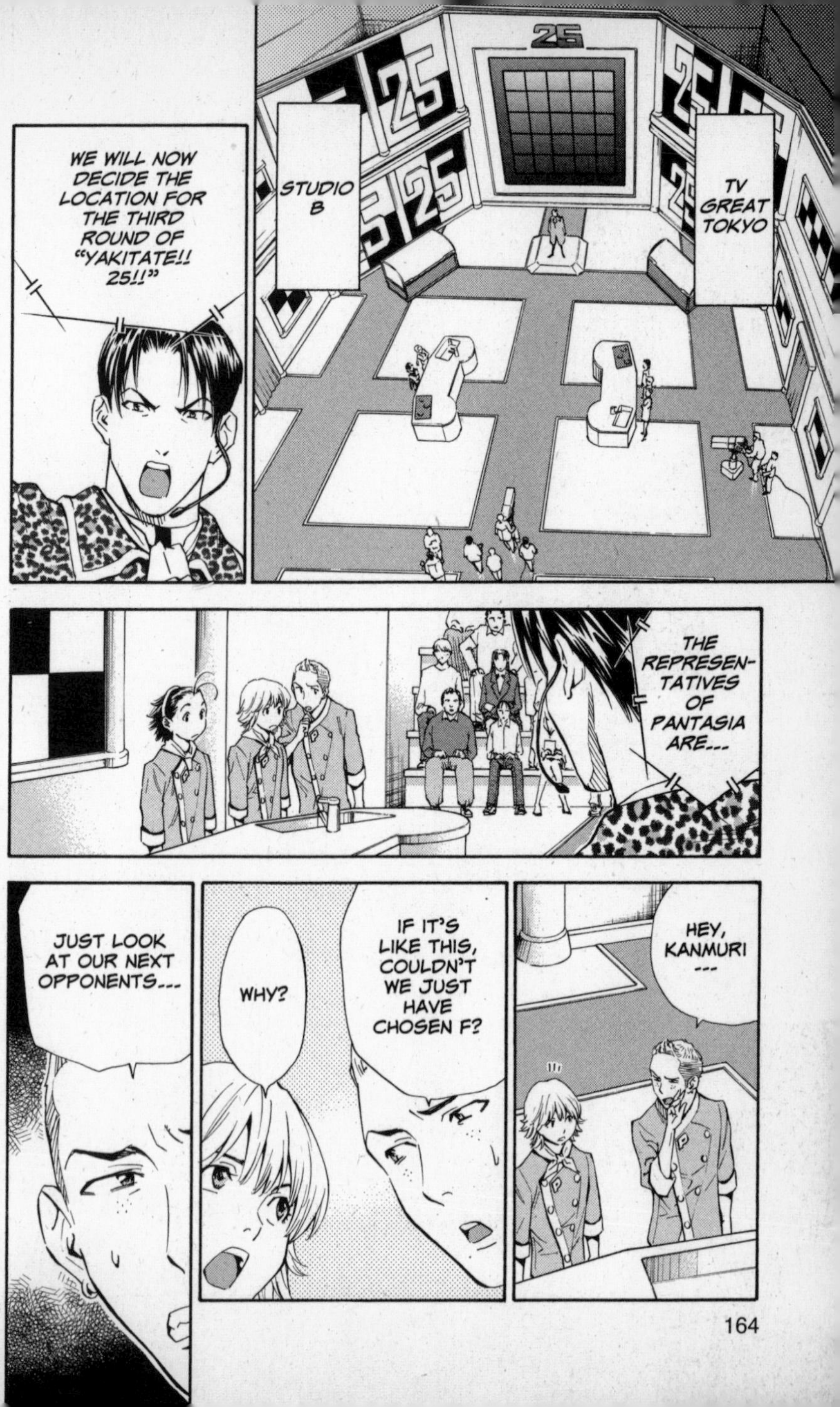

TV GREAT TOKYO
STUDIO B
WE WILL NOW DECIDE THE LOCATION FOR THE THIRD ROUND OF "YAKITATE!! 25!!"
THE REPRESEN-TATIVES OF PANTASIA ARE---
HEY, KANMURI ---
IF IT'S LIKE THIS, COULDN'T WE JUST HAVE CHOSEN F?
WHY?
JUST LOOK AT OUR NEXT OPPONENTS---

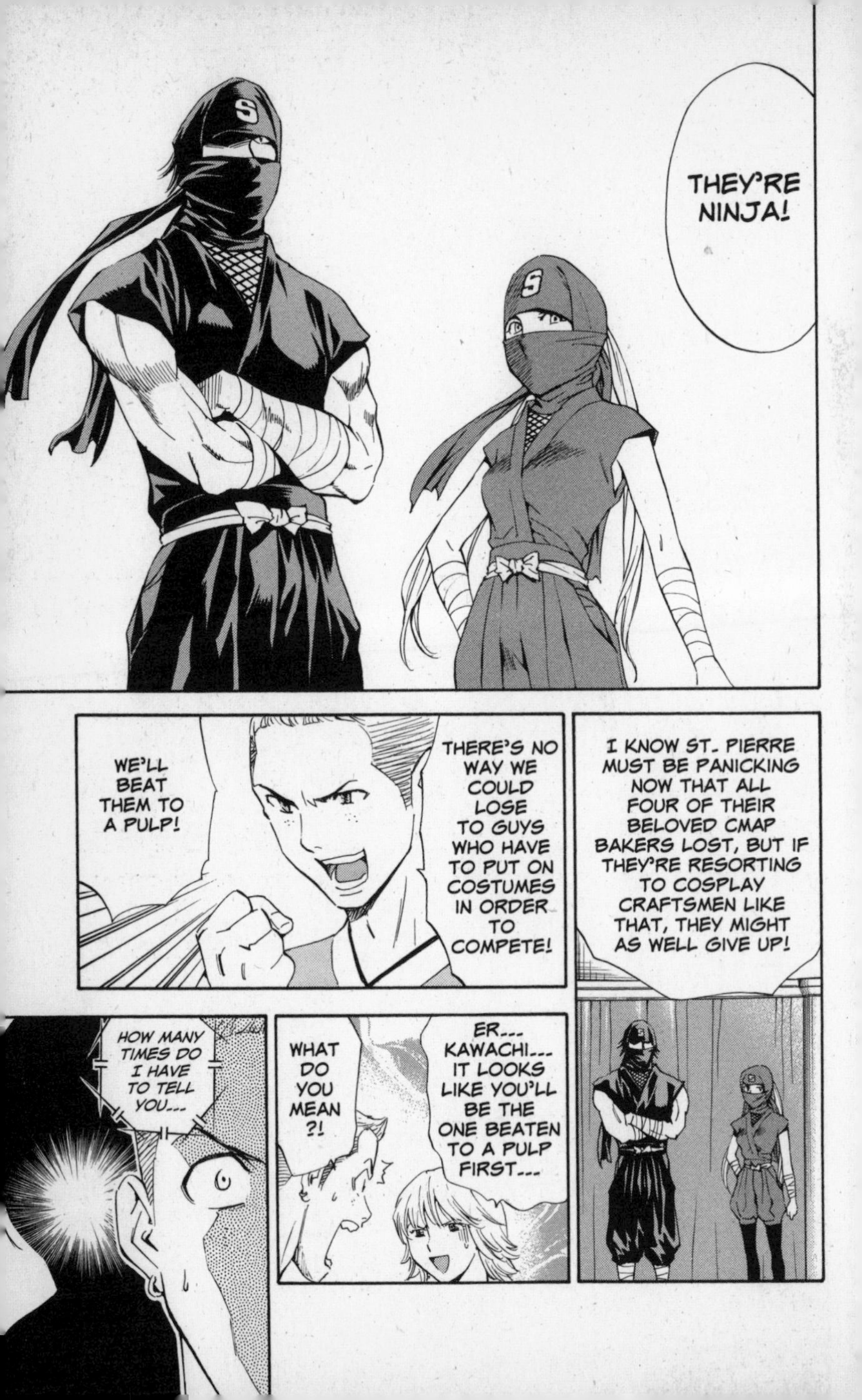
THEY'RE NINJA!
I KNOW ST. PIERRE MUST BE PANICKING NOW THAT ALL FOUR OF THEIR BELOVED CMAP BAKERS LOST, BUT IF THEY'RE RESORTING TO COSPLAY CRAFTSMEN LIKE THAT, THEY MIGHT AS WELL GIVE UP!
THERE'S NO WAY WE COULD LOSE TO GUYS WHO HAVE TO PUT ON COSTUMES IN ORDER TO COMPETE!
WE'LL BEAT THEM TO A PULP!
ER... KAWACHI... IT LOOKS LIKE YOU'LL BE THE ONE BEATEN TO A PULP FIRST...
WHAT DO YOU MEAN?!
HOW MANY TIMES DO I HAVE TO TELL YOU...

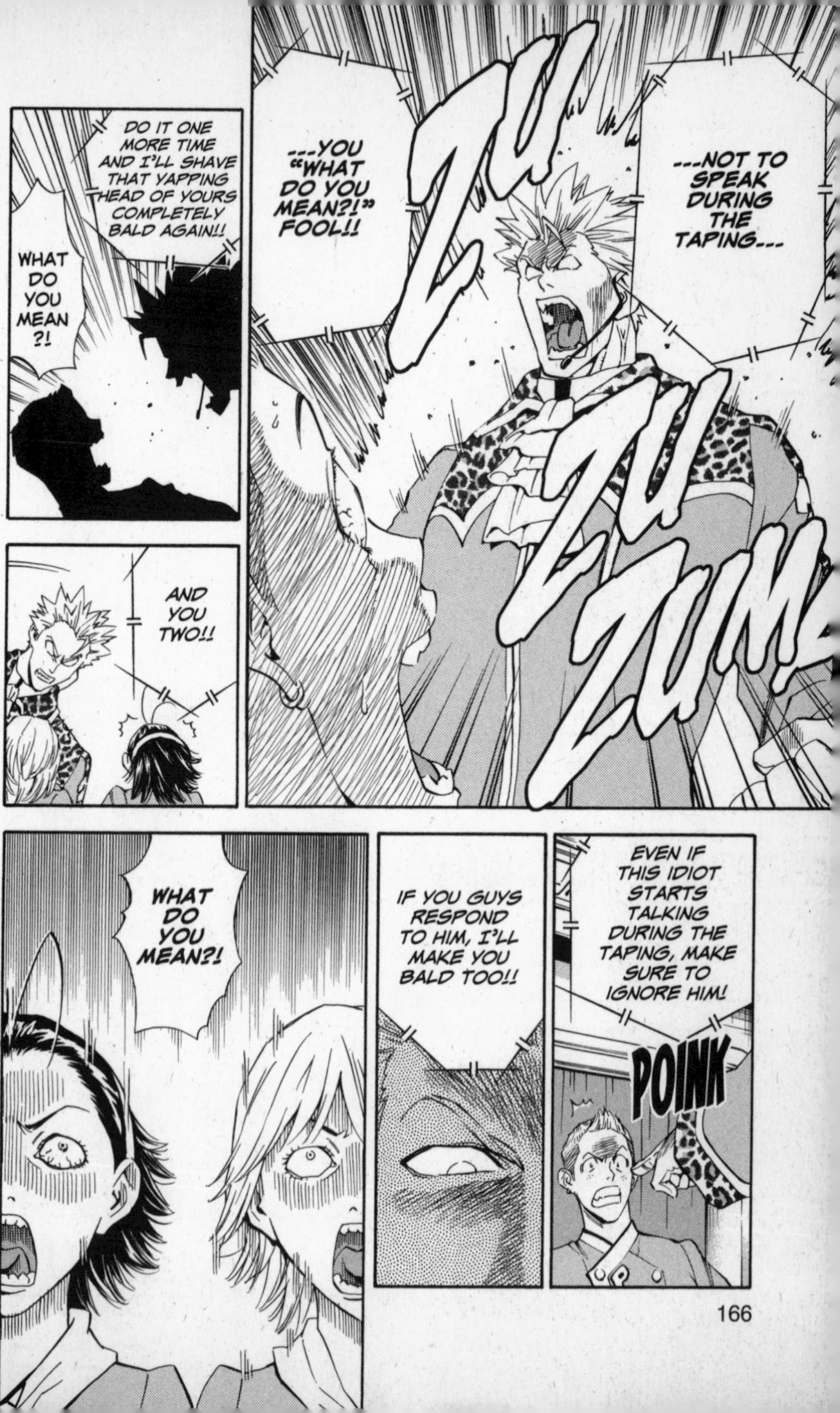
---NOT TO SPEAK DURING THE TAPING---
---YOU "WHAT DO YOU MEAN?!" FOOL!!
ZU ZU ZUN
DO IT ONE MORE TIME AND I'LL SHAVE THAT YAPPING HEAD OF YOURS COMPLETELY BALD AGAIN!!
WHAT DO YOU MEAN ?!
AND YOU TWO!!
EVEN IF THIS IDIOT STARTS TALKING DURING THE TAPING, MAKE SURE TO IGNORE HIM!
POINK
IF YOU GUYS RESPOND TO HIM, I'LL MAKE YOU BALD TOO!!
WHAT DO YOU MEAN?!

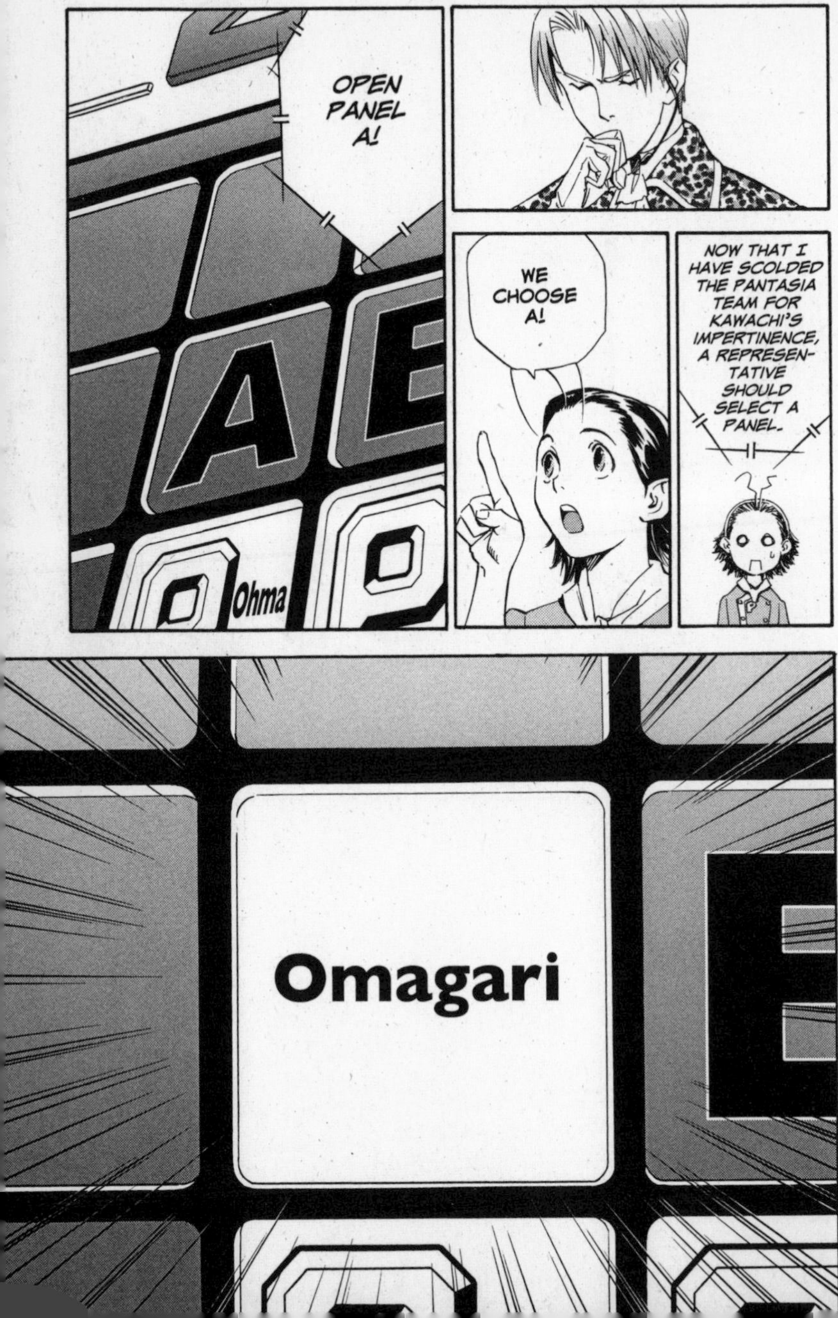
NOW THAT I HAVE SCOLDED THE PANTASIA TEAM FOR KAWACHI'S IMPERTINENCE, A REPRESEN-TATIVE SHOULD SELECT A PANEL.
WE CHOOSE A!
OPEN PANEL A!
A
Ohma
Omagari

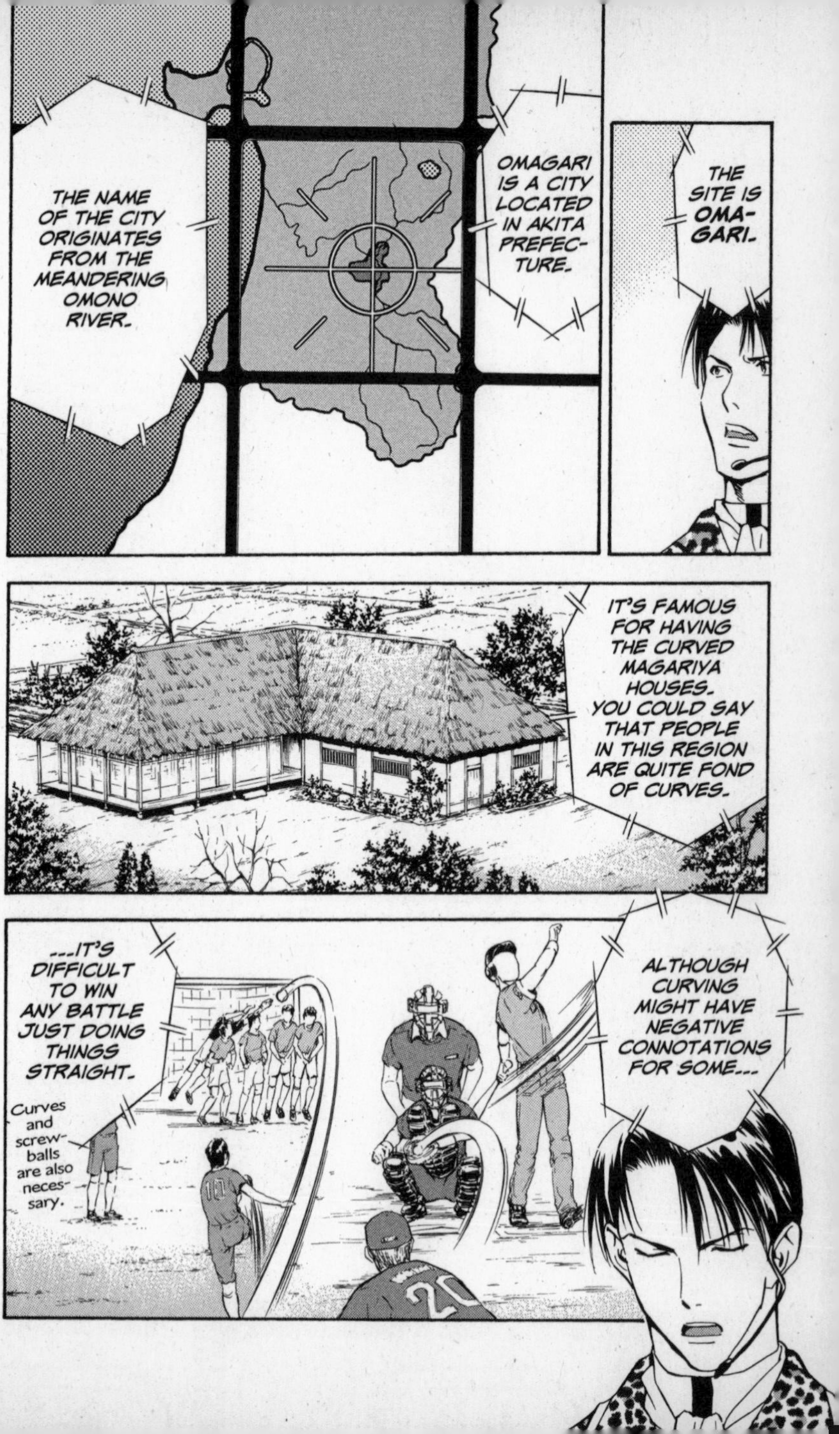
THE SITE IS OMAGARI.
OMAGARI IS A CITY LOCATED IN AKITA PREFECTURE.
THE NAME OF THE CITY ORIGINATES FROM THE MEANDERING OMONO RIVER.
IT'S FAMOUS FOR HAVING THE CURVED MAGARIYA HOUSES. YOU COULD SAY THAT PEOPLE IN THIS REGION ARE QUITE FOND OF CURVES.
ALTHOUGH CURVING MIGHT HAVE NEGATIVE CONNOTATIONS FOR SOME...
...IT'S DIFFICULT TO WIN ANY BATTLE JUST DOING THINGS STRAIGHT.
Curves and screwballs are also necessary.

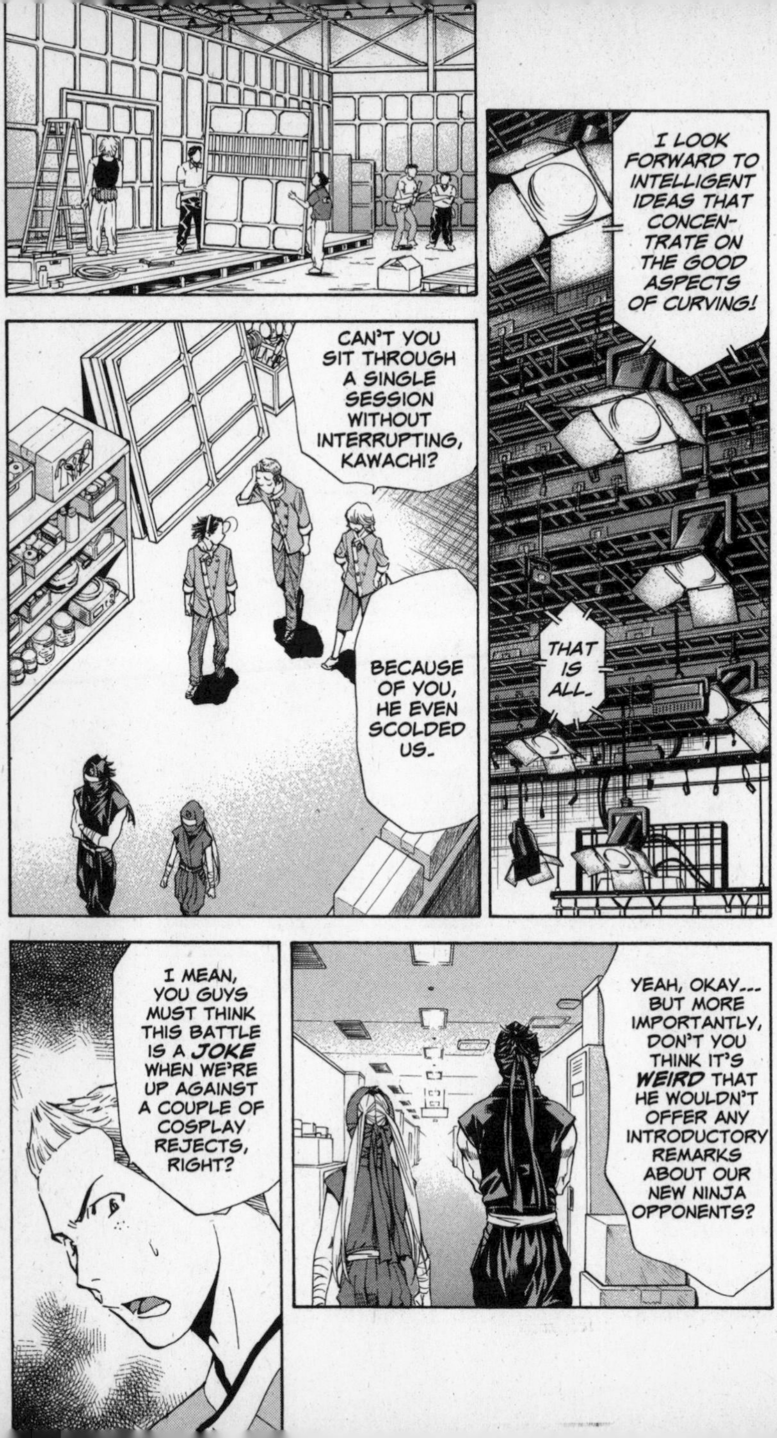
I LOOK FORWARD TO INTELLIGENT IDEAS THAT CONCEN-TRATE ON THE GOOD ASPECTS OF CURVING!
THAT IS ALL.
CAN'T YOU SIT THROUGH A SINGLE SESSION WITHOUT INTERRUPTING, KAWACHI?
BECAUSE OF YOU, HE EVEN SCOLDED US.
YEAH, OKAY... BUT MORE IMPORTANTLY, DON'T YOU THINK IT'S WEIRD THAT HE WOULDN'T OFFER ANY INTRODUCTORY REMARKS ABOUT OUR NEW NINJA OPPONENTS?
I MEAN, YOU GUYS MUST THINK THIS BATTLE IS A JOKE WHEN WE'RE UP AGAINST A COUPLE OF COSPLAY REJECTS, RIGHT?

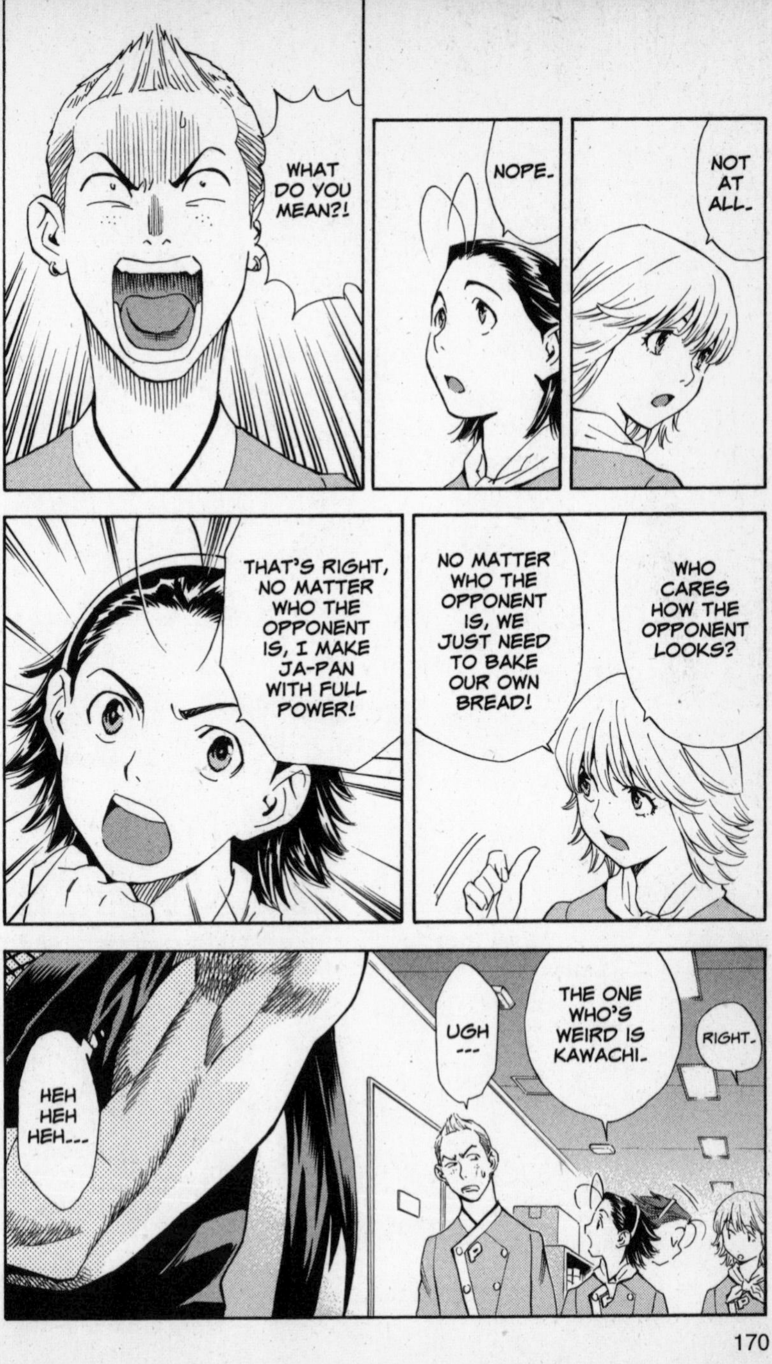
NOT AT ALL.
NOPE.
WHAT DO YOU MEAN?!
WHO CARES HOW THE OPPONENT LOOKS?
NO MATTER WHO THE OPPONENT IS, WE JUST NEED TO BAKE OUR OWN BREAD!
THAT'S RIGHT, NO MATTER WHO THE OPPONENT IS, I MAKE JA-PAN WITH FULL POWER!
RIGHT.
THE ONE WHO'S WEIRD IS KAWACHI.
UGH...
HEH HEH HEH...

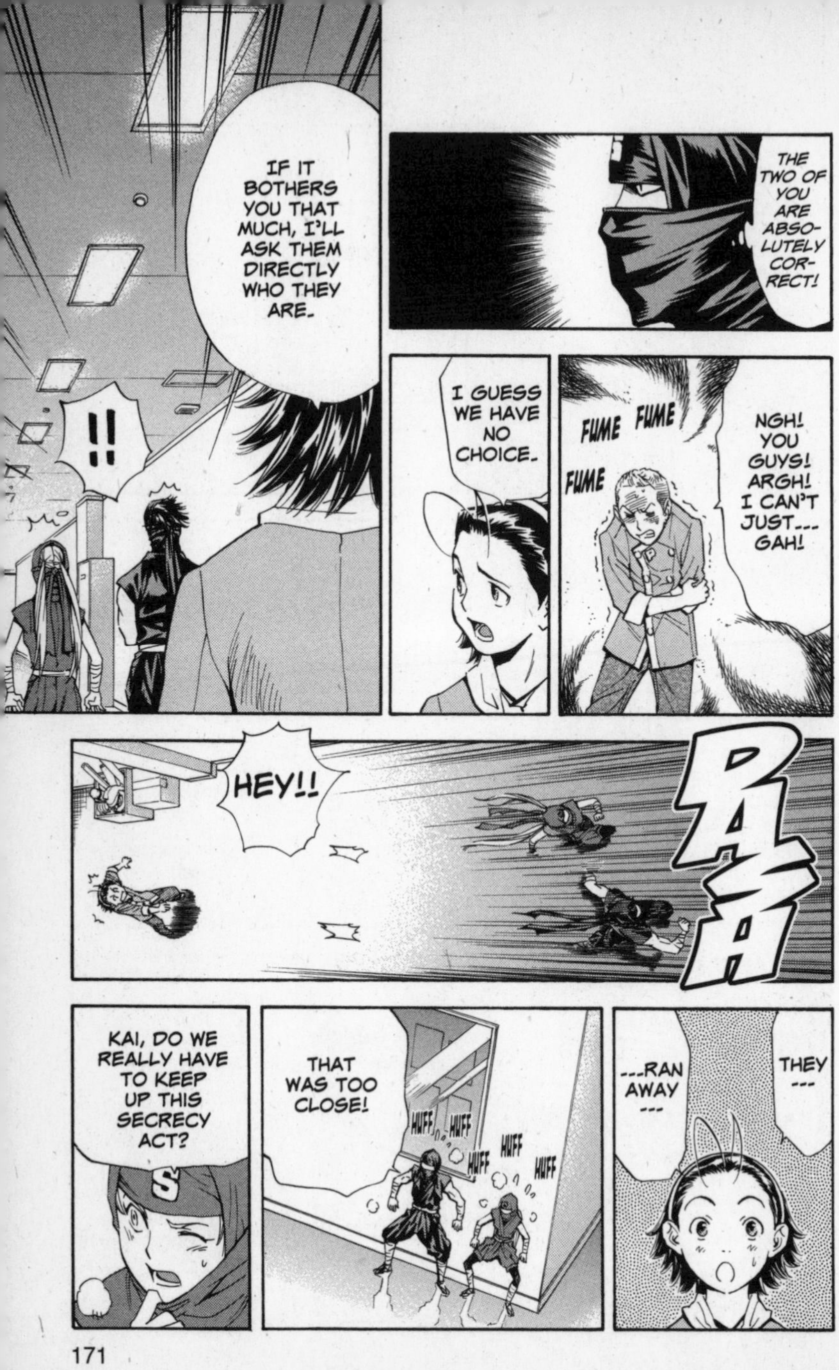
THE TWO OF YOU ARE ABSOLUTELY CORRECT!
NGH! YOU GUYS! ARGH! I CAN'T JUST--- GAH!
FUME FUME
FUME
I GUESS WE HAVE NO CHOICE.
IF IT BOTHERS YOU THAT MUCH, I'LL ASK THEM DIRECTLY WHO THEY ARE.
!!
DASH
HEY!!
THEY ---
---RAN AWAY ---
THAT WAS TOO CLOSE!
HUFF HUFF
HUFF HUFF
HUFF
KAI, DO WE REALLY HAVE TO KEEP UP THIS SECRECY ACT?

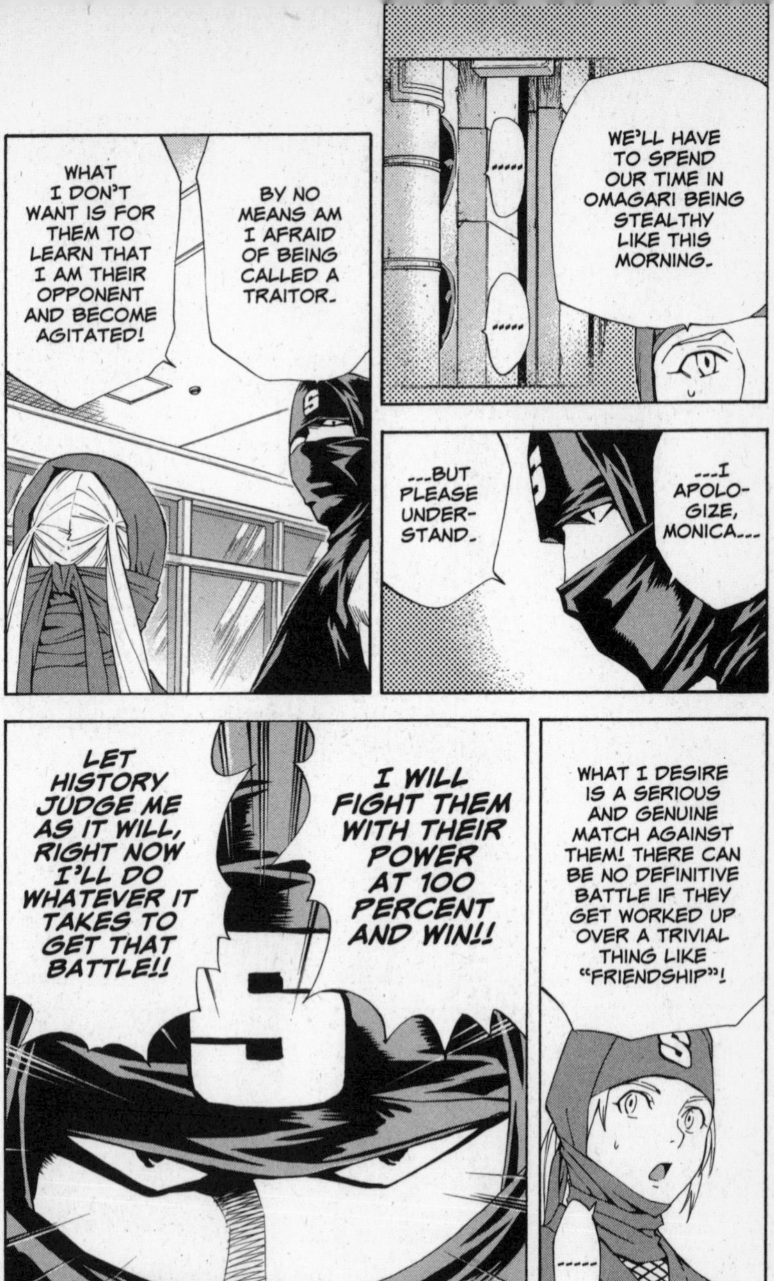
WE'LL HAVE TO SPEND OUR TIME IN OMAGARI BEING STEALTHY LIKE THIS MORNING.
......
......
...I APOLOGIZE, MONICA...
...BUT PLEASE UNDERSTAND.
BY NO MEANS AM I AFRAID OF BEING CALLED A TRAITOR.
WHAT I DON'T WANT IS FOR THEM TO LEARN THAT I AM THEIR OPPONENT AND BECOME AGITATED!
WHAT I DESIRE IS A SERIOUS AND GENUINE MATCH AGAINST THEM! THERE CAN BE NO DEFINITIVE BATTLE IF THEY GET WORKED UP OVER A TRIVIAL THING LIKE "FRIENDSHIP"!
......
I WILL FIGHT THEM WITH THEIR POWER AT 100 PERCENT AND WIN!!
LET HISTORY JUDGE ME AS IT WILL, RIGHT NOW I'LL DO WHATEVER IT TAKES TO GET THAT BATTLE!!

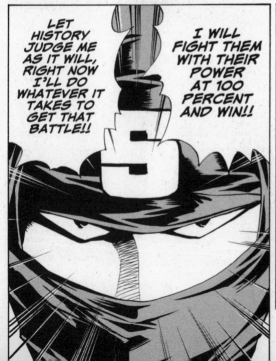

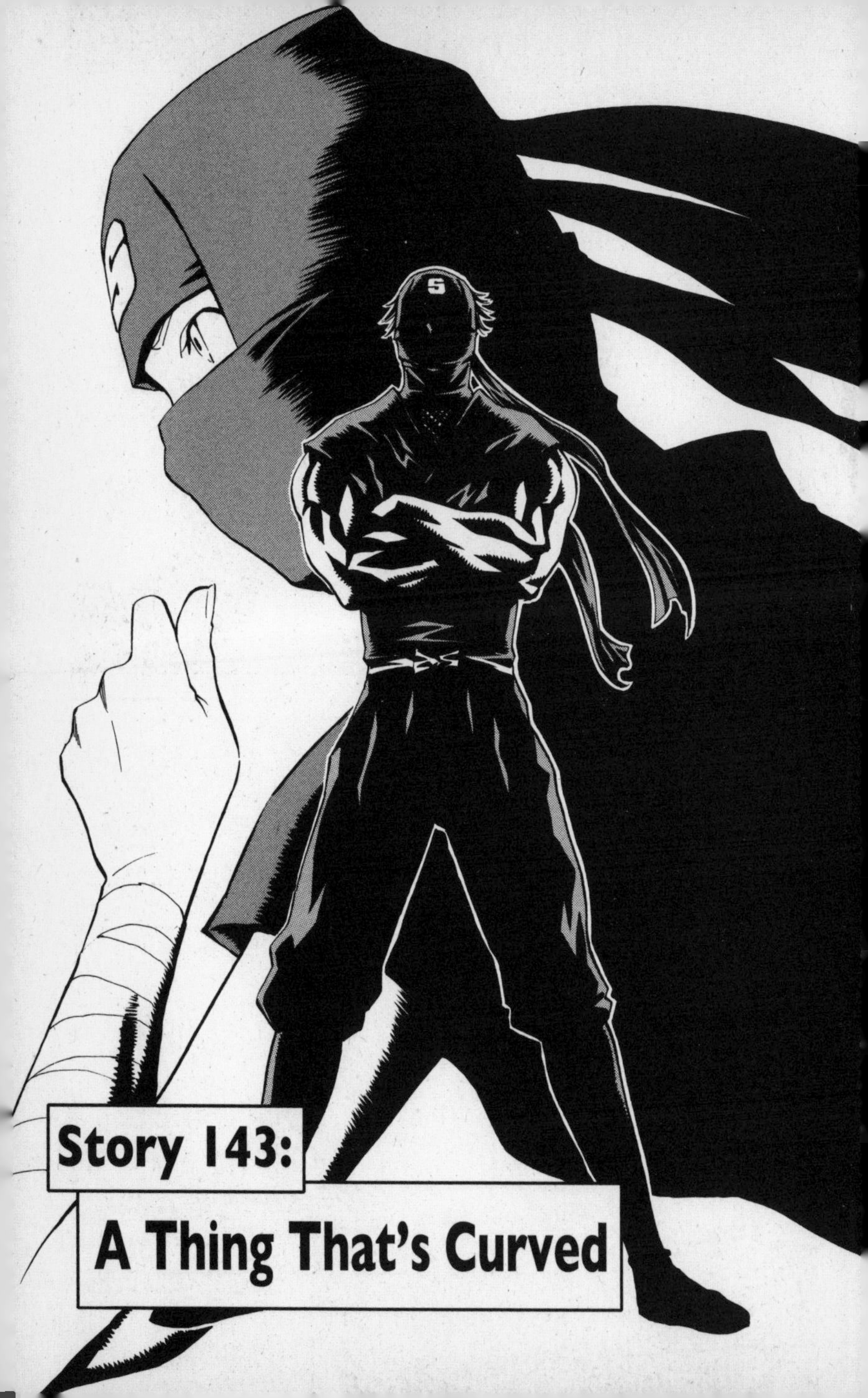
Story 143:
A Thing That's Curved

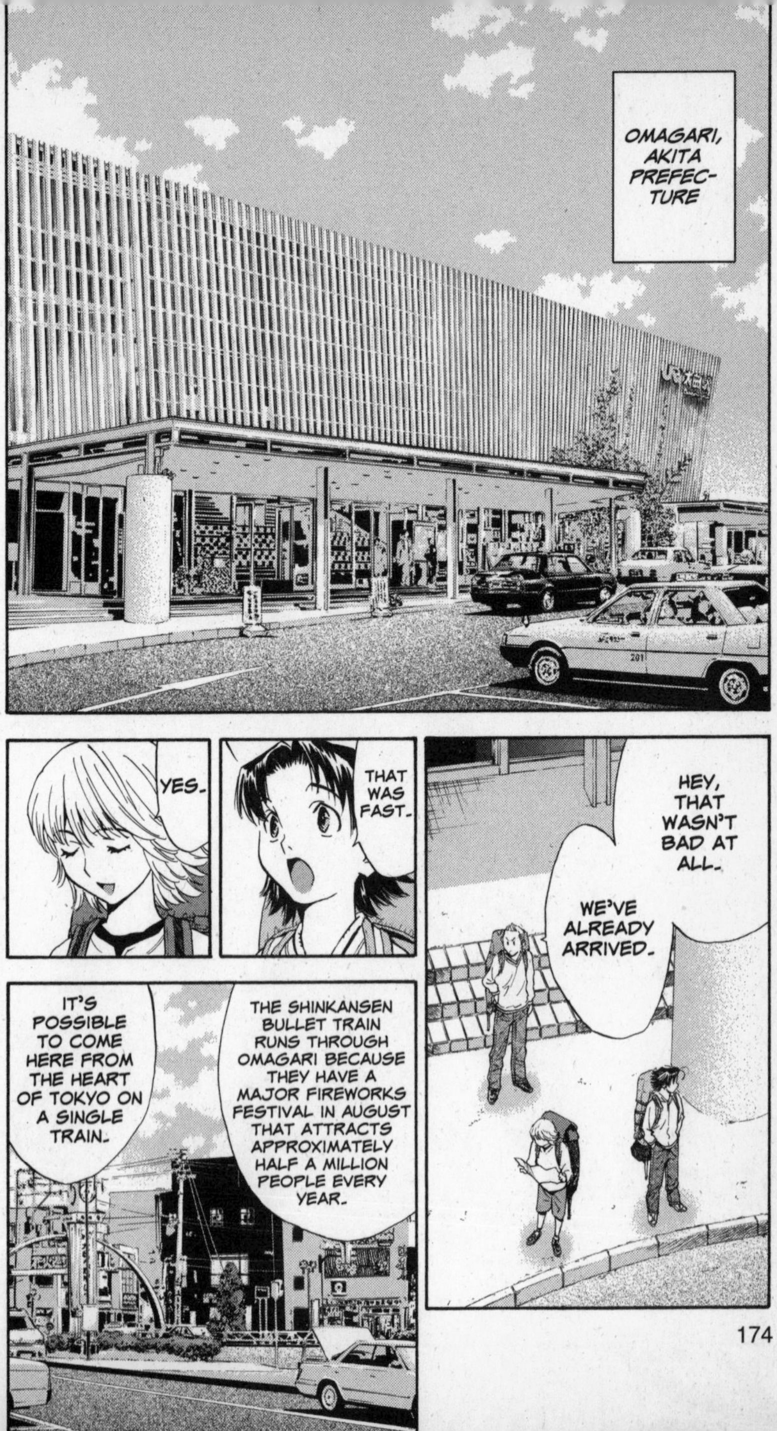
OMAGARI, AKITA PREFEC- TURE
HEY, THAT WASN'T BAD AT ALL.
WE'VE ALREADY ARRIVED.
THAT WAS FAST.
YES.
THE SHINKANSEN BULLET TRAIN RUNS THROUGH OMAGARI BECAUSE THEY HAVE A MAJOR FIREWORKS FESTIVAL IN AUGUST THAT ATTRACTS APPROXIMATELY HALF A MILLION PEOPLE EVERY YEAR.
IT'S POSSIBLE TO COME HERE FROM THE HEART OF TOKYO ON A SINGLE TRAIN.

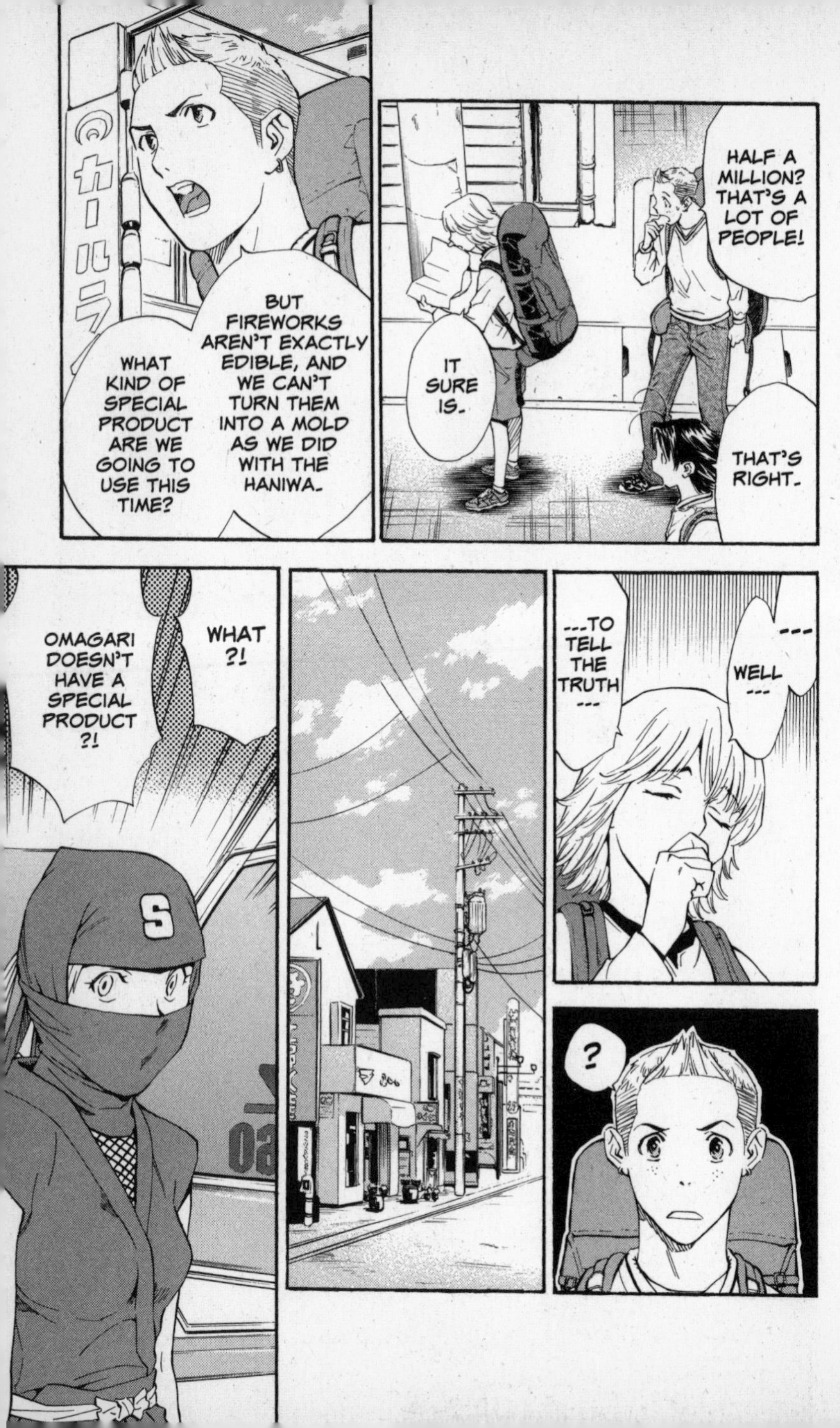
HALF A MILLION? THAT'S A LOT OF PEOPLE!
IT SURE IS.
THAT'S RIGHT.
BUT FIREWORKS AREN'T EXACTLY EDIBLE, AND WE CAN'T TURN THEM INTO A MOLD AS WE DID WITH THE HANIWA.
WHAT KIND OF SPECIAL PRODUCT ARE WE GOING TO USE THIS TIME?
---WELL---
---TO TELL THE TRUTH---
?
WHAT?!
OMAGARI DOESN'T HAVE A SPECIAL PRODUCT?!

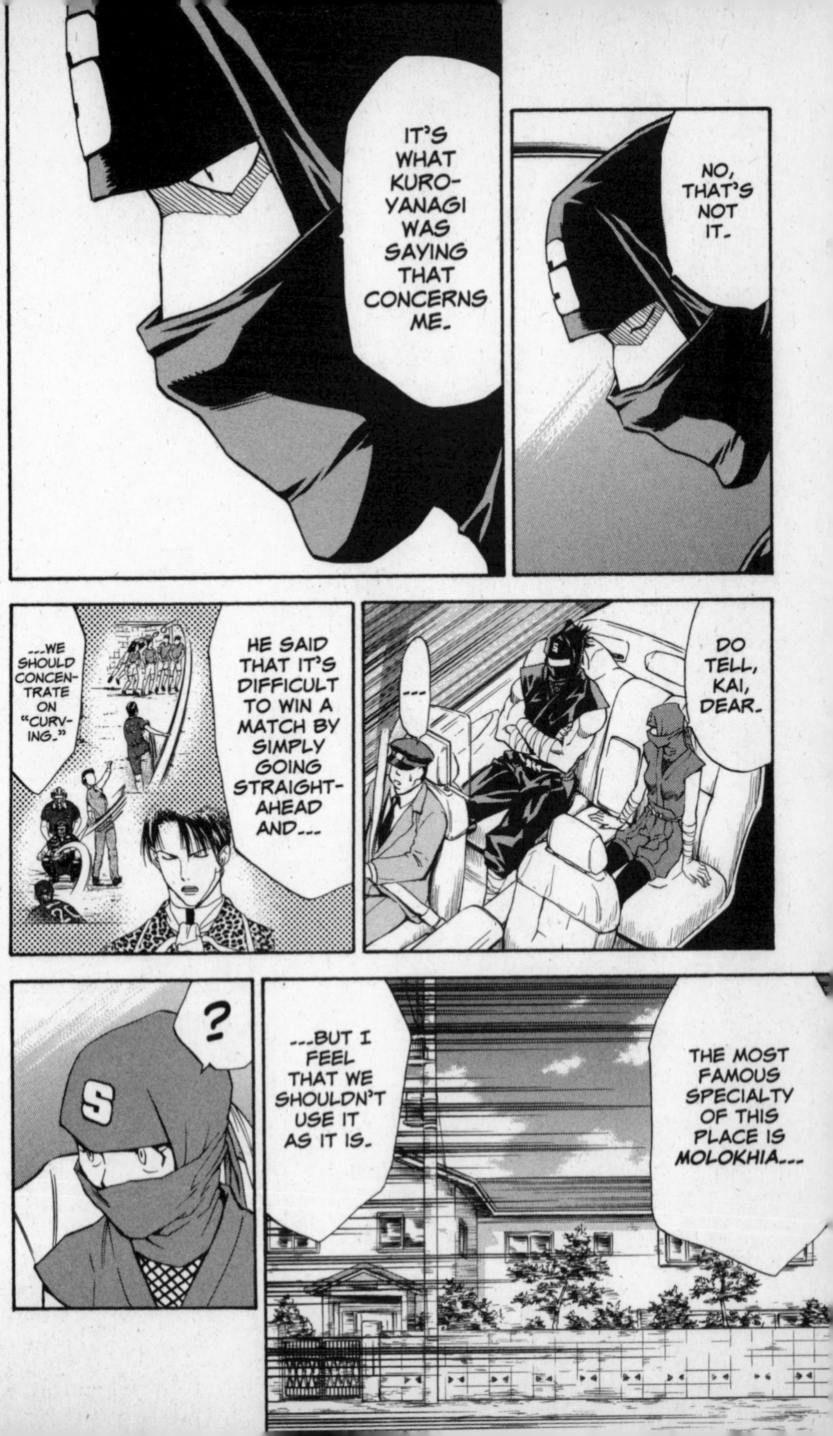
NO, THAT'S NOT IT.
IT'S WHAT KURO-YANAGI WAS SAYING THAT CONCERNS ME.
DO TELL, KAI, DEAR.
...
HE SAID THAT IT'S DIFFICULT TO WIN A MATCH BY SIMPLY GOING STRAIGHT-AHEAD AND...
...WE SHOULD CONCEN-TRATE ON "CURV-ING."
THE MOST FAMOUS SPECIALTY OF THIS PLACE IS MOLOKHIA...
...BUT I FEEL THAT WE SHOULDN'T USE IT AS IT IS.
?

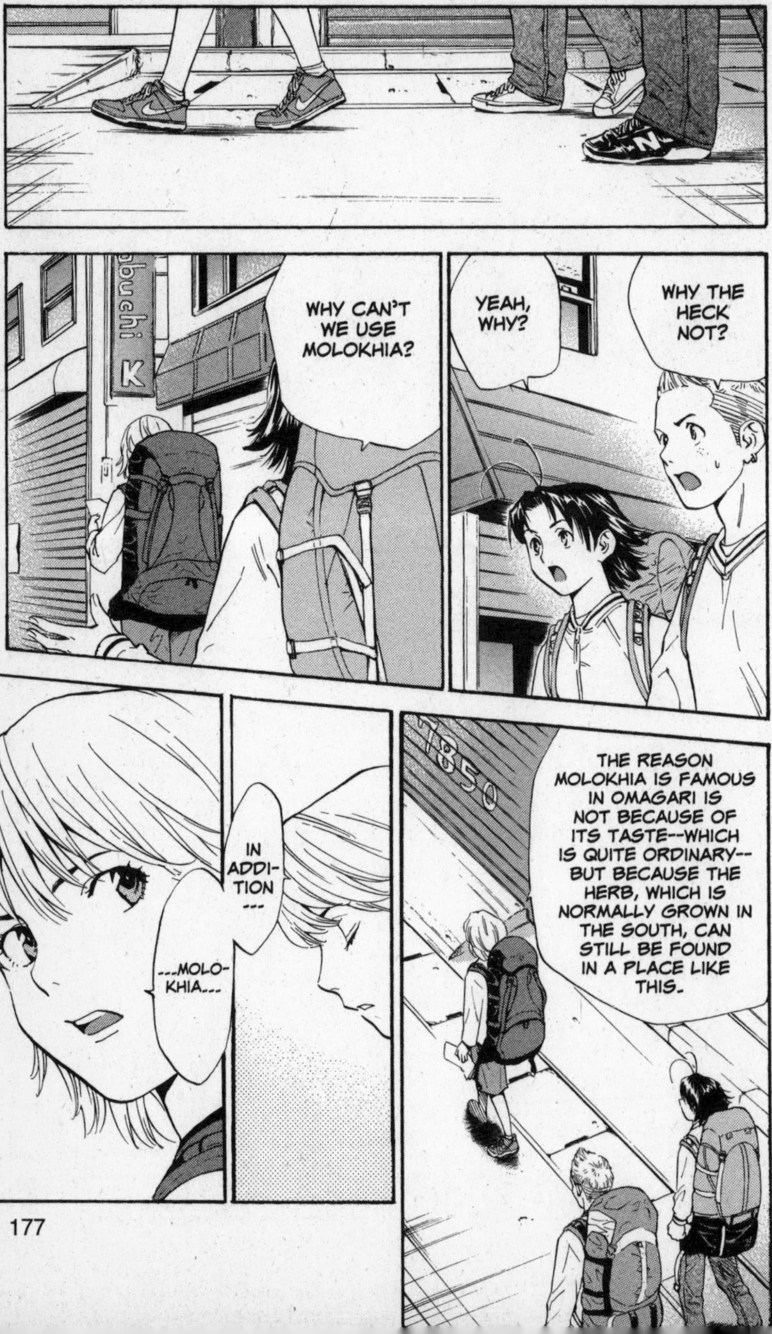
WHY THE HECK NOT?
YEAH, WHY?
WHY CAN'T WE USE MOLOKHIA?
THE REASON MOLOKHIA IS FAMOUS IN OMAGARI IS NOT BECAUSE OF ITS TASTE--WHICH IS QUITE ORDINARY--BUT BECAUSE THE HERB, WHICH IS NORMALLY GROWN IN THE SOUTH, CAN STILL BE FOUND IN A PLACE LIKE THIS.
IN ADDITION---
---MOLOKHIA---

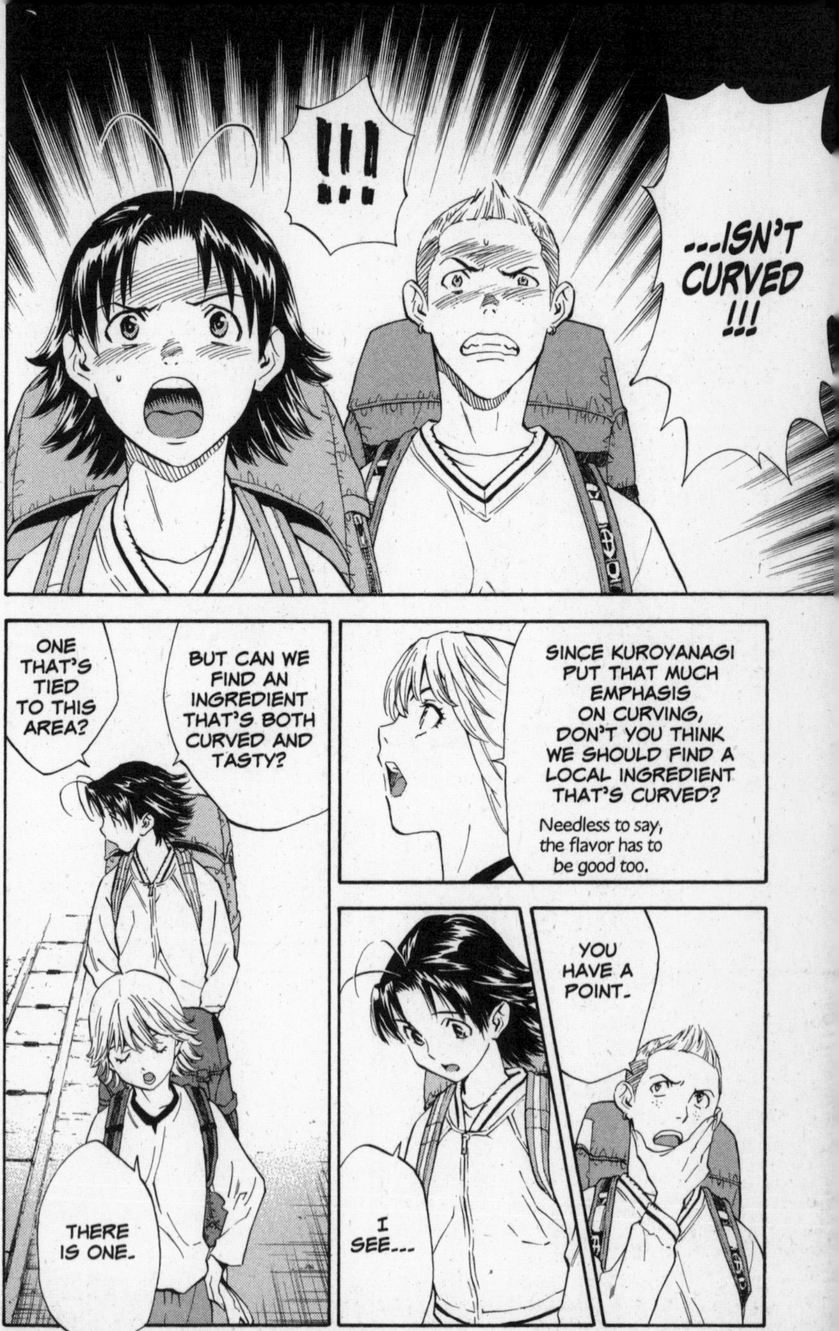
...ISN'T CURVED !!!
!!!
SINCE KUROYANAGI PUT THAT MUCH EMPHASIS ON CURVING, DON'T YOU THINK WE SHOULD FIND A LOCAL INGREDIENT THAT'S CURVED?
Needless to say, the flavor has to be good too.
YOU HAVE A POINT.
I SEE...
BUT CAN WE FIND AN INGREDIENT THAT'S BOTH CURVED AND TASTY?
ONE THAT'S TIED TO THIS AREA?
THERE IS ONE.

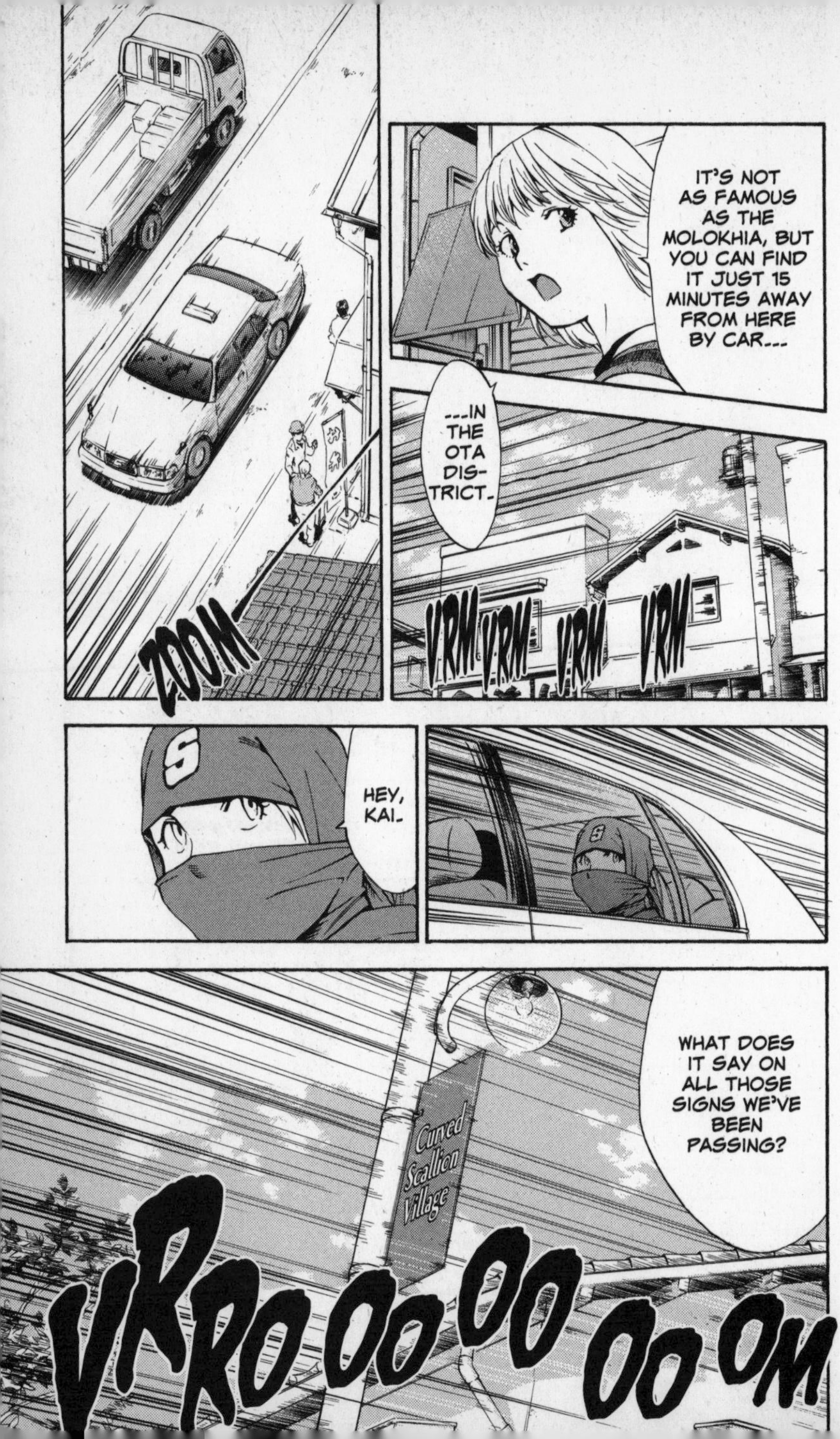
IT'S NOT AS FAMOUS AS THE MOLOKHIA, BUT YOU CAN FIND IT JUST 15 MINUTES AWAY FROM HERE BY CAR...
...IN THE OTA DIS-TRICT...
VRM VRM VRM VRM
ZOOM
HEY, KAI...
WHAT DOES IT SAY ON ALL THOSE SIGNS WE'VE BEEN PASSING?
Curved Scallion Village
VRROOOOOOOOOOM

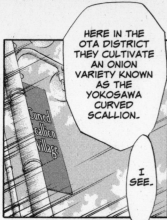

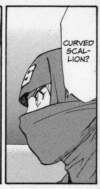

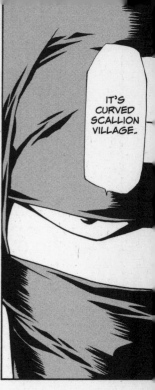

IT'S CURVED SCALLION VILLAGE.
CURVED SCAL-LION?
HERE IN THE OTA DISTRICT THEY CULTIVATE AN ONION VARIETY KNOWN AS THE YOKOSAWA CURVED SCALLION.
Curved Scallion Village
I SEE.
BUT WHY IS IT CURVED?
BE-CAUSE IT'S SOFT.
COMPARED TO NORMAL SCALLIONS, YOKOSAWA CURVED SCALLIONS ARE EXTREMELY SOFT AND WON'T GROW TO THEIR FULL POTENTIAL BY BEING PLANTED STRAIGHT.
THAT'S WHY THEY ARE UPROOTED AFTER GROWING TO A CERTAIN HEIGHT, THEN REPLANTED TO GROW SOME MORE.
PLANTED STRAIGHT AT FIRST
REPLANTED AT AN ANGLE DURING THE CULTIVATION
BE-CAUSE OF THIS---
THEY CURVE.
THEY GROW UPWARDS TOWARD SUNLIGHT
CURVES

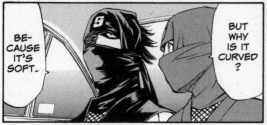

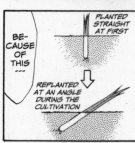

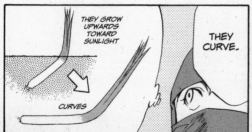

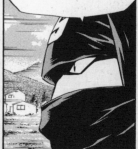

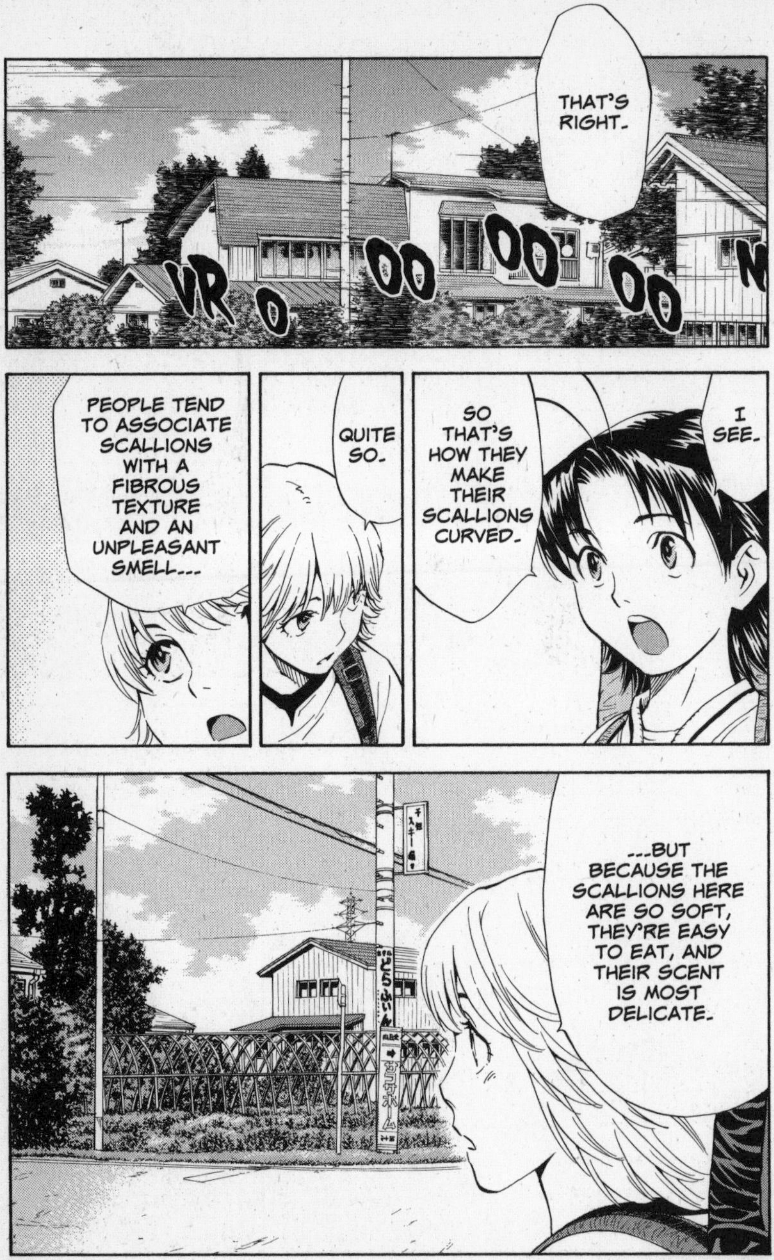
THAT'S RIGHT.
VROOOOOOOOOON
I SEE.
SO THAT'S HOW THEY MAKE THEIR SCALLIONS CURVED.
QUITE SO.
PEOPLE TEND TO ASSOCIATE SCALLIONS WITH A FIBROUS TEXTURE AND AN UNPLEASANT SMELL...
...BUT BECAUSE THE SCALLIONS HERE ARE SO SOFT, THEY'RE EASY TO EAT, AND THEIR SCENT IS MOST DELICATE.

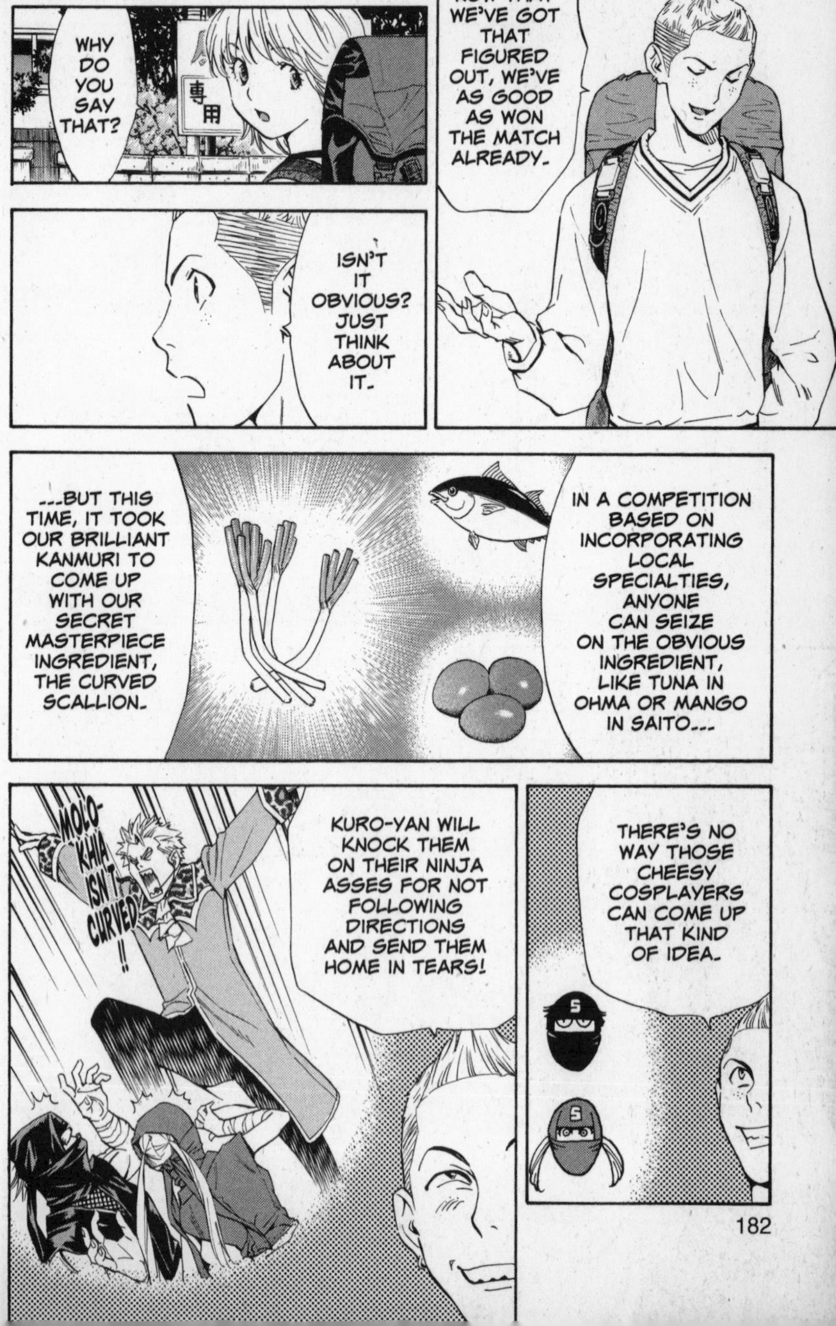
NOW THAT WE'VE GOT THAT FIGURED OUT, WE'VE AS GOOD AS WON THE MATCH ALREADY.
WHY DO YOU SAY THAT?
専用
ISN'T IT OBVIOUS? JUST THINK ABOUT IT.
IN A COMPETITION BASED ON INCORPORATING LOCAL SPECIALTIES, ANYONE CAN SEIZE ON THE OBVIOUS INGREDIENT, LIKE TUNA IN OHMA OR MANGO IN SAITO...
...BUT THIS TIME, IT TOOK OUR BRILLIANT KANMURI TO COME UP WITH OUR SECRET MASTERPIECE INGREDIENT, THE CURVED SCALLION.
THERE'S NO WAY THOSE CHEESY COSPLAYERS CAN COME UP THAT KIND OF IDEA.
KURO-YAN WILL KNOCK THEM ON THEIR NINJA ASSES FOR NOT FOLLOWING DIRECTIONS AND SEND THEM HOME IN TEARS!
MOLOKHIA ISN'T CURVED!!

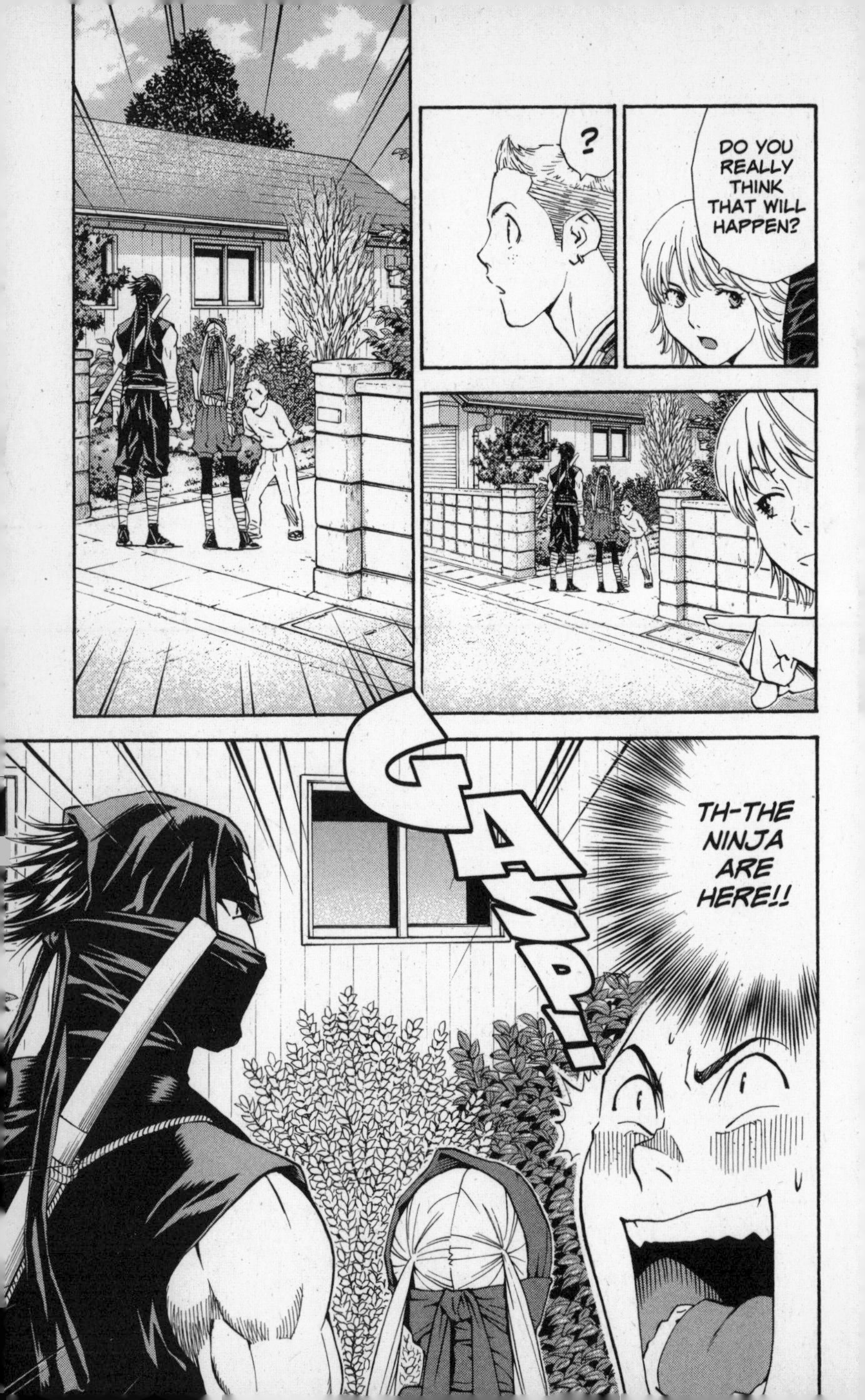
DO YOU REALLY THINK THAT WILL HAPPEN?
?
TH-THE NINJA ARE HERE!!
GASP!!

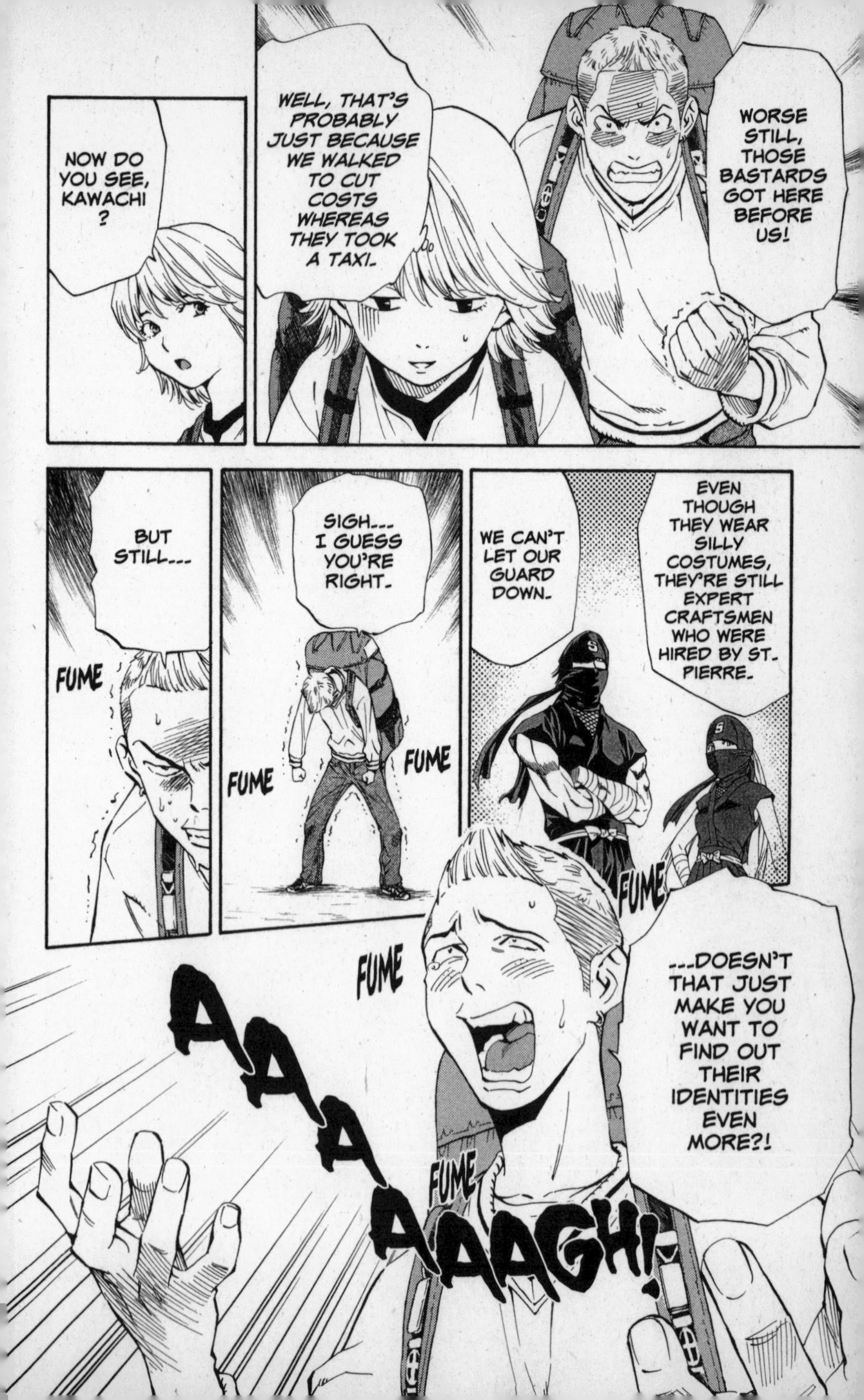
WORSE STILL, THOSE BASTARDS GOT HERE BEFORE US!
WELL, THAT'S PROBABLY JUST BECAUSE WE WALKED TO CUT COSTS WHEREAS THEY TOOK A TAXI.
NOW DO YOU SEE, KAWACHI?
EVEN THOUGH THEY WEAR SILLY COSTUMES, THEY'RE STILL EXPERT CRAFTSMEN WHO WERE HIRED BY ST. PIERRE.
WE CAN'T LET OUR GUARD DOWN.
SIGH... I GUESS YOU'RE RIGHT.
FUME
FUME
BUT STILL...
FUME
FUME
...DOESN'T THAT JUST MAKE YOU WANT TO FIND OUT THEIR IDENTITIES EVEN MORE?!
FUME
FUME
AAAAAAAGH!

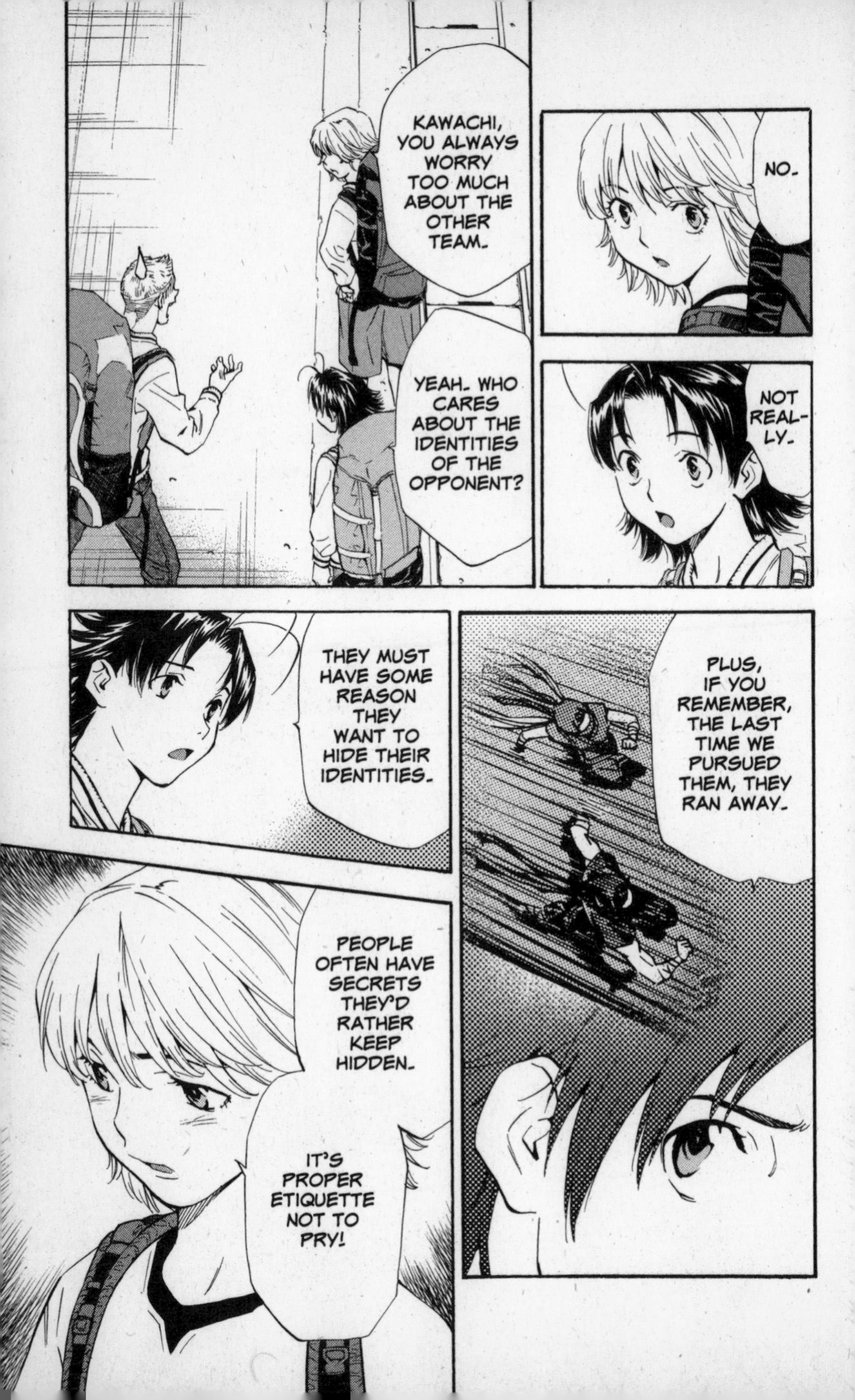
NO.
NOT REAL-LY.
KAWACHI, YOU ALWAYS WORRY TOO MUCH ABOUT THE OTHER TEAM.
YEAH. WHO CARES ABOUT THE IDENTITIES OF THE OPPONENT?
PLUS, IF YOU REMEMBER, THE LAST TIME WE PURSUED THEM, THEY RAN AWAY.
THEY MUST HAVE SOME REASON THEY WANT TO HIDE THEIR IDENTITIES.
PEOPLE OFTEN HAVE SECRETS THEY'D RATHER KEEP HIDDEN.
IT'S PROPER ETIQUETTE NOT TO PRY!

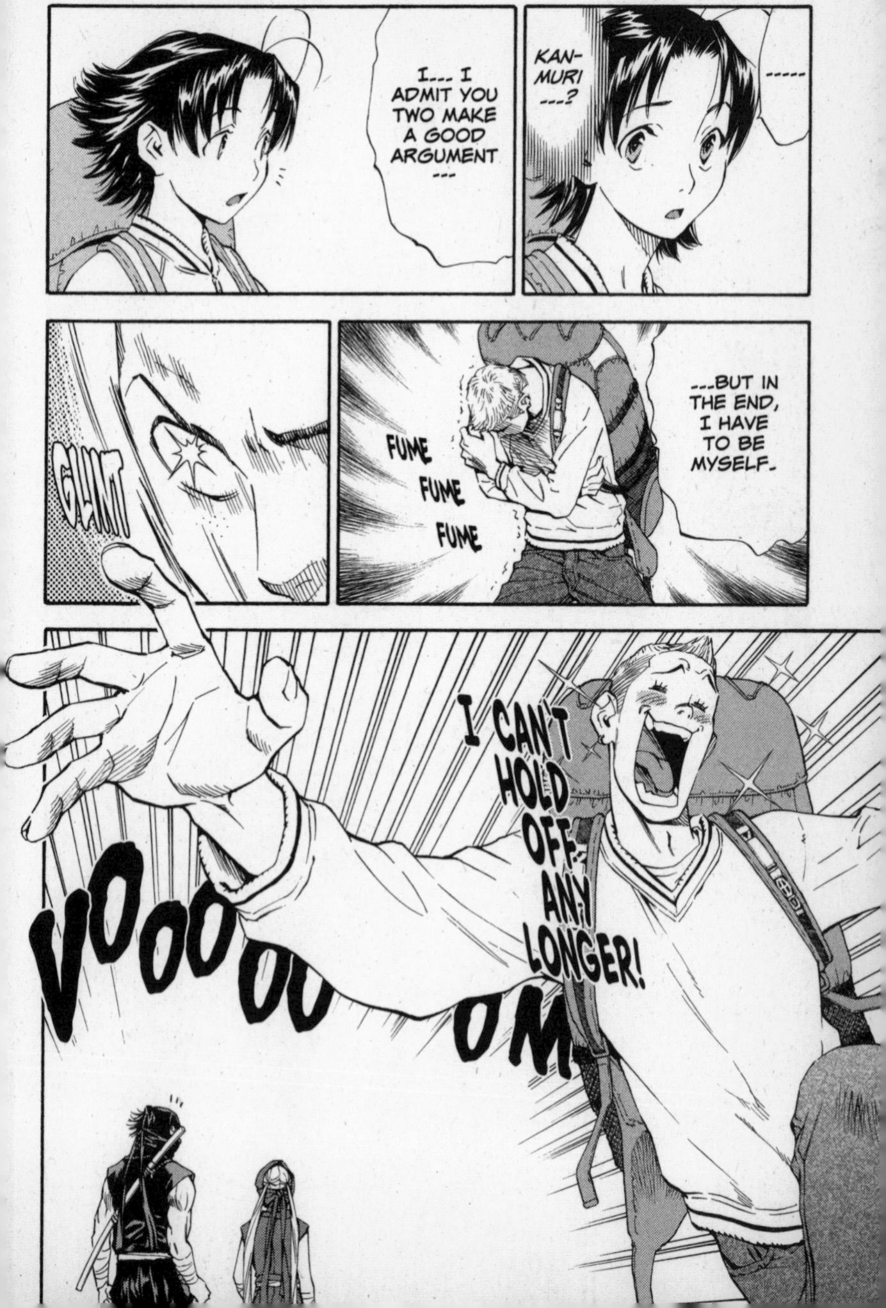

KAN-MURI ---?
I--- I ADMIT YOU TWO MAKE A GOOD ARGUMENT ---
---BUT IN THE END, I HAVE TO BE MYSELF-
FUME FUME FUME
GLINT
I CAN'T HOLD OFF ANY LONGER!
VOOOOOOOM

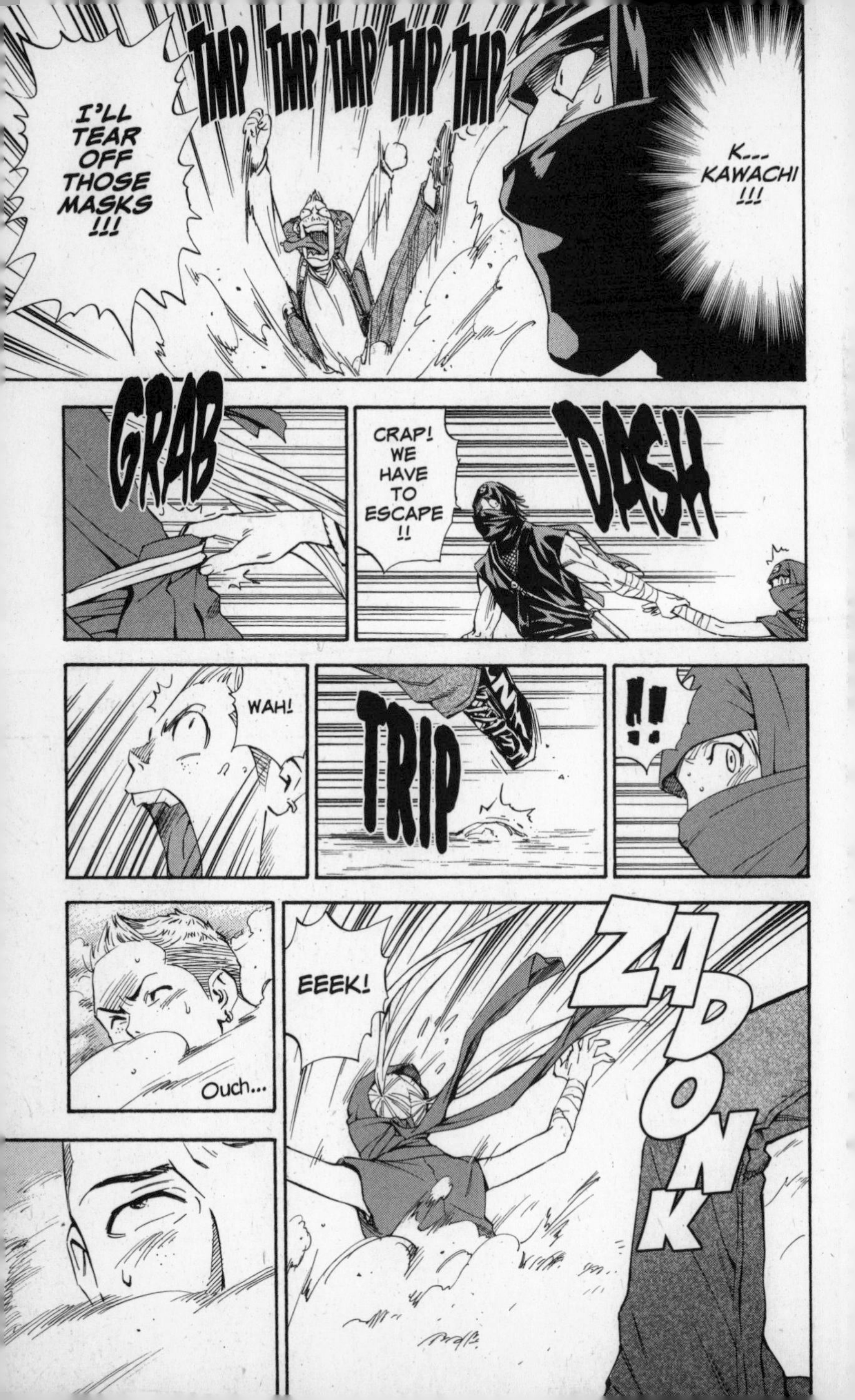
TMP TMP TMP TMP TMP
K... KAWACHI !!!
I'LL TEAR OFF THOSE MASKS !!!
CRAP! WE HAVE TO ESCAPE !!
DASH
GRAB
!!
TRIP
WAH!
ZADONK
EEEK!
Ouch...

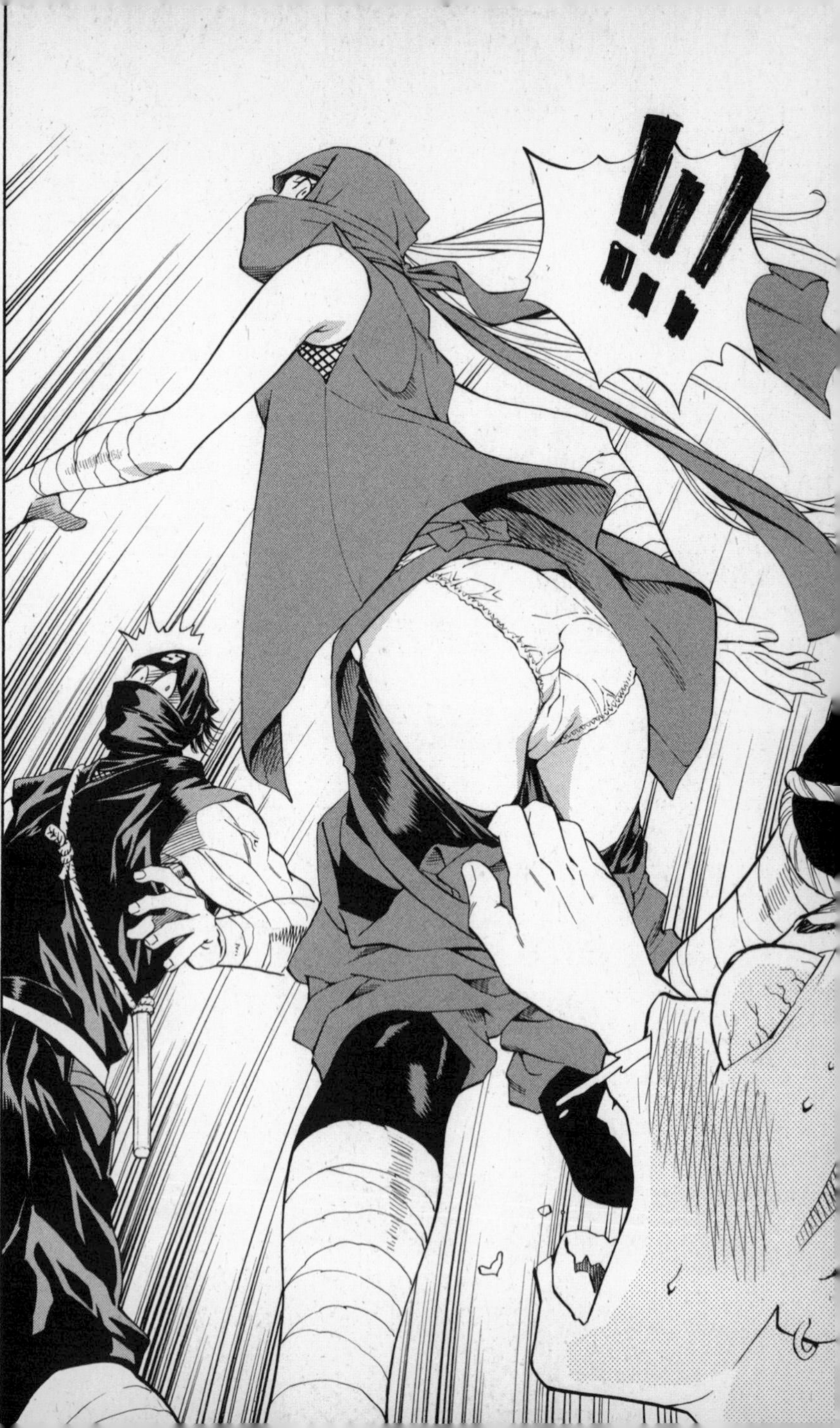
!!!

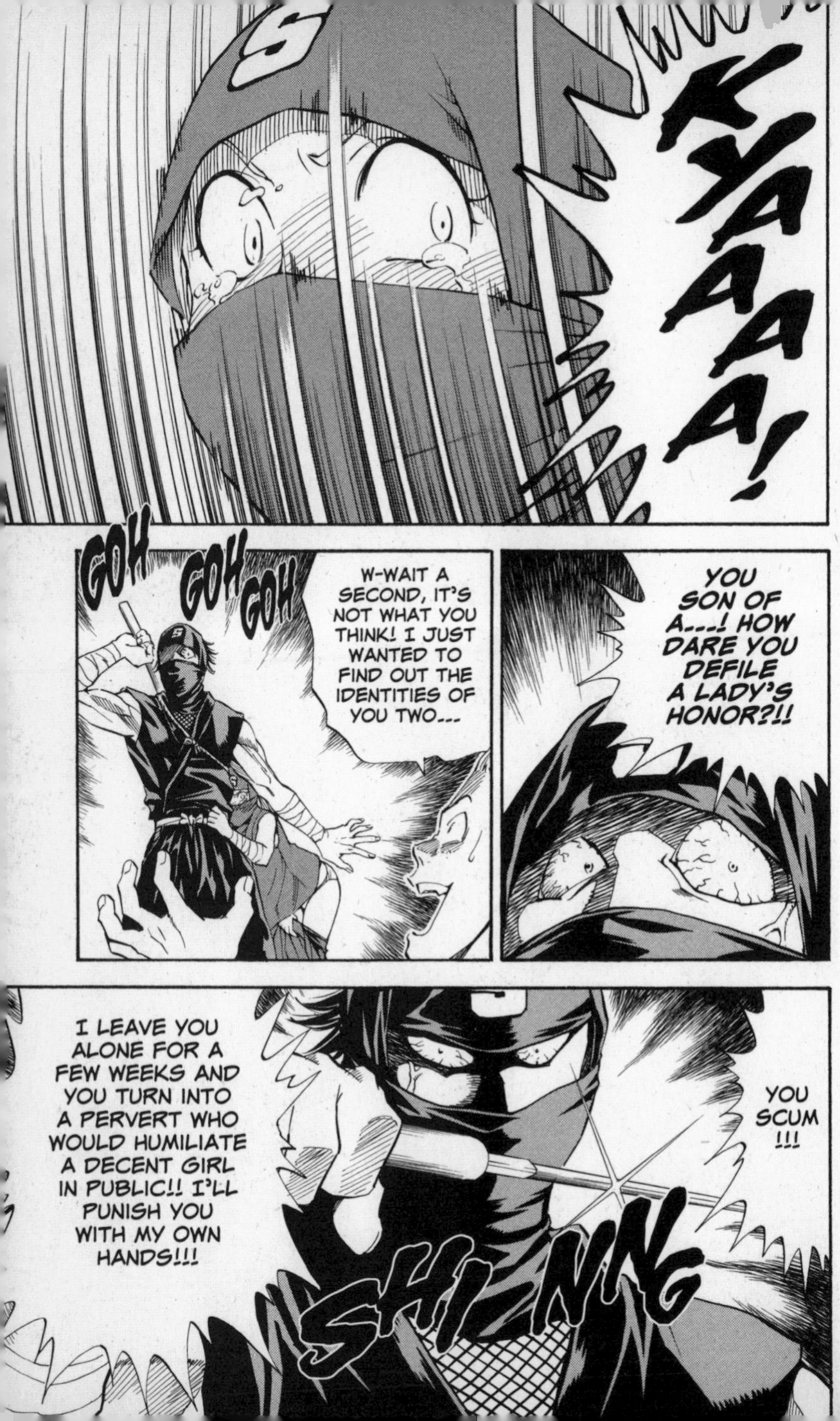
KYAAAA!
YOU SON OF A...! HOW DARE YOU DEFILE A LADY'S HONOR?!!
W-WAIT A SECOND, IT'S NOT WHAT YOU THINK! I JUST WANTED TO FIND OUT THE IDENTITIES OF YOU TWO...
GOH GOH GOH
YOU SCUM!!!
I LEAVE YOU ALONE FOR A FEW WEEKS AND YOU TURN INTO A PERVERT WHO WOULD HUMILIATE A DECENT GIRL IN PUBLIC!! I'LL PUNISH YOU WITH MY OWN HANDS!!!
SHI-NNG

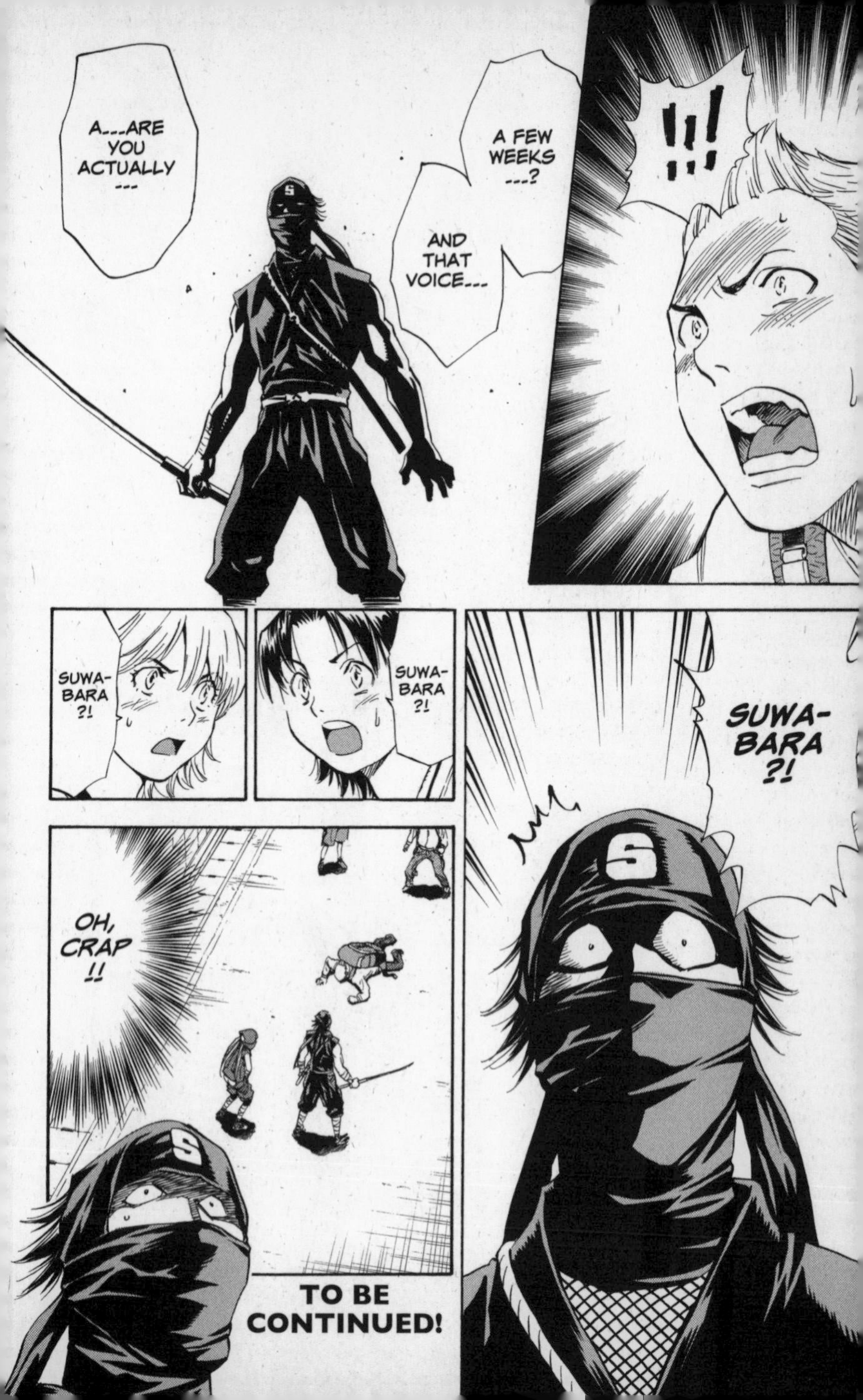
!!!
A FEW WEEKS ---?
AND THAT VOICE---
A---ARE YOU ACTUALLY ---
SUWA-BARA ?!
SUWA-BARA ?!
SUWA-BARA ?!
OH, CRAP !!
TO BE CONTINUED!

Freshly Baked!!
Mini Information

—— Malayan Tapir ——

The Malayan Tapir is said to be the most primitive of the large animals that exist today. It's hardly evolved over the last 20 million years. After seeing their lazy appearance in the photograph above, I almost want to tell them to evolve more (ha ha!). But that's science for you—what can you do?

By the way, the word for tapir in Brazil is "anta." Next time when you see a tapir at the zoo, please sing for them, "Anta, you are more than you tapir to be!"

YAKITATE!! JAPAN
VOL. 16

STORY AND ART BY
TAKASHI HASHIGUCHI

English Adaptation/Jake Forbes
Translation/Noritaka Minami
Touch-up Art & Lettering/Steve Dutro
Cover Design/Yukiko Whitley
Layout Design/Florian Fangohr
Editor/Megan Bates

Editor in Chief, Books/Alvin Lu
Editor in Chief, Magazines/Marc Weidenbaum
VP, Publishing Licensing/Rika Inouye
VP, Sales & Product Marketing/Gonzalo Ferreyra
VP, Creative/Linda Espinosa
Publisher/Hyoe Narita

Printed in the U.S.A.

Published by VIZ Media, LLC
P.O. Box 77010
San Francisco, CA 94107

10 9 8 7 6 5 4 3 2 1
First printing, March 2009

www.viz.com
store.viz.com

PARENTAL ADVISORY
YAKITATE!! JAPAN is rated T+ for Older Teen and is recommended for ages 16 and up. This volume contains alcohol and tobacco use, crude humor and mature situations.

RATED T+ FOR OLDER TEEN

ratings.viz.com

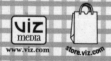